WANDERING
MONKS,
VIRGINS,
AND
PILGRIMS

ASCETIC TRAVEL IN THE MEDITERRANEAN WORLD, A.D. 300–800

MARIBEL DIETZ

THE PENNSYLVANIA STATE UNIVERSITY PRESS
UNIVERSITY PARK, PENNSYLVANIA

Library of Congress Cataloging-in-Publication Data

Dietz, Maribel, 1966–
Wandering monks, virgins, and pilgrims : ascetic travel in
the Mediterranean world, A.D. 300–800 / Maribel Dietz.
p.   cm.
Includes bibliographical references and index.
ISBN 0-271-02677-4 (alk. paper)
1. Monastic and religious life—Mediterranean Region—History—To 1500.
2. Travel—Religious aspects—Christianity—History—To 1500.
3. Christian pilgrims and pilgrimages—Mediterranean Region—History—To 1500.
I. Title.

BX2435 .D54 2005
263'.041'09015—dc22
2005001480

CONTENTS

In memory of my mother,
Marilu Remolina Sala Dietz,
September 11, 1941 to December 26, 2004

ACKNOWLEDGMENTS

I am deeply indebted to many people and institutions in the writing of this book, which grew out of my dissertation at Princeton University. I would like to express my deep gratitude to my advisors, Peter Brown and Bill Jordan, for their guidance, encouragement and faith in me. At Princeton I was also aided by Judith Herrin, Giles Constable, Slobodan Curcic, John Gager, and Tia Kolbaba, whom I would all like to thank. I would like to thank Princeton University, the History Department and the Late Antique Seminar. I would not have survived graduate school if not for the friendship and support of my fellow graduate students, especially Jennifer Delton, Jennifer Baszile, April Shelford, and Steve Kantrowitz. In addition to a Princeton University fellowship, I also received funding support for my research from the Group for the Study of Late Antiquity, the Council on Regional Studies, Princeton Graduate Alumni Association, Mellon Foundation, and the Stanley Seegar Fund.

Although the initial work in this project started while I was a graduate student, its true transformation into a book happened at my home institution of Louisiana State University. I would like to thank the College of Arts and Sciences for a Manship summer stipend and a pre-tenure research semester, the Council for Research for a summer stipend, and the Office of Research for travel support. In particular, I would like to thank Todd Pourciau in the Office of Research for his support, guidance, and friendship. My home at LSU has been the Department of History and I would like to thank the chair, Paul Paskoff, for his support of my project in many ways, including funds for conference travel and for piecing together liberal maternity and research leaves. The support of my colleagues, John Rodrigue, Victor Stater, Mark Thompson, Charlie Royster, Gaines Foster, John Henderson, David Lindenfeld, Steve Ross, and Katie Benton-Cohen, has been indispensable. Christine Kooi and

Suzanne Marchand merit special thanks since they read and commented on early drafts of this book and helped me tremendously during a particularly trying time. Chuck Shindo and Tiwanna Simpson, through their deep friendship, have provided needed shelter during many storms. I would also like to thank my students at LSU who have always kept me excited about history.

I have greatly benefited from discussions with and input from a number of scholars about my work, including Philip Rousseau, Constance Berman, Ralph Mathisen, Raymond Van Dam, Hagith Sivan, Giselle de Nie, Teofilo Ruiz, Claudia Rapp, Dan Caner, Georgia Frank, Phyllis Jestice, Noel Lenski, Dennis Trout, Richard Cusimano, and Michael Kulikowski. This book also benefited from my participation in a National Endowment for the Humanities summer seminar led by Dale Kinney and Birgitta Lindros Wohl at the American Academy in Rome. I would like to thank the National Endowment for the Humanities for this opportunity and thank all the participants of the seminar, especially Betsey Ayer, Polly Hoover, Felicity Ratté, Ann Kuzdale, and David Breiner.

I wish again to thank the National Endowment for the Humanities and the Louisiana State Board of Regents for grants that allowed for the creation of the Medieval and Renaissance Interdisciplinary studies (MARIS) project here at LSU. The scholars involved in MARIS, including Mary Sirridge, Lisi Oliver, Jan Herlinger, Mark Zucker, Susannah Monta, Greg Stone, Elaine Smyth, and Faye Phillips, have created a fertile and supportive environment for medievalists here at LSU that has helped me in the completion of this book. None of this would have happened if not for the unfailing work of my co-author in these grants, Kirstin Noreen. I cannot begin to thank Kirstin enough as both a colleague and friend. I have relied on her tenacity and generosity throughout my time at LSU. I also would like to thank my graduate student, Therese Champagne (now Dr. Champagne), who not only served as our grant coordinator, but also helped me as a informal research assistant bringing me Xeroxed articles and books from her own research trips.

This book would not have been possible without the resources of the libraries where I conducted research. I would like to thank the librarians and staff of Firestone library at Princeton, the Vatican Library, Library of the American Academy in Rome, Bibliothèque Nationale in Paris, and Middleton Library at Louisiana State University. I am especially indebted to the Office of Interlibrary Loan of Middleton library, where the staff, in particular Clare Castleberry, were tireless in locating obscure volumes for me and generous in overlooking overdue books in my possession.

I would also like to thank all of the anonymous readers who helped make this a better book. At Pennsylvania State University Press I would like to thank Cherene Holland, Patricia Mitchell, and especially Peter Potter. I would also like to thank Andrew B. Lewis who did a valiant job of copy-editing my text, saving me from many embarrassments. Sylvia Rodrigue helped me proof the final text and the index, but more important, she provided support and key advice when I needed it most. I will never be able to thank Sylvia enough.

I have been blessed throughout this project with the support of a network of old and new friends. I am grateful for the friendship of Joyce Tsuji, Amy Dagdigian, Jordan Susman, Todd Seidman, Mia Barker, Stuart Montgomery, Kristin Dobbs, Kevin and Sara Bongiorni, Michael Fontenot, Mary Farmer-Kaiser, Beth Paskoff, Vaughan Baker, Larry and Jeannie Kreamer, and Amanda Lafleur. I would also like to thank my family, Angela Dietz, William Dietz, Maedra Kellman. Herbert Kellman, Susan Parisi, Josh Kellman, Beth Fulkerson, Mia Kellman, Simon Kellman, and especially my father, Jim Dietz, and my brother, Steven Dietz. I would also like to thank my family in Mexico: Imelda Elizondo, Gerardo and Ely Varela, Gerardo and Ana Laura Aridjis, Patricia Aridjis, MariTere Aridjis, Pepe and Carmina Sala, Lalo and Tensi Sala. I would also like to thank my two children, Francisco and Gisele, who were born during the writing of this book. Their presence and love have kept me sane throughout this project. My greatest thanks go to my husband, Jordan Kellman, who has read and reread every word of this book, cooked nearly every meal for our family since this project began, explained to our children that mommy was busy, and provided constant encouragement and love, and without whom there would be nothing. Finally, I dedicate this book to my mother, Marilu Dietz, who died just before its publication and is terribly missed.

Advena sum et peregrine sicut omnes patres mei.

—PAULA, A MATRON OF ROME

For I am a stranger with thee, and a sojourner, as all my fathers were.

—PSALM 38.13

INTRODUCTION

In a letter of A.D. 399 to Oceanus, Jerome says of the travels of the Roman widow Fabiola, "Rome was not large enough for her compassionate kindness. She went from island to island, and traveled round the Etruscan Sea, and through the Volscian province . . . where bands of monks have taken up their home, bestowing her bounty either in person or by the agency of holy men of faith."[1] Eventually, and predictably, Fabiola sailed to Jerusalem. Though Jerome urged her to stay in the East, she instead wanted to resume her travels, living out of her "traveling baggage . . . a stranger (*peregrina*) in every city."[2] Fabiola did not take Jerome's advice, but instead followed another path, one that others before her, including many women, had followed. She left Jerusalem and resumed her travels, eventually returning to her home in Rome. Once again, Jerome states that she wanted to escape— she felt confined, and this time, against the advice of her Roman friends, she departed with a wealthy widower, Pammachius, and set up a *xenodochium,* a hostel for travelers, in Ostia, which quickly became popular and attracted huge crowds.[3]

Remarkable though her story is, Fabiola was not alone or even exceptional in combining travel and monastic life during late antiquity. Jerome's account of Fabiola's travels, her patronage of monks, and her foundation of a *xenodochium* is but one window into the world of late antique monastic

---

1. "Angusta misericordiae eius Roma fuit. Peragrabat ergo insulas, et totum Etruscum mare, Volscorumque provinciam . . . in quibus Monachorum consistunt chori, vel proprio corpore, vel transmissa per viros sanctos ac fideles munificentia circumibat." Jerome *Epistulae* (henceforth *Ep.*) 77.6. All translations of the letters of Jerome are from F. A. Wright, ed., *Select Letters of St. Jerome* (1933; reprint, Cambridge, Mass., 1991).

2. "Illa, quae tota in sarcinis erat, et in omni urbe peregrina." Jerome *Ep.* 77.8.

3. "Necdum dictum, iam factum: emitur hospitium et ad hospitium turba concurrit. . . . Xenodochium in portu Romano situm totus pariter mundus audivit." Ibid., 77.10.

travel. Her story hints at the riches that an exploration of the origins and development of Christian religious travel in the West might uncover. The relationship between monasticism and travel seems at first to be one of opposition, especially when seen in light of the *Regula Benedictina* and its precursor, the *Regula Magistri,* with their attacks on wandering monks.[4] Further study, however, reveals a broad intersection of early monastic practices and itinerancy. This book explores that intersection, the world of men and women, such as Fabiola, who traveled and promoted travel for religious reasons, as a form of monasticism, with the belief that there was spiritual meaning in the itineracy itself. Though pilgrimage is a more familiar mode of Christian religious travel, and the one that eventually eclipsed all others, it was in a monastic milieu that religious travel first claimed an essential place within Christianity.

Between the fourth and the eighth centuries there were many incentives leading the Christian toward a life of movement. Escape from hostility, escape from social pressures, escape from the mundane, and the urge to commune with holy men and women, both living and dead—these were all motives for travel. The life of movement that could result from these motives came to constitute a special form of monastic spirituality derived from a quest for the ascetic qualities of the state of detachment, detachment from homeland and from family. Douglas Burton-Christie traces this theme of exile and detachment in the early formation of desert monasticism in his seminal work on the essential role of scripture and the monastic urge to become the embodiment of scripture.[5]

Evidence from a wide variety of sources points to the special religious value placed on travel by monks and other religious figures. Monasticism in late antiquity was itself a loosely defined, multifaceted phenomenon that incorporated a wide variety of ascetic practices. Among the monastic practices that arose during this period and in the absence of a commonly accepted paradigm of monastic behavior were a variety of forms of religious travel. Much of this early Christian religious travel focused not on a particular holy place, but rather on travel as a practical way of visiting living and dead holy

4. For an interesting analysis of the relationship, see Giles Constable, "Monachisme et Pèlerinage au Moyen Age," *Revue Historique* 258, no. 1 (1977): 3–27, and idem, "Opposition to Pilgrimage in the Middle Ages," in *Religious Life and Thought (11th–12th centuries),* ed. Giles Constable (London, 1979), 125–46.

5. Douglas Burton-Christie, *The Word in the Desert: Scripture and the Quest for Holiness in Early Christian Monasticism* (Oxford, 1993).

people, and as a means of religious expression of homelessness and temporal exile.[6] The theme of travel and pilgrimage to living holy people has recently been explored by Georgia Frank.[7] Although her travelers are not monastic, the phenomenon of this sort of travel in Egypt helps to create a richer picture of religious travel in late antiquity, one that contains a multiplicity of meanings and practices. Though often criticized by contemporaries, monastic travel was clearly a reality of the late antique world.

Monastic travel mirrored an interior journey or quest on both an individual level, the journey of the soul toward God and heavenly Jerusalem, and on the level of the church as a whole, as manifested in Augustine's notion of the City of God's journey on Earth. This mirroring quality of the inward journey attracted many early Christians. Travel was viewed as an imitation of the life of Christ, a literal rendering of the life of a Christian, a life only "temporarily on this earth." One was a wanderer until death, and with death eternal life in the Christian's true homeland, heavenly Jerusalem. This idea was echoed by Orosius, Augustine's famous letter carrier and himself a long-distance traveler, when he wrote, "I enjoy every land temporarily as my fatherland, because what is truly my fatherland and that which I love, is not completely on this earth."[8]

The idea of perpetual pilgrimage, although in an allegorical form, is also found in the writings of the Church Fathers, who used it, curiously enough, to denigrate itinerant spirituality of the terrestrial sort. Authors such as Augustine, Jerome, and much later, Bede pointed to the notion of the spiritual "homelessness" of the Christian, whose true home was in the heavenly paradise, the idea that all Christians were always temporary sojourners on earth. Implicit and sometimes explicit in these discussions was a critique of those who took the image of homelessness *ad literam* by traveling constantly. Physical travel also served as a corporeal metaphor for spiritual progress and movement, with the journey itself reflecting the

6. On the themes of Christian exile and wandering, see Gerhart B. Ladner, *"Homo Viator:* Mediaeval Ideas on Alienation and Order," *Speculum* 42, no. 2 (1967); G. E. Gould, "Moving on and Staying put in the Apophthegmata Patrum," *Studia Patristica* 20 (1989): 231–37; and Elisabeth Malamut, *Sur la route des saints byzantins* (Paris, 1993).

7. Georgia Frank, *The Memory of the Eyes: Pilgrims to Living Saints in Christian Late Antiquity* (Berkeley and Los Angeles, 2000).

8. "Utor temporarie omni terra quasi patria, quia quae vera est et illa quam amo patria in terra penitus non est." Orosius *Historiarum adversum paganos libri VII* (henceforth *Hist.*) 5.2. All translations of Orosius's *Hist.* are from Roy J. Deferrari, trans., *Paulus Orosius: The Seven Books of History Against the Pagans* (Washington, D.C., 1964).

spiritual growth of the traveler. Augustine uses this metaphor in his *Confessions* with his discussion of his journey of the soul and his own physical journey from Thagaste to Carthage, Rome, Milan, and back to Africa.

Recently, Mediterranean culture and society in the transitional phase linking the ancient and medieval periods have been the focus of a great deal of historical study. The impact of monasticism on this world, however, was long obscured by the perceived nature of the institution, its isolation and separation from society. Monasticism in its many forms, scholars are now acknowledging, played an integral role in the social, cultural, and political history of this period. Path-breaking work in this area has been done by Philip Rousseau. His works have explored the development of early monasticism in relation to the greater fabric of late antique society.[9] Recent scholarship has made great strides in the investigation of monks and their relation to the society around them.[10] The wandering monks discussed by Daniel Caner were part of the economic and social fabric of the eastern Mediterranean.[11] These proto-mendicants claimed to offer their prayers and sanctity in return for material support, though not without some controversy and opposition from authorities. Caner views these monks as operating within a model of apostolic poverty. These studies have revealed monasticism as a socially and politically important phenomenon, which could challenge episcopal and civic authority. They have helped to reveal the role of the holy man and holy woman in society. Some scholars have traced the early tensions between anchoritic and cenobitic monasticism, and most recently turned their attention to the important role of women in early ascetic practices and in the spread of monasticism in Asia Minor.[12]

Large number of monks fleeing civic and familial duties in order to lead monastic lives had a profound effect on society. The movement spread quickly because of the rapid circulation of accounts of famous monks, such

9. Philip Rousseau made the most valuable contribution with his book, *Ascetics, Authority, and the Church in the Age of Jerome and Cassian* (Oxford, 1978). His subsequent books have concentrated on the study of Eastern monks, *Pachomius: The Making of a Community in Fourth-Century Egypt* (Berkeley and Los Angeles, 1985) and *Basil of Caesarea* (Berkeley and Los Angeles, 1994).

10. See Derwas Chitty, *The Desert a City: An Introduction to the Study of Egyptian and Palestinian Monasticism under the Christian Empire* (Crestwood, N.Y., 1966); Peter Brown, *The Body and Society: Men, Women and Sexual Renunciation in Early Christianity* (New York, 1988); and Susanna Elm, *Virgins of God: The Making of Asceticism in Late Antiquity* (Oxford, 1994).

11. Daniel Caner, *Wandering, Begging Monks: Spiritual Authority and the Promotion of Monasticism in Late Antiquity* (Berkeley and Los Angeles, 2002).

12. See Elm, *Virgins of God*.

as Antony, Pachomius, and Paul the Hermit.[13] It was hearing the story of Antony that triggered Augustine's final conversion; it was a monastic impulse, an impulse fulfilled in his first actions upon conversion: to resign his position in Milan, to not marry but instead begin a chaste life, and to flee society.[14] He retired to a life of monastic pursuits and contemplation at Cassiciacum with a small group of his friends, and when he returned to Africa, he started a similar community in Thagaste.[15] But Augustine is only one example of the effects of the monastic impulse. For women, monasticism offered an alternative to marriage or remarriage, as well as a way of fulfilling a religious vocation in a world where they were increasingly barred from leadership positions in the church.

The *Regula Benedictina,* written in Italy in the middle of the sixth century, presents a set of monastic regulations that was to become by the tenth century the most influential monastic rule in Western Europe. It prescribes for the monk a life of stability in a monastery, under a written rule and an abbot, emphasizing the isolation and otherworldliness of the monastery itself. Through the spread and dominance of the Benedictine Rule these attributes became so powerfully identified with monks and monasteries in the West that they have become part of their very definitions. The pervasive influence of the Benedictine Rule so overshadowed the early diversity of Western monasticism that it has often led some to project this identity even on monastic practices predating the rule. Thus the reification of stability as a defining element of Western monasticism from its beginnings has obscured the true diversity of early monasticism in the West and has in turn excluded travel as a possible monastic pursuit. One work that has avoided this pitfall is Marilyn Dunn's recent book, which explores the important relationship

---

13. Between 379 and 381, Jerome wrote the *Life of Paul the Hermit* in Latin, and by the 380s, Augustine had read a Latin translation of the *Life of St. Antony.* On Antony, see Chitty, *The Desert a City;* the Robert C. Gregg translation of Athanasius of Alexandria, *Vita Antonii;* Otto F. A. Meinardus, *Monks and Monasteries of the Egyptian Deserts* (Cairo, 1989 [1961]); and the Paul B. Harvey Jr. translation of Jerome's *Life of Paul.*

14. Augustine *Confessiones* 8.14–16. All translations of the *Confessions* are from Henry Chadwick, ed., *Augustine's Confessions* (Oxford, 1992).

15. "Ac placuit ei percepta gratia cum aliis civibus et amicis suis Deo pariter servientibus ad Africam et propriam domum agrosque remeare. Ad quos veniens et in quibus constitutus ferme triennio et a se iam alienatis, cum his qui eidem adhaerebant Deo vivebat, ieiuniis, orationibus, bonis operibus, in lege Domini meditans die ac nocte." Possidius *Vita Augustini* 3.2; translation from Thomas F. X. Noble and Thomas Head, eds., *Soldiers of Christ: Saints and Saints' Lives from Late Antiquity and the Early Middle Ages* (University Park, Pa., 1995), 33–73. All translations of Possidius's *Vita Augustini* are from Noble and Head. See also Augustine *Confessiones* 8.9.

between Eastern and Western monasticism, as well as the eventual development of Benedictine monasticism. Dunn is one of the few scholars who treats the full diversity of early monastic experience.[16]

The *Regula Benedictina* and its important predecessor, the *Regula Magistri*, both in fact discuss monastic travel in detail. Although both rules condemn the practice of monastic wandering, both clearly present travel as a fact of daily monastic life. The denunciations of the *gyrovague* have been interpreted as satires or rhetorical devices to better expound the virtues of proper monastic behavior based on stability. A great deal of internal evidence and evidence from other rules and a variety of other sources, however, points to a different interpretation of these canonical texts, and suggests that the monastic travel they condemn was a reality.

Pilgrimage is the most widely known of all forms of religiously motivated travel.[17] The title "pilgrim" has been bestowed on a wide variety of religious travelers, sometimes without careful attention to either the meaning of the term or to the precise motivation for and structure of the journey in question. Indeed, the word "pilgrimage" has taken on such a variety of powerful connotations that it has often distorted the actual practices it purports to describe.[18] The meanings the terms *peregrinus* and *peregrinatio* acquired in the Middle Ages have often served, since that time, to mask the diversity and unique structures of religious travel before that time, especially for the late antique period.

Many have assumed that Christian pilgrimage traces its roots to biblical injunction and that the practice began in the early church, thereafter existing

16. Marilyn Dunn, *The Emergence of Monasticism: From the Desert Fathers to the Early Middle Ages* (Oxford, 2000).

17. The best historical discussion of pilgrimage to date is David Frankfurter's introduction to a collection of articles on late antique Egypt, *Pilgrimage and Holy Space in Late Antique Egypt* (Leiden, 1998), 7–47. Frankfurter breaks away from the traditional view of pilgrimage as transcending history and place. He shows that if we place pilgrimage within its social, historical, and cultural contexts, it emerges not as a single, relatively uniform entity, but rather as a series of different practices. He distinguishes different types of pilgrimage—goal-oriented, peripathic, and stational—but perhaps the most useful part of his study is his belief that Christian pilgrimage is a construction, not an intrinsic part of Christianity.

18. This point is made in a recent paper by Gillian Clark, "Going Home: Soul Travel in Late Antiquity," in *Travel, Communication and Geography in Late Antiquity*, ed. L. Ellis and F. L. Kidner (Ashgate, 2004). Clark looks at Augustine's use of *peregrinatio* and *peregrinus* in his *De civitate Dei*. She states that *peregrinatio* should not be translated as "pilgrimage"—the City of God is not on pilgrimage, but rather is a stranger. Thus the City of God is full of foreigners, not pilgrims. Becoming a *peregrinus* is becoming a stranger or foreigner in your land rather than going on an edifying journey.

as a relatively unbroken and unchanging tradition, isolated from temporal, geographic, and cultural contexts.[19] Even the study of Christian liturgy, by its nature a conservative and defiantly unchanging topic, has not been accorded the static uniformity in practice and function that the study of pilgrimage has.[20] Pilgrimage appears to occupy a rarefied place in studies of the late antique and medieval worlds.[21]

In this study, I distinguish monastic travel from pilgrimage—that is to say, goal-centered, religious travel for an efficacious purpose. A close examination of late antique spiritual itinerants provides a clearer and more nuanced account of religious travel. It allows us to consider travel as part of a wandering and ascetic life, either on a voluntary basis or as a religious justification for forced migration. Many of what have been considered attacks on pilgrimage in late antiquity and the early Middle Ages might be better understood as attacks on ascetic or monastic travel.

The Mediterranean basin was the birthplace of Christian religious travel, and hence defines the geographical focus of this study. As a movement,

19. With the recent jubilee year there have been quite a few books published on Rome and her pilgrims. One of the best of these is by Debra Birch. Her treatment of pilgrimage to Rome in the Middle Ages is illuminating and convincing. The book, however, avoids the task of dealing with the origins of pilgrimage to the city by appearing to assume that pilgrimage is something innate within Christianity and therefore must have always existed. Birch seems to believe in the biblical origins of Christian pilgrimage. She states that the earliest evidence for pilgrimage to Rome comes from the second-century journey of Abercio, a Phrygian bishop, and that there is an unbroken continuity of pilgrimage to the city throughout the Middle Ages. Our evidence of Abercio's voyage comes from a single inscription, and the fact that he was a bishop may point to other reasons for his visit to Rome, rather than a pilgrimage. Debra J. Birch, *Pilgrimage to Rome in the Middle Ages: Continuity and Change* (Woodbridge, Suffolk, 1998), esp. 1, 6, and 23. Another excellent recent book that has a similar view of pilgrimage is Mario D'Onofrio, *Romei and Giubilei: Il pellegrinaggio medievale a San Pietro (350–1350)* (Rome, 1999).

20. The origins and variations of medieval liturgical practice have been carefully plotted and studied within a historical framework in works such as John F. Baldovin, *The Urban Character of Christian Worship: The Origins, Development, and Meaning of Stational Liturgy* (Rome, 1987); Pablo C. Diaz, "Monasticism and Liturgy in Visigothic Spain," in *The Visigoths: Studies in Culture and Society*, ed. Alberto Ferreiro (Leiden, 1999); and Victor Saxer, "L'utilisation par la liturgie de l'espace urbain et suburbain: L'exemple de Rome dans l'antiquité et le haut moyen âge," in *Actes du XIe Congrès International d'Archéologie Chrétienne* (Rome, 1989).

21. One of the major assumptions about pilgrimage is that it is a simple and easily definable set of actions. Pilgrimage is perceived as so obviously simple to comprehend that its origins need no explanation or examination. Peter Llewellyn refers to almost all travelers to Rome, no matter what their reason, as pilgrims. Refugees, episcopal visitors, wandering monks, and those seeking works from Rome's libraries are all grouped together into a discussion of pilgrimage to the city. See P. A. B. Llewellyn, "Rome of the Pilgrims," in *Rome in the Dark Ages* (London, 1993), 173–98. There have been some notable exceptions to this practice, such as the excellent study by Frankfurter, *Pilgrimage and Holy Space in Late Antique Egypt,* which truly treats pilgrimage as a multifaceted and historically contextualized phenomenon.

monasticism physically spread from the East to the West via the travels of people, books, and stories of the monks. Many in Spain and Italy wished to visit the legendary monks of Egypt, Palestine, and Syria, and the Mediterranean, rather than being an impediment, provided a convenient means of access. The Iberian Peninsula, Italy, and the Holy Land all had a special role in early Christian travel, and subsequently these regions provide the strongest evidence of religious travel and travelers. It was also here that by the Middle Ages, important pilgrimage sites first emerged: Santiago de Compostela in Spain, Rome in Italy, and Jerusalem in the Holy Land. This study also explores the special role of women in early Christian travel because women, in their roles as travelers and patrons, emerged as a crucial element in the source material. While it is accurate to say that both women and men traveled for religious reasons in this period, the conjunction of travel, monasticism, and patronage seems to have been particularly appealing to women. Women and their religious lives emerge throughout the chapters of this book. This culture of monastic travel comes to an abrupt end, particularly for women, by the ninth century with the emergence of a more fully cloistered monastic experience for women. An Egeria or Melania would be hard to imagine in the Carolingian period. Even royal or imperial travel by women—such as the voyage of the Byzantine princess Theophano to the Ottonian court for her wedding to Otto II—was considered exceptional and extraordinary in the tenth century.

The chapters of this study are thematic in nature, though they do roughly follow chronological order, exploring the development of ascetic travel between the fourth and eighth centuries. The earlier chapters primarily deal with the fourth through sixth centuries, and the last three chapters are concerned with the sixth through eighth centuries. The first chapter discusses travel in the ancient and medieval world, describing the rich culture surrounding movement in late antique Mediterranean society through a discussion of the logistics of travel, differing motives for travel, and the growing opposition to religious travel in particular. This points to a marked increase in travel that took place in the late antique period in spite of the many hardships travelers faced.

Chapter 2 explores the lives of two well-known travelers, Egeria and Orosius, who, though they made similar journeys only a generation apart, are rarely discussed together or seen in the same light. The voyages and writings of both these figures, viewed alongside the writing of Bachiarius, point to a particular form of religious travel within a monastic milieu. Defying the patterns and assumptions of the anachronistic category of "pilgrim," these Iberian travelers of the fourth and fifth centuries further elucidate the possibilities of an early interpretation of the monastic impulse that embraced travel and homelessness as essential to religious life and provide a model with which to analyze subsequent travelers.

Chapter 3 turns to evidence of the modes and meanings of monastic travel through a discussion of early written monastic rules and texts. It concentrates specifically on the emergence of the *gyrovague* or wandering monk as one of the categories of false monk within the developing typology of monks included in many Western monastic texts. The analysis of this typology serves as a way of understanding Western notions of legitimate monastic practices and highlights the importance of this often dismissed categorization. The *Regula Magistri* figures prominently in this chapter because of its invention of and near obsession with the gyrovague. The chapter finally turns to the regulations within the *Regula Magistri* concerning hospitality, reception of new members, and travel—all of which were viewed by the author of the rule as necessary but potentially dangerous to life in the monastery. I argue that the pervasiveness and vigor of these attacks on monastic travel and wandering serve as evidence that these practices were indeed present and provides us a unique insight into the structure and meaning of the religious wandering they sought to exclude from proper monastic behavior.

Chapter 4 focuses on the many Western women travelers to the East, exploring the role of monastic vocation and patronage in their journeys. Through a close examination of the women who traveled to Jerusalem, this chapter demonstrates the impact of travelers on the city and its Christian, and especially monastic, topography.

Much of the special nature of monastic travel can be traced to one crucial geographic region: the Iberian Peninsula, homeland of Egeria, Orosius, and Bachiarius. In Chapter 5, therefore, I trace the connections between Spanish monasticism and travel from the fourth century to the beginning of Islamic rule in the early eighth century. This chapter relies heavily on hagiographic evidence in addition to letters and monastic rules. Hagiography, or lives of the saints, is a special form of literature with its own conventions and a strong adherence to specific models, such as the *Life of Antony* and the lives written by Jerome. Previously historians shied away from using these sorts of texts because of their use of *topoi* and the overt attempts to mold facts into a story of the sanctity of a particular individual. By understanding the conventions of hagiography and the limitations inherent in its form, however, many modern-day historians have successfully used these texts to illuminate, not only the life of a particular individual, but also the social milieu, social interactions, and relations evidenced in the texts. By carefully peeling away the layers of *topoi,* and by exploring those areas where the text does not quite fit the conventions, one can begin to make use of hagiography. This is the case in Chapter 5, which relies on many Iberian works of hagiography, such as *Lives of the Fathers of Mérida,* the *Life of Saint Fructuosus,* and the *Life of Saint Emilian.*

Chapter 6 examines the evolution of Christian monastic travel in the seventh and eighth centuries, tracing the impact of Islam on the religious topography of Jerusalem and on Christian travel to the East, and the impact of Benedictine monasticism, with its emphasis on physical stability, on notions of monastic travel. The Mediterranean tradition of mostly first-hand accounts of monastic travel, like those of Egeria and the Piacenza Pilgrim, seems to vanish. Surprisingly, the only narratives of monastic travel in this period come from two insular writers, the Irish abbot of Iona, Adomnán, and the Anglo-Saxon nun, Huneberc, each of whom wrote a secondhand account of a long-distance, religious journey.

The epilogue explores how and why religious travel and monasticism diverged so greatly. It examines the importance of the Cluniac reform movement and the creation of the pilgrimage center of Santiago de Compostela in the emergence of a new model of religious travel: goal-centered, long-distance pilgrimage aimed at the laity rather than at monks.

CHAPTER ONE

THE CULTURE OF MOVEMENT

The nature, meaning, and perception of travel and of travelers changed during late antiquity. Refugees, Christian officials, women, and monks joined the ranks of the soldiers, Roman officials, merchants, and messengers who traditionally made up the majority of Roman travelers.[1] Many late antique travelers were on the road not by their own choice, but in flight from the urban upheaval resulting from Germanic migrations. As refugees headed first into Africa, and later, after the Vandal invasions, eastward to Egypt, Palestine, Syria, Greece, and Asia Minor, which were still under Roman control, long-distance travel increased dramatically, and upheaval and displacement became a way of life in the late empire.

As travel became more common, it became in many respects more difficult and more dangerous, and the stresses that this shift created caused a deep transformation in attitudes toward travel. Rather than being regarded as a desperate condition, wandering and homelessness could now be infused with meaning, including religious meaning.[2] Just as the ranks of Roman travelers were swelling, Christianity was beginning to have a major impact on the social and cultural fabric of Mediterranean society, not only bringing new ideas and rituals, but also providing new meanings and interpretations

---

1. Pleasure or tourism was not a factor in late antique and early medieval travel. Evidence of leisure travel is rare, though the surviving sources may not give an entirely balanced picture. There is ample evidence that by the tenth or eleventh century leisure travel, such as families gathering to celebrate weddings and festivals, was relatively common. S. D. Goitein, *A Mediterranean Society: The Jewish Communities of the Arab World as Portrayed in the Documents of the Cairo Geniza,* 3 vols. (Berkeley and Los Angeles, 1967), 1:273–75.

2. For discussions on wandering as part of a monastic life, see Malamut, *Sur la route des saints byzantins;* Bernhard Kötting, *Peregrinatio Religiosa: Wallfahrten in der Antike und das Pilgerwesen in der alten Kirche* (Regensberg, 1950), 302–7; and Salvatore Pricoco, "Il Monachesimo Occidentale dalle origini al maestro lineamenti storici e percorsi storiografici," in *Il Monachesimo Occidentale dalle origini alla Regula Magistri* (Rome, 1998), 17–18.

to many aspects of everyday life. At the same time, debate surrounded every attempt to define proper Christian behavior. In this world of new possibilities, Christian travel was open to seemingly limitless interpretation. Yet every form of religiously significant travel that arose was necessarily circumscribed by the practical limitations of travel in general during late antiquity.[3] To reconstruct the forms and patterns of religious travel that developed in the world of the late antique Mediterranean, therefore, we must first explore the physical conditions and possibilities of travel in general in that world.

LOGISTICS OF TRAVEL

Travel was an integral part of Roman identity and culture because travel had played an essential role in Roman society from its beginning. The empire was created through conquest, but kept together through communication, colonization, and the presence of the Roman military. Roads made an early appearance in this culture as a means of strengthening the cohesion of the empire. Roman expansion first occurred throughout Italy and later continued throughout the entire region surrounding the Mediterranean. The hub of the Roman Empire was this vast sea, which functioned as a water-highway linking the far reaches of the provinces. As provincial expansion moved inland, rivers and roads began to play an integral part in this cohesion.[4]

Movement existed at the heart of the Roman Empire. The enduring remains of the vast Roman road system serve as a physical reminder of the importance of travel in the Roman world. The army and its suppliers used the roads for efficient troop movements and kept in touch with the capital city by means of the *cursus publicus,* the imperial postal and transportation service, the backbone of communication in the Roman world. Roman vessels crossed the Mediterranean and sailed up its rivers. Two hundred years of relative peace and tranquility, beginning with the reign of Augustus, aided the process of Romanization of the Mediterranean basin, which caused the migration of many Romans to distant provinces.

3. For travel in late antiquity and the early Middle Ages, see Michael McCormick, *Origins of the European Economy: Communications and Commerce, A.D. 300–900* (Cambridge, 2001); L. Casson, *Travel in the Ancient World* (Toronto, 1974); and Albert C. Leighton, *Transport and Communication in Early Medieval Europe, A.D. 500–1100* (Devon, 1972).

4. On the early history of the Mediterranean, see Peregrine Horden and Nicholas Purcell, *The Corrupting Sea: A Study of Mediterranean History* (Oxford, 2000).

Sea travel was by far the fastest and most efficient form of transportation, but it, too, had its difficulties. Since sailors navigated by sight, sea voyages were restricted to the predominately clear months from April to October.[5] For the most part, boats clung to the coastline during voyages, within sight of land. Danger, however, could not always be avoided; piracy and shipwreck were ever-present threats.

The ships of the Mediterranean were sailing vessels, though many were equipped with oars that could be used when the winds were weak and during emergencies. These ships were for the most part square-rigged, the sails standing perpendicular to the hull. These sails could only be adjusted a few degrees, making it difficult to sail in any direction but downwind. During the sailing season, the prevailing winds were northerlies, making it faster and easier to sail to the southeast.[6] Thus, the voyage from Rome to Alexandria took some ten days, while the return trip took at least twice as long and sometimes up to two months.[7] Conditions on the Red Sea were different, with the majority of the ships being Egyptian, lateen-rigged vessels that were far more maneuverable and could sail closer to the wind. The Red Sea played a vital role in linking trade from the Arabian peninsula, Ethiopia, and even India to the Mediterranean provinces. To the North, the Irish Sea and the North Sea become important zones for travel in late antiquity and the early Middle Ages. Irish monks in particular made much use of these waterways.

During late antiquity, the majority of travel and movement had to do with trade and the commercial transport of goods. Grain shipment from North Africa and Egypt to the metropolitan areas of Rome and Constantinople constituted a major portion of Mediterranean shipping. Most of the vessels on the Mediterranean were either commercial boats, carrying cargo of various sorts, or small fishing boats. The majority of the cargo transported was grain, olive oil, and wine, but luxury items, animals for the arena, and building materials also made their way to cities via the Mediterranean.[8] Between the first and sixth centuries, the giant obelisks that still

---

5. A law of Gratian, Valentinian, and Theodosius states that there should be no shipping from November to the kalends of April in order to prevent shipwrecks. *Codex Theodosianus* (henceforth *CTh*) 13.9.3.

6. J. H. Pryor, *Geography, Technology and War: Studies in the Maritime History of the Mediterranean, 649–1571* (Cambridge, 1988); Kevin Greene, *The Archaeology of the Roman Economy* (Berkeley and Los Angeles, 1986).

7. Casson, *Travel in the Ancient World*, 151–52.

8. Lionel Casson, *Ships and Seamanship in the Ancient World* (Princeton, N.J., 1971), 172–73.

grace the cities of Rome and Constantinople were transported from Egypt, first via river barge, and then by cargo ship.[9] Shipping was a risky endeavor for merchants, not only in terms of potential loss of vessel and cargo to shipwreck; merchant vessels could also be confiscated. Surviving laws from the Theodosian Code reveal that privately owned boats could be commandeered as troop or grain transports.[10]

Passenger craft were virtually unknown in late antiquity. If someone wanted to travel on the seas, he or she had to book passage on a freighter. Passengers would most likely live on deck and bring their own provisions, while the captain usually supplied water. The largest vessels on the seas were the huge grain transport ships used to supply the great cities, such as Rome and Constantinople, with the *annona,* the imperial gift of free grain for the urban population.[11] Passage on these ships was costly for routine travelers, but many used them, sometimes secretly. Palladius relates the story of an Egyptian holy man named Sarapion who was a stowaway on one of the great grain carriers traveling from Alexandria to Rome.[12] When he was discovered, after the fifth day of the voyage, the sailors were initially angry, but when they realized that he had not eaten in five days, they took pity on him and fed him for the duration of the journey. It would have been tempting fate to throw the holy man overboard.

In the sixth-century *Life of Nicholas of Sion,* Nicholas travels to the Holy Land three times by ship. In this text the sailors are pleased to have him aboard. On his first voyage, it is the skipper of the boat who, upon hearing that Nicholas wants to travel to the Holy Land, seeks him out and offers passage.[13] The second voyage is plagued by storms that topple the mast and nearly sink the ship. It is only through Nicholas's prayers that the men are saved.[14] Nicholas uses his reputation as a useful passenger to persuade a

9. Recent underwater archaeologoical evidence has shown that vessels were often used to haul building material, such as giant columns and statues for decoration. See Greene, *Archaeology,* 17–35, and Casson, *Ships and Seamanship,* chap. 14.

10. The Theodosian code contains many laws dealing with shipping and shipwrecks. See, for example, *CTh* 13.5–9.

11. The masters of these ships received special imperial privileges and protection. See, for example, *CTh* 13.5.9. For the ships themselves, see Christoffer H. Ericsson, *Navis Oneraria: The Cargo Carrier of Late Antiquity, Studies in Ancient Ship Carpentry* (Åbo, 1984).

12. Palladius *Historia Lausiaca* (henceforth *HL*) 37.9–11. Translation from R. T. Myers, ed., *Lausiac History* (London, 1965).

13. *The Life of Saint Nicholas of Sion,* ed. and trans. Ihor Sevcenko and Nancy Patterson Sevcenko (Brookline, Mass., 1984), 8.

14. Ibid., 27–32.

Rhodian skipper to take him back to Asia Minor. He finds a boat stranded for three days in the port of Ascalon waiting for favorable winds and asks for passage for himself and his followers: "Take me in your boat, and the Lord will help you."[15] The favorable winds do eventually arrive, but then Nicholas is faced with a dilemma that passengers often confronted: the skipper refuses to stop at the port at which Nicholas and his company were to disembark, stating that he did not wish to risk losing such good winds. The boat's final destination is Constantinople, and the captain had not planned on stopping until they had reached Rhodes. Nicholas's attempts to change the captain's mind fail, and so he resorts to prayer. A sudden storm convinces the captain of the holy man's power, yet he still refuses to set into port, instead sending Nicholas and his men off in a small dinghy.[16]

The sources are replete with maritime disasters. The Theodosian Code contains an entire section on sea transport and shipwrecks.[17] A single shipwreck could quite easily ruin a long-distance trader and his investors. Roman law attempted to provide remedies for such disasters. Other sources also give us intriguing glimpses of how travelers actually experienced these dangers. In 423, the empress Galla Placidia and her two young children, the future emperor Valentinian III and his sister Honoria, were caught in a terrible storm in the Adriatic and promised to build a new church in Ravenna if they survived.[18] Once safely in Ravenna, she had two churches built, one of which, St. John the Divine, fulfilled her vow; the dedicatory inscription reads, "Galla Placidia, along with her son Placidus Valentinian Augustus and her daughter Justa Grata Honoria Augusta, paid off their vow for their liberation from the danger of the sea."[19]

15. Ibid., 36.

16. Ibid., 38.

17. See *CTh* 13.5–9.

18. Imperial travel constituted yet another form of late antique movement. The emperor and his family members frequently undertook special visits of imperial patronage to cities of the empire. These visits were celebrated with an *adventus* ceremony, a ritual procession of the imperial person into the city, with rounds of acclamations and displays of respect from the city's prominent citizens. Examples of such visits include the *adventus* of Julian to Antioch and of Constantius to Rome. Julian's was recorded by Ammianus Marcellinus in *Res Gestae* 22.9, 14–15. For Julian, see also R. L. Rike, *Apex Omnium: Religion in the "Res Gestae" of Ammianus* (Berkeley and Los Angeles, 1987), 52–68. Sozomen provides a Christian account of Julian's failed *adventus* in Antioch, in Sozomen *Historia ecclesiastica* 5.19–20. Constantius's *adventus* was also recorded in Ammianus Marcellinus *Res Gestae* 16.10, and in Themistius *Oratio*, bk. 3, ed. H. Schenkl et al. (Leipzig, 1965–74), to commemorate the event. See also Sabine G. MacCormack, *Art and Ceremony in Late Antiquity* (Berkeley and Los Angeles, 1981), and Michael McCormick, *Eternal Victory: Triumphal Rulership in Late Antiquity, Byzantium, and the Early Medieval West* (Cambridge, 1990).

19. S. I. Oost, *Galla Placidia Augusta: A Biographical Essay* (Chicago, 1968).

Sea travel played an important role in the spread of Irish monasticism, and Irish saints' lives are filled with maritime adventures. The sixth-century monk Columba, founder of the monasteries of Derry and Durrow, was later exiled from Ireland and wandered the seas before establishing the monastery of Iona on an isolated island off the Scottish coast.[20] Vessels could and did leave the confines of the Mediterranean and venture up the Atlantic coast to the British Isles. The island monasteries built by the Irish became stopping points for many sea travelers. The seventh-century abbot of Iona, Adomnán, based his *De locis sanctis* on a firsthand account of the Holy Land he heard during a conversation with a Gallic bishop, Arculf.[21] Arculf had traveled throughout the eastern Mediterranean and related his story to Adomnán after having been shipwrecked at Iona.

River travel was more difficult, time-consuming, and expensive than sea travel.[22] Given the limitations of the ships' rigging, it was nearly impossible to sail on most rivers. River boats were usually barges hauled by slaves or animals on the towpaths cleared on either side. The Tiber was a particularly difficult river to navigate because it is both narrow and shallow, which meant that it had to be dredged frequently. The twenty-two-mile stretch of the Tiber from the port of Ostia to Rome itself was an expensive addition to the price of grain shipments to the city. It could cost up to nine times more to move goods a few miles upriver than to ship them a similar distance by sea.

One exception to the general unnavigability of rivers was the Nile. The prevailing winds carried traffic south, and the current carried it north again. The ease of travel on the Nile caused some Red Sea traders to unload goods bound for the Mediterranean at an Egyptian port and transport them overland to the great river. At its closest point, the Nile is separated from the Red Sea by an eight-day trek across the desert.[23] These two water-ways were the principal commercial links between the Mediterranean world and Ethiopia, Yemen, and India.

---

20. See Adomnán of Iona, *Life of Saint Columba*, ed. A. O. Anderson and M. O. Anderson (London, 1961).

21. *Adamnan's De Locis Sanctis,* ed. Denis Meehan (Dublin, 1958). See Chapter 6 herein for more on Arculf's voyage.

22. The cost of transporting goods by river was around five to six times the cost by sea. For a discussion of the ratio of transportation costs by sea, river, and land, see Greene, *Archaeology,* 39–41.

23. Lionel Casson, *The Ancient Mariners: Seafarers and Sea Fighters of the Mediterranean in Ancient Times* (Princeton, N.J., 1991), 10.

Rivers in the northern provinces were essential to the defense of the empire and to the process of Romanization. The Rhine and Danube, rivers that marked the frontier between the Roman world and the Germanic tribes, were also used for the transportation of troops and supplies. Inland cities in Gaul and Spain were for the most part established on rivers. The Rhône served to link the interior of Gaul to the Mediterranean, as the Seine linked the interior to the English Channel and the North Sea. The city of Trier, one of Constantine's capitals, was established on the Moselle, a tributary of the Rhine. In Spain, the Ebro valley was an early center of Roman settlement on the peninsula. Most of the Roman cities of Spain, such as Saragossa, on the Ebro, Seville, on the Guadalquivir, and Mérida, on the Guadiana, were important river cities.

Overland transportation of goods and foodstuff was very costly, up to sixty times more than maritime transportation. Because of the high cost, ground transport of goods occurred only when absolutely necessary. Most people on the road were not traders, but instead soldiers, messengers, itinerant peddlers, refugees, and religious travelers. Military expeditions added to the traffic on Roman roads; roads were necessary for the mobilization of troops, a need that only increased in the late empire and during the establishment of the subsequent Germanic kingdoms in the West. Though slow and laborious, overland road travel was probably the most frequent choice for individual travelers, in that it gave them greater control over their journeys.[24] Overland travel did not require securing passage, and decisions about departure or stopping to rest were entirely left to the discretion of the individual traveler. Rivers and streams, so useful for trade and inland commerce, became impediments for the overland traveler, however, especially in the western and northern provinces. Although the Romans constructed many bridges, some of which still stand, most rivers, streams, and swamps had to be crossed in some other fashion.

The Roman road system was not initially constructed with state funds, but was instead built by wealthy elites as part of their duty when they served as public officials. Roads and bridges, though very durable, did need regular and costly maintenance. Even during the political upheavals in the late empire, the Roman road system was maintained and remained functional.[25]

---

24. Less costly in terms of personal travel, not transporting goods. See Greene, *Archaeology*, 40.

25. *CTh* 15.3.4, a law of Arcadius and Honorius, dated 399, in affirming the duty of landowners to repair the roads, does, however, state that the roads were in "immense ruin."

Upkeep of the roads was paid for by the localities through which they passed.[26] In theory, overland travel, unlike sea travel, could occur at any time of year. In the north, however, snow and ice prevented many from making journeys in winter. Regular markers, or mileposts, inscribed with the distances to and from various cities along the roadway, guided travelers toward their ultimate destinations. Some roads even had special stone stands to aid travelers on horseback to mount their horses. The Peutinger Map, a twelfth-century copy of a fourth-century road map, reveals that the Roman original was designed to be easy to use while traveling.[27] The map shows the entire Mediterranean basin, which is laid out in a strange, elongated form, with all the roads drawn in and cities and towns clearly marked to show proper routes and convenient stopping points. The map's function was clearly related to road travel. It was probably produced for official or military travelers, but some scholars suggest that similar, perhaps simpler roadmaps were available for common use. The early fourth-century text known as the Bordeaux itinerary opens and closes with a list of place-names and distances between towns, cities, changing stations or *mutationes,* and road markers for the journey from Bordeaux to the Holy Land and for a return trip via Rome and Milan.[28] Clearly the author of the Bordeaux itinerary created this work to aid other travelers.[29] For instance, he, or she, describes the city of Bordeaux

26. *CTh* 15.3, "The Construction and Repair of Roads," contains six laws, beginning with one from Constantine, affirming the duty of landowners to repair the roads. *CTh* 11.16.10, a law of Julian from 362, states that payment for the repair of roads was customary practice in the provinces. *CTh* 11.16.15 and 11.16.18 concern exemption from "compulsory public service of a menial nature," defined in each law to include the construction and care of roads and bridges. *CTh* 11.10.2, a law of Valentian, Valens, and Gratian dating from 370, freed provincial officials from certain services. An exemption, however, is made for the repair of the bridge at Livenza, "as often as the occasion requires, it shall be repaired by the landowners of the municipality in their own territory."

27. Annalina Levi and Mario Levi, *Itineraria Picta: Contributo allo Studio della Tabula Peutingeriana* (Rome, 1967).

28. The traditional English name of this account, the "Bordeaux Pilgrim's Guide," is another example of how ubiquitous is the assumption that any journey that includes the Holy Land must have been made by a "pilgrim." I do not believe that this work necessarily reflects a pilgrimage. *Itinerarium Burdigalense* (henceforth *Itin. Burd.*), in *Itineraria et alia geographica,* ed. P. Geyer and O. Cuntz, *CC* 175:1–26. At a recent conference Benet Salway presented some of his research on the Bordeaux itinerary and also agrees that is not a pilgrimage text. R. W. B. Salway, "Itineraries in Use," in *Travel, Communication and Geography in Late Antiquity,* ed. L. Ellis and F. L. Kidner (Ashgate, 2004).

29. Most scholars have viewed the function of this very schematic work as an aid to pilgrims traveling to the Holy Land. See, for example, Casson, *Travel in the Ancient World,* 307, and E. D. Hunt, *Holy Land Pilgrimage in the Later Roman Empire, A.D. 312–460* (Oxford, 1982), 55. Recently Laurie Douglas has questioned the intended use of the itinerary as a "pilgrim

as located on the Garonne river and specifies the distance between the city and access to the sea.[30] The distances between listed stopping points range from five to eighteen miles, which indicates its usefulness for travel by foot or by slow mule.[31] The Bordeaux itinerary was one of many such travel guides that were produced and used in late antiquity, and these accounts were probably written, not as reports of a personal voyage or pilgrimage, but rather as tools for travel by others.[32] They could have easily been copied, carried, and added to as the situation on the road changed.

The *cursus publicus,* the Roman postal service, operated throughout the empire. It not only transported messages, but also people traveling on official business.[33] Evidence from the Theodosian Code reveals that the system was often abused, and it was common for well-heeled travelers to bribe their way onto an official wagon.[34] Some emperors extended this service to bishops traveling to church councils.[35] At its swiftest, the *cursus publicus* could cover

guide" created for others, instead viewing it as a highly personalized account of one woman's voyage and return to the Holy Land. See Laurie Douglas, "A New Look at the *Itinerarium Burdigalense," Journal of Early Christian Studies* 4, no. 3 (1996): 313–33.

30. "Civitas Burdigala, ubi est Fluvius Garonna, per quem facit mare Oceanum accessa et recessa per leugas plus minus centum." *Itin. Burd.* 549. There is not enough evidence to determine the gender of the Bordeaux pilgrim. The account does seem to emphasize locations connected to biblical women and to display a concern with childbirth and fertility. One certainly cannot exclude a female writer simply on the basis of the difficulty of the journey, since it was not uncommon for women to make such expeditions. While most scholars assume a male author, Laurie Douglas and Joan Taylor assert female authorship. See Douglas, "New Look," and Joan E. Taylor, *Christians and the Holy Places: The Myth of Jewish-Christian Origins* (Oxford, 1993), 313.

31. There are two examples of stops above twenty miles apart, but the average is about ten miles, a typical distance for a day's travel. *Itin. Burd.* 600, 615.

32. Tsafrir, though writing specifically about the Holy Land, posits the existence of a wide variety of maps. Yoram Tsafrir, "Maps Used by Theodosius: On Pilgrim Maps of the Holy Land and Jerusalem in the Sixth Century C.E.," *Dumbarton Oaks Papers* 40 (1986).

33. The importance of the postal service can be seen in the many laws concerning it in the Theodosian Code. *CTh* 8.5 alone contains thirty laws on the postal service.

34. On the selling of illegal post warrants, see *CTh* 8.5.4. On the illegal use of the post, see *CTh* 8.5.54, *CTh* 8.5.57, and *CTh* 8.5.62. Julian issued a law (*CTh* 8.5.12) stating that only the praetorian prefect himself could issue a special post warrant. Gratian, Valentinian, and Theodosius reaffirmed Julian's law twice (*CTh* 8.5.40 and 8.5.43). They also issued a law mandating capital punishment for the illegal buying and selling of post warrants (*CTh* 8.5.41). *CTh* 16.10.15, a law of Arcadius and Honorius of 399, penalized those who issued false post warrants allowing the bearer to travel via the *cursus publicus.* This was added after a decree affirming the end of sacrifices, yet protecting public buildings, which also implies that false documents were being produced allowing the destruction of the buildings.

35. In describing Constantine's calling of the Council of Nicaea, Eusebius adds that "he allowed some the use of the public means of conveyance, while he afforded to others an ample supply of beasts of burden for their transport." Eusebius *Vita Constantini* 3.6. All translations of Eusebius's *Vita Constantini* are from *Eusebius, Life of Constantine,* trans. Averil Cameron and Stuart G. Hall (Oxford, 1999).

about a hundred miles per day, with riders changing horses at each station. The majority of overland travelers, however, covered a more modest twelve miles a day walking or twenty miles by mule. Road travel was facilitated by the many way stations and hostels that could be found along the route. By the fifth and sixth centuries, weary travelers, regardless of their religious status and reason for traveling, frequently stopped at monasteries to rest during their journeys. Monasteries slowly began to make provisions for this function, which the precept of hospitality required them to perform.[36]

The primary form of communication in late antiquity was epistolary, and the transportation of letters was a major motive for travel and could be an added duty on almost any type of journey.[37] Finding reliable letter carriers, however, was often difficult. Paulinus of Nola, in two separate letters to Sulpicius Severus, expresses disgust at the appearance and untrustworthiness of Marracinus, the messenger who delivered Sulpicius Severus's letters.[38] In fact, Paulinus devoted an entire letter to Sulpicius Severus describing the many faults of Marracinus, whom he calls a long-haired, overdressed drunk.[39] Paulinus was pleased when Marracinus, out of laziness, refused to travel the full distance to Nola and instead gave Severus's letter to a dependable monk named Sorianus. The shortage of reliable letter carriers is also hinted at in a letter Paulinus wrote to Augustine, a letter he was forced to write in haste, as the messenger was "impatient to get to the ship."[40] Clearly Paulinus was at the mercy of his letter carriers. It is understandable, then, that Augustine of Hippo was pleased when Orosius arrived in Africa; Orosius, whom he called an experienced traveler, had agreed to carry letters to Jerome for him.[41] The messenger's job was not always an easy one; the messenger Justus was accused of tampering with the *De gestis Pelagii* sent from Augustine to Cyril of Alexandria.[42] Justus was forced to return to Hippo to repudiate these

36. The precept of hospitality is present in many monastic texts. For a discussion of this precept in the *Apopthegmata patrum,* for example, see Helen Waddell, ed., *The Desert Fathers* (Ann Arbor, 1957), 113–14. Chapters 53 and 61 of the *Regula Benedictina* deal with hospitality and the proper reception of guests.

37. Stanley K. Stowers, *Letter Writing in Greco-Roman Antiquity* (Philadelphia, 1986).

38. Paulinus of Nola *Epistolae* (henceforth *Ep.*) 17 and 22. All translations of the *Epistolae* of Paulinus of Nola are from *Letters of St. Paulinus of Nola,* trans. P. G. Walsh (New York, 1966).

39. Ibid., 22.

40. Ibid., 50.

41. Augustine *Epistulae* (henceforth *Ep.*) 166.180–81. See also Carolinne White, *The Correspondence (394–419) Between Jerome and Augustine of Hippo* (Lewiston, N.Y., 1990).

42. "Hunc autem librum meum cum haberet iste servus dei Iustus, huius ad tuam venerabilitatem perlator epistolae, offendit quosdam, quod in eo disputatum est non omnes peccatores

charges and authenticate his copy of Augustine's work. Augustine gladly complied and included this story in a letter to Cyril that Justus also delivered.

Roman roads held many dangers; bandits and thieves were an unavoidable fact of late antique travel. The Iberian monastic traveler Egeria is known to have traveled for at least part of her journey—a particularly dangerous segment—with an armed escort of imperial soldiers.[43] The majority of overland travelers journeyed on foot. Expensive and also prone to injury of their hooves, horses were primarily used by the military and by the messengers of the *cursus publicus*. Romans were not known as great riders, in part because they lacked both stable saddles and stirrups and rarely shod their horses.[44]

Mules or donkeys were the animals of choice for the common traveler. Egeria's overland journey combined both foot and mule travel. Gyrovagues, the wandering monks of the *Regula Magistri,* were said to travel on weary donkeys laden with the monk's worldly goods, and according to the writer of the rule, these "false monks" also routinely beat their animals.[45] Some travelers used wagons and carts pulled by mules or oxen. Depictions surviving in Roman artwork show four-wheeled wooden wagons pulled by four to six animals, as well as simple two-wheeled carts, often pulled by a single animal.[46] Though well suited to hauling goods, neither vehicle had any shock-absorbing capacity, and lubricants for moving parts were often not available, making the vehicles quite uncomfortable to human passengers. When the Visigoths began their migration into the Roman Empire, they traveled primarily by foot, but were accompanied by some four thousand

---

aeterno igni puniri, et hunc libri locum, sicut mihi rettulit, non a me sic explicatum, sed ab ipso falsatum esse dixerunt. Unde permotus cum eodem ad nos codice navigavit, ne illum haberet fortasse mendosum, cum bene sibi fuisset conscius nihil in eo falsitatis a se fuisse commissum. Conferens itaque illum cum codicibus nostris me quoque percognoscente integrum habere compertus est." Augustine *Epistolae* 4*.3, in *Lettres 1*-29*, Nouvelle édition de texte critique et introduction,* ed. J. Divjak, Bibliothèque Augustinienne (Paris, 1987), 46B.108–17. All translations of the *Epistolae 1*–29** are from R. B. Eno, trans., *Saint Augustine, Letters, Volume VI (1*-29*)* (Washington, D.C., 1989).

43. "Ut cata mansiones monasteria sint cum militibus et prepositis, qui nos deducebant semper de castro ad castrum." Egeria *Itinerarium* (henceforth *Itin.*) 7.2, in P. Geyer and O. Cuntz, eds., *Itineraria et alia geographica,* CC 175:37–90. Egeria dismissed the soldiers at one point: "Nos autem inde iam remisimus milites, qui nobis pro disciplina Romana auxilia prebuerant, quandiu per loca suspecta ambulaueramus." Ibid., 9.3.

44. Ann Hyland, *Equus: The Horse in the Roman World* (London, 1990).

45. *Regula Magistri* (henceforth *RM*) 1.48–40.

46. For Roman depictions, see Leighton, *Transport and Communication,* 149–50. For a reconstruction of a Roman wagon, see Greene, *Archaeology,* 38.

wagons.[47] The wagons carried their possessions, as well the very young and very old, and those otherwise too feeble to walk. Covered litters, which were carried by slaves or hitched to mules, were a component of urban transportation but obviously impractical for long distance travel.

Travel by camel was the most efficient form of overland transportation. Though initially used in the Arabian peninsula, camels were later brought into the deserts of North Africa, Egypt, and even parts of Asia Minor.[48] The Arabian peninsula was the home of the Bedouin, a nomadic Arab people who traversed the desert in camel caravans, leading their flocks from oasis to oasis. Camels were the only effective mode of transportation in areas where roads did not exist, such as the desert and mountains. They were able to carry heavy loads, required little water, provided milk to the traveler, and could travel great distances without rest. While traveling in the Sinai, Egeria saw her first pack camels and wrote with astonishment about them and their ability to traverse areas without roads.[49]

As Rome slowly transformed itself after the economic and political crises of the third century, a new type of traveler emerged: the refugee. The degree of physical movement of people during this time was unprecedented, as was the impact these migrations would have on the Roman world. Beginning in the fourth century, a large number of Germanic people crossed the Roman frontier. The Germanic tribes were already known to the Roman Empire, but now were a new, threatening presence within its borders. The movements of the Germanic tribes ushered in a fundamentally new type of travel, brought on by hunger and the search for safety. This form of travel caused a chain reaction of displacement: as the Germanic tribes moved, invaded, and settled in areas of former Roman occupation, many inhabitants fled. The invasion of Italy by the Visigoths and the subsequent sack of the city of Rome in 410 spawned a wave of refugee migration to Africa and to the eastern provinces. Jerome, in his letter to Pacatula, notes the great number of Roman exiles throughout the Mediterranean.[50] With the invasion of Spain in the fifth century, many more Romans fled to Africa by sea. In

---

47. H. Wolfram, *History of the Goths,* trans. Thomas J. Dunlap (Berkeley and Los Angeles, 1988), 158–60.

48. R. W. Bulliet, *The Camel and the Wheel* (Cambridge, Mass., 1975).

49. "Via enim illic penitus non est, set totum heremi sunt arenosae. Faranite autem, qui ibi consueuerunt ambulare cum camelis suis, signa sibi locis et locis ponent, ad quae signa se tendent et sic ambulant per diem. Nocte autem signa cameli attendunt." Egeria *Itin.* 6.1–2.

50. "Nulla regio, quae non exules eius habeat." Jerome *Ep.* 128.5.

one of his sermons, Augustine writes of crowds of refugees in the city of Carthage. Orosius himself was one of these unfortunate travelers. The movement of refugees was not unidirectional: the sixth-century Vandal occupation of North Africa resulted in a wave of African refugees fleeing into Spain.

While the Germanic tribes traveled the overland routes in the western half of the empire, sea travel remained the domain of the Romans. Alaric, the leader of the Visigothic army that sacked Rome in 410, had another goal in mind with his entry into Italy: he intended to reach North Africa, the breadbasket of Rome, where a settlement was planned. The Visigoths were stopped in their tracks when they reached the tip of Italy, and every boat was gone; from the safety of Ravenna, the emperor Honorius had ordered their removal to trap the Visigoths. Marooned in the south, unable to reach their destination, many died, including Alaric. The quest for Africa was abandoned, and once again they traveled on foot through Italy, Gaul, and finally into Spain.

The migrations of Germanic peoples changed the western Mediterranean world. These movements, which themselves caused displacement of native Roman inhabitants, only served to increase the overall itinerant character of late antique society. Increased travel and trade continued in the West long after the initial migrations; in fact, the migrations left in their wake a new atmosphere in which travel and dislocation were commonplace. It was inevitable that within this context travel would become part of the experience of many Christians and even that of many monks. It is also clear that these very conditions created the opportunity for infusing travel with religious significance. It was in this world that monastic men and women began to explore the ascetic qualities of wandering itself.

Clearly late antique travel was not easy, nor was it an endeavor to be entered into lightly. It exposed the traveler to a variety of hardships, dangers, and difficulties. And yet the physical aspects and logistics of making a long journey provide the necessary context in understanding the concerns and experiences of individual travelers as well as how travel and movement itself could acquire religious and spiritual meaning. This does not mean that all late antique travel came to have a religious motive or is open to a religious interpretation; on the contrary, most travelers during late antiquity were the migrating tribes and Roman refugees. However many there were, religious travelers were only a small fraction of the total. Commerce, military campaigns, imperial business, communication, migration, and displacement were among the principal motives of those who crowded the roads and waterways of the late antique and early medieval Mediterranean basin. But travel, like other aspects of late antique Roman society, began to have a Christian dimension, one that would allow for religious travel and movement as an ascetic practice.

RELIGIOUS TRAVEL

The entangled origins of spiritual wandering and pilgrimage must be seen, not only in the context of these patterns of travel, but also in the context of different kinds of religious travel, travel with some connection to the church, but undertaken for a variety of reasons. In addition to spiritual wandering and pilgrimage, religious travel took the form of conciliar voyages, exile, and missionary expeditions.

Beginning in the fourth century many Mediterranean church councils attempted to spell out the daily functioning and beliefs of the church. In many cases, the bishops and priests who attended these councils traveled a great distance. The church was in this sense a highly mobile institution, with many important ecclesiastical and monastic leaders traveling to distant lands. The Spanish church held its own regional councils, including the earliest, the council of Elvira, *c.* 300, from which canons and the list of attendees survive.[51] The first Mediterranean-wide council was the Council of Nicaea; it was convened by the emperor Constantine in 324 to deal with the growing problem of theological disagreement within the church. The Council of Nicaea was originally presided over by Hosius, the bishop of Cordoba, who, though an old man, traveled the entire length of the Mediterranean in order to attend.[52] The lives of the Church Fathers themselves, such as Augustine and Jerome and even John Cassian, show that long journeys were commonplace within the church.

Flight and exile were two other important kinds of forced travel. The principal result of the Council of Nicaea was the condemnation of Arianism. After Constantine's death in 337, his son and successor Constantius favored Arianism over Catholic Christianity. The change in imperial policy

---

51. Canons of the Council of Elvira, in *Concilios Visigóticos e Hispano-Romanos, España Cristiana*, ed. José Vives (Barcelona and Madrid, 1963), 1–15.

52. E. A. Thompson, "The End of Roman Spain," pt. 1, *Nottingham Mediaeval Studies* 20 (1976): 3–28; Roger Collins, *Early Medieval Spain: Unity in Diversity, 400–1000*, 2d ed. (New York, 1995).

forced the exile of many bishops from their sees. Athanasius, the bishop of Alexandria and perhaps the most famous victim of these deportations, spent most of his episcopate in movement, including four separate exiles.[53] During some of these periods of banishment he traveled to the West, to Rome and Trier. Athanasius's counterpart in the West was the bishop of Poitiers, Hilary, who spent his exile, which was ordered by the Arian emperor Constantius, traveling to the East, to Phrygia and Constantinople. Isidore of Seville's less famous brother, Leander, bishop of Seville, was forced to flee Spain in 582 for having taken part in Hermanigild's conversion to Catholic Christianity.[54] Leander's exile led him to Constantinople where he met Pope Gregory the Great before eventually being recalled to Spain.

Missionary travel, voyages to spread Christianity to non-Christians, reaches back to the earliest days of the church and was responsible for a great deal of religious movement at that time. Indeed, most of the movement in the first three centuries of the church was linked to missionary endeavors. Members of the early church were highly mobile, traveling from city to city; this mobility, as many historians have argued, helped to spread Christianity throughout the Mediterranean.[55]

Missionary travel from the fourth to the seventh centuries was mostly confined to Northern Europe rather than to the Mediterranean.[56] The mid-fourth-century Arian mission led by Ulfilas traveled from Constantinople across the Danube in order to convert the Goths to Arian Christianity. A Gothic Bible was even created for this missionary endeavor. Arian missionary activities continued into the fifth century: Ajax, another Arian Christian missionary, was sent by the Visigothic king Theodoric II to Galicia in 464 to convert the Sueves.

In the fifth century, Patrick, a Roman Briton, traveled to Ireland, where he had earlier spent more than seven years in captivity, in order to spread Christianity. Patrick was quite successful, especially in appealing to the many

---

53. On Athanasius, see Timothy D. Barnes, *Athanasius and Constantius: Theology and Politics in the Constantinian Empire* (Cambridge, Mass., 1993); for his first exile, see Duane W. H. Arnold, *The Early Episcopal Career of Athanasius of Alexandria* (Notre Dame, Ind., 1991).

54. On Leander of Seville and his exile, see Ursicino Domínguez del Val, *Leandro de Sevilla y la lucha contra el Arrianismo* (Madrid, 1981).

55. Wayne Meeks, *The First Urban Christians: The Social World of the Apostle Paul* (New Haven, Conn., 1983); R. A. Fletcher, *The Conversion of Europe: From Paganism to Christianity, 371–1386 A.D.* (New York, 1997).

56. See Ian N. Wood, *The Missionary Life: Saints and the Evangelisation of Europe, 400–1050* (Harlow, Eng., 2001).

tribal kings of Ireland. Ireland had never been conquered by the Romans; it had not undergone the process of Romanization that the rest of Europe and the Mediterranean had, and it did not have the infrastructure necessary to support the fully episcopal form of Christianity that was prevalent in Roman Britain, Spain, and Gaul.[57] Even though Patrick called himself a bishop, Ireland came to possess a highly monastic form of Christianity. Irish monastic practices would include notions of movement and travel as part of spiritual expression. Thus, in Ireland we find evidence of diverse forms of ascetic and monastic practices, including wandering monasticism in the sixth and seventh centuries. Irish monastic travel, however, had an emphasis on missionary activity and penitential pilgrimage, distinguishing it from Mediterranean practices.[58]

Irish monks brought Christianity to Scotland and northern England through the foundation of monasteries, such as Iona and Lindisfarne, that became headquarters of missionary work. When Christianity in England all but disappeared in the face of the invasions by Angles, Saxons, and Jutes in the fifth century, it was the Irish who began the process of restoring it. Irish monks, such as the traveling Columbanus, moved to the Continent and founded monasteries, such as Luxeuil and Bobbio, where Irish-styled monasticism flourished.

In the late sixth century, papal initiation of missionary travel would begin to have an impact in northern Europe. Pope Gregory the Great sent Augustine, later of Canterbury, to southern England in order to convert the Anglo-Saxon kings.[59] This was an unusual occurrence. Gregory the Great was a unique pope and in many ways changed the nature of the papacy. More than any of his predecessors, he was interested in the Germanic kingdoms to the north. As Augustine's mission became successful, this new Rome-centered, episcopal form of Christianity often clashed with the more monastic Celtic Christianity spread by the Irish in the north. Disputes

57. Evidence also suggests strong interactions between Ireland and Spain during the sixth and seventh centuries. See J. N. Hillgarth, ed., *Visigothic Spain, Byzantium and the Irish* (London, 1985).

58. Kathleen Hughes, "The Changing Theory and Practice of Irish Pilgrimage," in *Church and Society in Ireland, A.D. 400–1200,* ed. David Dumville (London, 1987), 143–51. On penitential pilgrimage, see Jonathan Sumption, *Pilgrimage: An Image of Mediaeval Religion* (Totowa, N.J., 1975), 98–113.

59. Carole Straw, *Gregory the Great: Perfection in Imperfection* (Berkeley and Los Angeles, 1988); Jeffrey Richards, *Consul of God: The Life and Times of Gregory the Great* (London, 1980); Robert Markus, *Gregory the Great and His World* (Cambridge, 1997).

between these two forces ranged from proper forms of monastic tonsure and style of living to the dating of Easter, issues only resolved at the Council of Whitby in 664.

PILGRIMAGE

The quintessential form of religiously motivated travel is, of course, pilgrimage.[60] Yet the very ubiquity of the term has led to a haziness concerning exactly what the practice of pilgrimage entailed in the late antique period. The image conjured by the English word "pilgrimage" is powerful and precise: an organized religious journey to a particular holy place, the purpose of which is to be healed or absolved of sins. A pilgrimage is a temporary journey, always with a definite return, sometimes with souvenirs in tow, and pilgrims are viewed as common folk gathering for a voyage with strangers. This ahistorical image does not, however, mesh well with the reality of late antique Christian travel. The Latin word most commonly translated as "pilgrimage" is *peregrinatio*, with "pilgrim" being the usual translation of *peregrinus*. However, *Peregrinatio* can, and should most often, be translated simply as "journey," and *peregrinus* as "traveler" or even "foreigner."[61] Another Latin word commonly used to describe travel is *iter*, meaning "journey." This term, too, is often taken to imply a pilgrimage when used in a context of religious travel.

It is difficult to determine exactly when these Latin terms acquired the meanings and connotations that now surround the word "pilgrimage."[62] It

60. On pilgrimage in general during this period, see Hunt, *Holy Land Pilgrimage*; Kötting, *Peregrinatio Religiosa*; Pierre Maraval, *Lieux Saints et pèlerinages d'Orient: Histoire et Géographie des Origines à la Conquête Arabe* (Paris, 1985); Diana Webb, *Pilgrims and Pilgrimage in the Medieval West* (London, 1999); Birch, *Pilgrimage to Rome*; Frankfurter, *Pilgrimage and Holy Space*; and John Wilkinson, *Jerusalem Pilgrims Before the Crusades* (Warminster, 1977).

61. *Peregrinus* also had a specific meaning within Roman law: all free people under Roman law were either citizens or *peregrini*, foreigners who were either citizens of a foreign community or not citizens anywhere. *Peregrini* had their own praetor. See Cicero *De officiis* 1.125 and *Dig.* 1.2.2.28, and Gaius *Institutes* 1.iii–v. See also John Crook, *Law and Life of Rome* (Ithaca, N.Y., 1967), 36–45. I thank Carol Poster for this insight. In Rome, the *Castra Peregrinorum* housed soldiers detached from the provincial legions, that is, Roman soldiers from foreign parts. For the *Castra Peregrinorum*, see L. Richardson, *A New Topographical Dictionary of Ancient Rome* (Baltimore, Md., 1992), 78.

62. J. F. Niermeyer, *Mediae Latinitatis Lexicon minus* (Leiden, 1976), 787. Niermeyer includes several meanings for *peregrinari*, including to go on pilgrimage, to suffer penitential exile, and even to lead a monastic life. A *peregrinatio* is defined as a pilgrimage to the holy places. See also the discussion of the term *peregrinatio* in Constable, "Monachisme et pèlerinage."

is not always clear, for example, what late antique and early medieval writers had in mind when they used them. The late fourth-century traveler to the Holy Land and beyond, Egeria, used *iter* repeatedly to describe her journey, never *peregrinatio,* a term rarely used in this period. She did use the word *peregrinus* twice, but in each case the meaning is closer to "stranger" or "foreigner" than to "pilgrim."[63] The anonymous sixth-century Piacenza Pilgrim used the verb *peregrinari,* but only once, at the beginning of the account.[64] The specialized meaning of the word only begins to appear in the seventh century.[65] It acquired this meaning through its use in the context of the allegorical journey of the Christian in the world, as imagined by Augustine in the *De civitate Dei.*[66] Augustine speaks of the earthly pilgrimage of the "City of God," the true Christian community, a pilgrimage that will end with union with the City of God, which he also portrays as the heavenly Jerusalem. Augustine understood *peregrinatio* as religious travel, but allegorically.

Perhaps because of their interest in social stability, the Church Fathers tended more and more toward a metaphorical definition of travel. These writers often stressed the links between being a monk and being a pilgrim or foreign traveler. Basil of Caesarea, in a letter to a fallen monk, describes the demeanor of the ideal monk as "wholly uplifted, passing as a stranger and a pilgrim by fields and by cities, you hastened to Jerusalem."[67] Here Basil meant the heavenly Jerusalem. Bede shares the idea that the Christian

63. Egeria described the bishop of Ramesses as one who received travelers well: "suscipiens peregrinos valde bene." Egeria *Itin.* 8.4. She used the word again when discussing the difficulty, for foreigners or strangers to the bishop of Jerusalem, of being baptized in the city: "Si quis autem peregrinus est, nisi testimonia habuerit, qui eum noverint, non tam facile accedet ad baptismum." Egeria *Itin.* 45.4.

64. *Itinerarium Placentini* (henceforth *Itin. Plac.*), *CC* 175:127–74; see also G. F. M. Vermeer, *Observations sur le Vocabulaire du Pèlerinage chez Egerie et chez Antonin de Plaisance* (Utrecht, 1965).

65. Gregory the Great used the word in relation to travel to holy places in a letter to Rusticiana, *Registrum epistolarum VIII,* Ep. 22, *CC* 140A.

66. Augustine's *De civitate Dei* begins with a description of the "City of God" traveling as a stranger among the impious on the earth: "Gloriosissimam civitatem Dei sive in hoc temporum cursu, cum inter impios peregrinatur ex fide vivens." *De civitate Dei,* bk. 1, praefatio, *CC* 47. He repeats this metaphor and the use of the verb *peregrinari* throughout the work. See *De civitate Dei* 1.35, 10.7, 15.15, and 19.26. See Peter Brown, *Augustine of Hippo: A Biography,* revised edition with epilogue (Berkeley and Los Angeles, 2000), 323–24, and specifically on Augustine's use of *peregrinus* and *peregrinari* in the *De civitate Dei,* see Clark, "Going Home."

67. Basil of Caearea *Epistolae* 45. All translations of the *Epistolae* are from *Saint Basil: The Letters: Address to Young Men on Reading Greek Literature,* trans. Roy J. Deferrari, 4 vols., Loeb Classical Library (Cambridge, Mass., 1934).

is forever a pilgrim or traveler until returning to his or her true homeland in heaven.[68] While it is tempting to read later definitions of these words into the early texts, it is clear that they could have a variety of meanings at the time, and that the specialized sense of a religious journey to a specific holy place emerged only after the seventh century, if not much later.

Christian pilgrimage has long been an active area of study even outside the discipline of history. The anthropological work of Victor and Edith Turner, which has influenced a wide variety of scholars, has contributed greatly to the historiography of pilgrimage.[69] The Turners defined pilgrimage as a breaking down of the ordinary barriers and boundaries of society. They saw pilgrimage as containing certain key elements: travel to a specific, unique destination, for a set duration, with specific associated rituals and singularity of motivation. During a pilgrimage the participants enter a "semi-liminoid state"; they are temporarily, at least for the duration of the pilgrimage, outside the habitual constraints of society. This state is manifested physically by the participants' distinct dress and manner. The Turners also placed great importance on the final destination, the "sacred place," wherein most of the rituals pertaining to pilgrimage take place. This overt physical location becomes the primary location of the meaning of the pilgrimage. Though the goal is to connect in some way with the supernatural at the holy place, it is the physical place or *locus* that takes on, in the Turners' account, the greatest importance for the pilgrim. For the Turners, participants in pilgrimage lose their own identities, including their social status. The appeal of pilgrimage attracts men and women from all levels of society. Pilgrimage rituals create a special *communitas* among pilgrims, and for this reason the Turners emphasized the potentially subversive nature of pilgrimage.

By viewing pilgrims as being in a different state of mind from the ordinary, anthropologists have aided in our understanding of the phenomenon of pilgrimage and have provided historians with new ways of interpreting and viewing it. Historians have borrowed from the Turners the idea of pilgrimage as a way of breaking down social barriers and creating a kind of community or sense of community among those on the pilgrimage road.[70] They frequently

68. "Peregrinam pro aeterna patria duceret vitam." Bede *Historia Ecclesiastica* 3.13, in *Baedae Opera Historica,* ed. J. E. King (Cambridge, Mass., 1979), vol. 1.

69. Victor Turner and Edith Turner, *Image and Pilgrimage in Christian Culture: Anthropological Perspectives* (New York, 1978).

70. Alphonse Dupront, *Du Sacré: Croisades et pèlerinages, images et langages* (Paris, 1987). More recently see Thomas A. Idinopulos, "Sacred Space and Profane Power: Victor Turner

refer to the Turners' notion of liminality in understanding the pilgrim's relation to society.[71] Yet the Turners' work was primarily based on observations
and analysis of modern Christian pilgrimage, and on very selective use of
historical data.[72] On the whole, their interpretation was ahistorical, in that
they viewed Christian pilgrimage as a timeless, unchanging phenomenon
with structures and rules that transcend particular historical contexts.

Because the Turners' rather specific definition of pilgrimage eliminates
so many late antique religious travelers from consideration as "pilgrims,"
historians writing on this period have instead generally applied a looser
definition of pilgrimage: they label almost any religiously motivated journey
to a specific site, especially to the Holy Land, as a pilgrimage. This broader
definition, however, does not prevent many from applying the Turners'
interpretations to those travelers and their journeys, even though the Turners'
ideas themselves were based on a narrower definition and seem in important
ways to be at odds with much of the available evidence from this period.

Pilgrimage was not a uniform, regulated, or codified phenomenon in
the Mediterranean basin during late antiquity or the early Middle Ages. It
is difficult to see what was considered "the holy" as so neatly inscribed in a
specific location or holy place. Often it was the act of visiting holy people,
rather than their location, that was important to travelers.[73] Reaching a
particular destination was often less important than the journey itself. During
late antiquity there was no set form of pilgrim dress, no established routes
or rituals that defined a pilgrimage. The Turners' idea of pilgrimage stresses
a singularity of motivation and goal, yet many of the figures usually called
pilgrims in this period do not meet even this simple criterion. A multiplicity
of aims and motives, rather, seems to have shaped religious travel and
movement in late antiquity.

Recently, anthropologists themselves have problematized this mono-
lithic understanding of pilgrimage.[74] In 1989 an interdisciplinary conference
on pilgrimage was held in an attempt to challenge the Turners' paradigm of

---

and the Perspective of Holy Land Pilgrimage," in *Pilgrims and Travelers to the Holy Land,* ed.
Bryan F. Lebeau and Menachem Mor (Omaha, Nebr., 1996).

71. See, for example, Robert A. Markus, *The End of Ancient Christianity* (Cambridge,
1990), 154–55. For an example of overreliance on the Turners' work, see Joseph T. Rivers, "Pattern
and Process in Early Christian Pilgrimage" (Ph.D. diss., Duke University, 1983).

72. Turner and Turner, *Image and Pilgrimage.*

73. See Frank, *Memory of the Eyes.*

74. For the most recent critique, see Idinopulos, "Sacred Space and Profane Power."

pilgrimage and to provide a "new agenda in pilgrimage studies."[75] Here anthropologists, historians, and sociologists working on pilgrimage came together to compare their results and reassess those of the Turners. These scholars criticized the "generalizing thrust towards a universal model of pilgrimage, defined as a human quest for the sacred which generates a model of society based on fraternity and common well-being."[76] They attempted to analyze pilgrimage in its historical and cultural specificity rather than assuming a universal meaning of the term.

This new generation of anthropologists views pilgrimage as "an arena for competing religious and secular discourses," instead of a community-creating and uniform phenomenon.[77] Much of their work moves away from the model of pilgrimage to a particular site and instead emphasizes pilgrimage aimed at seeking the blessing of holy men and women. For these anthropologists, this lack of emphasis on a particular place is a contemporary development: "Today, living saints pose considerable problems for a centralized, bureaucratic religious institution like the Catholic church, for they obviate altogether the need for priestly intermediaries. The personification of the sacred centre is a movement to the limits of ecclesiastical control, a control which begins to be regained only with the death of the saint and his or her transformation into a mute, hieratic, domesticated shrine."[78] Although this revised model clearly takes better account of the historically specific circumstances surrounding religious travel, it also appears still to misread the historical origins of pilgrimage. The very phenomenon here ascribed to the unique context of modern Catholic pilgrimage, the emphasis on holy persons, in fact thrived in the earliest stages of the development of pilgrimage.[79]

Historians themselves are at odds when trying to pinpoint the origins of Christian pilgrimage. Some have tried to push the date of the earliest Christian pilgrimage to the era of the apostolic church, envisioning a continuity of pilgrimage throughout the ancient and medieval periods.[80] Others refuse

---

75. John Eade and Michael J. Sallnow, eds., *Contesting the Sacred: The Anthropology of Christian Pilgrimage* (London, 1990), 2.

76. Ibid., 27 n. 4.

77. See foreword by I. M. Lewis in Eade and Sallnow, *Contesting the Sacred*, x–xi.

78. Eade and Sallnow, *Contesting the Sacred*, 7.

79. For example, see Frank, *Memory of the Eyes*.

80. See, for example, Gisela Muschiol, "Zur Spiritualität des Pilgerns im frühen Mittelalter," in *Spiritualität des Pilgerns: Kontinuität und Wandel*, ed. Klaus Herbers and Robert Plötz (Tübingen, 1993), 25–38. For the stress on continuity of pilgrimage, see Jean Chelini and

to see pilgrimage as an entirely Christian invention, since there were important antecedents in both Judaism and polytheistic Mediterranean religions.[81] Travel to cult sites and oracle sites at Delphi and Didyma already had a long tradition in Hellenistic and Hellenic religion.[82]

The growth in the devotion to Asclepius, the central figure of another Hellenistic cult that also had great popularity in the Roman period, reveals the widespread appeal of healing cults.[83] The first complex was at Epidaurus, although the later complex at Pergamum, with its impressive modern remains, combined hospital, health spa, entertainment, and temple facilities.[84] It was partly outside the main city of Pergamum, and a paved road led to the complex. This road was lined with the epigraphic proof of the successes of the complex: stone inscriptions set up by grateful visitors. Clearly people journeyed to this site; it could not have been supported solely by the citizens of Pergamum. Important healing sites were also located in Palestine and on the Iberian Peninsula.[85]

Religious travel continued to play an important role in non-Christian religious life after the rise of Christianity. Wandering holy men were part of the Neoplatonic revival between the third and fifth centuries.[86] The fifth-century *Life of Proclus* by Marinus of Neapolis portrays a wandering pagan wonder-worker, who in his lifetime traveled from Alexandria to Constantinople and finally to Athens.[87] Other wandering pagan holy men are described in Eunapius's *Lives of the Philosophers and Sophists*, written in the late fourth century.[88] Plotinus's own life was mostly spent traveling

---

Henry Branthomme, *Les Chemins de Dieu: Histoire des Pèlerinages Chrétiens des origines à nos jours* (Paris, 1982); Raymond Oursel, *Les Pèlerins du Moyen Age: Les hommes, les chemins, les sanctuaires* (Paris, 1963); Sumption, *Pilgrimage;* and Taylor, *Christians and the Holy Places.*

81. See Kötting, *Peregrinatio Religiosa,* 12–79.

82. See Matthew Dillon, *Pilgrims and Pilgrimage in Ancient Greece* (London and New York, 1997). For the Eleusinian Mysteries and Eleusis's travel in the Hellenistic period, see Everett Ferguson, *Backgrounds of Early Christianity* (Grand Rapids, Mich., 1993).

83. For the Asclepius cult, see L. Edelstein and Emma J. Edelstein, *Asclepius* (Baltimore, 1998).

84. For the Pergamum compound, see Richard Tomlinson, *From Mycenae to Constantinople: The Evolution of the Ancient City* (London, 1992), 111–21. On Epidaurus, see Kötting, *Peregrinatio Religiosa.*

85. See "Sanctuaries," in Edelstein and Edelstein, *Asclepius.* See also Simon R. F. Price, *Rituals and Power: The Roman Imperial Cult in Asia Minor* (Cambridge, 1984), and Stephen McKenna, *Paganism and Pagan Survivals in Spain up to the Fall of the Visigothic Kingdom* (Washington, D.C., 1938).

86. Garth Fowden, "The Pagan Holy Man in Late Antique Society," *Journal of Hellenic Studies* 102 (1982): 33–59.

87. Marinus of Neapolis *Life of Proclus.*

88. Eunapius of Sardis *Lives of the Philosophers and Sophists.*

through Italy and Rome.[89] These pagan, Neoplatonic travelers played their part in the general culture of movement of the late antique Mediterranean. But their travels seldom resembled anything like "pilgrimage" and had little to do with later Christian notions of monastic travel.

Judaism, with its scriptural injunction for an annual pilgrimage to Jerusalem, has long been thought to be one of the roots of Christian pilgrimage. Jerusalem had long been revered as a holy city, historically as the city of David, and religiously as the site of the Temple, the sole temple to the Jewish God. Even after the destruction of the Temple the city remained important in Judaism. The origin of Jewish pilgrimage stems from the directive in Deuteronomy 16.16, commanding an assembly of all Israelite men to meet in Jerusalem three times a year. Jewish "pilgrimage," however, was ordinarily a communal rather than individual experience, though the individual type probably also existed.[90] The importance of a physical journey to the holy city surpassed the mortal lives of many Jews, as evidenced by the transportation of the bones of Diaspora Jews to Jerusalem for burial.[91]

Jewish religious travel continued well into the Christian era, which created a rivalry between Jews and Christians over sites in Jerusalem and the surrounding area.[92] In the late sixth century, the anonymous Piacenza Pilgrim wrote about his visit to the Oak at Mamre and described the basilica built there in this way: "The basilica has four porticoes and no roof over the central court. Down the middle runs a screen. Christians come in on one side and Jews on the other, and they use much incense."[93] Jewish emphasis on the importance of the place or *locus* of the holy was initially attacked by

89. For Plotinus and other late Neoplatonists, see Pierre Chuvin, *A Chronicle of the Last Pagans,* trans. B. A. Archer (Cambridge, Mass., 1990), and Robin Lane Fox, *Pagans and Christians in the Mediterranean World from the Second Century A.D. to the Conversion of Constantine* (London, 1986).

90. John Wilkinson, "Jewish Holy Places and the Origins of Christian Pilgrimage," in *The Blessings of Pilgrimage,* ed. Robert Ousterhout (Urbana, Ill., 1990), 41–53.

91. Robert L. Wilken, *The Land Called Holy: Palestine in Christian History and Thought* (New Haven, Conn., 1992), 131; Isaiah Gafni, "Reinterment in the Land of Israel: Notes on the Origin and Development of the Custom," *Jerusalem Cathedra* 1 (1981): 96–104.

92. Wilkinson, "Jewish Holy Places," 47, 51.

93. "Basilica aedificata in quadriporticus, in medio atrio discopertus, per medio discurrit cancellus et ex uno latere intrant christiani et ex alio latere Iudaei, incensa facientes multa." *Itin. Plac.* 30, in P. Geyer, ed., *Itineraria et Alia Geographica, CC* 175:129–53; translation in Wilkinson, *Jerusalem Pilgrims,* 85. It also becomes an important Islamic pilgrimage location. Amikam Elad, "Pilgrims and Pilgrimage to Hebron (al-Khalil) During the Early Muslim Period (638?–1099)," in *Pilgrims and Travelers to the Holy Land,* ed. Bryan F. LeBeau and Menachem Mor (Omaha, Nebr., 1996), 21–62.

the Christian Church as being too literal, yet the triumphant late fourth-century church, through Cyril of Jerusalem, aligned itself with the Jewish tradition.[94] The tension between the Jews and Christians over the religious identity of Jerusalem came to a head with the taking of the city by the Persians in 614, an event that the Christians blamed on Jewish collaborators who allegedly betrayed the city. The accusation itself reveals the growing tension between the two communities.

Within the apostolic church, long before the development of monasticism, there were early wanderers. To wander was to imitate Jesus and the apostles, and although it also served a practical purpose in the form of missionizing, it was much more than this.[95] Gerd Theissen writes of early itinerant movements within the apostolic church, wherein men and women literally followed the teachings of Jesus Christ, and lived a life of wandering and preaching.[96] The eschatological climate of the time, of course, had a great impact on this acceptance of a wandering lifestyle. The end of the world was at hand, and human society's temporary sojourn on the earth was drawing to a close. The *Didache,* a text from the late first to early second century, contains regulations on accepting visiting preachers and on mandatory hospitality.[97] Visitors were not allowed to stay for over two days; anyone doing so was to be considered a "false prophet" by the community.[98] These regulations reveal something of the tension caused by travelers. In the writings of the early Church Fathers, such as Cyprian of Carthage, Ignatius of Antioch, and Polycarp, we find additional evidence of travel relevant to this issue. There may be no absolutely demonstrable continuity of activity and belief with regard to wandering and hospitality from the apostolic church to the early medieval church and its notions of pilgrimage, but a link is certainly possible.

Historians sometimes date the first Christian pilgrimage to the second century, often using evidence from Eusebius's *Historia ecclesiastica.* Eusebius

94. Peter W. L. Walker, "Eusebius, Cyril and the Holy Places," *Studia Patristica* 20 (1989): 306–14; idem, *Holy City, Holy Places? Christian Attitudes to Jerusalem and the Holy Land in the Fourth Century* (Oxford, 1990).

95. On this *imitatio Christi* in the late antique East, see Caner, *Wandering, Begging Monks.*

96. Works by Gerd Theissen and Wayne Meeks focus on this movement. See Gerd Theissen, *Social Reality and the Early Christians: Theology, Ethics, and the World of the New Testament,* trans. Margaret Kohl (Minneapolis, 1992), and Meeks, *First Urban Christians.*

97. *Didache* 11–13. English translation in James A. Kleist, ed., *Didache, Epistle of Barnabas, Epistles and Martyrdom of St. Polycarp, Fragments of Papias, Epistle to Diognetus* (Westminster, Md., 1948).

98. *Didache* 11.

writes that a certain Alexander, a Cappadocian bishop, traveled to Jerusalem, "in consequence of a vow and for the sake of information in regard to its places."[99] Eusebius, however, relates that Alexander became the assistant to the elderly bishop of the city, and subsequently served as a co-bishop of Jerusalem. Alexander's journey to Jerusalem does not appear to have been motivated solely by the desire to visit its holy places. Melito of Sardis, who lived in the middle of the second century, has been considered by many as another candidate for the status of "first Christian pilgrim."[100] Melito was bishop of a small Christian community in Sardis, living amid a large traditional, polytheist population and a significant Jewish community. At some point he made a journey to the Holy Land for the purpose of obtaining better copies of the Christian scriptures.[101] Nowhere does he make any mention of visiting the holy places, of saying special prayers, or of doing other acts now associated with pilgrimage. When we apply the Turner pilgrimage criteria to either Alexander's or Melito's trips, they fall short on many counts. It could be argued that there is simply a lack of evidence, but in Melito's case, as we have seen, he provides us with his primary reason for traveling to the Holy Land, and it is not consistent with the Turners' criteria. It is, therefore, inaccurate to call Melito a pilgrim. Such a label not only obscures the motives behind his journey, but also provides a faulty starting point for a discussion of Christian pilgrimage.

The preceding analysis has served to problematize the definition of pilgrimage in late antiquity. It is important to differentiate between the various modes of religiously motivated travel while avoiding the error of applying "pilgrimage" as a label for all religiously motivated travel. By doing so one can allow for a multiplicity of motives for taking to the road for religious purposes. Stripped of the twin labels of "pilgrim" and "pilgrimage," we can begin to see the outline and form of a uniquely monastic and ascetic impulse to travel, one that sought spiritual fulfillment yet was open to accusations of instability and dangerously ill-defined wandering. Turning to evidence of opposition to religious, and particularly monastic, travel, we can view, from a different vantage point, the role of travel within a phenomenon that was born in late antiquity: monasticism.

---

99. Eusebius *Historia Ecclesiastia* 9.2.

100. "The presence of Melito of Sardis in the Holy Land in the middle years of the second century makes him the earliest known Christian 'pilgrim.'" Hunt, *Holy Land Pilgrimage,* 3. This is also the case in Sumption, *Pilgrimage,* 89.

101. Eusebius preserves a letter of Melito stating this in his *Historia Ecclesiastica* 4, 26.

OPPOSITION TO CHRISTIAN RELIGIOUS TRAVEL

As the frequency of Christian religious travel of various kinds spread, attacks began to appear, particularly on religious travel by monks, both male and female. Much of what has been interpreted as attacks on pilgrimage written during this period is better understood as attacks on monastic travel. In addition to the accounts of travelers, these attacks, found in monastic rules, decrees of church councils, letters, and other writings, provide key evidence of the nature of the travel they sought to suppress. Evidence of widespread opposition to monastic travel and pilgrimage begins to appear in the fourth century.[102] Fleeing compulsory civic service was a common social ill in late antiquity, and many laws were passed to increase the numbers of those obliged to serve their cities. In 370, the emperors Valens and Valentinian passed a law calling for the arrest of all men who fled civic service to join with the monks in Egypt: "Certain devotees of idleness have deserted the compulsory services of the municipalities, have betaken themselves to solitudes and secret places, and under the pretext of religion have joined with bands of hermit monks."[103] This law was the first to link the problem of desertion to the growth of monasticism, and it can be viewed as an attempt to control the popularity of the new movement. Interestingly, the law insinuates that there are many who became monks "under the pretext of religion" rather than out of legitimate monastic conviction, anticipating the accusations made of the gyrovagues in the *Regula Magistri*. Only twenty years later another edict was issued in reaction to the growth and spread of monasticism, and the inability of imperial authority to control it. Valentinian II and Theodosius I, taking the opposite stance of the previous emperors, ordered all monks expelled from the cities: "They shall be ordered to seek out and to inhabit desert places and desolate solitudes."[104] Monks represented a destabilizing presence in many cities and often an alternative to the spiritual authority of bishops.

Restrictions on itinerancy are contained in the canons of many church councils of this period. The Council of Laodicaea, in 360, issued canons stating that no clergy be allowed to undertake a journey with a "canonical

---

102. See the excellent article by Constable, "Opposition to Pilgrimage in the Middle Ages."
103. *CTh* 12.1.63. All translations of the Codex Theodosianus are from *The Theodosian Code and Novels and the Sirmondian Constitutions,* trans. Clyde Pharr (Princeton, N.J., 1952).
104. *CTh* 16.3.1.

letter," unless he is ordered to.[105] Almost a century later the Council of Chalcedon declared that every monk must be subject to a bishop.[106] Other canons of Chalcedon aimed at controlling the clergy as well. They were required to submit to the authority of a bishop, and they could only fall under the jurisdiction of a single city. "Strange and unknown clergy" were forbidden from officiating in another city without a letter.[107] Because of their role in the celebration of the sacraments, unknown clerics provoked far greater fear among the authorities and within the communities they visited than did "strange" monks. Monks who did move into the jurisdiction of another bishop, however, could create problems if they were viewed as a challenge to his authority.

Another expression of opposition to monasticism and especially to monastic travel was physical violence. Wandering particularly exposed one to the risk of physical attack, sometimes from imperial and even ecclesiastical authorities. The Piacenza Pilgrim was greeted with less than a warm reception while traveling in Samaritan villages. The Samaritans cursed at and spat on the travelers as they walked through their towns and villages.[108] The Samaritans forbade travelers from touching anything in the village, even the items offered for purchase. Commerce was a part of traveling; and even though the Samaritans were not happy with foreigners in their midst, provisions were made for economic exchange. The villagers had their customers deposit their money into a jug of water in order to purify it, rather than receiving the cash directly into their hands. The most vivid image of their cold reception was that of the Samaritans burning away the footprints left by the travelers.[109]

Augustine himself opposed physical wandering as a form of ascetic behavior. The central metaphor of his *City of God* was the notion of the heavenly City on a temporary pilgrimage on earth. This pilgrimage would end on judgment day when the earthly city of God would be joined with

---

105. Council of Laodicaea, canons 41 and 42.

106. Council of Chalcedon, canon 4.

107. Ibid., canons 8, 10, and 13.

108. "Et denuntiant tibi, quando ingrederis: non sputes, et si sputaveris, scandalum generas." *Itin. Plac.* 8.

109. "Et per plateas, unde transivimus sive nos sive Iudaei, cum paleas vestigia nostra incendentes; tanta illis est execratio utrisque. Christianis quidem responsum faciunt, ea sane ratione, ut quod habis emere non tangas, antequam pretium des; quod si tetigeris et non conparaveris, mox scandalum. Nam foris vico una condoma habent posita, qui faciunt responsum. Ipsos nummos in aqua iactas, nam de manu non accipiunt." Ibid., 8.

the heavenly, perfect city. The true homeland or native land for the Christian is in the heavenly city; thus, the Christian is but a temporary sojourner, as Augustine put it, in the midst of the city of Babylon.[110] For Augustine, these powerful metaphors of the Christian as a traveler or pilgrim were not meant to be taken literally; Augustine explicitly denies the need for a physical journey to Jerusalem in his *City of God*. In his *De opere monachorum*, Augustine attacks wandering and wearing long hair as part of his appeal to monks not to shun manual labor.[111] These false monks, according to Augustine, often claim to be on a journey to see relatives, but were in fact simply wandering and leading what he called "an easy life of leisure."[112] Augustine again used a travel metaphor when he wrote that instead of seeking the life of leisure through wandering and instability, one should follow "the narrow, confining path of this holy calling."[113]

In the mid-fifth century, Theodoret of Cyrrhus wrote *A History of the Monks of Syria,* which chronicled both living and recently deceased monks. In his description of the life of the monk Peter the Galatian, Theodoret subtly criticizes Peter's visit to the Holy Land. He writes that Peter wished to "see the places" in order to better worship God in them, but then adds, "not that He is circumscribed in place."[114] For Theodoret, physical pilgrimage was secondary to spiritual pilgrimage; Peter traveled to the Holy Land "in order to feast his eyes with seeing what he desired and so that the eyes of the soul should not through faith enjoy spiritual delight on their own, without the sense of sight."[115] Theodoret finally stated that Peter "did nothing unreasonable" in going to the Holy Land, a grudging acceptance

110. "Quantum oportebat signari etiam generationibus commemoratis cursum gloriossimae civitatis in hoc mundo peregrinantis et supernam patriam requirentis." Augustine *De civitate Dei* 15.15. "Quoniam, quamdiu permixtae sunt ambae civitates, utimur et nos pace Babylonis; ex qua ita per fidem populus Dei liberatur, ut apud hanc interim peregrinetur." Ibid., 19.26. He used this metaphor a number of times: see ibid., 1.35, 10.7, 19.17, and 22.30.

111. On wandering he calls these false monks hypocrites who "omni modo cupientes obscurare putoribus suis, tam multos hypocritas sub habitu monachorum usquequaque dispersit, circumeuntes provincias, nusquam missos, nusquam fixos, nusquam stantes, nusquam sedentes." Augustine *De opere monachorum* 28. He devotes two entire chapters (31 and 32) on the evils of monks wearing their hair long. English translation in Roy J. Deferrari, ed., *Saint Augustine: Treatises on various subjects* (New York, 1952), 384; all translations of *De opera monachorum* are from this edition.

112. Augustine *De opere monachorum* 28.

113. "Miseremini ergo et compatimini, et ostendite hominibus, non vos in otio facilem victum, sed per angustam et arctam vitam huius propositi, regnum Dei quaerere." Ibid.

114. Theodoret of Cyrrhus *A History of the Monks of Syria by Theodoret of Cyrrhus,* ed. and trans. by R. M. Price (Kalamazoo, Mich., 1985), 9.

115. Ibid., 82.

of his journey. What Theodoret approved of in Peter's life was his decision to leave his homeland and settle instead in Antioch, because "he preferred the foreign city to his homeland, counting as fellow-citizens not those of the same race and family but those of the same convictions, sharing the faith and bearing the same yoke of piety."[116] It was a life as a monastic exile that Theodoret endorsed, rather than pilgrimage to the Holy Land.

Criticism of the monastic life also came from outside Christianity. Libanius, for example, frequently attacked monks in his writings. In his *Oratio Pro Templis*, he calls them a "black-robed tribe, who eat more than elephants."[117] He considered these men no more than common criminals, for they went about destroying temples, which at the time were under the protection of the law. Eunapius of Sardis, too, spoke ill of monks. After the closing of pagan temples and shrines, he wrote that, "into the sacred places they imported monks, as they call them, who were men in appearance but led the lives of swine, and openly did and allowed countless unspeakable crimes."[118] Eunapius's observation is confirmed in the fifth-century life of Daniel the Stylite; before mounting a high column in Constantinople, Daniel, a Syrian holy man, lived for nine years in an abandoned temple in the capital city.[119] His daily battles with demons made him a popular attraction for visitors who viewed him as a powerful holy man. Growing opposition to monasticism in general suggests that monks and their supporters felt great pressure to reach an accommodation with the political and social structures around them, and this meant that wandering, taking over public property (as temples were still considered), and other ill-defined practices had to be brought under stricter control. In Daniel's case, he was repeatedly examined by the bishop of Constantinople, who tried to convince him to leave the temple and move to a more suitable place in the city.[120]

In many ways a spiritual journey was safer than actual religious travel. In the late fifth century Peter the Iberian, a Monophysite abbot of a monastery

116. Ibid.

117. Libanius *Oratio 30.8,* in Libanius *Orationes,* ed. R. Foerster (Berlin, 1909–27). English translation from *Libanius: Selected Works,* ed. and trans. by A. F. Norman, Loeb Classical Library (Cambridge, Mass., 1977), vol. 2.

118. Eunapius of Sardis *Lives of the Philosophers and Sophists,* in *Philostratus and Eunapius: The Lives of the Sophists,* trans. Wilmer Cave Wright (Cambridge, Mass., 1961), 423.

119. "The Life and Works of Our Holy Father, St. Daniel the Stylite," in *Three Byzantine Saints: Contemporary Biographies Translated from the Greek,* ed. Elizabeth Dawes and Norman H. Baynes (Crestwood, N.Y., 1977), 14.

120. Ibid., 17–18.

in Gaza, traveled around the Holy Land, where he met both Eudocia and Melania the Younger.[121] An account of his life was written by one of his companions and followers, John Rufus, a Monophysite monk at Maiumas.[122] Although John described Peter as visiting various holy sites, he included a reference to criticism leveled at Peter for not visiting Jerusalem: "How can this blessed man have been staying so long near Jerusalem without ever wanting to go into the holy City: even if it had to be by night he might have venerated the holy places, specially Golgotha and the lifegiving Tomb!"[123] In response, a vision came to one of Peter's followers in which Peter took him on a night tour of the holy places. John referred to this as a "holy circuit" in which Peter had "worshipped the Saviour in all the places."[124] The vision was a spiritual pilgrimage, which foreshadowed the actual visit that Peter made to Jerusalem. John Rufus believed that this spiritual pilgrimage was just as valid, if not more so, than the actual physical journey, and recounted the story to promote spiritual travel. John wrote, "This took place to persuade those who had murmured that in all the holy places—every day perhaps, and every hour—the blessed man was spiritually offering adoration to the Lord."[125] Apparently one did not have to be physically present in Jerusalem in order to venerate the holy places there.

This spiritual pilgrimage to Jerusalem was fundamentally different from Peter's holy wandering and visiting monks. In another part of the *vita*, John tells of his own visit, accompanied by Peter, to the mountain of Moses, Mount Nebo. At the top of the mountain there were a church and a number of monasteries.[126] Peter led John and the others into an empty cell where a holy ascetic from Scete whom Peter had visited long ago had lived for forty years. Like Egeria before him, Peter learned from the monks living on the mountaintop about the holiness of the place, in this case that the body of Moses had been buried there, even though the Bible said otherwise.[127] The combination of visions, monks' tales, and the physical presence

---

121. Peter was from Iberia in Asia Minor. He was educated in Constantinople and died around 491.

122. John Rufus, *Life of Peter the Iberian*, ed. R. Raabe as *Petrus der iberer* (Leipzig, 1885). The original was written around A.D. 500 in Syriac. An English translation can be found in Wilkinson, *Jerusalem Pilgrims*.

123. John Rufus, *Life of Peter the Iberian*, 99.

124. Ibid.

125. Ibid., 100.

126. Ibid., 85.

127. See Deut. 34.6.

of the monks provided more evidence for the sanctity of the place than did even scripture itself.

In addition to the idea of the heavenly Jerusalem, or making a spiritual journey rather than actually traveling to the physical Jerusalem, we find the idea of Jerusalem being "transported" to other closer locations—Constantinople, Rome, or even one's own monastic cell. The notion of a Jerusalem-near-at-hand is an element in the *Life of Nicholas of Sion,* which survives in a late sixth-century account. Nicholas twice set off on a journey to the Holy Land. After his first return home, a cross began to shine in his cell, and he said, "This spot is the counterpart of Holy Sion in Jerusalem."[128] When the possibility of pilgrimage to the Holy Land was thwarted for one reason or another, spiritual pilgrimage could then be emphasized or an alternative Holy Land could be suggested, as in the late fifth-century life of Daniel the Stylite. Daniel desired to visit Jerusalem, but while making the long journey he encountered a vision of Simeon the Stylite, who told him of unrest in the city and advised him to go instead to "the second Jerusalem, namely Constantinople."[129] Daniel reversed course and traveled to the imperial capital. Constantinople was the seat of both the emperor and the patriarch, and thus the center of political and ecclesiastic power in the eastern Mediterranean. Creating new "Jerusalems" in different places can in a sense show the importance of travel to the city but in actuality it is a way of de-emphasizing physical travel and promoting spiritual travel.

The ubiquity of travel and the movement of people during late antiquity led to the creation of new attitudes toward travel and new ways of thinking about the meaning of movement. Though we often concentrate on the fascinating continuities and areas of syncretism between pagan and Christian culture, we must bear in mind that the new religion forced a major reexamination of elements of Roman culture. The position of Christian bishop emerged from nowhere, with no real equivalent in the pagan priesthood.[130] Monasticism, too, born in the fourth century, had no pagan cognate. Sexuality, gender roles, and notions of identity, power, authority, and civic duty were all open to new interpretations, and these very elements

---

128. *Life of Nicholas of Sion,* 10.

129. "Life and Works," chap. 10, page 13 of translation.

130. The emperor Julian would, in fact, point to the role of Christian bishop as a model for his newly reestablished imperial cult priesthood. Julian *Fragment of a letter to a priest,* in *The Works of the Emperor Julian,* ed. Wilmer Cave Wright (New York, 1913), 2:295–339, esp. 337.

were often crucial in understanding the motivations of travelers and the sense they made of their journeys.[131]

The difficulties and hardships of the road and the experience of meeting holy people and becoming a "stranger" or *peregrinus* enabled travelers to see a spiritual or religious dimension in their journeying. Roman matrons, wealthy widows, educated men from the provinces, could all render themselves aliens and outsiders by embarking on a religious voyage and becoming "homeless." Their travel made them physical embodiments of the Christian as a temporary sojourner in the earthly world. This confluence of factors beginning in the fourth century led to a special role for travel in the cultural and religious landscape of the late antique Mediterranean. In an environment of religious, political, and social change, movement itself was now open to a multiplicity of meanings, interpretations, and purposes.

131. For excellent and recent examples of this, see Brown, *Body and Society;* idem, *Authority and the Sacred: Aspects of the Chistianisation of the Roman World* (Cambridge, 1995); and Elm, *Virgins of God.*

CHAPTER TWO

EARLY IBERIAN RELIGIOUS TRAVELERS:
EGERIA, OROSIUS, AND BACHIARIUS

Contrary to the image of the fourth-century Mediterranean world as rigid, stagnant, and dark, it was in many ways in constant flux, where displacement and itineracy resulted from a variety of causes and were in fact commonplace. It was this broad culture of movement and the relative ease of displacement that made travel an inevitable facet of early Christian religious experience. The spiritual significance some late antique figures found in travel and itineracy can only be understood within the context of the culture of travel and movement in the Mediterranean during this period. In the open climate of the early monastic movement, itineracy provided the possibility of a special form of monastic experience, one based on travel, but one that was clearly distinct from the later, more familiar forms of Christian pilgrimage. But where can we look to find evidence that early Christians might have actually engaged this possibility, and actively explored the ascetic qualities of travel, displacement, and homelessness?

Two figures who are rarely discussed together, Egeria (381–84) and Orosius (414–18), can tell us much about late antique religious travel. The assessment of the voyages of these two travelers has been colored by the labels that have been traditionally attached to them: Egeria's journey has been universally labeled a pilgrimage, while Orosius's has not. But this convention belies deep and significant similarities between the two voyages. Egeria and Orosius were near contemporaries. Evidence suggests that both were from Spain, or at least from the far western reaches of the Mediterranean, and both traveled eastward to Palestine and other provinces. A close examination of these two travelers, and a comparison with another figure of the period,

Bachiarius, an early fifth-century Spanish monk who also professed his faith through wandering, reveals strikingly similar patterns in religious expression through motion and travel, ones that were rooted in the late antique culture of movement and intimately tied to pre-Benedictine interpretations of the monastic impulse. What emerges from this comparison is a paradigm of early Christian travel that defies our assumptions about monastic stability and, while clearly containing the seeds of pilgrimage, just as clearly defies its definition and conventions.

The voyage of Egeria has been one of the most important pieces of evidence used to discuss early medieval pilgrimage. The number of publications on Egeria is astounding, especially considering the short span of time her text has been known to modern scholars.[1] In 1884, a long segment of an anonymous woman's travel account was discovered by the Italian historian and archaeologist G. F. Gamurrini, in an eleventh-century manuscript at the obscure library of the Pia Fraternità dei Laici in Arezzo, Italy.[2] The manuscript, which has come to be known as the Codex Aretinus 405, also contains Hilary of Poitiers's *De mysteriis* and fragments of his hymnbook, and originally belonged to the library at Monte Cassino, where it was listed in a catalog of 1532.[3] Since this discovery, no other manuscript containing this account has been located, though in 1909, eleven short fragments of the

---

1. For a good description of the historiographical problems surrounding Egeria and a good bibliography, see Pierre Maraval, ed., *Égérie: Journal de Voyage (Itinéraire)* (Paris, 1982). Agustín Arce, *Itinerario de la Virgen Egeria* (Madrid, 1980), is a Spanish critical edition and translation. M. Starowieyski, "Bibliographia Egeriana," *Augustinianum* 19 (1979): 297–317, is a bibliography of almost three hundred works on Egeria. See also Ursicino Dominguez Del Val, *Estudios sobre Literatura Latina Hispano-Cristiana, vol. 1, 1955–1971* (Madrid, 1986), 102–15. For an English translation, see John Wilkinson, *Egeria's Travels,* 3d ed. (Warminster, 1999), which includes much supporting material, and George E. Gingras, trans., *Egeria: Diary of a Pilgrimage* (New York, 1970).

2. See Augusto Campana, "La storia della scoperta del Codice Aretino nel Carteggio Gamurrini-De Rossi," in *Atti del Convegno Internazionale sulla Peregrinatio Egeriae, nel centenario della pubblicazione del Codex Aretinus 405 (già Aretinus VI, 3),* ed. Arezzo Accademia Petrarca Di Lettere Arti E Scienze (Arezzo, 1990), 77–84, and G. F. Gamurrini, "I misteri e gl'imni di s. Ilario vescovo di Poitiers ed una peregrinazione ai luoghi santi nel quarto secolo," *Studii e documenti di storia e diritto* 5 (1884): 81ff., and "Della inedita peregrinazione ai luoghi santi," *Studii e documenti di storia e diritto* 6 (1885): 145ff. The voyage was also published as Gamurrini, *S. Hilarii Tractatus de mysteriis et Hymni et S. Silviae Aquitanae Peregrinatio ad loca sancta quae inedita ex codice Arretino deprompsit I.F.G. Accedit Petri Diaconi Liber de locis sanctis* (Rome, 1887).

3. It is interesting that this account was preserved at Monte Cassino, the birthplace of the Benedictine Rule, which condemns the very forms of monastic wandering Egeria practiced.

account found in a ninth-century manuscript from Toledo at the Biblioteca Nacional in Madrid were published by Dom Bruyne.[4]

Unfortunately, none of the fragments of the travel account tell anything about the name or status of the woman traveler, leaving the topic open to heated scholarly debate. Various authors have been suggested, but three stand out in popularity. The first is St. Silvia of Aquitaine, who was mentioned by Palladius in his *Lausiac History* and who was the sister of Flavius Rufinus, a praetorian prefect of Theodosius I. Gamurrini believed her to be the author of the account. The second is Galla Placidia, the daughter of Theodosius I and sister of Honorius and Arcadius. She was kidnapped by the Visigothic king Athaulf shortly after the sack of Rome in 410 and was forced into marriage with him. It was perhaps the romantic leaning of the nineteenth century that led some scholars to believe that she was the author of the mysterious travel account. The third possibility was a nun mentioned in a seventh-century letter by Valerius of Bierzo, a Spanish monk.[5] Scholars finally came to agree that the author was indeed this woman. Unfortunately, surviving copies of the letter vary as to the woman's name, or at least its spelling, and so she was variously known as Aetheria, Echeria, Eucheria, and Egeria. After much debate, scholars have agreed with virtual unanimity on the name Egeria, but there still is much disagreement over where she came from and who she was. Yet our understanding of what she can tell us about early Christian travel hinges, in many respects, on just these biographical details.

The date of the journey has also been hotly contested. Internal evidence places the voyage anywhere between 363, the date when Nisibis fell into Persian hands (Egeria's reason for being unable to visit it), and 540, when the Persians destroyed Antioch, a city that Egeria was able to visit.[6] Gamurrini believed it was written in the late fourth century. But the German philologist Meister rejected that dating on the basis of Egeria's descriptions of

---

4. Dom de Bruyne, "Nouveaux fragments de l'*Itinerarium Eucheriae*," *Revue Benedictine* 26 (1909): 481–84. The Spanish provenance of this early manuscript further points to Egeria's Iberian origins.

5. Valerius of Bierzo, *Epistola Beatissime Egerie laude conscripta fratrum Bergidensium monachorum a Valerio conlata*, ed. and trans. Manuel C. Díaz y Díaz as *Valerius du Bierzo: Lettre sur la Bsa Égerie*, SC 296 (Paris, 1982), 336–49; idem, *Ordo Querimoniae*, in *Valerio of Bierzo: An Ascetic of the Late Visigothic Period*, ed. and trans. by Consuelo Maria Aherne (Washington, D.C., 1949), 70–71.

6. Gingras, *Egeria*, 12.

church life and monasticism, which seemed to him to belong to the sixth century,[7] while a group of Benedictine scholars placed the date of the voyage firmly in the fifth century.[8] Finally, a ground-breaking 1967 article by Paul Devos settled the question of date by using lists of Eastern, specifically Syrian bishops, and the dates of Easter to establish that Egeria must have been traveling in Jerusalem between Easter of 381 and Easter of 384.[9] Virtually all scholars now accept these dates for her voyage.

Another point of discussion and disagreement among scholars is Egeria's homeland. She most likely came from Spain, perhaps even the province of Galicia in the far northwestern corner of the peninsula, though the case has been made for Aquitaine and even Britain. There are several hints in her work. When she meets with the bishop of the city of Edessa, she writes that he said the following to her, "My daughter, I see that you have taken on yourself, because of your piety, the great task of journeying from very distant lands to these places. Therefore, if you are willing, we will show you whatever places there are here that Christians like to see."[10] Many scholars have used this evidence to show that Egeria was from the far western reaches of the empire, namely Spain. Others have argued that this passage simply reveals that the bishop of isolated Edessa would think that almost anyone was from a distant land. Although the quotation is meant to express what the bishop said to Egeria, it is in fact Egeria herself who reports what the bishop said, or should have said. While these interpretations have some merit, it is significant that these were not necessarily his words, but rather Egeria's own. She herself knew that she was from a far off land and had traveled a great distance. These "words of the bishop" also reveal the purpose behind Egeria's voyage, *gratia religionis*—she traveled for the sake of her piety.

If Egeria was from Galicia, then she was not the only Galician to have traveled as far as the Holy Land in this period. Hydatius, bishop of Iria Flavia in Galicia, visited Jerome in Bethlehem around 410, just a few years

---

7. K. Meister, "De itinerario Aetheriae abbatissae perperam nomini s. Silviae addicto," *Rheinisches Museum für Philologie*, n.s., 64 (1909): 337–92. See also Gingras, *Egeria*, 12–13, and Arce, *Itinerario de la Virgen Egeria*, xxiv.

8. A. Lambert, "L'Itinerarium Egeriae vers 414–416," *Revue Mabillon* 28 (1938): 49–69; E. Dekkers, "De datum der *Peregrinatio Egeriae* en het feest van Ons Heer Hemelvaart," *Sacris erudiri* 1 (1948): 181–205. Dekkers specifies 415–18 as the date of the voyage.

9. Paul Devos, "La date du voyage d'Égérie," *Analecta Bollandiana* 85 (1967): 165–94. See also Arce, *Itinerario de la Virgen Egeria*, xxiv.

10. "Quoniam video te, filia, gratia religionis tam magnum laborem tibi imposuisse, ut de extremis porro terris venires ad haec loca, itaque ergo, si libenter habes, quaecumque loca sunt hic grata ad videndum Christianis, ostendimus tibi." Egeria *Itin* 19.5.

after Egeria. He returned to Galicia and later wrote a chronicle of the history of Spain.[11] Galicia has often been considered a provincial backwater with little connection with the rest of the peninsula, let alone the eastern portions of the Mediterranean. The evidence of these two travelers who returned to their homeland should alter this conception.[12]

The question of who Egeria was is still unanswered and remains a topic of debate. Egeria has often been linked to the Theodosian ruling family.[13] This is partially due to the original belief that the text was composed by Galla Placidia, but other factors have also influenced this viewpoint. The identification of Spain as her homeland and the virtually uncontested dating of her journey point to a connection with the emperor Theodosius I, a Spaniard ruling the empire from 378 to 395. There is, however, no hint or mention of Theodosius or any other political figure in Egeria's account. Another reason for this identification is the existence of a "tradition" of imperial women who traveled to the Holy Land, namely Helena, the mother of Constantine, and Eudocia, wife of Theodosius II.[14] These trips, as I argue in Chapter 4, occurred in the fourth and fifth centuries and are best regarded as voyages of imperial patronage rather than pious pilgrimages.

Other scholars, while not necessarily considering Egeria a Theodosian, nevertheless see her as a wealthy aristocrat, traveling with a large entourage.[15] They point to her use of imperial guards during a particularly dangerous part of the voyage. Some have tried to link Egeria to a woman traveler described by Jerome in his letter to Furia. Jerome vehemently criticized the anonymous female traveler for her conspicuous display of wealth and regarded her journey as foolish.[16] Egeria, however, does not seem to have

11. Hydatius *Chronica,* in *The Chronicle of Hydatius and the Consularia Constantinopolitana: Two Contemporary Accounts of the Final Years of the Roman Empire,* ed. and trans. R. W. Burgess (Oxford, 1993). See also Collins, *Early Medieval Spain,* 14.

12. It should be noted, however, that by the reign of Theodosius, whose father came from the region, Galicia would become more connected to the rest of the Mediterranean world.

13. See Justo Pérez de Urbel, *Los Monjes Españoles en la edad media,* 2 vols. (Madrid, 1933), 1:114.

14. See Hunt, *Holy Land Pilgrimage.*

15. Hagith Sivan, "Who was Egeria? Piety and Pilgrimage in the Age of Gratian," *Harvard Theological Review* 81 (1988): 59–72.

16. Jerome *Ep.* 54.13 concerns a woman traveling in the Holy Land in the wrong company: "Vidimus nuper ignominiosum per totum Orientem volitasse; et aetas et cultus et habitus et incessus, indiscreta societas, exquisitae epulae, regius apparatus Neronis et Sardanapalli nuptias loquebantur." On women travelers in general, see Jerome *Ep.* 108; Susanna Elm, "Perceptions of Jerusalem Pilgrimage as Reflected in Two Early Sources on Female Pilgrimage (3rd and 4th centuries A.D.)," *Studia Patristica* 20 (1989): 219–23; and Vito Antonio Sirago, *Cicadae Noctium: Quando le donne furono monache e pellegrine* (Soveria Mannelli, 1986).

had a large entourage, and she relied on the hospitality and guidance of those whom she met on the way, mainly monks. She does not appear to have been traveling in a coach or carriage, but rather on donkeys and sometimes on foot. Her account provides little evidence for her having an elevated social or economic standing.

Another problem concerns Egeria's religious identity. Many have thought it impossible that Egeria could have been a nun, mainly because her journey lasted over three years.[17] These scholars believe that no nun or monastic would have been allowed to leave the monastery for such a long period. A voyage such as Egeria's was considered extremely dangerous, not only physically but spiritually. For this reason, scholars have preferred to label her a lay pilgrim, a label that has stuck. Though she never directly states that she is a *monacha,* there is abundant evidence that she was. Her account was written in the form of letters to women whom she refers to as "sisters."[18] Though a few scholars have believed that this was simply a form of endearment or that she was indeed writing to her "natural" sisters, it is more plausible that the "sisters" she was writing to are fellow monastics, members of her own small community. Though modern scholars have difficulties calling Egeria a monk, Valerius of Bierzo, a seventh-century Spanish monastic, apparently did not. Valerius refers to Egeria as a *sanctimonialis,* or nun.[19] His ability to recognize Egeria as a nun reveals that, at least in the seventh century, a Spanish cleric did not see any inconsistency between a relatively itinerant lifestyle and a monastic profession. We must also remember that the Benedictine Rule came late to Spain, and its emphasis on stability might have been absent from early Spanish monasticism.[20]

Egeria's voyage itself can help us to understand who she was and her reasons for setting out on such a long and difficult journey.[21] Egeria was

---

17. For example, Sivan, "Who was Egeria?" 70.

18. For example, in her *Itinerarium:* "dominae venerabiles sorores" (3.8), "dominae" (23.10), "dominae sorores" (46.1), and "dominae sorores" (46.4). She also refers to them as "your charity/affection" (affectio vestra) (24.1).

19. Valerius of Bierzo *Epistola,* chap. 1. The connection between the letter of Valerius and the text of Egeria's voyage was first made by M. Férotin, "Le Véritable auteur de la *Peregrinatio Silviae,* la vierge espagnole Ethéria," *Revue des Questions Historiques* 74 (1903): 367–97. See Chapter 5 for further discussion on Valerius of Bierzo.

20. See A. Linage Conde, *Los Orígenes del monacato Benedictino en la península Iberica* (Leon, 1973), and idem, "El monacato femenino entre la clausura y la peregrinación: en torno a Egeria," *Studia Monastica* 34, no. 1 (1992): 29–40.

21. Some scholars believe that this is an impossibility: "Indeed almost nothing about Egeria personally can be safely inferred from her text." Peter Dronke, *Women Writers of the Middle*

not unique in being a woman who traveled to the Holy Land, as well as to Egypt and Asia Minor, in this period. Most of the women who traveled did so for reasons similar to hers. They were monastics, consecrated virgins, who, as part of their ascetic practice, went wandering to visit holy places and, more important, holy people. Paula and Eustochium went to Jerusalem in order to be close to Jerome and other holy monks, as well as to visit the holy city. Many of these women set up their own monasteries and eventually remained there. These women, though clearly religious travelers, do not easily fit our image of pilgrims.

Geographically, Egeria's voyage covered a large territory—Palestine, Egypt, Syria, Mesopotamia, and Asia Minor. She did not simply go to the Holy Land to see the sacred places and then return to her homeland; she was on the road for at least three years, if not longer. In order for her to have covered the territory that she did, she must have been in constant motion. Clearly, Egeria's goal was not simply the Holy Land or the city of Jerusalem.

Unfortunately, only a part of Egeria's travel account survives. Valerius of Bierzo, in the seventh century, had a fuller text, as did Peter Damien in the eleventh century. Using their writings, we can thus reconstruct some of the missing portions. What we have is written in a simple, almost oral Latin style that seems to be transcribed into a text. This is clear from her use of transliterations of Greek and Syriac words. Her prose style and dry descriptions of liturgical details have often been criticized by modern historians as simplistic, barbaric, or boring,[22] but it is this very style that makes her account vivid, immediate, and real. Egeria was not writing for herself or for posterity; she was writing for a specific group of individuals—her monastic sisters at home. She is careful in her recounting of details in order that they could share her experience—she even collects objects to bring back to these sisters. What comes through Egeria's account most vividly is the immense excitement she feels in meeting various holy men and women, in traveling to biblical and historical sites, and in observing the local customs.

From her surviving text it appears that Egeria traveled largely alone. Although she does use the plural "us" or "we," perhaps implying that she

Ages: A Critical Study of Texts from Perpetua (203) to Marguerite Porete (1310) (Cambridge, 1984), 20. Also see Ora Limor, "Reading Sacred Space: Egeria, Paula, and the Christian Holy Land," in De Sion exibit lex et verbum domini de Hierusalem: Essays on Medieval Law, Liturgy, and Literature in Honour of Amnon Linder, ed. Yitzhak Hen (Turnhout, 2001), 1–15.

22. Dronke calls her account "boring" and wishes that she had included mishaps or a description of at least one rude monk. Dronke, Women Writers, 21.

has travel companions, she makes no reference to a husband, other family members, friends, or "sisters" traveling with her.[23] She does, however, employ numerous guides along her voyage, including monks, priests, and even bishops. "The holy men who were with us on this journey, the priests and monks, that is, showed us all the places which I was always seeking out, following the Scriptures."[24]

The journey must have been difficult, yet there is no hint of problems in her account. Egeria's voyage is entirely her own; all along the way she makes her own decisions. She alone chooses where to visit and when to go: "Some time afterwards I decided to go next to the land of Ausitis to visit the tomb of the holy man Job in order to pray there."[25] In another place she writes, "I wished to go to Mesopotamia of Syria, to visit the holy monks who were said to be numerous there and to be of such exemplary life that it can scarcely be described."[26] There is a strong current of independent thought running throughout the account. Her plans are flexible, and she seems to change them at times along the way. Much of her travel seems to be on foot, including her ascent to the top of Mount Sinai, though sometimes she rides on mule back. Her decisions often are based on what she hears from the people, especially holy men and women, whom she meets. By no means did Egeria follow a fixed or prearranged itinerary.

Egeria is interested in visiting the historical and sacred places mentioned in scripture, but she places an even greater emphasis on visiting holy *people*. Many have noted that Egeria refers to Old Testament figures as "sancti," such as *sanctus Moyses, sanctus Abraam, sanctus Melchisedech, sancta Rebecca*. Egeria uses the same word in describing the various monks, *sancti monachi,* she meets during her travels, and the usage is significant. In Egeria's estimation, the places she visits are not inherently holy, they are made holy by the continuity of the sanctity of the people there.[27] It is the *sancti monachi* on Mount Sinai who tell her where *sanctus Moyses* spoke

---

23. For example, "Interea ambulantes pervenimus ad quendam locum." Egeria *Itin.* 1.1.

24. "In eo ergo itinere sancti, qui nobiscum erant, hoc est clerici vel monachi, ostendebant nobis singula loca, quae semper ego iuxta Scripturas requirebam." Ibid., 7.2.

25. "Item post aliquantum tempus volui etiam ad regionem Ausitidem accedere propter visendam memoriam sancti Iob gratia orationis." Ibid., 13.1.

26. "Volui, iubente Deo, ut et ad Mesopotamiam Syriae accedere ad visendos sanctos monachos, qui ibi plurimi et tam eximiae vitae esse dicebantur, ut vix referri possit." Ibid., 17.1.

27. For some examples of monks referred to as "sancti monachi," see Egeria *Itin.* 3.6, 11.3, 12.3, 16.5, 19.4, 20.6, 20.11, and 20.13.

with the burning bush.[28] She is not simply visiting empty "holy places," but instead places populated with monks, true holy people worthy of the places. During this period many of the holy places were populated with monks eager to explain the significance of the site and their devotion to it.

Though Egeria is universally considered a pilgrim, her journey, at least what we know of it, does not seem to stand up to the Turners' criteria and observations of pilgrimage experience.[29] Her time frame is immense; Egeria herself tells us that she has been away from her homeland for three years.[30] Her destination is not singular, nor is her motivation. She does not seem to be aware of being on a semi-liminal journey. She does mention other visitors to certain sites, and she has heard stories about other visitors, but there does not seem to be any real sense of a shared experience with other pilgrims. Unlike many pilgrims she is unconcerned with receiving healing or absolving a sin. Only once does she mention visiting a healing shrine, a holy sycamore tree in the city of Ramesses, but she is not personally interested in it, writing matter-of-factly, "Those who are ill go there and take away twigs, and it helps them. We learned this from the holy bishop of Arabia who spoke about it."[31]

Does Egeria's voyage fit other, wider definitions of pilgrimage? On the surface it clearly seems to: she undertakes a journey to the Holy Land and eventually returns home. She is also a Christian and visits Christian holy sites. However, she did not travel to any specific place seeking absolution or an efficacious cure. She was not as interested in the holy places themselves as much as in the holy people she met. There is, in her account, more of an emphasis on people rather than on a *locus* or place. Jerusalem, for example, does not appear to be the primary goal of her journey, though she probably did reside there for some time. Indeed, Egeria was in constant motion, moving from city to city, town to town throughout her journey, and this motion seems to be more significant to her than any particular place along the way.

---

28. "Locus etiam ostenditur ibi iuxta, ubi stetit sanctus Moyses, quando ei dixit Deus: 'Solue corrigiam calciamenti tui,' et cetera . . . et sic, quia sera erat, gustavimus nobis loco in horto ante rubum cum sanctis ipsis." Ibid., 4.8.

29. Turner and Turner, *Image and Pilgrimage*. See my discussion in Chapter 1.

30. "Transacto aliquanto tempore, cum iam tres anni pleni essent, a quo in Ierusolimam venisse." Egeria *Itin.* 17.1.

31. "Nam cuicumque inquomoditas fuerit, vadent ibi et tollent surculos, et prode illis est. Hoc autem referente sancto episcopo de Arabia cognovimus." Ibid., 8.3–4.

Were her motives for traveling those we usually associate with pilgrimage? We can only infer them from her account. Many later pilgrims state healing or remission of sins or fulfilling a vow as their central motivating force, yet these seem absent from Egeria's account. Egeria may be placing the reasons for her journey in the mouth of the bishop of Edessa when she quotes him saying, "My daughter, I see that you have taken on yourself, because of your piety, the great task of journeying from very distant lands to these places."[32] She is traveling for reasons of *religio,* in order to pursue her own personal religious expression, which, in fourth-century terms, would mean not pilgrimage but monasticism. Egeria is interested in visiting, meeting, and observing the lives of the holy men and women, the *sancti monachi,* living at various holy sites. She often describes in detail how they live, including their cultivation of land. She only mentions one of these people by name, the deaconess Marthana, whom she meets in Jerusalem and later visits in Seleucia.[33]

Marthana was the leader of a monastic community of women, and possibly the leader of a dual community of both men and women.[34] The importance Egeria places on Marthana in her account suggests commonalties between the two. Egeria was also a member or perhaps leader of a small community of women in Spain. Evidence of this is apparent in her account of her visit to Edessa, where she receives copies of the King Abgar letters from the bishop of the city. She then writes, "Although I had copies of them at home, I was clearly very pleased to accept them from him, in case the copy which had reached us at home happened to be incomplete; for the copy which I received was certainly more extensive. If Jesus Christ our Lord wills it and I return home, you, ladies dear to me, will read them."[35] Her interest in having a correct copy is significant. Clearly this shows that she came from some sort of monastic community with a library extensive enough to have the Abgar letters.[36]

32. "Quoniam video te, filia, gratia religionis tam magnum laborem tibi imposuisse, ut de extremis porro terris venires ad haec loca." Ibid., 19.5.

33. "Nam inveni ibi aliquam amicissimam michi, et cui omnes in oriente testimonium ferebant vitae ipsius, sancta diaconissa nomine Marthana, quam ego aput Ierusolimam noveram, ubi illa gratia orationis ascenderat." Ibid., 23.3.

34. See the discussion on Marthana in Elm, *Virgins of God.*

35. "Et licet in patria exemplaria ipsarum haberem, tamen gratius mihi visum est, ut et ibi eas de ipso acciperem, ne quid forsitan minus ad nos in patria pervenisset; nam vere amplius est, quod hic accepi. Unde si Deus noster Iesus iusserit et venero in patria, legitis vos, dominae animae meae." Egeria *Itin.* 19.19.

36. Evidence for the existence of extensive monastic libraries in this period, however, is scanty. See Lionel Casson, *Libraries in the Ancient World* (New Haven, Conn., 2001), 141–45.

Egeria's strong interest in the differences between the liturgy of the churches she visits and that of the churches in her own region also points to her being some sort of monastic herself. This interest shows that she was aware of and concerned with the structure of her religion, especially in the proper and "authentic" way to worship. This interest does not suggest a member of the laity. Egeria must have been involved in the church and was probably a consecrated virgin and, at least in this way, a type of monastic.[37] As for her other motives, throughout her account she writes that she wants to visit places in order to pray there, *gratia orationis*. At one point she gives an overview of what she does at these places, "For this was always very much our custom, that, whenever we should come to places that I had desired to visit, the proper passage from Scripture would be read."[38]

The importance of scripture in Egeria's experience in the Holy Land must not be overlooked. The *lectio* or reading passages of scripture is essential to Egeria's understanding of the world around her. The Bible is the sacred lens through which she views the places and people she visits. She stresses how she and her party used passages of scripture to understand what they were viewing. In a similar way, the *sancti monachi* she meets become personal embodiments of the scriptures. They are the *dramatis personae* who bring scripture to life in the very places sacred events occurred years before.

We do not know of any relics Egeria picked up along the way to take back to her sisters. It was a common practice among pilgrims to buy lead or ceramic *ampullae* decorated with scenes from the scriptures or the Holy Land and filled with holy oil. Many of these *ampullae* have been found in the West.[39] Relics were among the more difficult souvenirs of the Holy

---

Egeria may have been referring to her own personal book collection, but my impression still centers on a collection possessed by her community.

37. See Anscari Mundó, "Il monachesimo nella penisola iberica fino al sec. VII," in *Il Monachesimo nell'alto medioevo e la formazione della civiltà occidentale* (Spoleto, 1957), 73–108. See also Sivan, "Who was Egeria?" 59–72. See Josep Amengual i Batle, "Manifestaciones del Monacato Balear y Tarraconense según la correspondencia entre San Agustín y Consencio (415–420)," in *Il Monachesimo Occidentale dalle origini alla Regula Magistri*, XXVI Incontro di studiosi dell'antichità cristiana, Roma, 8–10 maggio 1997 (Rome, 1998), 341–59.

38. "Id enim nobis vel maxime desideraveram semper, ut ubicumque venissemus, semper ipse locus de libro legeretur." Egeria *Itin.* 4.3.

39. On pilgrimage souvenirs, see Cynthia Hahn, "Loca Sancta Souvenirs: Sealing the Pilgrim's Experience," in *The Blessings of Pilgrimage*, ed. Robert Ousterhout (Urbana, Ill., 1990), 85–96, and Maggie Ducan-Flowers, "A Pilgrim's Ampulla from the Shrine of St. John the Evangelist at Ephesus," in ibid., 125–39. See also Gary Vikan, *Byzantine Pilgrimage Art* (Washington, D.C., 1982), and "Guided by Land and Sea: Pilgrim Art and Pilgrim Travel in Early Byzantium," *Jahrbuch für Antike und Christentum* 18 (1991): 74–92.

Land to obtain,[40] and when Egeria mentions relic taking, she seems to be referring to something other people do, such as the men and women who take the healing sticks from the Oak of Mamre or bite off a piece of the True Cross.[41] Egeria distances herself from these people and even seems to disdain them; these are things she would never consider doing herself.

Egeria's souvenirs of the Holy Land are her experiences.[42] The one thing we know she takes with her are the Abgar letters, and here we have another example of the importance of written proof of the holiness of the places Egeria visited. Her own written account of travels thus becomes a type of proof that she wishes to share with her companions at home, perhaps by reading her story out loud to them. In a sense, hers is a voyage framed by texts: scripture acts as her initial guide, and her own writings become the product of her odyssey as well as a physical or spiritual guide for her sisters. Scripture is embodied by the sanctity of the holy men and women living in the *terra sancta*.

If we believe Valerius of Bierzo, Egeria did complete her journey and arrived safely at home, where she became an abbess. Her firsthand experiences of monasticism in the East probably influenced the monastic practices of her "sisters." Egeria may have encouraged others to go traveling as well. Egeria's journey demonstrates something much more than an example of late antique pilgrimage; her trip was part of her monastic vocation, one that included travel at its very core.

It is useful to compare Egeria's journey to a similar one, taken only twenty-five years later, the journey of Orosius. Unlike Egeria's account of her travels, Orosius's works were very well known and survived in numerous copies.[43] Although more of his writing survives and he is mentioned by a number of his contemporaries, Orosius in many ways is a far more elusive character than Egeria. First of all, he provides conflicting accounts of the reasons for his journey from Spain to Africa. These range from some "unknown force" that compelled him, to barbarian enemies chasing him,

40. Patrick Geary, *Furta Sacra: The Theft of Relics in the Central Middle Ages* (Princeton, N.J., 1990).

41. On the cross incident, Egeria writes, "Et quoniam nescio quando dicitur quidam fixisse morsum et furasse de sancto ligno, ideo nunc a diaconibus, qui in giro stant, sic custoditur, ne qui veniens audeat denuo sic facere." Egeria *Itin.* 37.2.

42. On letter writing in this period, see Stowers, *Letter Writing in Greco-Roman Antiquity.*

43. Orosius's *Seven Books Against the Pagans,* written around 418–19, was a medieval best seller, rivaling Augustine's own *De civitate Dei,* a Christian history of the world written a few years after Orosius's. For a bibliography on Orosius, see Dominguez Del Val, *Estudios,* 175–90.

to, as he told Augustine, his priestly concern to try to combat the Pelagian controversy. In other places he speaks of himself as a citizen of no particular place, but instead a sort of Christian wanderer. Orosius is an anomaly among the travelers discussed in this book: he is the only one who traveled to the Holy Land whom modern scholars never consider a pilgrim.

Orosius was a young priest from Spain who fled to North Africa in 414, shortly after the invasions of the Iberian Peninsula by the Vandals, Alans, and Sueves. In his *Commonitorium* to Augustine, written around 414, he writes, concerning his departure from Spain, "I do not know why I came: involuntarily, without necessity and without resolution I left my homeland, moved by an unknown force, until I arrived on the shore of this land. Here I have come to understand that I was ordered to come to you."[44] Yet the coincidence with the invasions and his oblique references to them in his writings reveal that they were probably a strong motivating force in his decision to leave. In his *Historiarum adversum paganos,* Orosius occasionally interjects comments about his own personal experience. When writing about the death of Alexander the Great, he was overcome with emotion, and added the following reflection:

> And yet, if I at times speak about myself, how for the first time I saw barbarians previously unknown to me, how I avoided enemies, how I flattered those in authority, how I guarded against infidels, how I fled from those lying in wait for me; finally, how suddenly enveloped in a mist I evaded those pursuing me on sea and seeking me with stones and spears, even almost seizing me with their hands, I would wish that all who hear me be moved to tears and I would grieve in silence for those who do not grieve, reflecting upon the insensibility of those who do not believe what they have not experienced.[45]

44. "Agnosco, cur venerim: sine voluntate, sine necessitate, sine consensu de patria egressus sum occulta quadam vi actus, donec in istius terrae littus allatus sum. Hic demum in eum resipiui intellectum, quod ad te venire mandabar." Orosius *Consultatio sive Commonitorium Orosii ad Augustinum* 1. Orosius also writes that he was sent by God to Augustine: "Ad te per deum missus sum." Ibid.

45. "Cum tamen, si quando de me ipso refero, ut ignotos primum barbaros viderim, ut infestos declinaverim, ut dominantibus blanditus sim, ut infideles praecaverim, ut insidiantes subterfugerim, postremo ut persequentes in mari ac saxis spiculisque adpetentes, manibus etiam paene iam adprehendentes repentina nebula circumfusus evaserim, cunctos audientes me in lacrimas commoveri velim et tacitus de non dolentibus doleam, reputans duritiae eorum, qui quod non sustinuere non credunt." Orosius *Hist.* 3.20.

It is obvious from this passage that Orosius had experienced some dangerous times, apparently in Spain, and that he placed a great emphasis on actual experience as proof of the authenticity of his account. This melodramatic passage provides insight into Orosius's reasons for fleeing: it appears to have been a coerced flight with an element of subterfuge.

In North Africa, Orosius made contact with the great bishop of Hippo, Augustine, and had the good fortune of making a very favorable impression. North African ports were teeming with Italian and Iberian refugees who had fled the Germanic invasions. Augustine normally was critical of priests and bishops who left their posts, but somehow Orosius convinced him that he was a legitimate traveler. Augustine took an immediate liking to the young man and asked him to undertake a journey to the Holy Land in order to deliver two letters he had written to Jerome and to attend a church council on Pelagianism.[46] Many of Augustine's previous letters to Jerome had been undelivered or, worse yet, misdelivered.[47] Jerome was also angry with Augustine because of the rumors he had heard concerning harsh criticism contained in some of these letters. Augustine was happy to have a reliable person such as Orosius as his letter carrier, and he began his first letter to Jerome on Pelagianism with a glowing description of the young priest.

> There came to me just now a devout young man, a brother in the Catholic faith, in age my son but in worthiness my fellow presbyter; he is Orosius, a man with an alert mind, ready eloquence and burning with eagerness to be a useful instrument in the house of the Lord for he longs to be able to refute the false and dangerous doctrines which are slaughtering the souls of the Spanish in a more terrible way than the barbarian sword slaughters their bodies. He has hastened to come here right from the Atlantic coast, stimulated by the report that he could hear from me whatever he wanted of those topics in which he was interested. . . . I also encouraged him to visit you. . . . For I was looking for someone to send to you but it was not easy to

---

46. Augustine *Ep.* 166 and 167. See White, *The Correspondence.*

47. Augustine had already gained quite a reputation on theological matters by this time. This made his correspondence popular, and one assumes that his letters were often intercepted along the way by bishops and others, in order that they might make their own copies. Often the originals never made it to their destinations. Combined with the uncertainties of mail delivery, this probably resulted in lost letters.

find someone suitable who was reliable and keen to obey as well as an experienced traveler. When I got to know this young man, I could not doubt that he was exactly the sort of person I was asking for from the Lord.[48]

Augustine's description has become the standard scholarly picture of Orosius. Augustine portrays him as an ardent foe of heresy, someone who feared Pelagianism more than barbarian invaders. It is doubtful that Orosius would have agreed with Augustine's comparison between the dangers of the "barbarian sword" and the doctrines of Pelagius. The letter also provides more than simply evidence of the esteem Augustine had for Orosius; it reveals the nature of the explanation Orosius gave Augustine concerning his flight from his homeland. Orosius left in order to seek information about the heresy of Pelagianism that was running rampant in Spain and help from Augustine in fighting it. Yet this account of his departure differs from what Orosius wrote in either his *Commonitorium* or his *Historiarum.* Augustine calls Orosius an "experienced traveler," which suggests that Orosius's travels were not simply confined to his departure from Spain and arrival in Africa. Travel seems to have been an important part of his life. The passage also gives evidence of his homeland as being on the "Atlantic coast," probably Galicia.

Orosius seems purposefully elusive about his specific reasons for leaving Spain. He may have wanted to protect himself from accusations of wandering or abandoning his flock (if he had one) during times of trouble. Travel to distant places also presented the danger of being "a stranger," without a friend or patron to vouch for one's identity or orthodoxy. This presented a particular problem for priests, since they had the ability to celebrate the sacraments, and late antiquity was a period in which issues concerning the orthodoxy of those performing baptisms and offering the Eucharist were still being hammered out.[49] A traveler, even with letters of introduction, which Orosius probably had, was still a stranger. If this stranger also claimed

---

48. Augustine *Ep.* 166.

49. In North Africa, the Donatist controversy centered around this very issue, and Augustine, a bishop and staunch anti-Donastist, was well aware of the dangers posed by priests of questionable morality and orthodoxy. At almost the same time that Orosius came to Africa Pope Anastasius (399–401) issued a decree stating "that no cleric from overseas should be received unless he had a certificate signed by five bishops, because at that time Manichaeans were discovered at Rome." *The Book of the Pontiffs (Liber Pontificalis),* ed. and trans. Raymond Davis (Liverpool, 1989), chap. 41, p. 31. (Henceforth *LP.*)

to be a priest, then it became more important for someone to "test" him, in order to prove his identity and orthodoxy. In this respect, it was easier for a woman, who at this time was barred from any sacramental office, to travel. From Egeria's incomplete account of her travels, there are no hints that her orthodoxy or identity were ever questioned.

Orosius successfully delivered the letters to Jerome. His attendance at the church council of 415 against Pelagius, however, brought him trouble. Judging from Augustine's description, Orosius was someone who told people what they wanted to hear, especially when protecting himself from accusations. It may have been this trait that caused him difficulties at the council. Bishop John of Jerusalem had asked Orosius to take the stand and answer questions to test his own orthodoxy. Orosius's account of the proceedings, his *Liber apologeticus,* states that his answers were mistranslated and this prompted John to accuse him of heresy.[50] One might wonder if this was truly the case, or if in fact Orosius had misspoken in an attempt to curry favor.

Orosius returned to Africa in May or June of 416, with his own eyewitness account of how Pelagius had escaped condemnation, yet without the official proceedings.[51] It was around this time that Orosius claimed that Augustine asked him to write a Christian history of the world to counter both pagan histories and recent pagan attacks on Christianity that blamed the religion for the sack of Rome in 410. It is unclear whether or not this was the case, and it also appears that Orosius had already started his work while in the East. Orosius's prologue to his *Historiarum* contains unambiguous statements of exactly what Augustine requested Orosius to write.[52]

> You bade me speak out in opposition to the empty perversity of those who, aliens to the city of God, are called "pagans" from the crossroads and villages of country places or "heathen" because of their knowledge of earthly things . . . accordingly you bade me set

---

50. "Concedendum et magis, ut interpres errasse dicendo quam episcopus audiendo finxisse videatur." Orosius *Liber apologeticus* 8.1.

51. In one of the newly discovered sermons of Augustine, Dolbeau 30, which is a lost section of Sermon 348, Augustine refers to Orosius's recent arrival from the East, without the official proceedings, and his presence in the congregation. English translation by Edmund Hill in John E. Rotelle, ed., *The Works of Saint Augustine: A Translation for the 21st Century,* part 3, vol. 11, *Newly Discovered Sermons* (Hyde Park, N.Y., 1997), 312–13.

52. On the possibility that Orosius did not receive Augustine's consent to write his history, see E. Corsini, *Introduzione alle 'Storie' di Orosio* (Turin, 1968), 35–51.

forth from all the records available of histories and annals whatever instances I have found recorded from the past of the burdens
of war or ravages of disease or sorrows of famine or horrors of
earthquakes or of unusual floods or dreadful outbreaks of fire or
cruel strokes or lightning and storms of hail or even the miseries
caused by parricides and shameful deeds, and unfold them system-
atically and briefly in the context of this book. . . . I gave myself to
the task and I was especially overcome with confusion, to whom,
as I repeatedly considered the matter, the calamities of the present
times seemed to boil over beyond measure. For I found the days of
the past not only equally oppressive as these, but also the more
wretched the more distant they are from the solace of true religion.[53]

Orosius is usually classified as a friend of Augustine, but never as his
equal. This friendship has been exaggerated, and ironically, there may even
have been a falling out between the two relating to their different accounts
of the Christian history of the world. Augustine may have indeed asked
Orosius to write a history, but evidence points to his disappointment with
the final product, and he noted his displeasure with much of the content
and the theory behind Orosius's efforts in his own *City of God*.[54] Augustine

53. "Praeceperas mihi, uti adversus vaniloquam pravitatem eorum, qui alieni a civitate Dei
ex locorum agrestium conpitis et pagis pagani vocantur sive gentiles quia terrena sapiunt. . . .
praeceperas ergo, ut ex omnibus qui haberi ad praesens possunt historiarum atque annalium
fastis, quaecumque aut bellis gravia aut corrupta morbis aut fame tristia aut terrarum motibus
terribilia aut inundationibus aquarum insolita aut eruptionibus ignium metuenda aut ictibus
fulminum plagisque grandinum saeva vel etiam parricidiis flagitiisque misera per transacta
retro saecula repperissem, ordinato breviter voluminis textu explicarem . . . dedi operam et
me ipsum in primis confusione pressi, cui plerumque reputanti super modum exaestuavisse
praesentium clades temporum videbantur. Nanctus sum enim praeteritos dies non solum
aeque ut hos graves, verum etiam tanto atrocius miseros quanto longius a remedio verae religionis
alienos." Orosius *Hist.*, bk. 1, prologue.
54. One of strongest pieces of evidence revealing Augustine's disappointment concerns
Orosius's claim that Christians have endured ten persecutions, which he links to the ten plagues
of Egypt, and that the eleventh will be that of the Antichrist; the clearest expression of this
theory occurs in Orosius *Hist.*, book 7, chaps. 26–27. This theory did not sit well with Augustine.
De civitate Dei includes an entire chapter (chapter 52 of book 18) angrily refuting Orosius's
ten-persecutions theory. It begins with the statement, "Accordingly, I do not imagine that we
should rashly assert or believe the theory that some have entertained or still do entertain: that
the Church is not going to suffer any more persecutions until the time of Antichrist, beyond
the number she has already endured, namely ten." Augustine then summarizes Orosius's ten
persecutions and then goes on to list a series of other possible "persecutions," including
the crucifixion of Jesus and reign of the Apostate Julian, that were ignored by Orosius. He
concludes with the following: "Haec atque huius modi mihi cogitanti non videtur esse

was already in the middle of writing his own Christian history of the world when Orosius started his.[55] Orosius included in his text hints of Augustine's wariness and caution in asking him to write this history. Orosius wrote, "Indeed, you have already labored at this decision, whether I was equal to this task which you bade me, yet I am content with the evidence of obedience alone, if at least I have distinguished it by my will and my effort."[56] Of course, this could simply be a literary commonplace of self-deprecation, but this would be incongruous with the style of the work. Orosius's history, far shorter than Augustine's, was aimed at a popular audience, written in a simple style and full of vivid imagery of battles and disasters; in short, there is little subtlety in his account. Augustine's *City of God,* on the other hand, is a masterly and erudite work of Christian history. Although both works survived into the later Middle Ages, it was Orosius's account that became the popular and accepted one.[57] It is striking, however, that Orosius's *Historiarum adversum paganos* does not seem to be influenced in its descriptions by his own travels in Palestine. Yet it is from these seven books of history that we learn of his trip to Jerusalem, his experiences with barbarians, and his views on travel and the world.

One of the themes of his history is the Christianization of the "whole world." Christianity, for Orosius, creates a boundless brotherhood of people of various nations. Though his history consists almost entirely of a simple account of a number of important historical events, all temporally defined

---

definiendus numerus persecutionum, quibus exerceri oportet ecclesiam" [When I think over events like these it seems to me that no limit can be set to the number of persecutions which the Church is bound to suffer for her training]. Augustine *De civitate Dei* 18.52; English translation by Henry Bettenson in *Concerning the City of God Against the Pagans* (Harmondsworth, U.K., 1984), 837.

55. Orosius states that Augustine was finishing writing the eleventh book of the *City of God:* "Maxime cum reverentiam tuam perficiendo adversum hos ipsos paganos undecimo libro insistentem — quorum iam decem orientes radii mox ut de specula ecclesiasticae claritatis elati sunt toto orbe fulserunt." Orosius *Hist.,* bk. 1, prologue.

56. "Tu enim iam isto iudicio laborasti, utrumne hoc, quod praeciperes, possem; ego autem solius oboedientiae, si tamen eam voluntate conatuque decoravi, testimonio contentus sum." Ibid.

57. Indeed, when Alfred the Great selects works to be translated into Anglo-Saxon, it is Orosius's history rather than Augustine's *De civitate Dei* that he chooses. For the manuscript history and popularity of Orosius in the Middle Ages, see J. N. Hillgarth, "The *Historiae* of Orosius in the Early Middle Ages," in *De Tertullien aux Mozarabes. Antiquité Tardive et Christianisme Ancien (IIIe–VIe siècles). Mélanges offerts à Jacques Fontaine membre de l'Institut à l'occasion de son 70e anniversaire, par ses élèves, amis et collègues,* ed. Louis Holtz and Jean-Claude Fredouille (Paris, 1992), 1:157–70.

in relation to the founding of the city of Rome, Orosius often turns to his own personal experiences in order to make his account more vivid and authentic. Nowhere is this more evident than when he writes of the manner in which a Christian can travel wherever he or she wants and expect to receive hospitality: "When I flee at the first disturbance of whatever commotion, since it is a question of a secure place of refuge, everywhere there is native land, everywhere my law and my religion. Now Africa has received me as kindly as I confidently approached her."[58]

Chapter 2 of the fifth book begins with an emotional and personal digression, which provides an interesting look at Orosius's view of his own time, a time of great turmoil. He portrays Africa as a safe haven and place of secure refuge for those, like himself, fleeing the danger of wars in Spain. After recounting his own personal experience with barbarians, Orosius explains, in the third book, how this experience caused him to do a very unroman thing—to abandon his *patria,* both physically and figuratively. No longer is Spain his homeland, but rather Christendom itself, and those provinces still under Roman rule are now his new home. Orosius asserts his identity as both a Roman and a Christian, but he does not refer to his provincial identity as an Iberian, as when he writes, "The breadth of the East, the vastness of the North, the extensiveness of the South, and the very large and secure seats of the great islands are of my law and name because I, as a Roman and a Christian, approach Christians and Romans."[59]

It is in this context that Orosius writes about the motives behind his travels. "I enjoy every land temporarily as my fatherland, because what is truly my fatherland and that which I love, is not completely on this earth."[60] Orosius's *patria* is not Spain, but the *patria* of all Christians, the heavenly Jerusalem. This sentiment is at the heart of a new interpretation of monastic life centered around motion.[61] For the wandering ascetic, there was no homeland, for the true homeland could only be paradise after death. Time

58. "Mihi autem prima qualiscumque motus perturbatione fudienti, quia de confugiendi statione securo, ubique patria, ubique lex et religio mea est. Nunc me Africa tam libenter excepit quam confidenter accessi." Orosius *Hist.* 5.2.

59. "Latitudo orientis, septentrionis copiositas, meridiana diffusio, magnarum insularum largissimae tutissimaeque sedes mei iuris et nominis sunt, quia ad Christianos et Romanos Romanus et Christianus accedo." Ibid.

60. "Utor temporarie omni terra quasi patria, quia quae vera est et illa quam amo patria in terra penitus non est." Ibid.

61. On the themes of Christian exile and wandering, see Ladner, "*Homo Viator,*" and Gould, "Moving on and Staying Put."

on earth, one's physical life, is actually an exile from Eden. As an exile, the Christian must move constantly, never stopping too long in one place, never becoming too comfortable. This is what Orosius adopted as a justification for his fleeing Spain and for his itinerant lifestyle. This justification could only have been possible if a life of wandering asceticism was considered legitimate.

And justification was needed. Augustine himself was very critical of priests and bishops who left their posts even in the face of extreme danger. In a long letter replying to the anxious inquiries of a fellow bishop, Honoratus, who was facing the invasion of the Vandals, Augustine strongly advised him not to leave his post. "Whoever, therefore, flees from danger in circumstances in which the Church is not deprived, through his flight, of necessary service, is doing that which the Lord has commanded or permitted. But the minister who flees when the consequence of his flight is the withdrawal from Christ's flock of that nourishment by which its spiritual life is sustained, is a 'hireling who seeth the wolf coming, and fleeth because he careth not for the sheep.'"[62] Indeed, shortly after writing this letter, Augustine himself died, his health broken by the privations suffered during the Vandals' six-month siege of Hippo.

Orosius's voyage from Africa to Palestine was probably made by boat. He stopped at Alexandria and promptly moved on to Palestine. Like a pilgrim, he probably visited the many churches in the city, and like Egeria, he visited monks, including Jerome, and traveled to other nearby places. Jerome, a Dalmatian who studied in Rome, converted to a monastic life and lived in a small community at Aquileia, left for the Holy Land by 373, residing first in Jerusalem, then in Bethlehem, but not before another short stay in Rome between 382 and 385. Jerome had a dedicated following among a group of wealthy Roman women who sought his spiritual advice and companionship, and in turn helped him financially. Jerome was a magnet for many visitors to the Holy Land, including the young Galician Hydatius, who visited him in 407.[63] While Orosius was there, he met a man from the

---

62. "Quicumque igitur isto modo fugit, ut ecclesiae necessarium ministerium illo fugiente non desit, facit, quod dominus praecepit sive permisit. qui autem sic fugit, ut gregi Christi ea, quibus spiritaliter vivit, alimenta subtrahantur, mercennarius ille est, qui videt lupum venientem et fugit, quoniam non est ei cura de ovibus." Augustine *Ep.* 228, in *S. Aureli Augustini Hipponiensis Episcopi Epistulae,* ed. A. Goldbacher (Lispiae, 1911), 496. English translation in P. Schaff, ed., *The Confessions and Letters of St. Augustin, with a Sketch of His Life and Work* (Grand Rapids, Mich., 1994), 577–81.

63. See Chapter 5 for a discussion of Hydatius and his journey.

West visiting Jerome.[64] Like a pilgrim, Orosius acquired important souvenirs of his visit; he left the Holy Land in early 416 with the relics of St. Stephen the Protomartyr, whose tomb had been discovered outside of Jerusalem while Orosius was in city. Avitus of Braga, a fellow Spaniard who was also in Jerusalem during Orosius's visit, had managed to obtain some of the relics and asked him to carry them to the bishop Palchonius of Braga. Avitus also gave Orosius a copy of his Latin translation of Lucian's account of the discovery of the relics.[65] Orosius mentioned this Avitus and another Avitus in his *Commonitorium*. Both were fellow Spaniards, both on journeys, one to Jerusalem and the other to Rome.[66] As we already know, Orosius stopped in Africa first on the journey home in 416, but by early 417 he arrived at Minorca, just off the coast of Spain. The relics of St. Stephen never arrived in Spain, but instead remained on the island of Minorca, left there by Orosius, who probably never completed his journey home. A fifth-century letter about the relics by Bishop Severus of Minorca explains how the relics came to the city of Magona in Minorca:

> In those days, when I, though unworthy, was promoted to clerical office, a certain priest of known holiness stayed here in Magona for a few days, having just come from Jerusalem. Unable to travel to Spain as he wished, he then decided to return to Africa. Having previously resolved to take the relics of the blessed saint Stephen to Spain, which had only recently been discovered, he instead placed them in the church of the previous mentioned town, a deed which was without a doubt inspired by the martyr himself.[67]

64. "Nam ego quoque ipse virum quendam Narbonensem inlustris sub Theodosio militiae, etiam religiosum prudentemque et gravem, apud Bethleem oppidum Palaestinae beatissimo Hieronymo presbytero referentem audivi, se familiarissimum Athaulfo apud Narbonam fuisse." Orosius *Hist.* 7.43. Orosius's encounter with this fellow traveler is analyzed in A. Marchetta, *Orosio e Ataulfo nell'ideologia dei rapporti Romano-Barbarici* (Rome, 1987).

65. Avitus *Epistola ad Palchonium, de reliquiis Sancti Stephani, et de Luciani epistola a se e graeco in latinum versa, PL* 41:805–8.

66. "Tunc duo cives mei, Avitus et alius Avitus, cum iam tam turpem confusionem per se ipsam veritas sola nudaret, peregrina petierunt. Nam unus Ierosolymam, alius Romam profectus est. Reversi unus rettulit Origenem, alius Victorinum; ex his duobus alter alteri cessit. Priscillianum tamen ambo damnarunt." Orosius *Commonitorium* 3.

67. "Namque diebus pene hiisdem, quibus ego tanti sacerdotii nomen, licet indignus, adeptus sum: presbyter quidam sanctitate praecipuus, a Hierosolyma veniens, Magonae non longo tempore immoratus est. Qui postquam transvehi ad Hispanias, sicut desiderabat, requievit, remeare denuo ad Africam statuit. Hic beati Stephani martyris reliquias, quae nuper revelatae sunt, cum ad Hispanias portare constituisset: ipsas, sine dubio martyre inspirante,

The relics remained there and had their own stormy history.[68] At this point Orosius disappears from the historical record; however, more relics of Stephen the Protomartyr began to arrive in Africa at this same time. Evodius, the bishop of Uzalis, just outside Carthage, obtained relics of Stephen by 417. I believe that Orosius did return to Africa after his aborted journey to Spain, but to Carthage rather than Hippo. Even though Augustine wrote about the many miracles surrounding Stephen's relics in Uzalis and later in Calama, he never mentions any connection between the relics and Orosius, nor does he explain how the relics arrived in Africa. Eight years later, Augustine himself obtained relics of Stephen the Protomartyr while visiting Carthage. He set up a shrine in the church of Hippo that became the site of many miracles.[69] Clearly Augustine was purposefully avoiding any mention of Orosius.

Orosius does not fit the specific "pilgrim" criteria as described by Victor and Edith Turner, but he does clearly fit into our broader definition of pilgrim as one who undertakes a religiously motivated journey and return, specifically to the Holy Land.[70] Orosius's return with relics in tow only further reinforces the image of a pious pilgrim wanting to bring home a piece of the Holy Land. Orosius, however, is surrounded by the special aura of being a friend of Augustine of Hippo. He was also a priest and did, in fact, attend a church council in Jerusalem, and these factors seem to have precluded him from consideration as a mere pilgrim.

But the question remains, can we meaningfully draw such a distinction between Egeria and Orosius? The fact that Egeria is a woman has probably made it convenient for scholars to view her simply as a pilgrim, whereas Orosius was a priest and a friend of Augustine's, not a likely candidate for the pilgrim label. Clearly both Egeria and Orosius could be considered pilgrims, but I believe they can best be understood as ascetic wanderers, practicing a form of monasticism based on itinerary.[71]

---

immemorati oppidi ecclesia collocavit." *Epistola Severi Episcopi: Edición paleográfica y Transcripción latina seguidas de las versiones castellana y catalana de su texto,* ed. Eusebio Lafuente Hernández (Menorca, 1981), 27. See also Scott Bradbury, ed., *Severus of Minorca: Letter on the Conversion of the Jews* (Oxford, 1996).

68. The relics were used in the forced conversion of the Jews living in Minorca.

69. Augustine *De civitate Dei* 22.8.

70. See my Chapter 1 for a discussion of definitions of pilgrim and pilgrimage. See also Turner and Turner, *Image and Pilgrimage.*

71. For an early view of Egeria and Orosius in light of a possible Spanish form of wandering monasticism, see Mundó, "Il monachesimo." Mundó's ideas have been mostly

One way of trying to understand the travels and religious lives of both Egeria and Orosius is to compare them to a fellow countryman, Bachiarius. Bachiarius, an interesting and little studied figure, was a fifth-century monk who apparently encountered difficulties and criticism for his wandering, which he defended in his writing.[72] Two of his works survive, *Libellus de Fide* and *De reparatione lapsi ad Januarium*. Gennadius of Marseilles, in his continuation of Jerome's *Lives of Illustrious Men,* described Bachiarius as "a Christian philosopher" who "chose travel as a means of preserving the integrity of his purpose"; his purpose being to "devote his time to God."[73] Gennadius continued to describe the book and the reasons for which it was written: "He is said to have published acceptable small works but I have only read one of them, a work *On faith,* in which he justified himself to the Pope, defending himself against those who complained and misrepresented his travel, and asserting that he undertook his travel not through fear of men but for the sake of God, that going forth from his land and kindred he might become a co-heir with Abraham the patriarch."[74] In this passage, Gennadius hints at possible accusations against wandering monks, such as fleeing their homes out of fear. Bachiarius wrote in the early 400s and

neglected, but recently Amengual i Batle wrote the following concerning early Spanish monasticism: "No sabemos cómo estos monjes concretaban su ideal. Mundó dedicó unas páginas al monacato hispánico itinerante. No nos atrevemos a aplicar esta condición a los monjes que hemos mencionado; pero tampoco la excluiríamos del todo, puesto que la agilidad de movimientos les caracteriza." Amengual i Batle, "Manifestaciones."

72. See bibliography on and introduction to Bachiarius in Dominguez Del Val, *Estudios,* 86–90. See also J. Marique, *Leaders of Iberean Christianity (50 to 650 A.D.)* (Boston, 1962); J. N. Hillgarth, "Visigothic Spain and Early Christian Ireland," in *Visigothic Spain, Byzantium and the Irish* (London, 1985), 167–94; Jose M. Bover, "Bachiarius Peregrinus?" *Estudios eclesiasticos* 7 (1928): 361–66; Joseph Duhr, *Aperçus sur l'Espagne chrétienne du IVe siecle ou le 'De Lapso' de Bachiarius* (Louvain, 1934); and Germain Morin, "Pages inédites de deux pseudo-Jéromes des environs de l'an 400. I: Deux lettres mystiques d'un ascète espagnol," *Revue Bénédictine* 40 (1928): 289–310. In a forthcoming article, Michael Kulikowski shows Bachiarius's work to be more in line with Origenist controversies than Priscillianist and thus posits an Illyrian rather than Iberian background for Bachiarius. See Michael Kulikowski, "The Identity of Bachiarius," *Medieval Prosopography,* forthcoming.

73. "Bachiarius vir Christianae philosophiae, nudus et expeditus vacare Deo disponens, etiam peregrinationem propter conservandam vitae integritatem elegit." Gennadius of Marseilles *Liber de viris inlustribus,* chap. 24, *PL* 58:1053. Translated by Ernest Cushing Richardson as "Jerome and Gennadius: Lives of Illustrious Men," in *A Select Library of Nicene and Post-Nicene Fathers of the Christian Church* (reprint, Grand Rapids, Mich., 1979), 390.

74. "Satisfacit pontifici Urbis adversum querulos et infamatores peregrinationis suae, indicans se non timore hominum, sed Dei causa peregrinatione suscepisse, ut exiens de terra sua et cognatione sua cohaeres fieret Abrahae patriarchae," Gennadius *Liber de viris inlustribus,* chap. 24.

probably died in 425, making him a contemporary of both Egeria and Orosius. In addition to being criticized for wandering, he was also accused of Priscillianist tendencies and was compelled to travel to Rome to defend himself. In the *De fide*, Bachiarius looks to scripture in order to defend his wandering lifestyle; he quotes from the Psalms, writing, "I am a sojourner, as all my fathers were."[75]

Bachiarius is probably one of the few voices of a wandering monk that remains in the historical record. This was a time of changing definitions of proper monastic conduct. With Bachiarius we are perhaps reading the words of an actual "gyrovague," defending his ascetic method. Although he might have been fleeing charges of Priscillianism, Bachiarius's life and his defense of travel as a means of professing his faith shed new light of the question of the wandering monk and on the concept of itinerant spirituality. By comparing Bachiarius to both Egeria and Orosius, we gain a clearer understanding of their journeys and of their spiritual expressions.[76] Egeria and Orosius were, in their interest in meeting ascetics, monastics, and other travelers, not exhibiting the traditional motivations and actions of a pilgrim, but instead wandering and meeting people as a "religious" way of life. This was a life of permanent pilgrimage and journey, or *instabilitas*. Pilgrimage, with its limited duration and singular geographic goal fails to capture the essence of this journey. These travelers take the words of scripture literally; they are "but temporary travelers in this world," constantly journeying until they find their peace and stability in the world to come, the heavenly Jerusalem.

With the passage of the Edict of Milan, in 313, and the official recognition of Christianity, came the reining-in of religious belief and expression within the church. Heresy, both its definition and eradication, was the primary problem of the church in the fourth and fifth centuries. Attempts at regulation of belief and practice were widespread: the church also needed a way of controlling the swelling ranks of monks throughout the empire. Church canons and imperial legislation attempted to place monks firmly under the control of their local bishops, preferably through an abbot.

---

75. "Peregrinus ego sum, sicut omnes patres mei," Bachiarius *Libellus de fide*, PL 20:1024. Bachiarius is quoting Psalm 38.13; the full line is "quia advena ego sum apud te et peregrinus sicut omnes patres mei." This is the same line from the psalms that Paula, mother of Eustochium and friend of Jerome, used to frequently recite: "Advena sum et peregrina sicut omnes patres mei." See Jerome *Ep.* 108.1. See also A. M. Mundó, "Estudios sobre el *De fide* de Baquiari," *Studia Monastica* 7, no. 2 (1965): 247–303.

76. For an early comparison of Bachiarius and Egeria (called Eteria), see chapter 2 of Pérez de Urbel, *Los Monjes Españoles en la edad media.*

Monasticism itself was in a formative period when Egeria and Orosius traveled. In the wake of the diffusion of Athanasius's account of Antony, the "first" monk, monasticism had spread across the Mediterranean from its birthplace in the East. Augustine himself writes in the *Confessions* of hearing Antony's story and being profoundly moved by it; following his own conversion, Augustine returned to Africa and set up a small monastic community. This type of "spontaneous" monasticism was not uncommon; monastic practice, especially in the West, was far from standardized. Men and women often gathered in small communities, agreeing to live together under the monastic yoke. These enthusiasts wrote rules, took vows, and renounced worldly concerns, yet in many instances, they lived outside of what would traditionally be considered a monastic environment.

Philip Rousseau writes that the "early history of Christian asceticism was not one of smooth development," that it was a "period of debate," and that there was a "fluid situation" within monasticism at this time.[77] He also speaks of competition among different types of ascetic practices, warning the historian to be aware of their extreme variety.[78] Susanna Elm's recent book heeds this advice, clearly outlining the various forms Eastern monastic practice took in the fourth century, and making a strong argument for acknowledging a multiplicity of valid monastic practices in this period.[79] In the case of Western monasticism, this variety can best be studied by a thorough rereading of sources outside the framework of structured Benedictine monasticism.

One approach is through a careful reading of the opposition to monasticism, both from within and outside the church. This opposition can be seen in legislation, both secular and ecclesiastical, such as the laws making monks responsible to their local bishops. Many acts of the Spanish councils were aimed at controlling monks. We also have evidence of opposition to pilgrimage, and the downplaying of the holy places in and around Jerusalem.

The following chapter will explore the complicated question of that "most terrible" type of monk, the gyrovague of the *Regula Magistri*. A long and detailed "satire" of the gyrovagues is included in this monastic legislation, and many scholars have dismissed the description of the gyrovagues as "a digression" or a "literary flourish," or have wholeheartedly heeded the Master's

---

77. Philip Rousseau, "Christian Asceticism and the Early Monks," in *Early Christianity: Origins and Evolution to A.D. 600, In Honour of W. H. C. Frend,* ed. Ian Hazlett (Nashville, 1991), 112–22:117. See also Rousseau, *Ascetics, Authority, and the Church.*

78. Rousseau, "Christian Asceticism," 119–22.

79. Elm, *Virgins of God.*

condemnation of the gyrovagues as false monks, propelled by gluttony and indolence, and not by spiritual needs. This portrayal of the gyrovague must be reexamined, and the possibility that the term *gyrovagus* refers to a real and once legitimate form of monastic practice must be explored.

CHAPTER THREE

MONASTIC RULES AND WANDERING MONKS

Early monasticism was an exceedingly diverse phenomenon that drew in Christian men and women who were eager to commit themselves to a religious life "outside" traditional civic society. Withdrawal from the societal conventions of marriage, public life, and trade did not, however, denote complete separation and intensive seclusion. Monks, male and female, became a part of late antique society and even civic life through charity, hospitality, and patronage. They also functioned as supporters or sometimes opponents of the local bishop in this period of fluid relations.

The late antique period witnessed a solidification of the definitions of proper monastic behavior that would eventually deny any spiritual value in wandering in favor of physical stability, staying in one place, as a reflection of spiritual and institutional stability. This chapter explores this development in the Christian centuries and examines what we can learn about monastic travel and wandering asceticism from evidence provided by its detractors. Denigrators of wandering and of pilgrimage complained that religious travelers employed an overly literal interpretation of the "homelessness" and state of exile of the Christian.[1] It was difficult enough for the authorities of the church to control the popularity of a sedentary charismatic holy man or woman; a wandering charismatic was even more dangerous, since he or she would inevitably cross boundaries of episcopal authority and power.[2] For many early Christian writers culminating with Benedict, physical stability

---

1. For a discussion, see Muschiol, "Zur Spiritualität des Pilgerns"; Constable, "Monachisme et Pèlerinage"; Kathleen Hughes, "On an Irish Litany of Pilgrim Saints," in *Church and Society in Ireland, A.D. 400–1200,* ed. D. Dumville (London, 1987), 302–31; and Rousseau, *Ascetics, Authority, and the Church.* See also Amengual i Batle, "Manifestaciones."

2. The spread of heresy was another potential danger of wandering monk or clerics. See Chap. 2, note 49.

was the answer. Church fathers downplayed and even attacked the benefits of spiritual wandering and physical visits to holy people and places. The true journey for the Christian, they asserted, was an inward one.[3]

Evidence of the disapproval of the ecclesiastical hierarchy and church authorities takes many forms, including denunciations of itineracy in letters, the limiting or abolishing of religious wandering through conciliar and imperial legislation, and the creation of monastic rules that emphasize physical stability. Monastic rules are a unique literary invention of the late antique period. There are many early monastic *regulae,* but most are of unknown authorship, uncertain provenance, and even uncertain date. A reevaluation of all of these sources, letters, laws, and rules—not simply as documents on the regulation of life within the monastery's gates, but as efforts to deal with, define, and control proper monastic behavior—illuminates the diverse reality of monastic practice that the authors of rules hoped to limit and control. The long excursus on the gyrovague, the dissolute wandering monk, in the anonymous sixth-century *Regula Magistri (RM)* is perhaps the best example of monastic criticism of ascetic travelers.[4] When considered along with other early monastic writing, the *RM* provides much information on the existence and nature of religious wandering and the monastic authorities' reaction to it.

The fifth and sixth centuries were a veritable golden age in monastic legislation and monastic diversity in the West. Descriptive accounts of monastic behavior were soon joined with prescriptive texts ranging from collections of sayings to well-organized precepts and regulations regarding proper monastic life. The earliest rules in the East were those of Pachomius and Basil, written in the fourth century and written for specific communities of monks. In the West, the fifth and sixth centuries witnessed the emergence of a variety of monastic rules, including the most celebrated monastic text, the *Regula Benedictina (RB)*, written in the mid-sixth century. It would be

3. This argument would be made by Augustine, Jerome, Eusebius, and Evagrius Ponticus, among others.
4. I use the edition of Adalbert de Vogüé, ed., *La Règle du Maître* (Paris, 1964). All further reference to this volume will be designated by *RM* and the appropriate chapter and section number. I also consulted the alternative edition: *La Règle du Maître: Edition diplomatique des manuscrits latins 12205 et 12634 de Paris,* ed. Hubert Vanderhoven and François Masai, with collaboration by P. B. Corbett (Paris, 1953). Translations of the Latin come from the English edition, Luke Eberle, ed., *The Rule of the Master* (Kalamazoo, Mich., 1977), unless otherwise noted. This translation is based on the Vogüé edition. From this point onward I will refer to the author of the *Regula Magistri* as the Master.

a mistake, however, to conclude that these surviving monastic rules were the basis of all forms of early monasticism. The vast majority of early Western monks lived, not under a formal rule, but instead, as with the communities that Augustine described in the *Confessions,* in small communities of like-minded friends, perhaps under the pastoral care of the local bishop. This was the case, for example, with some early communities outside Milan.[5]

The surviving monastic texts and rules from this period point both to the diversity of monasticism as well as to increasing attempts to define, regulate, and control legitimate monastic activity; however, further analysis must proceed carefully, as most are anonymous and of uncertain provenance. I have relied on the authoritative work of Adalbert de Vogüé in dealing with such textual problems.[6] Vogüé suggests that some of the so-called rules may not have been written as such, and in any case there is no strict definition of *regula.*[7] These rules often borrowed liberally from other rules and monastic documents, making understanding of specific contexts ever more complicated. Moreover, these surviving monastic texts present us with only part of the story of early monasticism in the West. They represent what later writers and copyists thought important to preserve, so it should not surprise us that many reveal similarities with the *Regula Benedictina.* The *RM,* only surviving in three known copies, with its long discussion of the gyrovague and the dangers of travel of all sorts, may not have been quite as unique as it now appears.

Before we move to a close examination of the *RM,* we must explore some of its precursors. Most Western monastic rules from late antiquity contain descriptions of different classes of monks. This monastic typology provided a kind of definition of proper and improper monastic behavior.

---

5. On Ambrose and monasteries surrounding Milan, see Rita Lizzi, "Ambrose's Contemporaries and the Christianization of Northern Italy," *Journal of Roman Studies* 80 (1990): 156–73.

6. Adalbert de Vogüé, a monk himself of the *La Pierre-qui-vire* monastery in France, is the foremost expert on the *RM* and probably also on all the pre-Benedictine rules. Vogüé has done much work in dating and placing these rules in their geographic settings. In his influential article, "The Cenobitic Rules of the West," Vogüé discusses a number of early monastic rules and their relation to one another and arranges the rules into "generations" based on the date of their composition and into families based on their borrowings. Adalbert de Vogüé, "Cenobitic Rules of the West," *Cistercian Studies* 12 (1977): 175–83.

7. Vogüé defines a *regula* as "a written rule, proper to a particular time and place, to a monastery or group of monasteries." Adalbert de Vogüé, "Sub regula vel abbate: A Study of the Theological Significance of the Ancient Monastic Rules," in *Rule and Life: An Interdisciplinary Symposium,* ed. M. Basil Pennington (Spencer, Mass., 1971), 52.

The development of a standard typology of monks can be traced through various rules and monastic commentary. The two earliest texts about the different types of monks are the anonymous *Consultationes Zacchaei et Apollonii (ConZA)*, *c*. 360–80, and Jerome's *Epistula ad Eustochium,* dated 384.[8] Both of these texts were written before the monastic rules in question and were influential in monastic circles. This chapter also considers the *Regula IV Patrum (RIVP)*, and *De Institutis Coenobiorum* and *Conlationes* of John Cassian, texts that Vogüé places in the second generation of monastic rules.[9] The *RM,* which, according to Vogüé, was probably written in Italy, near Rome, around 530, belongs to what he considers the fourth generation of monastic rules.[10]

An important commonplace in Western monastic rules was a list classi-fying the various types of monks, including both "good" and "bad" types.[11] This form of classification served to define the proper form of monastic profession and echo the apparent diversity of monastic practices between the fourth and sixth centuries. Each author inherited a model of a monastic typology, which was in turn added to or manipulated according to individual needs and beliefs. When the Master came to write his rule, a standard Western typology already existed. It included the cenobite, the anchorite, and either one or two categories of false monks of various names. Careful examination of the attributes of these monastic types and the role they play in the rules and texts is key to understanding the fundamental character of monasticism

---

8. Jerome *Ep.* 22.

9. Cassian's work here is being considered as a proto-rule and as a monastic text. The first generation consists of the "mother rules," written around 400. From this generation, I primarily looked at the *Regula Basilii (RFT* and *RBT)* and the *Regula Augustini (RA)*. Basil's rule consists of two parts, the Longer Rules or *Regulae Fusius Tractatae,* and the Shorter Rules or *Regulae Brevius Tractatae.* These were translated from Greek into Latin in the early fifth century by Rufinus. See W. K. L. Clarke, *The Ascetic Works of Saint Basil* (London, 1925), 9–55, and George Saint-Laurent, "St. Basil of Caesarea and the Rule of St. Benedict," *Diakonia* 16 (1981): 71–79. On Augustine's possible authorship of this rule and for a summary of the argu-ments for and against, as well as the text of the rule itself, see George Lawless, *Augustine of Hippo and his Monastic Rule* (Oxford, 1987).

10. Vogüé, "Cenobitic Rules," 177. The case has also been made for southern Gaul as the *RM's* provenance. From this fourth generation of monastic rules I also look at the *Regula Orientalis (RO)* and at the *Regula Ad Virgines (RV)* of Caesarius of Arles, this last one being a rule for nuns.

11. For an interesting discussion on the chapter *De generibus monachorum* in both pre- and post-Benedictine monastic rules and texts, see Gregorio Penco, "Il capitolo *de generibus mona-chorum* nella tradizione medievale," in *Medievo Monastico,* ed. P. Giustino Farnedi (Rome, 1988), 493–513. Penco relates this chapter in the rules to the way it appears in the *RB,* even in his pre-Benedictine examples. Also see Caner, *Wandering, Begging Monks.*

in the era before Benedictine hegemony. It was in the category of the false monk that the Master made his innovation. By contrasting the Master's typology with other typologies, much can be learned about his attitudes concerning proper monastic behavior, in particular, his attitude toward monastic wandering and travel.

MONASTIC TYPOLOGIES

From the beginnings of monasticism in the fourth-century deserts of Egypt, there had existed a tension between the monastic desire for solitude and the benefit of sharing in the difficulties and rewards of the monastic life with others, either other monks or the local laity whose charitable gifts supported these heroes of spiritual combat. Antony, widely considered the "first" monk, was an Egyptian who gave up everything he possessed for a life of asceticism and solitude. In the *vita* of Antony, most probably written by the embattled local bishop, Athanasius of Alexandria, the young monk is often portrayed in the company of visitors, fellow monks, and the bishops to whom he defers.[12] This solitary monk, therefore, was often in company. The tension between solitary versus communal life is also evident in the life and writings of Pachomius, another early Egyptian monk. Pachomius gathered desert solitaries into large monastic communities and wrote a monastic rule to regulate their lives.[13] From its Egyptian beginnings to the westward spread of its ideals and practices, monasticism would always manifest this tension between isolation and community.

The monastic movement quickly spread to the West, aided by the Latin translation of the *Life of Antony,* which provided the basic model for Christian monastic and ascetic behavior. It was this text that introduced the very word *monachus* into Latin.[14] Antony, though a solitary, gave rise to a form of communal retreat from society toward a life of prayer and contemplation.

12. Athanasius of Alexandria, *Vita Antonii,* ed. G. J. Bartelink, trans. Pietro Citati and Salvatore Cilla as *Vita di San Antonio,* vol. 1 of *Vite dei Santi,* ed. C. Mohrmann (Milan, 1974).

13. On Pachomius, see Rousseau, *Pachomius.* For his writing and *regulae,* see *Pachomian Koinonia: The Lives, Rules and Other Writings of Pachomius and His Disciples,* 3 vols., translated by Armand Veilleux (Kalamazoo, Mich., 1981).

14. The word *monachus* appears in the anonymous Latin translation of Athanasius's *Life of Antony,* not the translation by Evagrius of Antioch. Jerome, who some believe was the first to use the term in Latin, did not employ "monachus" until 375 in his third letter. See Jaime Sepulcre, "Dos 'etimologías' de monachus: Jerónimo y Agustín," in *Il Monachesimo Occidentale dalle origini alla Regula Magistri,* XXVI Incontro di studiosi dell'antichità cristiana, Roma, 8–10 maggio 1997 (Rome, 1998), 197–211.

Augustine himself was a witness to the impact of Antony's life on the formation of small communities of friends in Italy and his own small North African community. Augustine's final conversion was triggered by his hearing the story of Antony; it was a monastic impulse, an impulse fulfilled in his first actions upon conversion: to resign his position in Milan, to not marry but instead begin a chaste life, and to flee society.[15] He retired to a life of monastic pursuits and contemplation at Cassiciacum with a small group of his friends; and when he returned to Africa, he started a similar community in Thagaste.[16] As monasticism began in the West, it would be the model of the anchorite, or solitary monk, that would be ranked as the most perfect and most difficult model to pursue. But it would be the communal form of monasticism that would take an early hold on Western monks.

The *ConZa*, probably written between 360 and 380, contain a section on the different kinds of monks, "under the one name 'monk' are included various types."[17] Here, unlike in subsequent examples, there is no set number of the different types of monks, possibly because the author believed there was too much variation: "The cause of this variety is . . . the various types of characters [with] . . . various intentions."[18] The anonymous author started his description with the "lowest rung" of monks and worked his way to the "highest." The monks on the "topmost rung of monastic practice" are anchorites, who "live alone in the wilderness, in arid tracts of the desert, and true to the name of monk lead a lonely life."[19] Below the anchorite, the author of the *ConZa* discusses five types of monks: two false monks, two true monks (cenobites), and one "lay" monk, who is "content with little observance, [and] merely live[s] unmarried."[20] Placing the anchorite on the "highest rung" of monasticism followed the model of Antony of Egypt, already made famous by this time as a result of Athanasius's written account of his life.

15. Augustine *Confessiones* 8.14–16, CC 27.

16. Possidius *Vita Augustini* 3.2. See also Augustine *Confessiones* 8.9.

17. *Consultationes Zacchei christiani et Apollonii philosophi*, trans. by Caedmon Holmes as "The Discussions of Zacchaeus and Apollonius," trans. rev. Adalbert De Vogüé, *Monastic Studies* 12 (1976): 278. (Henceforth *ConZA*.)

18. *ConZA* 280.

19. *ConZA* 280. This image of a "ladder" of monastic perfection becomes the basis of the sixth-century work by John Climacus, *The Divine Ladder of Heavenly Ascent*, aimed at a monastic audience. The monastic ladder also becomes a frequent motif in Byzantine icons.

20. *ConZA* 279.

Jerome offers a slightly modified form of the *ConZa* typology. In a letter to Eustochium, the daughter of his patroness Paula, on the merits of virginity, Jerome includes a long digression on the various kinds of monks that differs significantly from the typology found in the *ConZa*.[21] He begins his discussion with the following classification: "There are in Egypt three classes of monks. First, there are the cenobites, called in their Gentile tongue *Sauhes,* or, as we should say, men living in community. Secondly, there are the anchorites, who live in the desert as solitaries, so called because they have withdrawn from the society of men. Thirdly, there is the class called *Remnuoth,* a very inferior and despised kind, though in my own province they are the chief if not the only sort of monks."[22] For Jerome, Egyptian practice was the ideal that monks in the West should emulate.[23] Partly for this reason, Jerome draws a contrast between the monks in Egypt and those in his own province, Palestine, whom he viewed as mostly false monks.

In beginning his list of monks with the cenobite rather than the anchorite, who was in other typologies supposed to be leading the "perfect" life, Jerome created a new standard ranking. The best or "most perfect" monk was now the cenobite. But his most interesting remarks relate to false monks, whom he calls *Remnuoth,* a Coptic word unknown elsewhere. These offensive monks, the most common in his own province, were full of danger. He dismisses them abruptly: "Avoiding these then as though they were the plague, let us come to the more numerous class who live together and are called, as we have said, cenobites."[24] He continues the passage with a detailed and flattering description of the cenobites. Only after the long excursus on cenobites does he then turn to a description of anchorites. In his short account, he mentions the model anchorites, Paul the hermit and Antony, and John the Baptist as the "first example" of a solitary life, but

---

21. The letter was probably written in 384. Jerome *Ep.* 22, in *Epistula ad Eustochium,* in *Select Letters of St. Jerome,* trans. F. A. Wright (New York, 1933), 52–159.

22. "Tria sunt in Aegypto genera monachorum: coenobium, quod illi 'sauhes' gentili lingua vocant, nos 'in commune viventes' possumus appellare; anchoretae, qui soli habitant per deserta et ab eo, quod procul ab hominibus recesserint, nuncupantur, tertium genus est, quod dicunt 'remnouth,' deterrimum atque neglectum et quod in nostra provincia aut solum aut primum est." Jerome *Ep.* 22.34.

23. For more on early Egyptian monasticism and asceticism, see Chitty, *The Desert a City,* and Rousseau, *Pachomius.*

24. "His igitur quasi quibusdam pestibus exterminatis veniamus ad eos, qui plures in commune habitant, id est, quos vocari coenobium diximus." Jerome *Ep.* 22.35.

fails to give any information about their lives.[25] Jerome ends his digression on monks at this point, writing, "The struggles of the anchorites and their life, in the flesh but not of the flesh, I will unfold to you on some other occasion, if you wish."[26] This silence seems strange, since Jerome himself lived as an anchorite, or at least a quasi-anchorite. The solution to this contradiction may lie in the addressee of the letter, Eustochium, a young woman. Jerome knew the difficulties and pitfalls of the anchoritic life; and though he was aware of the existence of female anchorites, he believed that it was not the proper model for a woman's religious life. Within the same long letter he would later provide the model of the Virgin Mary for Eustochium to emulate.[27] Monastic legislators and writers *were*, however, deeply concerned about the negative aspects of the anchorite's life. The anchorite, in living alone, lived according to his own will and was not subject to the authority of an elder. He, or she, was liable to become confused and succumb to the temptations of evil spirits in disguise.[28] Anchorites were also vulnerable to the sin of pride if successful in their efforts to live a life of severe asceticism and isolation.

Isolation in many cases was only relative. Popular anchorites attracted many followers and devotees, who came seeking cures and access to holy power and who brought food and other gifts. It was anxiety about potentially uncontrollable charismatic ascetics that prompted monastic legislators to promote the cenobitic life over the anchoritic life and to define the proper anchorite as someone who lived many years in a monastic community before becoming an anchorite.

25. "Huius vitae auctor Paulus, inlustrator Antonius et, ut ad superiora conscendam, princeps Iohannes baptista fuit." Ibid., 22.36. Jerome probably mentions Paul the Hermit here because he authored the life of this monk, whose very existence his critics had recently questioned.

26. "Horum laborem et conversationem in carne, non carnis, alio tempore, si volueris, explicabo." Ibid.

27. "Propone tibi beatam Mariam, quae tantae extitit puritatis, ut mater esse domini mereretur." Ibid., 22.38.

28. Discernment of spirits, *discretio spirituum*, is a discussed in the *Vita Antonii* and is a frequent topic in the *Apophegmata Patrum*. In the *Vita Antonii*, Antony discusses the problem of discerning good and evil spirits and how God can grant this ability: "Cum ergo venerint ad vos nocte, et voluerint dicere vobis futura, aut dixerint: 'Nos sumus angeli', nolite adtendere illis. Mentiuntur enim. . . . Distantiam enim adventus malorum et bonorum possiblile est scire, Domino praestante." *Vita Antonii* 35.1 and 35.4. In the Latin version of the *Apophegmata Patrum*, translated by Pelagius the Deacon as *Verba Seniorum*, book 10 is devoted to discernment in monastic life. See Helen Waddell's translation, *The Desert Fathers* (Ann Arbor, Mich., 1957).

A remarkably similar classification of monks appears in the work of John Cassian, probably a Westerner from southern Gaul, who was sent by his parents to Bethlehem to be educated and apparently to become a monk.[29] By the 390s he was traveling across the Egyptian desert and visiting monks there in order to learn about their lives. After living in both Constantinople (*c.* 403) and Rome (*c.* 405), he eventually settled in southern Gaul and founded monasteries in Marseilles. He is best known for his two monastic works, the *Institutes* and the *Conferences*. About thirty-five years after Jerome wrote his letter to Eustochium, John Cassian, in his *Conferences,* wrote:

> There are in Egypt three classes of monks. Two of them are quite excellent. The third is an indifferent class and is to be avoided in every way. The first class is that of the cenobites, namely, those who live together in one community under the authority of an elder. Most of the Egyptian monks are of this class. The second is that of the anchorites, who are first trained in the monasteries, have achieved perfection in their way of life and have chosen the hidden life of solitude. And our wish is to belong to this profession. The third—and one to be deplored—is that of the sarabaites.[30]

The similarity with Jerome's descriptions is obvious, but two interesting differences stand out. Cassian's anchorite is defined as someone who was initially a cenobite and turns to a solitary life only after "training" in a monastery. Second, Cassian gave the third variety of monks a different name, sarabaite. Cassian's sarabaites, like Jerome's false monks, appear to have been pseudo-cenobites, possibly a group of monks who had broken away from a community and formed their own fellowship. Although in his

---

29. Although Gennadius writes that he was born in Scythia, most scholars believe this was a misunderstanding based on the time Cassian spent in Scetis, Egypt. It is not at all clear where Cassian was from, and scholars have made the assumption that Provence was his homeland, since it was the region he chose to settle in and establish monasteries.

30. "Tria sunt in Aegypto genera monachorum, quorum duo sunt optima, tertium tepidum atque omnimodis evitandum. Primum est coenobiotarum, qui scilicet in congregatione pariter consistentes unius senioris iudicio guberantur: cuius generis maximus numerus monachorum per universam Aegyptum commoratur. Secundum anachoretarum, qui prius in coenobiis instituti iamque in actuali conversatione perfecti solitudinis elegere secreta: cuius professionis nos quoque optamus esse participes. Tertium reprehensibile Sarabaitarum est." John Cassian *Conferences* 18.4, in *Conférences,* ed. E. Pichery, 3 vols., SC 42, 54, 64 (Paris, 1955, 1958, 1959). The English translation is mine, but is based on Colm Luibheid's, in *John Cassian: Conferences* (New York, 1985), 185.

introduction Cassian wrote that there were only three varieties of monks, he amended his description by discussing a fourth, unnamed type: "Now there is a fourth class which we have seen emerging lately, men who flatter themselves with seeming to look like anchorites. At the beginning of their career such is their zeal for a short while that they seem to be in active pursuit of monastic perfection."[31] This category of false anchorite was to become a standard part of monastic type and crucial, as we have seen, for the Master's own elaboration of the typology.

REGULA MAGISTRI

The *Regula Magistri* establishes a new "type" or class of monk, the "gyrovague," who is placed within the category of "false" monk. Through a comparison of the Master's typology to those of previous monastic writers, writers whom the Master used as models, the unique characteristics of the gyrovague emerge. Far from being merely a rhetorical device, the identification of the gyrovague as a monastic "type" was certainly the Master's response to what he viewed as a general problem of unsupervised monastic wandering. That he is lamenting the existence of gyrovagues as a "type" suggests that this is not a reaction to isolated incidents of vagrant monks taking advantage of his monastery, but a false step too many are choosing to take. The Master, here, was attempting to tighten the definition of a monk and to lay down strict rules of legitimate monastic practice, rules that excluded any form of itinerant spirituality. Though the Master was the only pre-Benedictine legislator to identify the gyrovagues as a type, evidence for their existence, or at least for the existence of the abuses and problems they typify, is present in most other early monastic rules. These *regulae* and monastic texts further reveal problems in the isolation of the monastery and its relationship to the outside world.

In addition to the Master's attitude toward monastic wanderers, a detailed analysis of his depiction of the gyrovague reveals his concern about authority, and particularly the crucial role of the power of an abbot over his community. The role of clerical authority in relation to monastic authority also troubled the Master, and his treatment of the issue includes various

---

31. "Sane est etiam aliud quartum genus, quod nuper cernimus emersisse in his qui anachoretarum sibi specie atque imagine blandiuntur quique in primordiis suis fervore quodam brevi coenobii perfectionem videntur expetere." Ibid., 18.8.

restrictions on the involvement of clergy in the monastery.[32] The Master's ideal monastic community was not governed by the many or the few, but by the firm pastoral hand of one strong leader.

Throughout the *RM,* there is a clear distinction between the world within the gates of the monastery and the world outside them. The idealized portrait of the monastery is of a fellowship of believers cut off from society at large. Monks were supposed to live in isolation so that they could become one with God, but the Master interpreted isolation to mean life in a separate *community* of religious men or women, under a single leader. In this way monks could more readily achieve the perfect life, avoiding the dangers and pitfalls of the absolutely eremitic life. In an unstable world, the Master sought to bring order and stability to the lives of his monks.

Most studies of early monastic rules focus on the relationship of these rules to the *Regula Benedictina (RB).*[33] The tremendous hold the *RB* had and still has on monastic scholars has caused one major controversy to rage for many years: the question of precedence. Like the majority of monastic scholars, I believe that the *RM* predates the *RB,* though this question has no real effect on the argument I am making concerning monastic travel.[34] Even apart from concern over the place of the *RB,* scholars have gone to great lengths to date and situate these rules. They look for borrowings and similarities among rules as well as possible interpolations. A great deal of effort in recent years has also gone into translating and editing these rules, making them accessible to a wider range of scholars.[35] Monastic scholars

---

32. "Peregrinorum loco habeantur in monasterio sacerdotes, maxime quorum primatus et honor in ecclesiis continetur et militat" (*RM* 83.1–2), and "Aliud vero nihil aut praesumant aut eis liceat vel aliquid ordinationis aut dominationis aut dispensationis Dei vindicent, sed omnem formam licentiae vel ordinandae dominationis monasterii abbas, qui super gregem universum est ordinatus a regula, adiudicet vel defendat" (*RM* 83.6–7).

33. On the relationship of other rules to the *RB,* see de Vogüé, "Cenobitic Rules" and *Les Règles Monastiques Anciennes (400–700)* (Turnhout, 1985), and P. B. Corbett, "The *Regula Magistri* and Some of Its Problems," *Studia Patristica* I, no. 1 (1957): 82–93. See also the excellent discussion of the historiography of the *Regula Magistri* in Pricoco, "Il Monachesimo Occidentale."

34. For a summary of this controversy and its participants, see David Knowles, *Great Historical Enterprises: Problems in Monastic History* (London, 1963). For a contrasting view, see Marilyn Dunn, "Mastering Benedict: Monastic Rules and Their Authors in the Early Medieval West," *English Historical Review* 416 (July 1990): 567–94, who gives philological evidence supporting the primacy of *RB.* The *RM* is more explicit than the *RB* in the matter of monastic travel and the problem of the wandering monk, but whether or not it was written prior to the *RB* is irrelevant to my analysis of the rules here.

35. Recently a conference was held on the *Regula Magistri,* and its proceedings are published as *Il Monachesimo Occidentale dalle origini alla Regula Magistri,* XXVI Incontro di studiosi

less concerned with textual intricacies are usually interested in the way early monks followed a religious life, tracing the history and development of certain monastic practices. A few others are interested in theology and spirituality within the early monasteries. In both cases, most of the scholarship on early monastic rules and their early followers focuses on the world within the monastery's gates. Though these studies have brought us a much greater understanding of early monasticism, they have also left certain questions unanswered. Who were the monks regulated by the rules and what were their reasons for joining a community? Where did they come from and what was the monastery's relationship to the world outside its gate?

The *Regula Magistri* is the longest surviving pre-Benedictine monastic rule. Thorough and detailed, it was probably intended for a specific monastery, unlike the Benedictine Rule, which is more general and adaptable in nature. Cassian, Jerome, and the anonymous author of the *ConZA* had placed their classification of monks within the body of their works; indeed, for Jerome, it came merely as a digression in a letter. The Master, however, highlighted his concern with the issue by setting out a lengthy typology of monks at the beginning of his rule. He also introduced an entirely new type of monk, the gyrovague.

That the Master borrowed from Cassian and Jerome is especially clear from the following excerpt from the beginning of his chapter on *de generibus monachorum*.

> Of monks, it is well known, there are four kinds. The first are the cenobites, namely, those who live in monasteries and serve under a rule and an abbot. Then the second kind are the anchorites, that is, hermits, who are no longer in the first fervor of conversion but by long probation in the monastery have learned, taught by association with many others, to fight against the devil; well-equipped, they leave the ranks of the brethren for the single combat of the desert. . . . The third kind of monks the sarabaites, is the worst. I would do better to call them still of the world, except that the tonsure of their religious intent prevents me from doing so. Untested, as gold in the furnace, by the rule or by experience as a master, soft as lead, they still

---

dell'antichità cristiana, Roma, 8–10 maggio 1997 (Rome, 1998). See also the discussion of the *Regula Benedictina* in the context of sixth-century Italy in Dunn, *Emergence of Monasticism*. See also Friedrich Prinz, "Il Monachesimo occidentale," in *Passaggio dal mondo antico al medio evo da Teodosio a San Gregorio Magno* (Rome, 1980), 415–34.

keep faith with the world and manifestly lie to God by their tonsure. Two or three together, or even alone, without a shepherd, enclosed not in the Lord's but in their own sheepfold, they have as their law the willfulness of their own desires; whatever they think and decide, that they call holy, and what they do not want, that they consider forbidden. . . . The fourth kind of monks, who should not even be called that and about whom I would do better to keep silence than to say anything, are called gyrovagues. They spend their whole life as guests for three or four days at a time at various cells and monasteries of others in various provinces. Taking advantage of hospitality, they want to be received every day anew at different places.[36]

The Master, although he clearly followed the example of Jerome and Cassian, never claims that these are "Egyptian" types of monks, and it seems reasonable to assume that he was writing about monks from his own region, using the earlier Egyptian typology. His vivid descriptions also suggest that he had a personal knowledge of them, especially of the gyrovagues.

The cenobite was the first type of monk discussed by Jerome, Cassian, and the Master. Although the Master considered the life of the anchorite to be ideal, he recommended following that of the cenobite in practice. After describing the different types of monks, the Master returned to the cenobite; "And now, in accordance with our high esteem for the first kind of monks, the cenobites, whose service and probation are the will of God, let us return to their rule."[37] They were the monks at whom the rule was aimed.

36. "Monachorum quattuor esse genera manifestum est. Primum coenobiorum, hoc est monasteriale, militans sub regula vel abbate. Diende secundum genus est anachoritarum, id est heremitarum, horum qui non conversionis fervore novicio, sed monasterii probatione diuturna, qui didicerunt contra diabolum multorum solacio iam docti pugnare, et bene instructi fraterna ex acie ad singularem pugnam heremi. . . .

"Tertium vero monachorum deterrimum genus est sarabaitarum, quem melius adhuc laicum dixissem, si me propositi sancti non inpediret tunsura. Qui nulla regula adprobati et experientia magistro sicut aurum fornacis, sed in plumbi natura molliti, adhuc factis servantes saeculo fidem mentiri Deo per tunsuram noscuntur. Qui bini vel terni aut certe singuli sine pastore, non dominicis sed suis inclusi ovilibus, pro lege eis est desideriorum voluntas, cum quidquid putaverint vel elegerint, hoc dicunt sanctum, et quod noluerint, hoc putant non licere. . . .

"Quartum vero genus est monachorum nec nominandum, quod melius tacerem quam de talibus aliquid dicerem, quod genus nominatur gyrovagorum, qui tota vita sua per diversas provincias ternis aut quaternis diebus per diversorum cellas et monasteria hospitantes, cum pro hospitis adventu a diversis volunt cottidie noviter suscipi." *RM* 1.1–15.

37. "Unde ergo magnum existimantes primum genus coenobitarum, cuius militia vel probatio voluntas est Dei, ad ipsorum regulam revertamur." *RM* 1.75.

The principal characteristics of Jerome's cenobites were their hierarchical organization and their obedience to their leaders. He describes an almost militaristic organization. "They [cenobites] are divided into sections of ten and a hundred; each tenth man is over nine others, while the hundredth has ten such officers under him."[38] Silence, fasting, work, prayer, and study of the scriptures occupied the cenobites' lives. To make sure the brothers were not breaking any of the rules, they were constantly and secretly watched over by elders: "At night, besides the common prayers, each man keeps vigil in his own chamber; and so the deans go round to each cell, and putting their ears to the door carefully ascertain what the inmates are doing."[39] Jerome, displaying his erudition, concluded his discussion of the cenobites by stating that the Jewish Essenes lived according to the same rules; and although he did not elaborate on the comparison, and he clearly did not mean to affirm any continuous tradition, he was indirectly attesting to the ancient origins of cenobiticism.[40]

For Cassian, the cenobite was *primus* in more ways than one. Not only was the cenobite the best type of monk, it was historically the oldest type, contradicting the then commonly held belief that the life of the hermit was the earliest form of monastic practice.[41] According to Cassian, the history of monasticism originated in the early church with the apostles, who were the "perfect" cenobites and converted many to a "monastic" lifestyle. After the death of the apostles, Christians turned indifferent, causing this primitive monasticism of the entire Christian society to die out—at least publicly. Cassian believed that some continued the tradition and traced a continuous cenobitic history from the apostles to the present. He emphasized the importance of living within a monastic community; his cenobites were to live in *congregatione*.[42] The community of the monastery was to be a heavenly sanctuary in the world.

The Master takes up this idea near the end of the *RM*, when he writes about the monastery gates: "Therefore, since all these things are located

38. "Divisi sunt per decurias atque centurias, ita ut novem hominibus decimus praesit et rursus decem praepositos sub se centesimus habeat." Jerome *Ep.* 22.35.

39. "Et quia nocte extra orationes publicas in suo cubili unusquisque vigilat, circumeunt cellulas singulorum et aure adposita, quid faciant, diligenter explorant." Ibid., 22.35.

40. "Tales Philo, Platonici sermonis imitator, tales Iosephus, Graecus Livius, in secunda Iudaicae captivitatis historia Essenos refert." Ibid.

41. "Istud ergo solummodo fuit antiquissimum monachorum genus." Cassian *Conferences* 18.5.

42. Ibid., bk. 14.

inside, let the gate of the monastery be always shut so that the brothers, enclosed within, with the Lord, just as if they were already in heaven, separated from the world for the sake of God."[43] Echoing Cassian's vision, the Master goes a step further: the monastery can only retain its heavenly environment by isolating and protecting itself from outsiders. According to the Master, to keep the community running smoothly required strong leadership and strict obedience. Living "under a rule and an abbot" distinguished the cenobites most clearly from the other types of monks.[44] Jerome also referred to the necessity of living under a rule and an abbot in his letter to Eustochium; "Among them [cenobites] the first principle of their association is to obey superiors and do whatever they command."[45] The importance of the abbot was echoed by Cassian, who defined cenobites as "those who live together in one community under the authority of an elder."[46] In these rules, submission to the will of the abbot was often expressed in analogy to the monks' submission to God. In the *RIVP*, an early fifth-century rule, the author saw the need for one person to rule over all the brethren, who in turn must obey him as they do God: "Therefore, we wish that one presides over all, so that they will not slide into evil from their own judgment and command, but just as following the will of the Lord, all will obey with joy."[47] Likewise, the Master's monks were to abandon their own will entirely and follow, with complete obedience, the judgment of their abbot.

> Those whom love urges on to eternal life, on the contrary, take the narrow way. Not living according to their own discretion or obeying their own desires and pleasures, but walking by the judgment and command of another, they not only exercise self-control in the

---

43. "Cum ergo haec omnia intus fuerint constituta, clausa sit semper monasterii regia, ut intus clausi cum Domino fratres veluti a saeculo sint iam causa Dei in caelestibus separati." *RM* 95.22; my translation.

44. "Sub regula vel abbate." *RM* 1.2.

45. "Prima apud eos confoederatio est oboedire maioribus et, quidquid iusserint, facere." Jerome *Ep.* 22.35. In this example Jerome uses the plural because he is not speaking of a single abbot but instead of various leaders or senior monks presiding over a group of monks, with these seniors, in turn, having other seniors over them.

46. "Qui scilicet in congregatione pariter consistentes unius senioris iudicio guberantur." Cassian *Conferences* 18.4.

47. "Volumus ergo unum praeesse super omnes, nec ab eius consilio vel imperio quicquam sinistrum declinare, sed sicut imperio Domini cum omni laetitia oboedire." *Rule of the Four Fathers* (henceforth *RIVP*), in *Early Monastic Rules,* edited and translated by Carmela Vircillo Franklin, Ivan Havener, and J. Alcuin Francis (Collegeville, Minn., 1982), 18.

aforesaid desires and pleasures and do not want to do their own will even if they could, but they also submit themselves to the authority of another. Living in monasteries, they wish to have an abbot over them and not bear this title themselves.[48]

The Master linked obedience to the abbot with obedience to God; "They follow God whithersoever the command of the abbot leads them."[49]

The Master's view of the importance of the monk's complete submission to the will of the abbot led him to argue that a monk was not responsible for his actions when obeying the orders of his abbot. "This is so because, whether for good or for ill, what happens among the sheep is the responsibility of the shepherd, and he who gave orders is the one who will have to render an account when inquiry is made at the judgment, not he who carried out the orders, whether good or bad."[50] No other author adopted such an extreme view, whatever importance they attributed to the abbot. This further reveals the Master's fear of monks acting on their own concerning their pursuit of a monastic life.

The proper cenobite lived under a written rule as well as an abbot. There were many of these rules, often associated with particular communities, yet there was no universal rule followed by all monks. The rules were read to the brethren daily, so that the written word could be reinforced orally,[51] a crucial procedure considering the number of semiliterate brothers and children comprising a community. By the time of the Master, a written rule was regarded as essential to life in a monastery: "If, on the other hand, you do not put into practice what is here written and which I am going to read to you, you will be consigned to the eternal fire of hell with the devil whose will you preferred to follow."[52]

---

48. "E contrario, quibus vero ad vitam aeternam ambulandi amor incumbit, ideo angustam viam arripiunt, ut non suo arbitrio viventes vel desideriis suis et voluptatibus oboedientes, sed ambulantes alieno iudicio et imperio, non solum in supradictis desideriis suis et voluptatibus coartantur et facere suum nolunt, cum possunt, arbitrium, sed etiam alieno se imperio subdunt et in coenobiis degentes abbatem sibi praesse, non nomen ipsud sibi inesse desiderant." *RM* 7.47–50.

49. "Sequuntur Deum, quocumque abbatis praeceptio duxerit." *RM* 7.52.

50. "Quia sive bene, sive male, pastori incumbit, quod in ovibus exercetur, et illum tanget in discussionis iudicio rationem reddere, qui imperavit, non qui imperata perfecit, sive bona, sive mala." *RM* 7.55–56.

51. "Custodienda sunt ista praecepta et per singulos dies in aures fratrum rescensenda." *RIVP* 26.

52. "Si autem hanc scripturam, quam tibi lecturus sum, factis non adinpleveris, in aeternum ignem gehennae cum diabolo, cuius voluntatem magis secutus es, deputaberis." *RM,* prologue, 21.

In the *ConZa* the anchorites, modeled on the life of Antony, were at the highest level of monasticism. Anchorites lived "alone in the wilderness" where "they have present there a varied crowd of demons" and "they often clash victoriously with the wiles of the unclean spirits."[53] Jerome's anchorites also lived far from society, in the desert, but unlike those following the model of Antony, his anchorites originated in a monastery: "They go out from the monastery and live in the desert, taking nothing with them but bread and salt."[54] Cassian continued Jerome's example, stating, "[Anchorites] are first trained in monasteries, have achieved perfection in their way of life and . . . have chosen the hidden life of solitude."[55]

Cassian looked to scripture for models of monasticism, rather than to the famous monks who lived in the recent past. Though he regarded both Antony and Paul the Hermit as anchorites, Cassian employed John the Baptist as his model: "[Anchorites] are surely the imitators of John the Baptist, who remained in the desert throughout the whole of his life."[56] This was a way of linking monasticism, a relatively recent phenomenon born in the fourth century, to the Bible. By using scriptural models, such as John the Baptist, he thus avoided the risk of choosing someone who might later be condemned in a church council. Cassian himself knew the dangers of illegitimacy—he had wandered the Mediterranean for many years, visiting numerous monks in Palestine, Egypt, and Syria. In the fifth-century West, the tide in monasticism was shifting toward stability in a physical sense, a state in which the monk could be more easily controlled and held in check by church authorities, especially bishops. Wandering as a form of spiritual activity was growing increasingly difficult to defend.

The Master's anchorites had to first find perfection through a "long probation in the monastery" before leaving for the desert, and they were to maintain a relationship with the monastery after they left.[57] It was only in the company of the brethren that the monk could acquire the necessary tools to do battle in the desert. Evidence from Western monasteries reveals that the model had echoes in reality: at the southern French monastery at

53. *ConZA* 280.
54. "Quos anchoretas vocant et qui de coenobiis exeuntes excepto pane et sale amplius ad deserta nil perferunt." Jerome *Ep.* 22.36.
55. "Qui prius in coenobiis instituti iamque in actuali conversatione perfecti solitudinis elegere secreta." Cassian *Conferences* 18.4.
56. "Ad imitationem scilicet Iohannis Baptistae, qui in heremo tota aetate permansit." Ibid., 18.6.
57. "Monasterii probatione diuturna." *RM* 1.3.

Lérins local anchorites were considered part of the monastery community.[58] Known to and part of the community, a *true* anchorite would be under a measure of control. Those men and women living hermetic lives in the wilderness, without a relationship to a monastery, would be in danger of being classified as sarabaites or worse, as gyrovagues.

Although the authors of these rules saw potential perfection in the life of the anchorite, they also saw great danger, and therefore portrayed it as a virtually unattainable ideal. Basil's *Regulae Fusius Tractatae,* written in the mid-fourth century and translated into Latin by Rufinus in 397, points out some of the problems inherent in the life of the anchorite. "In such separation the man will not even recognize his defects readily, not having anyone to reprove him and to set him right with kindness and compassion. . . . And many commandments are easily performed by a number living together, but not by a solitary man . . . for example, when we visit a sick man we cannot receive a stranger."[59] Cassian expressed a similar view about anchorites and even included a false anchorite as his unnamed fourth monk. "Out of reverence for the monk's cell no one dares to give open evidence of the sins of a man living alone, sins which he himself preferred to ignore rather than to cure."[60] No one questioned the life of the solitary, not even the solitary himself. Cassian related the story of a certain Abbot John, an anchorite who decided to return to his original community. In the desert John realized firsthand the difficulty in leading the life of a true anchorite. He found himself overly concerned with physical matters, such as providing himself with food and shelter and finally decided to return to the monastery to submit himself to the will of another: "I may console myself by fulfilling the precept of the gospel, and what I lose in sublimity of contemplation, may be made up to me by submission and obedience."[61] Through Abbot John, Cassian was able to show the importance of scripture

58. Jeremiah F. O'Sullivan, "Early Monasticism in Gaul," *American Benedictine Review* 16 (March 1965): 44: "At Lérins those advanced in spirituality lived in cells, somewhat as the anchorites of Egypt. Their objective was perfection and contemplation. They were regarded as part of the community, meeting with the coenobites for prayers on Saturday and Sunday . . . and for spiritual conferences with the abbot."

59. Basil, *Regulae Fusius Tractatae,* trans. W. K. L. Clarke, in *The Ascetic Works of Saint Basil* (London, 1925), 163–64; Greek on pages 481–82.

60. "Pro reverentia enim singularis cellae nullus iam vitia solitarii audet arguere, quae ille ignorari maluit quam curari." Cassian *Conferences* 18.8.

61. "Evangelici me praecepti consummatio consoletur, et id, quod mihi de illa theoretica sublimitate subtrahitur, hac oboedientiae subiectione pensetur." Ibid., 19.5, referring to Matt. 6.34.

in the pursuit of the monastic life, while revealing both the dangers of the anchoritic pursuit and his own preference for the life of the cenobite: "For it is better to seem earnest with smaller promises than careless in larger ones."[62]

Cassian introduced the name *sarabaitae* for the traditional category of false monk.[63] Sarabaites were the third type of monk Cassian and the Master described; and although Jerome did not use this name in his account, his third monk, apparently a false cenobite, seems to fit the same category: "Thirdly, there is the class called *Remnuoth,* a very inferior and despised kind. . . . These men live together in twos and threes, seldom in larger numbers, and live according to their own will and ruling. A portion of what they make they contribute to a common fund which provides food for all."[64] These leaderless monks nevertheless expressed a sense of community by sharing their food and traveling together. Jerome hints at their constant interactions with society when he complained that they sold their crafts for too much money: "And anything they sell is very dear, the idea being that their workmanship, not their life, is sanctified."[65]

Cassian's and, as we shall see, the Master's argument was essentially the same as Jerome's, but his attack on the sarabaite was stronger. "A very bad and unfaithful band of monks . . . [the] sarabaites . . . are so called because they cut themselves off from the monastic communities and take care of their own need. . . . They have no interest in monastic discipline. They do not submit to the direction of elders and they do not learn their instructions in how to overcome their own desires. They do not accept any of the correct and formative rules deriving from sensible guidance."[66] Cassian conceived of these monks as having once been a part of a cenobitic community, and then having broken away from it. Unlike anchorites, however,

---

62. "Melius enim est devotum in minoribus quam indevotum in maioribus promissionibus inveniri." Ibid., 19.3.

63. He probably did not invent the word, since, as Vogüé has shown, it has a Coptic origin. Adalbert de Vogüé, *Community and Abbot* (Kalamazoo, Mich., 1979), 52.

64. "Tertium genus est, quod dicunt 'remnuoth,' deterrimum atque neglectum . . . Hi bini vel terni nec multo plures simul habitant suo arbitratu ac dicione viventes, et de eo, quod laboraverint, in medium partes conferunt, ut habeant alimenta communia." Jerome *Ep.* 22.34.

65. "Et quasi ars sit sancta, non vita, quidquid vendiderint, maioris est pretii." Ibid.

66. "Illud deterrimum et infidele monachorum . . . Sarabaitarum genus, qui ab eo, quod semet ipsos a coenobiorum congregationibus sequestrarent ac singillatim suas curarent necessitates . . . coenobiorum nullatenus expetunt disciplinam nec seniorum subduntur arbitrio aut eorum traditionibus instituti suas discunt vincere voluntates nec ullam sanae discretionis regulam legitima eruditione suscipiunt . . . illi autem qui districtionem ut diximus coenobii declinantes bini vel terni in cellulis commorantur." Cassian *Conferences* 18.7.

who had become perfected within a monastery before entering the desert alone, the sarabaites left improperly prepared. Not surprisingly, the Master uses very similar language to make the same point. "The third kind of monks, the sarabaites, is the worst . . . [they are] untested . . . by any rule or by experience as a master . . . two or three together, or even alone, without a shepherd, enclosed not in the Lord's but in their own sheepfold, they have as their law the willfulness of their own desires."[67] The Master's description of the sarabaite reveals that a true monk, by contrast, holds goods in common and leads a spiritual life with brethren apart from worldly society.

The problem of the sarabaite, for both Jerome and Cassian, is that he lives according to his own will and judgment, without rule and without a master. Cassian's criticism in particular dwells on the sarabaites' reliance on themselves and their lack of discernment or *discretio*. The concept of *discretio* has a long monastic history dating from the Egyptian desert fathers. Cassian's use of the term is closer to the original biblical meaning of discernment of spirits, and it becomes the skill of telling good from evil: "Life must be lived with due measure and, with discernment for a guide, the road must be traveled between the two kinds of excess so that in the end we may not allow ourselves to be diverted from the pathway of restraint which has been laid down for us nor fall through dangerous carelessness into the urgings of gluttony and self-indulgence."[68] Discernment becomes a practical skill that every monk should possess so that one is not fooled by demons. The sarabaite, thus, is an unknowing fool, and the label "sarabaite" becomes a sort of accusation of foolishness and of hidden monastic impropriety. It becomes a flexible category to be used for any so-called false monk—yet not for the Master, who was driven to create a new category and label, the gyrovague.

THE GYROVAGUE

The Master's innovation to the received monastic typology was the category of the gyrovague, the wandering monk; "The fourth kind of monks, who

---

67. "Tertium vero monachorum deterrimum genus est sarabitarum. . . . Qui nulla regula adprobati et experientia magistro. . . . Qui bini aut terni aut certe singuli sine pastore, non dominicis sed suis inclusi ovilibus, pro lege eis est desideriorum voluntas." *RM* 1.6–8.

68. Cassian *Conferences* 2.2. Cassian's conference on discernment in the *Conferences* mostly relates stories of monks deceived by Satan.

should not even be called that and about whom I would do better to keep silence than to say anything, are called gyrovagues."[69] Though he thought it best to keep silent about these false monks, the chapter on the gyrovague is among the longest in the *Regula Magistri*. While most of the other chapters are prescriptive in nature, merely stating regulations, the chapter on the gyrovagues describes the life and practices of this new monastic type in great detail. These two factors, the innovation and the amount of detail provided, point to the importance of the gyrovague in understanding the Master and his view of proper monasticism. Whereas most scholars have been dismissive of the Master's excursus on the wandering monk and have singled it out as a flaw of the *RM* that was corrected in the much shorter *Regula Benedictina*, I believe that the Master's discussion of the gyrovague presents us with a unique insight into the monastic world of the sixth-century West.

The gyrovagues were the worst type of monk because they did not live "under a rule and an abbot," but, like sarabaites, according to their own judgment and will.[70] What infuriated the Master most, however, was that gyrovagues disrupted the life of the monastery and of the "proper" monks whom they visited. Wandering monks who spent "their entire lives as guests in various cells and monasteries in diverse provinces staying three or four days at a time,"[71] the gyrovagues never joined in the life of prayer and work of the communities or hermits on whom they depended. Using the hardships of their travel as an excuse, they did not fast, and even overate and drank to the point of illness: "And when after the double excess of food and drink they are stuffed to the point of vomiting, they attribute to their laborious journey all that their gluttony has got them."[72] The Master's portrayal of the gyrovagues may be read as a commentary on the problem of the monastery's wider relation with the outside world.

The graphic language of the Master's indictment of the gyrovague is unique in the rule. Gyrovagues were barbarous; they even mistreated their donkeys. "The poor donkey is whipped, prodded, singed, but it hunches its back and does not budge. They beat its ears when its haunches are down.

---

69. "Quartum vero genus est monachorum nec nominandum, quod melius tacerem quam de talibus aliquid dicerem, quod genus nominatur gyrovagorum." *RM* 1.13.

70. "Sub regula vel abbate" and "sub propio arbitrio." *RM* 1.1.

71. "Qui tota vita sua per diversas provincias aut ternis aut quaternis diebus per diversorum cellas at monasteria hospitantes." *RM* 1.14.

72. "Et postquam ex utraque nimietate cibi et potus percalcati usque ad vomitum fuerint, totum laboriosae viae inputant, quod gula lucravit." *RM* 1.21.

And so the poor thing is almost killed and, [already] worn out, is beaten, because they are in a hurry and cannot wait to get to another monastery for a meal."[73] The inclusion of this strange discussion of donkeys is unique in a monastic rule. The Master's apparent compassion for the poor, half-dead donkey served to dramatize the bestial nature of the gyrovague. The gyrovagues, the Master alleged, lied about their true lives. When they arrived at a monastery or hermit's cell, they would pretend to be so tired that they could not work; they lied about fasting in order to get a greater portion of food; and they lied about their journey, making it seem so rough and wearying that they were unable to arise from bed to pray the psalms.[74] The gyrovagues would purposely arrive at monasteries wearing ragged clothing only to obtain new garments more easily. The Master accused them of carrying many tunics, clothing that had been given to them by other monks.[75]

Similar accusations against false monks were made in other rules and texts as well. Cassian describes monks who, while hiding their money, asked others for shoes and clothing and became upset if these others were slow in responding to their pleas.[76] In the *ConZA,* the worst kind of monk was one who "simulate[s] fasting temporarily."[77] Jerome described his third type of monk as one whose entire life was a masquerade evidenced by affectations in his actions and in the way he dressed. "Everything with them [*Remnuoth,* the third kind of monk] is done for effect: loose sleeves, big boots, clumsy dress, constant sighing, visiting virgins, disparaging the clergy, and when a feast day comes, they eat so much that they make themselves ill."[78] The concern with monks' proper appearance emerges in all the texts examined

---

73. "Caeditur, pungitur, ustulatur, lordicat miser asellus et non vadet. Vapulant aures eius, postquam clunes defecerint. Ideo miser perocciditur et manibus lassus inpingitur, quia festinatur et satagitur, ut ad alterius monasterii prandium occurratur." *RM* 1.48–40.

74. Prayer of the psalms was a traditional mark of a true monk: "Vel cum quidem occupatione gulosae ambulationis psalmos aliquando neglexerint meditare, ipsorum ore respondunt se lassis post viam ossibus non posse de lectulo surgere." *RM* 1.63–64.

75. "Et noviter restratus et diversis tunicis et cucullis resarcinatus, quas aut inportunitas a diversis exigerat aut inventa occasio fraudis diversos hospites nudaverat, et ut alio petant, fingunt se pannos advestiri." *RM* 1.45–46.

76. "Cumque furtim possideat reconditam pecuniam, ne calciamenta quidem ac vestimenta se habere conqueritur darique sibi tardius indignatur." Cassian *Institutiones* 7.9.2, in *Jean Cassien: Institutiones cénobitiques,* trans. Jean-Claude Guy, *SC* 109 (Paris, 1965).

77. *ConZA* 278.

78. "Apud hos affectata sunt omnia: laxae manicae, caligae follicantes, vestis grossior, crebra suspiria, visitatio virginum, detractatio clericorum, et si quando festior dies venerit, saturantur ad vomitum." Jerome *Ep.* 22.34.

here. In the absence of introductory letters, visual examination was paramount in establishing any stranger's identity and credentials in this period. This was especially so in monastic circles, where hospitality was a great concern.

In his *De opere monachorum,* Augustine attacked both wandering and wearing long hair as part of his appeal to monks not to shun manual labor.[79] After proceeding through a carefully argued statement on the importance of such labor, Augustine began a diatribe on those who called themselves monks, but in reality were "false monks." His principal complaints were two: the physical appearance of the monks and the fact that they wandered: "[There are] in every place many hypocrites in the garb of monks, who go through the provinces, sent by no authority, never stationary, stable, or settled."[80] Augustine includes a harsh attack on their clothing and specifically on their long hair, which though it echoed Jerome's criticisms, it was in fact a response to a practice he himself had seen. Augustine also makes it clear that "false" monks were not the only ones wearing their hair long: "For, what is the reason, I wonder, why men wear their hair long contrary to the precept of the Apostle? . . . I refrain from saying more concerning this vice because of certain long-haired brethren whom, in almost all other respects, we hold in high esteem."[81] Though Augustine attacks the practice by using Paul's writings as evidence, he reveals that those being attacked were also relying on the words of the apostle: "The very Apostle on whose authority these persons support their argument says that long hair is as a veil. As a matter of fact, he openly declares: 'For a man to wear his hair long is degrading.' 'We assume this disgrace,' they say, 'because of our sins,' thus extending over themselves the shade of humility, so that under it they may display their venal pride."[82] Outward physical appearance

79. This text was written in 400 at the behest of Aurelius, the bishop of Carthage, who had asked Augustine to judge the practice of a two competeing groups of monks in Carthage concerning the role of manual labor in the monastery. See the discussion of this text in Caner, *Wandering, Begging Monks,* 117–20.

80. "Omni modo cupientes obscurare putoribus suis, tam multos hypocritas sub habitu monachorum usquequaque dispersit, circumeuntes provincias, nusquam missos, nusquam fixos, nusquam stantes, nusquam sedentes." Augustine *De opere monachorum* 28.

81. "Nam et hoc quo pertinet, quaeso, tam aperte contra Apostoli praecepta comari? . . . Vereor in hoc vitium plura dicere, propter quosdam crinitos fratres, quorum praeter hoc multa et pene omnia veneramur." Ibid., 31.

82. "Nam idem apostolus etiam comam pro velamento esse dicit, cuius auctoritate isti urgentur. Aperte quippe ait: Vir quidem si comatus sit, ignominia est illi. Ipsam ignominiam, inquiunt, suscipimus merito peccatorum nostrorum: ad hoc obtendentes simulatae humilitatis umbraculum, ut sub eoproponant venalem typhum; quasi Apostolus superbiam doceat, cum

was considered an important manifestation of inner monastic spirituality and legitimacy.[83] In a world of movement, filled with travelers, religious and otherwise, discerning the truth about one's identity becomes paramount. It is for this reason, as we shall see, that monastic legislators such as the Master provide detailed regulations on such presumed mundane topics as proper attire, hairstyle, and how to judge the character of those arriving at the monastery.[84]

According to the Master's account, gyrovagues were opposed to living permanently in a monastery: "Since the manner of life at these various places and the discipline of all monasteries does not please them, they choose to travel rather than to settle down."[85] The lifestyle of the gyrovague was an affront to the monastic world that the Master envisioned. He did, however, suggest a possible solution to the problem in the following passage. "Now, since they do not want to be under the regime of a monastery or to have an abbot to look after all their needs, they should put up a cell somewhere and stay there, living as they please, and should provide the necessities of life for themselves. If our way of life does not please them, they should let us see theirs."[86] The Master appears to be suggesting that the gyrovagues transform themselves into anchorites of some sort, possibly sarabaites. He does not suggest physical stability in order to heighten their spirituality, but rather to provide an alternative to interfering with the lives of monks in monasteries.

The gyrovagues depicted in the *RM* did give reasons (characterized as excuses by the Master) for their wandering. They claimed to be on pilgrimage or in flight from captivity.[87] If they were pilgrims, it would mean that

dicit: Omnis vir orans aut prophetans velato capite, confundit caput suum; et: Vir quidem non debet velare caput, cum sit imago et gloria Dei." Ibid.

83. It must also be noted that long hair and a disheveled appearance was also typical of the penitent in ancient Mediterranean society and that in Roman practice, as early as the Republic, one could solicit sympathy or inflame feelings against a political or legal opponent by publicly appearing with long, disheveled hair and wearing dirty or torn clothing. See Andrew Lintott, *Violence in Republican Rome,* 2d ed. (Oxford, 1999), 16–20. I thank one of my anonymous readers for this insight.

84. It may be the case that the emphasis in the *RM* on properly receiving the monastic tonsure, with the abbot himself cutting the monk's hair in front of the assembled brethren, relates to the earlier meanings of long, disheveled hair in Mediterranean society. On the tonsuring, see *RM* 90.81.

85. "Et veluti quibus diversorum vita et actus et omnium monasteriorum disciplina non placeat, eligunt magis ambulare quam sistere." *RM* 1.73.

86. "Nam cum sibi nolunt sub imperio monasterii abbatem de omnibus necessariis cogitare, vel ipsi alicubi suo viventes arbitrio facta cellula persistando, vel ipsi sibi necessaria vitae debuerant cogitare, et si nostra illis displicet vita, vel suam nobis ostenderent formam." *RM* 1.68–70.

87. "Rationem erroris sui per peregrinationem et captivitatem celando excusat." *RM* 1.23.

the monastery of the Master was under even more obligation to provide them food and shelter. Pilgrimage was growing in popularity when the Master wrote his rule, and his equation of pilgrims with gyrovagues reveals the low esteem he held even for pious travelers. The refugee excuse testifies to the political instability of the period and reinforces the correlation between, on the one hand, the emergence of itinerant spirituality and an asceticism of wandering, and, on the other, the great movements of people discussed in Chapter 1.

The sudden appearance and elaboration of the gyrovague in a monastic typology has caused some scholars to speculate that the section is a later interpolation.[88] While Vogüé discredits this hypothesis, he sees little significance in the Master's discussion of gyrovagues. He views the section on the gyrovague as a literary outburst, revealing the Master's "excess of satirical spirit" and his "verbal intemperance and triviality."[89] Vogüé claims that the Master was only trying to emulate Cassian's model, even though, as he apparently recognizes, the Master's gyrovague bears no resemblance to Cassian's unnamed fourth monk.[90] Vogüé then goes on to praise the *RB*, writing, "Prudently, *RB* summarized this interminable satire into a few verses."[91]

The Master's writing on the gyrovague should not be so hastily dismissed, nor should the *RM* be viewed only in comparison with the *RB*. It is clear that the Master was reacting to problems in his monastic environment. Even Vogüé admits that the Master "plainly had in mind certain disorders he had witnessed and from which both he and his community had suffered."[92] The Master was clearly motivated to include the gyrovagues by long-standing problems in the monastery's relationship to the outside world.

The ideal of a complete separation from society was difficult to accomplish, and thus tended to remain merely an ideal. The Master conceived of a perfect community, where the monastery had complete control over its relationship with external society. The gyrovagues upset this control and

88. Vogüé tells us that François Masai believes that the "digression on gyrovagues was itself an interpolation within [the chapter] *De generibus.*" Vogüé, *Community and Abbot,* 37. In one of the manuscripts of the *RM* the section on the gyrovague is missing, but, according to Vogüé, even if the section were an interpolation, it happened very soon after the *RM* was written, for it is clear that the author of the *RB* based his rule on a text of the *RM* that included the gyrovagues. Ibid., 30.

89. Ibid., 57–58.

90. Ibid., 53.

91. Ibid.

92. Ibid., 54.

thus became a symbol of the monastery's actual lack of control over the intrusion of the outside world. The Master's attempt at establishing control over these interactions and over gyrovagues meant the creation of strict regulations on the reception of guests, on travel by the brethren outside the gate, and on the admission of new members.

If "gyrovagues" or wandering monks existed, we should expect to find evidence for them in the rest of the rule, and we do. The Master's concern about gyrovagues is especially evident in the precepts concerning reception of guests, reception of novices, and monastic travel. How the image of gyrovagues infuses the entire *RM* is also further proof that the passages explicitly devoted to them were not later interpolations.

In his long discussion of the gyrovague, the Master never wrote that they should be excluded from entrance to the monastery. Many people came as guests and visitors to monastery gates, and anyone who did might, for all the abbot knew, be a gyrovague. Who were these visitors? The Master wrote that brethren of other monasteries, priests, and bishops often visited his monastery.[93] The laity also visited the monastery, and even the aristocratic parents of a novice visited in order to question their son on his decision to join a monastic community.[94]

There is a direct relationship between the Master's development of the picture of the gyrovague and the amount of material in the rule dealing with visitors. One of the complaints the Master had with gyrovagues was how they would unload their packs even before being announced, let alone received, by the abbot.[95] The Master wanted the arrival of visitors to be as formal as possible in order to prevent such an abuse. The last chapter of the *RM* is entirely devoted to the gates of the monastery: how they were to be manned by two trustworthy monks, "advanced in age," who would announce all visitors directly to the abbot, and how they would keep the entrance secure. "Posted there [at the gates], let them at all times close up the monastery behind those who leave and open it for those who are coming in, and also announce arrivals to the abbot."[96]

---

93. "Fratres cum monasterio extranei supervenerint." *RM* 65.1. "Cum oblagiae a ponticfice summo vel a sacerdotibus sequentibus monasterio advenerint." *RM* 76.1.

94. "Quod si magis fuerint consentientes eius voto parentes, convocatis eis ab abbate in monasterio." *RM* 91.5.

95. "Et intrantes regias, adhuc non nuntiati et suscepti excarricant." *RM* 1.53.

96. "Qui deputati ibi et claudant monasterium omni hora post exeuntes et aperiant ingredientibus et advenientes nuntient abbati." *RM* 95.2–3.

The Master's strictest regulation about visitors prohibits anyone from staying more than two days without earning his keep by working.

> A VISITOR, BE HE A BROTHER OR A LAYMAN, SHOULD NOT BE FED MORE THAN TWO DAYS WITHOUT WORKING. When any brother comes to the monastery as a guest, out of respect for his status as a guest and because of the fatigue of travel let him, if he wishes to remain unoccupied, be seated at table in common with the brothers at the regular time for two days. But after Prime has been said on the third day, when the abbot leaves the oratory, let the weekly servers and the cellarer detain the guest within the oratory and say to him: 'Would you please work with the brothers at whatever the abbot assigns either in the field or at craft. If you do not so please, be on your way, because the rule limits your stay as a guest to two days.'[97]

Interestingly, the abbot was not to be the one to confront the guests or even to be in the room at the time of the confrontation. The Master was treading a very fine line with this precept. Hospitality was one of the primary duties of the monastery in relation to the outside world, and this regulation attempted to put limits on that duty. Involving the abbot in this questionable precept would have put him in a difficult position. The Master made it quite clear that this rule applied to all visitors, even legitimate visiting brethren.

Although this regulation seems to be related to the gyrovague, the Master does not mention him by name in this precept. The word he uses for guests who are abusing hospitality is *peregrini* and not *gyrovagui*. If he and his monastery were simply disturbed by gyrovagues abusing the hospitality of the monastery, they would certainly have been mentioned here. Instead, the Master clearly states that this precept applies to *all* visitors to the monastery. In the following passage the Master seems to hint at a hierarchy of abuses. A *peregrinus* who still refuses to work is implicitly a gyrovague. "Therefore, if he does not want to work let the weekly servers

---

97. "NON DEBERE ALIQUEM ADVENIENTEM AUT FRATREM AUT LAICUM PLUS A BIDUO OTIOSUM PASCI. Cum aliquis frater in monasterio ut hospis advenerit, in hospitis honorem vel viae lassitudinem, si voluerit otiosus esse, biduo mensae fratrum hora sua conmunis adsedeat. Tertio vero die post primam dictam, exeunte abbate de oratorio, retineant hospitem intus in oratorio eudomararii et cellararius, dicentes ei: 'iube cum fratribus operari quidquid abbas praeceperit aut in agro aut in arte. Si non iubes, abscedere, quia regula hospitalitatem vestram conplevit in biduo.'" *RM* 78.1–5.

and the cellarer tell him to depart . . . such strangers [*peregrinos*] who, because of wretched laziness, do not settle down anywhere but visit monasteries under the pretext of religion and remain idle while devouring the bread due to workers."[98]

The Master made detailed provisions about where to house visitors of all stripes. In chapter 79, called *de cella peregrinorum*, he wrote that they should be sequestered away from the brethren. He also specified that none of the monastery's belongings be kept in the same room as the visitors: "The guest quarters should be set apart in the monastery, with beds made up, where the brothers who come, especially those who are unknown, may sleep and deposit their bags. Things belonging to the monastery, whether iron tools or utensils, should not be put into this room, lest it happen that guests who were thought to be spiritual guests are suddenly and with consequent loss found to be thieves."[99] The Master had little trust in his guests, which is why he had two of the brothers act as guards, to the extent that they even slept in the guest quarters. The guards were to lock the door of the guest quarters from inside and outside and keep the key, though the Master constantly stressed that the guests were to be unaware of the brothers watching over them.[100] These guards were to follow the guests everywhere they went in the monastery, even if it was during the middle of the night. Physically, the monastery would have probably had separate guest quarters, located at a distance from the brothers. The Master attempted to show that this type of vigilance could also be interpreted as hospitality. "In this way they [the monastic guards] will manifestly be fulfilling the requirements of charity toward guests by accompanying them, while protecting the goods of the monastery from persons who are not trusted though they are not aware of this."[101] One doubts whether the guests would have been

98. "Ergo si noluerit laborare, dicatur ei ab eudomarariis et cellarario ut abscedat, . . . peregrinos, qui per inertiam miseriae nusquam fixi stando, laborantium debitos panes sub praetexto religionis visitando monasteria devorant otiosi." *RM* 78.10–13.

99. "Cella vero peregrinorum semote in monasterio constituatur cum lectis stratis, ubi supervenientes fratres, maxime ignoti, dormiant et bisacias suas ponant. In qua cella re monasterii aut ferramenta aut usitilia non sint posita, ne forte cum putantur hospites spiritales, subito in damno fures inveniantur." *RM* 79.1–4.

100. "Nam et propter cautelam custodiendi duo fratres, de quorum decada alii concinam exercent, tamdiu ex ipsa decada deputati vicibus a suis praepositis fratres peregrinos ex inproviso custodiant." *RM* 79.5–6.

101. "Ut caritatem solacii videantur hospitibus adinplere et res monasterii ab incertis ex inproviso custodiant." *RM* 79.14.

unaware of the monastic guards, watching their every move. The Master's fear of "outsiders" clearly had an impact on the precept of hospitality at his monastery.

One important adjustment in the routine of the monastery caused by visitors was the suspension of reading the rule out loud daily to the brothers. This was forbidden in the presence of lay visitors.[102] The Master's reasoning for this reveals his low opinion of these guests to the monastery. He believed that if lay people learned the secrets of life in the monastery, they would then expose and ridicule monastic life when they returned to the outside world. Once again, the Master constrained the precept of hospitality by an atmosphere of secrecy, in order to preserve his community from the scrutinizing incursions of the outside world. The Master expressed this same fear in other parts of the rule as well. The paradox of separation from the outside and the requirement of hospitality made the Master an unusually cautious and suspicious leader.

An alternative way to characterize the gyrovague is as a traveling monk, rather than a dangerous monastic misfit. While the Master complained of the number of visitors to the monastery, he also admitted that some sort of monastic travel was necessary for his own brethren. No fewer than twelve chapters of the *RM* deal with monks undertaking journeys, suggesting that monastic travel was common.[103] Indeed, travel was important enough in the Master's monastery that the brethren kept pack animals that they regularly used on their travels.[104] In the section on the reception of a novice of noble blood, the Master suggested that all the novice's property be sold and the money given to charity and to his family, except for one third which he should bring with him to the monastery and use partly as his travel fund.[105] But the very frequency of monks' travel contributed to the problems associated with large numbers of guests at monasteries. Consequently, the Master tried to regulate travel as much as he did the reception and retention of guests.

---

102. "Nam si supervenerint forte mensae monasterii laici, propter detractionem futuram in saeculo, cum secreta Dei saecularis agnoverit, si placuerit abbati, iam lectionem cuiuscumque codicis legat, ut secretum monasterii vel mensuras vitae sanctae constitutas in disciplinam ab inrisoribus non sciatur." *RM* 24.20–21.

103. Chapters 56 through 67 of the *RM* concern brethren on journeys.

104. "Vel de conponendis sarcinis animalium vel de constrictione honeris bisaciarum suarum reddantur solliciti." *RM* 58.7.

105. "Tertiam vero partem viatici sui utilitate deferat secum monasterio sanctorum usibus profuturam." *RM* 91.52.

Before anyone was to leave the monastery, the Master wrote that the abbot should give him special instruction and advice concerning his journey.[106] The abbot was also allowed to give traveling brothers extra bread and wine for the difficult journey, provisions that they could give to companions whom they might meet on the road.[107] The Master was careful to lay out detailed instructions for dealing with the many hardships of travel, revealing his sensitivity to the varying capacities of different monks.

> Furthermore, the abbot should have the traveling brothers take a meal if after very careful attention to considerations of time and necessity, whether in winter or summer, he has fears about the heavy frost of the plains or the burning heat of the roads or the precipitous heights of the mountains or the weight of the heavy packs, and has taken into account the weaknesses and incapacities of some brothers, in such cases he should have them eat something before dispatching them from the monastery.[108]

This passage perhaps reveals that the Master had personal experience with the difficulties of long-distance travel.

The Master included entire chapters on how to follow the rule properly while traveling. These chapters detail the various prayers to be recited, as well as the proper occasions for eating and fasting.[109] For long journeys, the Master made the special provision that the brother should carry a small book containing lessons or, if he did not know all the psalms, a tablet with psalms written on it by one of his superiors.[110] An illiterate brother ideally

106. "Nam et hoc praeceptum abbatis vel praepositorum exeuntes in via fratres accipiant." *RM* 57.19.

107. "Considerans abbas fratrum debitum cottidianae mensurae necnon et longinquitatem itineris vel moras agendi actus, simul et perpensans substantiae monasterii quantitatem in nummis aut in his quae cruda possunt portari, sufficientibus consuetae mensurae sumptibus aliquantulum pro labore intineris, magis propter adiuncti forte viae collegae vel socii caritatem, quantum abbas voluerit, panis aut vini sed et aliarum rerum vel nummorum iungat mensurae." *RM* 60.1–4.

108. "Nam tunc abbas in via ambulantes fratres faciat reficere, considerata perpensatione aut temporis aut necessitatis, sive in hieme sive in aestate, si gravia gelicidia camporum aut ferventes aestus viarum aut montium excelsos subitus aut grave sarcinum pondus extimaverit vel inbicillitates quorundam et inpossibilitates fratrum consideraverit, tunc refectos aliquid faciat de monasterio properare." *RM* 59.5–8.

109. For prayers, see *RM* 56; for eating and fasting, see *RM* 59–62.

110. "Si vero in viam longiorem dirigatur, codiciclum modicum cum aliquibus lectionibus de monasterio secum portet, ut quavis hora in via repausaverit, aliquantulum tamen legat.

was to travel with a literate monk, so he could practice his letters while on the journey.

Nonetheless, the Master did not stipulate that brothers had to travel together and even made a reference to one traveling alone.[111] Perhaps he wanted as few monks as possible to travel, so as to expose the fewest possible brethren to the dangers of travel. Or perhaps (unhappily for the Master), monastic travel was so frequent an occurrence that the monastery could not spare enough brothers to allow them to travel in groups. Whatever the case, there seems to have been a significant amount of traveling, so much so that if a brother refused to go on a journey, he was punished by excommunication. "As for the brother who either does not want to go out on monastery business, or who would indeed go but murmurs about it and wants to delay his departure a while, let him now, if the abbot so please, not be sent out. Furthermore, let him be immediately punished with excommunication, and let him know that by clinging to pride he is rejecting a divine command—divine, because the Lord says to our teachers: 'Anyone who rejects you rejects me.'"[112] This is strong language and severe punishment; obedience to the abbot was far more important for the monk than the obligation of physical stability.

It appears as if few in the Master's monastery were spared the difficulties of travel. Even children were sent out on journeys, as is suggested by a precept stating that children under twelve years old did not have to fast while on a journey, unless it lasted a half-day or less.[113] Children were indeed part of the community, and many of them, as well as some of the older brothers who had also been raised in the community, knew only life in the monastery. Their

---

Ita tamen si fuerit psalteratus. Si vero non fuerit, tabulas a maiore superpositas psalmis secum portet, ut ad refectionem prandii aut ad mansionem cum adplicaverit, aliquantulum quantum occucurrerit tamen meditetur, ut cottidie regulae reddat quod suum est. Ita et frater qui adhuc litteras discit, tabulas superpositas a maiore de monasterio secum portet, ut si cum litterato vadit, cum ad refectionem aut mansionem adplicaverit, ab eo tamen aliquantulum quantm occucurrerit meditetur." *RM* 57.4–11.

111. "Si solus vadit." *RM* 57.12.

112. "Item frater qui pro actibus monasterii aut noluerit ire aut certe ambulans murmuraverit vel cum aliqua tarditate exire voluerit, si placuerit abbati, iam non mittatur et statim excommunicationis poenam suscipiat et sciat se adeptum superbiam praeceptioni repugnare divinae; ideo divinae, quia dicit Dominus doctoribus nostris: 'Qui vos spernit, me spernit.'" *RM* 57.14–16.

113. "Infantuli vero intra duodecim annos non solum nullo tempore in via non ieiunent, sed etiam nullo die ieiuni de monasterio egrediantur, dumtaxat si in proximo non mittuntur, unde ante tertiam in aestate aut ante sextam in hieme expectentur, in quibus horis constitutum est eis debere reficere." *RM* 59.10–11.

presence certainly affected some of the regulations about contact with the outside world.

In the last chapter of the rule, on the keepers of the gates, the Master stressed that all necessary things should be available within the walls of the monastery: "oven, machines, lavatory, garden and all that is required, so there may not be frequent occasion for the brothers to go outside repeatedly and mingle with people of the world."[114] Nearly his last, these words again stressed the ideal of complete separation, which the Master visualized and attempted to realize by the creation of the rule. Of course, despite his ambition, this could never be achieved. The brethren of his monastery frequently traveled *viae necessitatibus* or *pro monasterii utilitate*.[115] Ironically, the Master also wrote that *necessitas* was one of the reasons the gyrovagues gave for their travel.[116]

Throughout the rule there is much discussion of the proper dress of the monk.[117] It was during travel that dress played its most crucial role in defining identity, for on the road, there was no other way, besides dress and manner, of showing who one was. What could prevent monks from being mistaken for gyrovagues? The Master ordered the brothers to say *Benedicite* when they arrived at a monastery.[118] Unfortunately, as the Master knew, when gyrovagues arrived, they yelled out the same word: "As soon as they have arrived at another monastery or monk's cell, they cry out *Benedicite* gaily and loudly, from outside."[119] The existence of travelers made the concern for how to discern a true monk from a false monk a critical challenge.

The Master's concern about the appearance of monks emerges in the *RM* with the inclusion of a chapter on proper clothing and shoes. The Master was specific about the material for the clothing and even gave an implicit critique of the clergy by forbidding the brothers from wearing

114. "Omnia vero necessaria intus intra regias esse oportet, id est furnus, macinae, refrigerium, hortus vel omnia necessaria, ut non sit frequens occasio, propter quam fratres multotiens foras egressi, saecularibus mixti." *RM* 95.17–18.

115. *RM* 50.74.

116. "Et nesciunt quia, ut eis non liceat ieiunare aut abstinere, aut aliquo nesciant aliquando loco stare, non eos aliqua ambulare conpellit necessitas, sed gulae cogit voluntas." *RM* 1.60.

117. Even Vogüé believed that "the way of dressing was a serious matter." Adalbert de Vogüé, "To Study the Early Monks," *Monastic Studies* 12 (1976): 75.

118. "Primo ad ingressum suum mox voce sua *benedicite* salutent." *RM* 65.3.

119. "Et cum pervenerint ad alterius monasterii aut monachi regias, ita hilari et clamosa voce de foris *benedicite* clamant." *RM* 1.51.

linen drawers, lest they be mistaken for clerics.[120] One of many complaints about gyrovagues was that they extorted clothing from the monasteries they visited; when, in the *RM,* a gyrovague is preparing to leave, he loads up his donkey with tunics and cowls from various places visited.[121] The gyrovague could at least look the proper part if not act it.

The Master also placed great significance on the tonsure of monks. The tonsure was so important to the Master that the novice had to wait an entire year before receiving it.[122] The actual tonsuring of a brother was a central ritual in his joining the community: "He is tonsured thus: this brother kneels in the middle of the oratory and, with everyone round about chanting psalms, the abbot tonsures him."[123] The tonsure and the habit were instrumental in defining the monk's identity when he traveled outside his own monastery. Here too, however, the gyrovagues followed suit; to do otherwise would have caused them to be taken as laymen and deemed ineligible for some of the benefits of hospitality.[124] The gyrovague thus showed how even the tonsure could be abused by someone who was not following the holy profession properly.

The relationship between the monastery and its novices and even potential novices can reveal much about its relationship with outside society. Vogüé has shown that by the early sixth century, a change began to occur in monastic rules, and along with this change, "the formalities of admission become more numerous and precise."[125] In the *RM,* gyrovagues allegedly complained that they wished to serve God and join a community, but the monasteries denied them entry. "Feigning fatigue, as if the whole world were shutting them out and as if in all of it there were neither place nor forest nor the wide expanse of Egyptian desert itself to take them in, not even any monastery to receive them for the service of God—as if, as it

120. "Lineas vero uti Dei homines prohibemus, ut aliquid distet a clerico monachus." *RM* 81.6.

121. "Et noviter restratus et diversis tunicis et cucullis resarcinatus, quas aut inportunitas a diversis exigerat aut inventa occasio fraudis diversos hospites nudaverat, et ut alio petant, fingunt se pannos advestiri." *RM* 1.45–46; *RM* 151.

122. "Ingresso in monasterio cuiquam laico non debere intra annum mutari res nec caput eius secundum propositum tonderi." *RM* 90, title.

123. "Tondatur enim sic: stat ipse frater medio oratorio curvatis in genibus, tondente eum abbate, psallentibus in circuitu cunctis." *RM* 90.81.

124. "In hoc enim via lata a talibus creditur ambulari, cum in nomine monachi communi more viventes cum laicis, solo tunsurae habitu separati." *RM* 7.31.

125. Vogüé, "Cenobitic Rules," 180.

were, the whole world were rejecting them."[126] In a sense, the "gyrovague" was correct in bemoaning the difficulty in joining a monastic community; the Master made it especially difficult for potential members to join the community permanently. He tried to enact a stronger sense of separation from the world, including separation from family and freedom from obligations on the outside.

The Master showed a distrust of all who wanted to join, similar to his distrust of guests and the prospect of travel.[127] An abbot was to make certain that the novice was not simply escaping from something such as hunger, taxes, or familial obligations, but that he was entering into a religious profession, one which sought a separation from worldly desires. When someone arrived seeking admission to the community, the abbot first warned him that he might not be able properly to live under the rule of the monastery and then read him the rule and explained it in his own words.[128] The candidate was told to sell everything in the fashion of Antony. Finally, the potential brother also swore an oath stating that he would not steal anything from the monastery or hide monastic goods in an unknown place.[129]

The Master never mentioned whether or not the novice was to wait outside the gates, but he prescribed a two-month probation period in the guest quarters under surveillance by the same brothers who watched over the guests.[130] After the two months, if the novice chose to remain (*stabilitas eligatur*), he was read the rule again and took an oath.[131] The Master's use of the word *stabilitas* emphasized the contrast with the *instabilitas* of the outside world and of the gyrovague. A highly detailed ritual of admission confirmed transition to *stabilitas*,[132] but as noted before, the novice did not

---

126. "Velut lassi et quasi quibus iam universus clausus sit mundus, et ex toto eos nec loca nec silvae nec latus ipse Aegypti heremus capiat, nec universa monasteria ad servitium Dei eos suscipiant, et eos, ut diximus, totus mundus non capiat." *RM* 1.25–26.

127. "Cum aliquis novellus de saeculo ad servitium Domini in monastherium confugerit et indicaverit se velle converti non credatur tam facile." *RM* 294.

128. "Cum vero ille dixerit posse se ad omnia obaudire, tunc haec monasterii regula ei legatur. Qua regula in lectione expleta et omnia abbatis verbis praedicta." *RM* 87.3–4.

129. "Prius iuret se de rebus monasterii nulla furti conmissione aut foris antecessus commendasse aut absconse secum portare." *RM* 87.52.

130. "In quibus duobus mensibus sub cura illorum fratrum, qui peregrinos custodiunt, et ipsi similiter ex inproviso custodiantur et in cella illa peregrinorum dormiant." *RM* 88.7–8.

131. "Cum expletae duorum mensuum ad tractandum indutiae fuerint et placibili disciplina ab eis magis stabilitas eligatur et perseverantia, repromissa lectae regulae firmitate, ab eis placeat adinpleri." *RM* 89.1.

132. See the rest of chapter, *RM* 89.2–35, for details on the ritual surrounding the final oath-taking by the novice.

receive the tonsure or the monastic habit until he had remained in the community for one year.[133]

The Master described other methods of joining the community. If guests were staying at the monastery, working with the brethren for their food, and seemed as though they might want to join the community, the brothers guarding them were to inform the abbot.[134] He was then to read them the rule; and if they wished to stay, the days they had already spent in the monastery were to count as part of the probation period. If they were unsure about the decision, a special provision in the rule stipulated that they would be permitted to join the community on a provisional basis.[135] The Master made it clear that they were to provide for their own necessities, such as clothing. These "temporary" monks, like the guests and novices, were still to be watched over by the guards.[136]

The Master was uncomfortable with the reception of priests into the community. They were to be considered as guests or travelers in the monastery, with no special privileges.[137] If they chose to enter the monastery, the Master would allow it, but only conditionally. "Let them [the priests] not presume or be allowed anything else, nor may they lay claim to any part in God's organization or government or administration, but it is the abbot, set over the whole flock by the Rule, who is to adjudge and reserve to himself every kind of authority and ruling power over the monastery."[138]

Priests would have no distinctive dress after they joined the community. Moreover, "if these priests choose to use the monastery's fare, clothing, and footwear every day, they must also work in common with the brothers."[139]

133. "Ingresso in monasterio cuiquam laico non debere intra annum mutari res nec caput eius secundum propositum tonderi." *RM* 90, title.

134. "Iam si forte tales inventi fuerint hospites, qui diu persistando fideliter et animo laborando indicaverint se monasterio perfirmare, suggerant eorum custodes abbati, et lecta eis regula, videant quot dies iam habent in monasterio." *RM* 79.23–24.

135. "Quod si non se voluerint firmare, sed sic laborando cotidie cum fratribus monasterio voluerint remorari, si contenti sunt pannos suos vel indumenta in alieno opere stricare, sola tamen conmunis mensae vel vitae mensura eis de monasterio praebeatur." *RM* 79.29–30.

136. "A fratribus illis custoditi dumtaxat die noctuque cotidie." *RM* 79.34.

137. "Peregrinorum loco habeantur in monasterio sacerdotes, maxime quorum primatus et honor in ecclesiis continetur et militat." *RM* 83.1–2.

138. "Aliud vero nihil aut praesumant aut eis liceat vel aliquid ordinationis aut dominationis aut dispensationis Dei vindicent, sed omnem formam licentiae vel ordinandae dominationis monasterii abbas, qui super gregem universum est ordinatus a regula, adiudicet vel defendat." *RM* 83.6–7.

139. "Nam ipsi sacerdotes, si victum et vestitum et calciarium monasterii uti magis cottidie eligunt, et operari communiter . . . cum fratribus debeant." *RM* 83.10–11.

Refusal to work would require the abbot to confront the priest in the presence of "a large number of religious persons as witnesses" and ask him to leave the monastery.[140] When writing about this difficult issue, the Master was very cautious, both in language and in the precepts he provided. However, the tone of the *RM* and of the confrontation itself changes if the priest refuses to leave the monastery. "But if, God forbid, they do not want to leave peacefully but instead make a scene, let them be held and stripped of clothing that belongs to the monastery, provided there is no serious injury, then let them be ousted and the door closed. For they themselves ought by all means to do what they preach to others: it is a universal precept of God that the workers' bread must be refused to the idle."[141] There is little doubt that this passage indicates that the relationship between the monastery and the clergy was at times a strained one. The clergy was an ever-present force attempting to control monastic activities. The Master's words were a defensive gesture, an attempt to keep control in the hands of the abbot. Ideally, the monastery itself was ruled by an abbot with absolute power; any attempt at questioning this power or wresting it away had to be dealt with severely.

Analysis of travel in early monastic rules reveals that monastic legislators knew much about the practice of religious wandering and vigorously tried to eliminate it, or at least, in the case of the Master, to control its disruptive influence on monasteries. By narrowly defining proper monastic behavior and dress, and by emphasizing physical stability and submission to the authority of an abbot and rule, the Master and the writer of the *Regula Benedictina* created a form of monasticism in the West that would be acceptable to ecclesiastic and secular authorities. The potential danger of "false" monks who traveled constantly was particularly of concern in the sixth century, an era of social and political flux as well as economic hardships in the West. It is, however, essential to remember that monasticism emphasizing physical stability, the absolute power of an abbot and adherence to a written rule, would only become normative in the West in the

---

140. "Ergo quod si diutissime otiosi labore manuum suarum quaerere victum noluerunt, cum reverentia permultorum religiosorum testimonio conventi ab abbate, ecclesiis revertantur." *RM* 83.17–18.

141. "Si vero, quod absit, non pacifice, sed magis per scandalum exire voluerint, tenti et exuti rebus monasterii, dumtaxat sine gravi iniuria, clausa regia excludantur, quia magis ipsi amplius agere debent, quod aliis praedicant, generaliter a Deo esse praeceptum, otiosis debere laborantium panes negari." *RM* 83.19–22.

ninth century. Viewing Benedictine-style monasticism as normative during the sixth century or even earlier only serves to obscure the wildly varied monastic practices of late antiquity, just as accepting the judgments of monastic legislators concerning "true" or "false" monks shrouds the real, if marginal, practice of spirituality based on wandering behind the label "gyrovague."

CHAPTER FOUR

WOMEN AND RELIGIOUS TRAVEL

As the evidence from monastic rules and other forms of monastic literature has shown, there may indeed have existed monks who used wandering and homelessness as part of their ascetic practice. Evidence from fourth- and early fifth-century Spain also points to the crucial role religious travel played in the lives of Bachiarius, Orosius, and Egeria. The example of Egeria, in particular, suggests that women may have been drawn to a form of monastic travel. The question remains, however, just how "normal" Egeria and her voyages were: did other Western women undertake such travels? This is difficult to answer firmly, yet the evidence shows clearly that she was not at all unique. A number of women emerge as religious travelers in the sources, a fact that may itself reveal other sides to monastic travel previously not considered.

Recent studies have revealed a number of special modes of spiritual and religious expression among late antique women. The field is indebted to the work of Elizabeth Clark, whose pioneering research in the late 1970s and 1980s opened the door to studies of the religious life of late antique women.[1] More recently Susanna Elm and Gillian Cloke have provided much more insight into early female asceticism and spirituality.[2] Elm not only reconstructed the ascetic landscape around Macrina, sister of Basil of Caesarea, but also revealed the centrality of women's monastic and ascetic developments in the eastern Mediterranean. Cloke carefully delineates the

---

1. Elizabeth A. Clark, *Ascetic Piety and Women's Faith: Essays on Late Ancient Christianity* (Lewiston, N.Y., 1986).

2. Elm, *Virgins of God,* and Gillian Cloke, *This Female Man of God: Women and Spiritual Power in the Patristic Age, A.D. 350–450* (New York, 1995).

spiritual lives and possibilities created by "holy women" of late antiquity. Each of these studies have revealed major differences between male and female ascetic and monastic expression as well as differing perceptions of the religious life of men and women.

Though their exact number will never be known, women made up a considerable portion of the religious travelers during late antiquity. There was little preventing women from traveling as a form of religious devotion. In fact, the cloistered and isolated life of the women living in one of the monasteries of Jerusalem that pilgrim Theodosius wrote about in the sixth century seems to have been out of the ordinary.[3] When we look only at woman travelers, certain common traits emerge: most were either widows[4] or unmarried virgins,[5] and many traveled in family units, such as mother and daughter, grandmother and granddaughter, or sister and sister.[6] Women travelers were frequently drawn to other monastic or pious women whom they met during their travels, as Egeria was drawn to Marthana, and as the

3. The only specific reference to monks in his entire account is to virgins living in a cloistered monastery below the Temple Mount in Jerusalem. His description of these women and their monastery emphasized how isolated and separated they were, so much so that their food was delivered to them over the high walls of the convent and when they died they were buried within its walls. "A pinna templi subtus monasterium est de castas, et quando aliqua earum de saeculo transierit, ibi intus in monasterio aliqua earum de saeculo transierit, ibi intus in monasterio ipso deponitur, et a quo illuc intraverint, usque dum vivunt, inde non exeunt. Quando alilqua de sanctimonialibus illuc converti voluerit aut aliqua poenitens, huic tantummodo ipsas portas aperiuntur, nam semper clausae sunt, et victualia eis per muros deponuntur, nam aquam ibi in cisternas habent." Theodosius *De situ terrae sanctae* 11. On the emergence of cloistered life for women, see Donald Hochstetler, *A Conflict of Traditions: Women in Religion in the Early Middle Ages, 500–840* (Lanham, Md., 1992); Adalbert de Vogüé, "Cesáreo de Arlés y los orígenes de la clausura de las monjas," in *Mujeres del Absoluto: El monacato femenino, historia, instituciones, actualidad,* ed. Fray Clemente de la Serna Gonzalez (Burgos, 1986), 183–95; Jane Tibbetts Schulenburg, "Strict Active Enclosure and Its Effects on the Female Monastic Experience (ca. 500–1100)," in *Medieval Religious Women: Distant Echoes,* ed. John A. Nichols and Lillian Thomas Shank (Kalamazoo, Mich., 1984), 51–86.

4. Cloke, *This Female Man of God,* chap. 5, pp. 82–99, on the "order of widows."

5. Melania the Younger was an exception to this as was the empress Eudocia, but both had a certain degree of freedom from their husbands at the time of their journeys. Melania had a chaste relationship with her husband Pinianus, who traveled with her, and Eudocia was estranged from her husband Theodosius II, having been exiled from the court in Constantinople.

6. Sometimes this familial community was enlarged to include close friends, as in the case of Fabiola. Egeria, apparently traveling alone, wrote to her "sisters" in Spain. See Elm's discussion, in *Virgins of God,* of a similar female monastic movement in Asia Minor, centered around Macrina, sister of both Basil of Caesarea and Gregory of Nyssa, their mother, and other women close to the family. See also Jo Ann McNamara, "Muffled Voices: The Lives of Consecrated Women in the Fourth Century," in *Medieval Religious Women: Distant Echoes,* ed. John A. Nichols and Lillian Thomas Shank (Kalamazoo, Mich., 1984), 11–29; Anna Ewing Hickey, *Women of the Roman Aristocracy as Christian Monastics,* ed. Margaret R. Miles (Ann Arbor, Mich., 1987); and Sirago, *Cicadae Noctium.*

evidence of their frequent establishment of female monastic communities suggests.[7] These women did interact with men, mainly monks, but generally men played roles such as spiritual adviser, local guide, or holy man to be visited.

Women on religious journeys during late antiquity were not simply pilgrims. If they were *peregrini*, strangers in distant lands, they were also monastic travelers whose vocation included the desire to commune, not so much with the holy places, as with the holy people who occupied them. Travel itself became part of their monastic identity. In the case of journeys to Jerusalem, some women remained there for their entire lives, while others returned to their homelands, sometimes after long stays; some made multiple journeys. In the city of Jerusalem, the Mount of Olives emerged as the prime location of female monasticism and patronage in many of the accounts we possess. The monastic foundations established by these women, especially those on the Mount of Olives, might best be seen as monastic hostels, temporary dwellings for the women, like Mary or Marthana, who came to the city as part of their ascetic practice. These women travelers helped to shape Jerusalem as a holy Christian city. Patronage by Western women travelers would not only change the urban fabric of Jerusalem, but also the meaning of and perception of Jerusalem in the West.

Egeria's voyage came just a generation before the most famous fourth-century journey of a women to Jerusalem, that of the empress Helena. Helena Augusta, mother of the emperor Constantine, was the first wife of Constantius Chlorus and a woman of humble origins.[8] When Constantius Chlorus was made Caesar in 293, Helena was cast off by her husband for a marriage to a politically well-connected younger woman, Theodora, the daughter of the emperor Maximianus.[9] Constantine was the only child of this first union—the second union produced six children.[10] Constantine appears to have been very attached to his mother; after the death of his

---

7. The only exception to this appears to be the strange and vivid account of Pelagia, who joined a male monastic community. Her account is discussed later in this chapter.

8. Ambrose referred to her as a *stabularia*, an innkeeper. *Oratio de obitu Theodosii* 42. The sixth-century historian Zosimus, who based much of his work on a now-lost work of Eunapius of Sardis (fourth century), wrote that Constantine was "the son of the illegal intercourse of a low woman with the emperor Constantius." *Historia Nova* 2.8.

9. Theodora was also the half-sister of both Maxentius and Fausta, Constantine's future wife. *PLRE*, vol. 1, "Theodora 1," and Jan Willem Drijvers, *Helena Augusta: The Mother of Constantine the Great and the Legend of Her Finding of the True Cross* (Leiden, 1992).

10. These children included Constantia and the father of the future emperor Julian. *PLRE*, vol. 1, "Constantius 12."

father in 306, Helena joined her son in Britain and later moved with him to Trier, and he began at this time to strike coins with her image. After his victory over Maxentius in 312, she moved to Rome, which she made her principal residence. By 314, at the latest, Helena was in possession of the Sessorian palace complex and a large estate along the Via Labicana, just on the other side of the Aurelian walls. Constantine himself spent very little time in Rome; it was Helena who embodied Constantinian imperial presence in the city. She became an important patroness in Rome, particularly in the region around the Sessorian, as attested to in both documentary and epigraphic evidence.[11] By 324 when Constantine defeated Licinius and became the sole Roman emperor, he gave his mother the title *augusta* and, shortly thereafter, he restored and renamed her home town in her honor, Helenopolis.[12] Constantine increased the number of coins minted in her name, now Helena Augusta, until her death at the age of eighty, in 329.[13] Helena was clearly important to Constantine, and she appears to have been a strong supporter of and adviser to her son.

In the year 326, Helena left Rome for a journey that would include a visit to Jerusalem. The visit would soon cast Helena as one of the first Christian "pilgrims" to the city and therefore an exemplar for later pilgrims. Other Christian women traveling to the Holy Land soon after Helena have been cast in this same light, as pilgrims, on temporary and "liminal" journeys. A steady stream of women, as well as men, did indeed travel to the Holy Land in this period, but the particular patterns of these journeys have not been explored, and the meaning of these journeys to those women who undertook them remains unexplained.

The association between Helena and the holy city of Jerusalem resulted from her journey to the Holy Land in 326; it was an association that was recognized by her family and by many Romans. Constantine sent Helena

---

11. Three inscriptions have been found near Santa Croce concerning Helena: one commemorates her restoration of a nearby bath complex; the others praise her as both a mother and grandmother; and one appears to have been on a base of a statue of her. See *CIL*, vi.1134, 1135, 1136.

12. Sozomen *Historia ecclesiastica* 2.2.5. Constantine also made his wife Fausta an *augusta* at the same time.

13. "He had honored her so fully with imperial dignities, that in every province, and in the very ranks of the soldiery, she was spoken of under the titles of Augusta and empress, and her likeness was impressed on golden coins. He had even granted her authority over the imperial treasures, to use and dispense them according to her own will and discretion in every case for this enviable distinction also she received at the hands of her son." Eusebius *Vita Constantini* 3.47.

on her journey to the Holy Land, during which she dispensed imperial patronage and even supervised the building of the churches ordered by her son. Eusebius, who wrote about Helena's journey in his biography of Constantine, gave as the motivation for her travels her desire to offer prayers of thanks for her son and grandsons in the Holy Land. She wanted, according to Eusebius, to offer prayers where Jesus had stood.[14] Eusebius stressed her personal connections with the Holy Land as reasons for her visit, writing that she established many churches there, including the Church of the Nativity in Bethlehem and, in Jerusalem, the Church of the Ascension on the Mount of Olives.

These reasons, however, were overshadowed by what Eusebius himself said in his first introduction to her trip, that she was "to inspect with imperial concern the eastern provinces with their communities and peoples."[15] He gives further details about this aspect of her journey after a careful and slightly forced account of her purely "Christian" intentions in the Holy Land. "As she visited the whole east in the magnificence of imperial authority, she showered countless gifts upon the citizen bodies of every city, and privately to each of those who approached her; and she made countless distributions also to the ranks of the soldiery with magnificent hand."[16] He also related how she recalled exiles and had people released from prison and from forced labor in the mines. Helena was not merely on a trip to Jerusalem, but rather on a "circuit" of the eastern provinces, only a year or so after her son had become the sole ruler of the empire. The deeds Eusebius wrote of are acts of imperial patronage, part of a grand tour by the imperial mother promoting the humanity of the new emperor with the requisite show of pomp and splendor. For Helena, the Holy Land and Jerusalem were not primarily pilgrimage destinations, but rather stops on a political journey.[17] As a voyage of Constantinian imperial patronage, it necessarily contained strong Christian elements, and it was these elements that contemporary interpreters seized upon, portraying Helena as a "pilgrim." Many of these elements may correspond more closely, however, to the patterns of female monastic travel later embodied by women such as Paula, the Melanias, and Fabiola rather than site-specific pilgrimage.

14. Ibid., 3.42.
15. Ibid.
16. Ibid., 3.44.
17. See Kenneth G. Holum, "Hadrian and St. Helena: Imperial Travel and the Origins of Christian Holy Land Pilgrimage," in *The Blessings of Pilgrimage*, 66–81.

It is likely that Helena set up churches in other eastern provinces as well. Eusebius himself wrote that she left gifts at all the churches she visited, even in the smallest cities.[18] Eusebius, as bishop of Caesarea, which was at the time the metropolitan see in the province of Palestine, intended to promote the importance of the Holy Land.[19] His account of Helena's journey certainly convinced many, including later historians, of the appropriateness of the city as a destination for pious Christians because of its unique sacred history, but there is in fact no evidence that Helena visited the city as a pilgrim, or that the city had a recognized identity as a Christian pilgrimage destination.

Just as Helena embodied the Constantinian presence in Rome, so she embodied the imperial presence through her travels.[20] Helena visited the actual city of Jerusalem not so much as a pilgrim, but as an emissary of her son, who favored Christianity. Her visit occurred only a year after Constantine's calling of the Council of Nicaea; Constantine saw himself as the most important patron of Christianity, and he used his mother's voyage as a means of showering largesse on churches throughout the Holy Land. Helena did this while simultaneously bestowing more traditional imperial favors, such as freeing prisoners and giving money to the poor.[21]

There may have been another, rather more sinister motive for her journey. Her voyage began shortly after executions of her oldest grandson, Crispus, and Fausta, Constantine's wife and stepmother of Crispus. These executions took place in Rome and were ordered by Constantine, who was in the city celebrating his *vicennalia,* marking twenty years of his rule. Fausta, who was born and raised in Rome, was, in addition to being Constantine's wife, the sister of Maxentius, whom Constantine had of course defeated at the battle of the Milvian bridge in 312. Her family estate in Rome was located next to the Lateran, and she, like Helena, was an embodiment of imperial presence in the city. In a sense she was, for Helena, a competing female Constantinian presence who possessed her own independent claim on the city and people of Rome. Constantine had elevated Fausta to the rank of *augusta* at the same time as Helena, in 324. Creating further complication in their relationship, Fausta was also the half-sister of Theodora, the second

18. Eusebius *Vita Constantini* 3.45.

19. Walker, "Eusebius, Cyril and the Holy Places," 311; idem, *Holy City, Holy Places.*

20. She had access to imperial funds according to Eusebius: "He even remitted to her authority over imperial treasuries, to use them at will and to manage them at her discretion, in whatever way she might wish and however she might judge best in each care, her son having accorded her distinction and eminence in these matters too." Eusebius *Vita Constantini* 3.47.

21. Ibid., 3.44.

wife of Helena's husband Constantius Chlorus.[22] The rivalry between Helena and Fausta, whose Roman residences were less than a mile apart, as patronesses of imperial prestige, Constantinian largesse, and Christianity would be physically played out within the urban fabric of Rome.

Rumors were circulating that Fausta had unjustly accused her stepson Crispus of a sexual relationship with her, causing Constantine to immediately order his death, before his own arrival in the city.[23] This execution conveniently resulted in Fausta's own son, Constantine II, replacing Crispus as the emperor's eldest son. When Constantine learned of his mistake in believing his wife's charges, perhaps through the influence of Helena, he ordered Fausta's death.[24] Some have viewed Helena's journey to the Holy Land as a form of penance on behalf of Constantine for the unjust murder of Crispus. The building of the churches in Jerusalem and Bethlehem thus could be viewed as a sort of votive offering.[25] But this explanation appears to rely too heavily on the idea of penitential pilgrimage, developed only later; it is more likely that Helena left Rome to avoid being present for the execution of Fausta.

Helena presents us with a special case, for she is remembered for much more than simply being Constantine's mother; just a generation after her death, Ambrose, the bishop of Milan, attributed the finding of the True Cross in Jerusalem to her in his eulogy for Theodosius I.[26] The legend of Helena's discovery of the True Cross has a complicated history. Although it appears quite early in the historical record, most modern scholars dismiss any actual connection between Helena and the discovery of this important

---

22. *PLRE*, vol. 1, "Fl. Maxima Fausta."

23. Zosimus perhaps preserves a fourth-century opinion implicating Constantine in these murders. *Historia Nova* 2.29. Also in Sozomen *Historia ecclesiastica* 1.5.

24. Fausta was suffocated in an overheated bath near her palace on the Lateran. Crispus was considered the favorite (perhaps because he was the oldest) grandchild of Helena and thus Helena is viewed as implicating Fausta to avenge the death of Crispus.

25. A recent paper posits another reason for Helena's swift departure: Helena's journey to the Holy Land, rather than being in the name and with the approval of Constantine, was instead as a way for the *augusta* to get out of town and atone for her own role in the death of Fausta. Noel Lenski, "Empresses in the Holy Land: The Making of a Christian Utopia in the Fourth and Fifth Centuries," in *Travel, Communication and Geography in Late Antiquity*, ed. L. Ellis and F. L. Kidner (Ashgate, 2004).

26. Ambrose *Oratio de obitu Theodosii* 45–48. According to the early legend, Helena went to the city, discovered relics and brought them back with her and gave some to her son, Constantine. Helena may have visited Constantine in Constantinople, but she eventually returned to her home in Rome. Socrates Scholasticus (see his *Historia ecclesiastica* 1.17) and Sozomen (*Historia ecclesiastica* 2.1) both mention Helena's return with relics of the Crucifixion.

relic.[27] The principal reasons for this skepticism are the lack of references to the discovery in Eusebius's account of Helena's journey to Jerusalem, the silence of the *Liber Pontificalis* in the section about Santa Croce (the Constantinian church created out of Helena's Sessorian Palace in Rome[28]) and the True Cross, and the absence of Helena in the early accounts concerning the relic by Cyril of Jerusalem, Egeria, and Paulinus of Nola.

Eusebius claims that Helena returned from her trip to the East with various relics of the Passion, which were then set up in Constantinople, not Rome. Writing after the death of Constantine in 337 and the establishment of Constantinople, Eusebius would of course have emphasized the city in his account.[29] In fact, Eusebius hardly mentions Rome, so if Helena or Constantine had set up relics there, he would not necessarily have described them. Returning to Rome, Helena would probably have housed the souvenirs she brought from the Holy Land in a private oratory, most likely within her home, the Sessorian Palace, or she may have presented them to a church. The *Liber Pontificalis,* a collection of papal biographies first compiled in the early sixth century, states that Constantine placed a fragment of the True Cross in Santa Croce, then, of course, called "Jerusalem," though

27. Ambrose mentions it in 395. For discussions of Helena's association with the discovery of the cross, see Drijvers, *Helena Augusta;* Hans A. Pohlsander, *Helena: Empress and Saint* (Chicago, 1995); H. A. Drake, "Eusebius on the True Cross," *Journal of Ecclesiastical History* 36 (1985): 1–22; Timothy D. Barnes, *Constantine and Eusebius* (Cambridge, Mass., 1981); and Sible de Blaauw, "Jerusalem in Rome and the Cult of the Cross," in *Pratum Romanum. Richard Krautheimer zum 100. Geburtstag,* ed. Meredith J. Gill, Renate L. Colella, Lawrence A. Jenkens, and Petra Lamers (Wiesbaden, 1997), 55–73.

28. There is some dispute over when the transformation of Santa Croce was initiated and who initiated it. Richard Krautheimer, the foremost authority on early Roman churches, originally believed that the brickwork indicated a mid-fourth-century date, but probably one after Constantine's reign. Before his death he revised his position, claiming instead that the transformation occurred during Helena's lifetime. See Richard Krautheimer, *Corpus Basilicarum Christianarum Romae: The Early Christian Basilicas of Rome,* 5 vols. (Vatican City, 1937–77), 1:191–92, and Richard Krautheimer and Slobodan Curcic, *Early Christian and Byzantine Architecture,* 4th ed. (London, 1986), 460 n. 28. Krautheimer does not give the reasons for change in his opinion here. Grabar does not consider Santa Croce a foundation of Constantine, but instead credits Helena herself. Andre Grabar, *Martyrium: Recherches sur le culte des reliques et l'art chrétien antique,* 2 vols. (London, 1946; reprint, 1972), 1:205.

29. Drake argues that Eusebius perhaps purposely omitted mentioning the discovery of the True Cross and Helena association because the cross was far more of an imperial and Constantinian symbol than a Christian one. He also states that there is no reason to believe Eusebius's account over that of Cyril of Jerusalem. See Drake, "Eusebius on the True Cross." Walker makes a similar argument; he believes that Eusebius wanted to downplay the importance of Jerusalem and was opposed to pilgrimage, emphasizing "spiritual" rather than "physical" pilgrimage. It must also be remembered that Eusebius was bishop of Caesarea, the provincial capital and rival to Jerusalem. Walker, "Eusebius, Cyril and the Holy Places," 311.

the text does not describe Helena as its discoverer.[30] In addition, the *Liber Pontificalis* contains a long account of the treasures given to the other Roman churches by Constantine, yet the relic of the holy cross is only placed at Santa Croce.[31] This, too, makes it appear that Rome and the "Jerusalem" church would be the logical place for the relic of the True Cross.

Although the connections of the discovery of the cross and Helena's journey are contested, it is generally agreed that this relic was "discovered" in the fourth century. Cyril, the bishop of Jerusalem, includes references to the discovery of the True Cross as early as twenty-five years after Helena's visit.[32] Independent sources confirm this discovery, and pieces of the cross clearly begin circulating in the fourth century. Egeria, who was in Jerusalem between 381 and 384, visited the relic of the True Cross housed at the Holy Sepulcher, and her travelogue gives much evidence about the great popularity of the cross for visitors, one of whom tried to bite off a piece while kissing the relic.[33] Melania the Elder, returning to Rome from Jerusalem in 400, was able somehow to bring back a piece of the cross as a gift for Paulinus of Nola.

Eusebius preserves a letter written by Constantine to Bishop Macarius of Jerusalem, in which the emperor discusses his wish to construct "beautiful buildings" over the location of the Holy Sepulcher. Eusebius places the letter within the context of the discovery of a cave, the tomb of Jesus, behind a temple to Venus that had just been destroyed. Eusebius stresses the importance of the locality as a reminder of the Resurrection, whereas Constantine's letter appears to stress the discovery of some object connected to the Crucifixion. Constantine writes,

> So great is our Saviour's grace, that no words seem enough to match the present miracle. For the evidence of his most sacred passion, long since hidden under the ground, to have remained unknown for such a long period of years. . . . The thing therefore which I consider clear to everybody is what I want you in particular to believe, namely that above all else my concern is that that sacred

30. For the issues surrounding the compilation and dating, see the introduction to Raymond Davis, ed., *The Book of the Pontiffs (Liber Pontificalis)* (Liverpool, 1989).

31. *LP* 34.

32. Cyril of Jerusalem *Catechetical Lectures* 4.10, 10.19, and 13.4. See also Anatole Frolow, *La Relique De La Vraie Croix: Recherches Sur Le Developpement D'un Culte* (Paris, 1961).

33. "Et quoniam nescio quando dicitur quidam fixisse morsum et furasse de saancto ligno, ideo nunc a diaconibus, qui in giro stant, sic custoditur, ne qui veniens audeat denuo sic facere." Egeria *Itin.* 37.2.

place, which at God's command I have now relieved of the hideous burden of an idol which lay on it like a weight, hallowed from the start by God's decree, and now proved yet holier since it brought to light the pledge of the Saviour's passion, should be adorned by us with beautiful buildings.[34]

Could this "evidence of his most sacred passion" and "pledge of the Saviour's passion" be the cross or perhaps Golgotha, rather than simply the tomb as Eusebius indicates? Indeed, Constantine's Holy Sepulcher complex would encompass not only the location of Christ's tombs but also Golgotha, the location of the Crucifixion. By the mid-fourth century, a relic of the True Cross would also be displayed at the complex. It is, perhaps, impossible to know if Helena's trip to the East can indeed be associated with the discovery of the relic of the True Cross, but it is certain that Helena's name gets associated with the discovery by 395 and that parts of her former home in Rome were transformed into a church called "Jerusalem," which at least by the fifth century housed a relic of the True Cross.

Constantine was present at Helena's death and had her buried in Rome next to the cemeterial basilica of Saints Marcellinus and Peter, near her own suburban properties.[35] She was buried in a large mausoleum adjoining the basilica, just a few miles away from the Sessorian Palace on the Via Labicana. Ss. Marcellinus and Peter, a richly endowed Constantinian cemeterial foundation, stands over a vast network of early Christian catacombs, which appear in the earliest lists of Roman burial sites.[36] Some believe that the

34. Eusebius *Vita Constantini* 3.30.

35. Eusebius states that Constantine was present at her death, but he is not clear about where she died. He writes that she was buried in the "imperial city," which some have assumed meant Constantinople, yet Eusebius uses the term for Rome. He writes, "with a great guard of honour she was carried to the imperial city, and there laid in the imperial tombs." Eusebius *Vita Constantini* 3.47. The *Liber Pontificalis* (see *LP* 34) states she died in Rome. Marcellinus and Peter were Roman martyrs—this Peter was an exorcist and not the apostle Peter. Marcellinus and Peter were killed in 304 during the great persecution instigated by Diocletian. The *Liber Pontificalis* states that Constantine gave Helena's estates to the Church of Saints Marcellinus and Peter; they are described as "the farm laurentum close to the aqueduct, with a bath and all the land from the Porta Sessoriana as far as the Via Praenestina, by the route of the Via Latina as far as Mons Gabus, the property of the empress Helena, revenue 1120 solidi." It is interesting that Constantine chose the burial site of these Roman martyrs, killed while he was Caesar, as the location for Helena's burial, which he may have intended for himself.

36. "Ubi mater ipsius sepulta est Helena Augusta, via Lavicana, miliario III. In quo loco et pro amorem matris suae et veneratione sanctorum posuit dona voti sui: [list follows]." *LP* 34.26. These catacombs are also known for their beautiful artwork, and they were on the circuit

mausoleum was originally built for Constantine's own burial, though he was instead buried in the Church of the Holy Apostles in Constantinople, his new Rome and personal imperial foundation.[37] In fact, Helena's impressive porphyry sarcophagus may also have been originally intended for Constantine.[38] It is decidedly militaristic and imperial in decoration, though one of the portrait heads carved near the lid of the tomb is of a woman.

Helena's mausoleum on the Via Labicana, whether or not it was originally meant for her or her son, was a tall rotunda bearing some similarity to the mausoleum of Constantina on the Via Nomentana, now the Church of Santa Constanza. Santa Constanza is located outside the walls and also on Constantinian imperial property associated with Constantine's daughters, Constantina and Helena the Younger.[39] Constantina, like her grandmother, was an *augusta* (proclaimed such by Constantine in 335) and a patroness in Rome, but far more of a patroness of Christianity in the city; she established the Church of Sant'Agnese fuori le mure and an associated monastery, which she may have joined at one point.[40] During the period of her widowhood,

---

of catacombs visited by Christians seeking out the tombs of the martyrs. Although the basilica no longer exists, remains of the mausoleum still stand, showing it to have been an impressive structure. The current church of SS. Marcellino e Pietro is a later construction. The original basilica stood behind the mausoleum, which is today called the Tor Pignatta or Torpignattara. See the excellent article by Jean Guyon, "Dal praedium imperiale al santuario dei martiri. Il territorio *ad duas lauros*," in *Società romana e impero tardoantico,* ed. Andrea Giardina (Rome, 1986), 299–332, and Davide Dionisi and Gennaro Della Pietra, *Torpignattara: I luoghi della memoria* (Rome, 1994).

37. This was Grabar's opinion, and most have agreed with him. Grabar, *Martyrium,* 205.

38. The *Liber Pontificalis* states that her sarcophagus was "of hard porphyry, carved with medallions." *LP,* chap. 34, entry on Silvester. The sarcophagus had resided at her mausoleum on the Labicana for many centuries until it was "reused" by a Renaissance pope; it is currently in the Vatican museum near a similar, but smaller and less ornate, sarcophagus of Constantina, daughter of Constantine and Fausta. Constantina's sarcophagus was moved from its position in Santa Constanza, her mausoleum next to Sant'Agnese on the via Nomentana. Interestingly, the layout of mausoleum, cemeterial basilica, and catacombs at SS. Marcellino e Pietro is strikingly similar to the complex of Sant'Agnese. Amato Pietro Frutaz, *Il Complesso Monumentale Di Sant'agnese,* 5th ed. (Rome, 1992). For more on the connections between these two complexes and the Honorian mausolea attached to St. Peter's, see Krautheimer and Curcic, *Early Christian and Byzantine Architecture,* 64. Krautheimer believed that Constantina's mausoleum had brickwork similar to that of the remodeling of Santa Croce. Krautheimer, *Corpus,* 1:191. See also Guyon, "Dal praedium imperiale."

39. Constantina married Gallus, while her sister Helena married Julian. Gillian Mackie has proposed that S. Constanza was originally intended to be Julian's mausoleum. See Gillian Mackie, "A New Look at the Patronage of Santa Costanza, Rome," *Byzantion* 67 (1997): 383–406.

40. The *Liber Pontificalis* states that Constantine established the church at the request of his daughter Constantina. It also states that both Constantina and Constantine's sister, Constantia,

from 337 to 351, between her marriages to Hanibalianus and Gallus Caesar, she lived in Rome, probably on the imperial estate on the Via Nomentana near Sant'Agnese. During this time she housed Pope Liberius, who had been deposed and exiled by her Arian-supporting brother, Constantius, at Sant'Agnese.[41] It was through her efforts that Liberius and Constantius reconciled, and the emperor eventually recalled the elderly pontiff during his month-long stay in Rome. Constantina, at her brother's request, entered into another political marriage with their cousin Gallus Caesar in 351. Four years later, their younger sister Helena, named after her grandmother, would be married to Gallus's brother Julian. Both Constantina and her sister Helena were buried together in the mausoleum of Santa Constanza, attached to Sant'Agnese.[42] These Constantinian women were living in Rome during the time of the transformation of the Sessorian Palace into Santa Croce and may have been instrumental in the establishment of the church. Scholars who believe that the transformation in fact took place after Constantine's death often look to his surviving sons, Constantius II, Constans, and Constantine II, as possible patrons, but these men spent very little time in Rome and were not a strong presence in the city.[43] Rarely considered are Constantine's two daughters, both of whom lived in Rome and were viewed as Christian patronesses.[44] The inscriptions honoring the elder Helena found near Santa Croce all refer to her as a devoted mother and, significantly, grandmother. After her death in 329 it would be left to her two granddaughters to continue the imperial and decidedly female presence in the city.

---

were baptized there by Pope Silvester. There has been much confusion between these two women because of the similarity of their names. Constantia had been married to Licinius, who was killed by Constantine in 324. There is no evidence of her ever becoming an *augusta*. She probably spent her widowhood in Rome. The evidence from Prudentius's *Peristephanon* points to the daughter Constantina as the founder of the church. *LP* 34, entry on Silvester. See also Krautheimer, *Corpus*, 1:34, and Frutaz, *Il Complesso Monumentale Di Sant'agnese.*

41. *LP* 37, entry on Liberius.

42. For a discussion of Constantina's sarcophagus, see John Beckwith, *Early Christian and Byzantine Art* (New Haven, 1979; reprint, 1993), 29–30.

43. Constantius's *adventus* in 357, the first time he personally had been in Rome, was an important occasion; it was a rare occurrence in this period for an emperor to come to Rome, and consequently, Constantius's month-long visit was quite ceremonial in nature. We know that he erected an obelisk and removed the altar of victory from the forum. Symmachus *Relatio* 6. See also Ammianus Marcellinus *Res Gestae* 16.10.

44. Even the Helena who was married to Julian is called devout and pious in Christian sources. *LP* 37.4. Ammianus Marcellinus wrote of Helena's Christian burial near her sister in Rome. *Res Gestae* 21.1.5.

The *Liber Pontificalis* clearly states that Constantine himself placed the relic of the True Cross at Santa Croce. The entry for Pope Sylvester states: "Then the emperor Constantine built a basilica in the Sessorian Palace; there he placed some of the wood of the our Lord Jesus Christ's holy Cross and sealed it with gold and jewels; and from this he chose the name for the dedication of the church, which today is still called Jerusalem."[45] Perhaps the *Liber Pontificalis,* begun almost two centuries after the events, has conflated Constantine with his daughters, Constantina and Helena, or with one of his sons, all of whom were likelier candidates. At the same time Constantine donated two other crosses; one went to Saint Peter's and is described as a 150-pound cross of gold, with an inscription stating that it came from Constantine Augustus and Helena Augusta.[46] This was not a piece of the True Cross but a golden treasure and an emblem of imperial and Christian victory, given by both Constantine and his mother. Here the cross is not only an imperial symbol, but also a symbol associated with Helena. The third cross was given to Saint Paul's; it, too, was a 150-pound jeweled cross given by Constantine and positioned "over the burial place" of Paul.[47] It is clear why Constantine or his children would have donated giant jeweled crosses to the great basilicas of Peter and Paul; what is not as clear is the placement of the piece of the True Cross, sealed in a jeweled, golden reliquary, to a small and isolated church built from two rooms of the Sessorian Palace. Constantine himself is said to have named this new church, his only church foundation within the walls of Rome, "Jerusalem" because of the gift of the relic of the cross.[48] This was a special church, one intimately connected to Helena and to Constantinian imperial presence in Rome.

The jeweled crosses in Rome had both an association with Jerusalem and, at least in the case of the fourth-century examples, a connection to the Constantinian imperial family. Even if we discount the story of Helena finding the True Cross, she nonetheless became associated with both Jerusalem and the cross by the late fourth century. She certainly returned

45. "Basilicam in palatio Sessoriano . . . ubi et nomen ecclesiae dedicavit, quae cognominatur usque in hodiernum diem Hierusalem." *LP* 34, entry on Silvester.

46. "Over St. Peter's body, above the bronze in which he had sealed, he provided a cross of finest gold weighing 150 lb, made to measure; on the cross itself is written in <fine> niellowed letters, 'Constantine Augustus and Helena Augusta. He surrounds this house with a royal hall gleaming with equal splendour.'" *LP* 35.

47. *LP* 35.

48. "Basilicam in palatio Sessoriano . . . ubi et nomen ecclesiae dedicavit, quae cognominatur usque in hodiernum diem Hierusalem." *LP* 34, entry on Silvester.

with souvenirs, including, according to Eusebius, relics of the Passion. Tradition holds that the rear room of the church had once been Helena's own bedroom, but it just as easily could have been a private oratory where the empress could display the souvenirs of her journey to the East.[49]

The Constantinian placement, either by Helena, Constantine, his daughters, or his sons, of the True Cross relic in a church then called "Jerusalem," which was originally part of the Helena's imperial residence, and in close proximity to the Lateran, cannot have been coincidental. By placing the relic in the "Jerusalem" church, a conscious connection was created between Jerusalem and Helena, who died and was buried in Rome shortly after her return from the Holy Land. The church was therefore both a memorial to Helena and to her journey to Jerusalem and thus the logical place to house the relic of the cross.

Thus Santa Croce, created from rooms of the Sessorian Palace, was Jerusalem—Jerusalem in Rome. As such, "Jerusalem" had a very different function from other Roman churches—it was not a *titulus,* or a cemeterial basilica, or the episcopal seat of Rome. It manifested holy space within the confines of Rome—holy space not associated with Rome's traditional *sancti*— Peter, Paul, and other martyrs in the catacombs. It was instead associated with Christ himself and the Constantinian imperial family, particularly Helena Augusta, mother and grandmother of emperors.

Whether it was a journey of imperial patronage or a religious journey, Helena's travels left their mark on future women religious travelers. Her journey was popularized by both Eusebius and, in the West, Ambrose. By the end of the fourth century her name would be forever associated with the relic of the True Cross. Perhaps it was this journey by an elderly imperial mother that revealed the possibilities of long-distance travel to other women, such as Egeria.

Egeria's account sheds light not only on her own journey but on the travels of others as well, for the holy sites within Jerusalem that she described were frequently visited by other travelers, especially during festivals. Although her account provides evidence of a wide variety of travelers, the only one she identified by name was a woman named Marthana, leader of a Syrian

---

49. This is different from Krautheimer's opinion that Santa Croce itself was turned into a private, palace church during Helena's lifetime. I think that the transformation of the structure occurred after Helena's death and that it was clearly turned into public space. During Helena's long stay in the Sessorian, I believe these rooms were private, and that the rear room could have served the *augusta* as a depository of special Holy Land relics.

monastic community. Egeria first met Marthana in Jerusalem, while the latter was visiting the city. Later, Egeria traveled to Seleucia in order to visit Marthana and her sisters, because she felt a connection to Marthana that she did not feel with many other pilgrims and travelers, including those seeking a cure with branches from the Oak of Mamre.[50] This suggests that Marthana, too, saw travel and meeting holy people as part of a monastic vocation. If Egeria recognized herself in Marthana, Marthana must have recognized herself in Egeria as well when she invited the Spanish woman to visit her community.

Western travelers to the East had at their disposal models for religious travel in the Eastern travelers they met. Egeria makes much of her meeting with Marthana; one can imagine Marthana telling Egeria of the ways and methods of travel in the East, particularly for women on a spiritual quest. Marthana presents us with a mystery; we wish we knew more about her and her monastic community, and, for the purposes of the present study, more about her travels. Did Egeria see her as an Eastern model for a traveling woman? If so, what sort of model did she represent? A slightly later example of Eastern female religious travel can be found in an account written by John of Ephesus in the sixth century. Mary and Euphemia, Syrian sisters who lived in the middle of the sixth century, were, in a sense, the successors of Egeria's friend Marthana. John of Ephesus, a Monophysite monk, portrayed the two sisters as practicing different forms of monastic life. Mary, the elder, wandered: "This Mary was a pure virgin, and from her childhood she chose for her part quiet, abstinence, great feats of fasting, many vigils, constant prayers, exertion in charity, and wandering."[51] She spent much of her life traveling to Jerusalem and wandering through the city in prayer. John saw her travel as an essential part of her extreme asceticism; even the heat of the summer apparently did not stop her wandering.[52]

John's portrait of her sister Euphemia both contrasts and complements his description of Mary's ascetic practices. Euphemia was a widow with a young daughter when she decided to begin her monastic life. Instead of wandering, Euphemia and her daughter set up a large xenodochium in the

---

50. "Nam cuicumque inquomoditas fuerit, vadent ibi et tollent surculos, et prode illis est." Egeria *Itin.* 8.3.

51. John of Ephesus *Lives of the Eastern Saints: Mary, Euphemia and Susan* 12, in *Holy Women of the Syrian Orient*, ed. Sebastian P. Brock and Susan Ashbrook Harvey (Berkeley and Los Angeles, 1987), 125.

52. Ibid., 129.

city of Amida, initially to provide a home for Monophysite monks who had been driven out of their monasteries by the orthodox. Her house grew and soon, "like a harbor that receives ships from everywhere for mooring and peaceful rest, that blessed woman in this way took in and gave relief to the exiled and oppressed from all places."[53] Euphemia sheltered strangers and holy travelers alike, and for thirty years "her house was resounding day and night with the praises of holy men from everywhere."[54] When Euphemia faced opposition from certain citizens of Amida, who complained that her home was full of thieves, she and her daughter took to the road and traveled to Jerusalem to visit her sister Mary. John of Ephesus ended his story with the death of the two sisters, and he again emphasized the differences in their choices. "The blessed Mary had lived sixty years in the way of holiness from her birth until her death, traveling on the road of perfection and laboring toward God. The blessed Euphemia, too, had passed thirty-five years of that way of perfection: thirty in serving the holy men and five in sufferings and trial of persecution."[55] Both of these women made travel and homelessness part of their monastic lives: travel itself in the case of Mary and providing hospitality to holy travelers in the case of Euphemia. In each of their lives, Jerusalem, the city, played an important role, but it was not the focus or goal of their asceticism. Mary, Euphemia, and Euphemia's daughter present us with Eastern models of female ascetic practice that centered on travel and travelers. It is certainly plausible that these models would have an influence on Western women visiting the East.

Egeria's journey was one of many journeys of Western, Latin-speaking women to the East. In some cases, we know much more about the backgrounds and lives of some of these other traveling women than we know of Egeria's. An important fourth-century visitor to Jerusalem, for example, was the traveler Melania the Elder, a member of a powerful and rich Roman family of Spanish origin.[56] Married early to a pagan, she was already widowed, as well as very wealthy, at the age of twenty-two. Shortly thereafter, in 372, she left her young son Publicola in the care of a guardian in Rome and

---

53. Ibid.

54. Ibid.

55. W. K. Lowther Clarke, trans., *The Lausiac History of Palladius* (New York, 1918); Robert T. Meyer, "Palladius as Biographer and Autobiographer," *Studia Patristica* 17 (1982): 66–71; idem, "Holy Orders in the Eastern Church in the Early Fifth Century as Seen in Palladius," *Studia Patristica* 16, no. 2 (1985): 38–49.

56. *HL* 46.5. See also Brown, *Body and Society*, 281.

began a monastic journey abroad. She first visited Egypt, birthplace of monasticism, and met with the "living holy people," the monks, whom she brought many gifts. In 377, she moved to Palestine and founded a monastery on the Mount of Olives, living there with about fifty women and supporting other monastic travelers during their stay in Jerusalem. Rufinus of Aquileia became her spiritual adviser, joining her in Jerusalem in 381 and staying until he returned to Rome in 399.[57] A few years later, Melania too would return to Rome, but only temporarily. Melania, like Egeria, seems to have traveled and met with other monks, both men and women, not just out of necessity but as a way of life and as a form of asceticism.

As we have so often seen, however, it was the disapproval of monastic wandering that provides the most telling evidence for its existence. The disapproving letter written about Melania by Evagrius Ponticus provides perhaps the strongest indicator of how seriously she took her journeying and of its centrality in her spiritual life: "I praise her intentions but I do not approve of her undertaking. I do not see what she will gain from such a long walk over such a laborious route; . . . Thus, I beseech your holiness to prevent those [women] who have renounced the world from needlessly walking around over such roads; . . . Such behavior is misguided for those who live in chastity."[58] In a letter Evagrius wrote to Melania herself, he stated that she should "teach your sisters and your sons not to take a long journey or to travel through deserted lands without examining the matter seriously. For this is misguided and unbecoming to every soul that has retreated from the world. . . . And I wonder whether a woman roaming about and meeting myriads of people can achieve such a goal."[59] Evagrius was clearly critical of the idea that wandering could be part of a monastic life. Interestingly, he also seems to have believed it was a particularly female form of monasticism. Melania, however, did not heed his advice, and her travels continued.

Returning to Italy around the year 400, Melania visited Paulinus of Nola and brought him an important gift from Jerusalem, a relic of the True Cross.[60] Even outside the Holy Land, gift exchange was an important part

---

57. Evagrius Ponticus, quoted in Elm, *Virgins of God*, 277.

58. Ibid., 278.

59. Paulinus of Nola *Ep.* 31, to Septimius Severus. Paulinus then sent this gift to Severus to "enhance both the consecration of [his] basilica and [his] holy collection of sacred ashes."

60. Her life was written by Gerontius. Gerontius, *Life of Melania*, in *Handmaids of the Lord: Contemporary Descriptions of Feminine Asceticism in the First Six Christian Centuries*, ed. Joan M.

of her religious life. When she returned to Rome for a brief visit, she stayed with her son Publicola, who was then a prominent married senator with a young daughter named Melania, known as Melania the Younger.[61] The two women shared more than a name: Melania the Younger admired her grandmother and had wanted to lead a monastic life as well, but her parents, especially her father, forbade it. Publicola had been left behind as a young boy, and was critical of the life his mother was leading. So while Melania the Elder left once more for Jerusalem, Melania the Younger, at age thirteen, was forced to marry her cousin Pinianus, the son of the wealthy prefect of Rome, Valerius Severus.[62] Pinianus and Melania would have two children together, but when both children died, she was able to convince her husband that this was a sign that they should lead monastic lives. Their marriage then became a chaste one, in which they lived "as brother and sister."[63] Melania began to give away their property to the poor, and when her grandmother returned from Jerusalem she fell further under her influence.

Among the people fleeing Rome in large numbers with the Visigothic invasion of Italy and eventual sack of Rome in 410 were both Melanias, Pinianus, and Albina, the mother of Melania the Younger. The group first escaped to Sicily, before going on to North Africa, where they had a family estate near Thagaste.[64] They remained in Africa for seven years, befriending Augustine and Alypius, and establishing monasteries. Eventually the group left for Palestine, probably in 417. Shortly after their arrival in Jerusalem, the elder Melania died, but her granddaughter persisted in her vocation. Pinianus remained with her as a companion and chaste husband-brother. Together they traveled to Egypt and visited numerous monks, but the holy woman traveler was not always hospitably received. She made it her habit to give gifts of gold to the holy hermits, sometimes hiding the gold in their cells after they had refused the gifts. One monk, upon finding an unwanted gift, even ran after Melania in an attempt to return it. When Melania refused to take it back, the story goes, the monk threw the gold into a river.

Petersen (Kalamazoo, Mich., 1996). (All page references to this work are to this translation.) For an excellent discussion of Melania the Elder, see Elizabeth A. Clark, " Piety and Propaganda," in *Ascetic Piety and Women's Faith*.

61. See Clark, "Piety and Propaganda," 61. See discussion of the Valerii family and their property in Rodolfo Lanciani, *The Ruins and Excavations of Ancient Rome* (New York, 1897; reprint, 1967), 345.

62. See discussion of Melania in Malamut, *Sur la route des saints byzantins*.

63. Clark, "Piety and Propaganda," 62.

64. Gerontius *Life of Melania* 334.

Even with this rejection, her hagiographer Gerontius maintained that this form of gift-giving was proper for Melania: "Many other holy hermits and devout virgins were also unwilling to accept gold. The blessed lady therefore left it in their cells, by means of a spiritual subterfuge."[65] Gift-giving and gift-receiving were an important part of travel for these traveling ascetic women; exchanges sealed the meeting between travelers and their monastic hosts. They were crucial in legitimizing visits, and in addition, they functioned to enhance the sanctity of the holy people.

Melania the Younger was far more successful in charitable acts toward monks through the establishment of monasteries in Jerusalem, including a woman's monastery on the Mount of Olives and, near the church of the Ascension, one for men, which she established shortly after Pinianus's death. Her traveling did not come to an end with the death of her husband. In 436 she made a journey to Constantinople to see her still-pagan uncle Volusianus who was visiting the city from Rome. Gerontius wrote that she was concerned that this trip might be "contrary to the purpose of God." She immediately turned for advice to the monks around her: "She shared the problem with all the holy men and asked them to pray fervently that her journey might be in accordance with the will of God."[66] The monks gave her the reassurance she needed, and she continued with her travels, which Gerontius described in rich detail.

In Constantinople she met with both the emperor Theodosius II and his new wife Eudocia, and in fact Gerontius states that it was Melania's prompting that convinced Eudocia to undertake her own trip to the Holy Land.[67] Eudocia made this trip partly to visit Melania. Gerontius put the following words in the empress's mouth: "I have discharged a two-fold vow to the Lord; to venerate the Holy Places and to see my mother, for I wished to have the honor of seeing Your Holiness, while you are still serving the Lord in the flesh."[68] Melania's final days were spent traveling back and forth between various Eastern shrines and her monastery in Jerusalem. She died in 439 and was buried with many of the items she had collected from the holy people she had visited throughout her life: "She had the tunic of one holy man, the veil of another handmaid of God, a piece of a sleeveless tunic which had belonged to another holy man, the girdle of a

---

65. Ibid., 342.
66. This trip and her second permanent trip are discussed later in this chapter.
67. Gerontius *Life of Melania* 348.
68. Ibid., 358.

third (with which she always girt herself when alive), the cowl of a fourth, and, as a pillow the haircloth cowl of a fifth—from it we made a cushion and placed it beneath her honored head. It was fitting that she should be buried in the garments of those whose virtues she had acquired in her lifetime."[69] In this passage, Gerontius associates Melania's visits with holy people not only with gathering physical reminders of the meeting, but with the attainment of religious qualities of the holy people she visited. The physical gifts mirrored the spiritual gifts that came from encounters through travel.

Jerome, the great translator of the Vulgate, was himself a spiritual guide and adviser to a group of Roman aristocratic women who, like the two Melanias, would eventually travel to the East and follow monastic lives.[70] One of these women was Paula, a Roman matron married to a pagan, Toxotius, who had four daughters, all of them Christian. Upon the death of her husband, Paula adopted an ascetic life, and Jerome became her spiritual adviser. He also helped two of her daughters, Blesilla and Eustochium, in their pursuit of monastic life. Blesilla died suddenly in 384, and some in Rome blamed her death on the austere life that Jerome had convinced her to lead.[71] Jerome was forced to leave Rome during this scandal, but a few months later, Paula, Eustochium, and other devout women decided to follow Jerome on a journey to the East.[72] Paula faced much opposition, primarily from her own family; her young son and remaining two daughters tried in vain to convince her to stay. As with Melania the Elder and Melania the Younger, so too with Paula, monastic vocation involved separation from family, a separation that generated much disapproval.

Like journeys of the two Melanias, Paula and Eustochium's voyage centered around visiting monks and monastic centers. Before arriving in Palestine

---

69. See discussion of these Roman aristocratic women and their monastic lives in Dunn, *Emergence of Monasticism*, 46–56.

70. Jerome *Ep.* 39, to Paula. For an excellent discussion of Jerome's views on monasticism, particularly female monasticism, see Adalbert de Vogüé, *Histoire Littéraire du Mouvement Monastique dans L'Antiquité: Première Partie: Le monachisme Latin de l'épitaphe de sainte Paule à la consécration de Démétriade (404–414)* (Paris, 1998).

71. Jerome's departure from Rome also coincided with the scandal surrounding Pope Damasus. On Paula and Eustochium, see Jo Ann McNamara, "Cornelia's Daughters: Paula and Eustochium," *Women's Studies* 11 (1984): 9–27. See also Kate Cooper, *The Virgin and the Bride: Idealized Womanhood in Late Antiquity* (Cambridge, Mass., 1996), 68–115.

72. "Post virorum monasterium, quod viris tradiderat gubernandum, plures virgines quas e diversis provinciis congregarat, tam nobiles, quam medii, et infimi generis, in tres turmas, monasteriaque divisit." Jerome *Ep.* 108.19.

they went to Egypt to visit monks in Nitria. By 386 they had settled in Bethlehem, where Paula established four monasteries, one for men and three for women.[73] What we know about Paula and her life comes primarily through Jerome, including the eulogy he wrote for her and dedicated to her daughter Eustochium. It opens by stating very clearly Paula's repeated claims concerning her status as a permanent sojourner. According to Jerome, Paula was inspired by the Psalms and would quote them often, especially Psalm 38.13: "For I am a stranger with thee, and a sojourner, as all my fathers were."[74] Jerome used these statements in his eulogy to show that now, in death, this sojourner was finally in her "true home." Paula, he insisted, believed these words from Psalms and, though she had faced much familial and social pressure to remain in Rome, she had chosen a life of travel. After noting her noble lineage and how she decided to devote her life to Christ after the death of her husband, Jerome then recounted Paula's journey to the East.

Jerome appears to portray her journey as a Holy Land pilgrimage, but his description tells us less about her actual journey and motives than it does about Jerome's own interest in linking biblical and classical places to their geographical location, and his interest in the etymology of names. At the beginning of this description he states, "I say nothing of her journey through Coele-Syria and Phoenicia (for it is not my purpose to give you a complete itinerary of her wanderings). I shall name only such places as are mentioned in the sacred books."[75] He did not follow this declaration exactly, since he did digress at various points and refer to important political and mythological sites, such as the site where Andromeda was tied to the rock. Jerome clearly wished to downplay any travel undertaken outside his influence and control.

There is little about Paula's own sentiments in Jerome's description. Her personality does emerge, however, in a few of his vignettes, such as that of the ecstatic Paula, who when she arrived at the Holy Sepulcher in Jerusalem,

73. "Advena sum et peregrina sicut omnes patres mei" Ps. 38.13, quoted in Jerome *Ep.* 108.1. The fifth-century Spanish monk Bachiarius used the same line in his defense of his own wandering life. "Peregrinus ego sum, sicut omnes patres mei." Bachiarius *Libellus de fide, PL* 20:1024.

74. "Omitto Coeles Syriae, et Phoenicis iter (neque enim hodoeporicon eius disposui scribere): ea tantum loca nominabo, quae sacris Voluminibus continentur." Jerome *Ep.* 108.8, translation in Petersen, *Handmaids of the Lord,* 131.

75. "Et ipsum corporis locum in quo Dominus jacuerat, quasi sitiens desideratas aquas, fideli ore lambebat." Jerome *Ep.* 108.9.

had an immediate physical reaction: she threw herself to the floor, kissed the stone that had covered the entrance of the tomb, and finally "she even licked with her mouth the very spot on which the Lord's body had lain, like one athirst for the river which he had longed for."[76] Egeria, whose own journey was contemporary with Paula's, described similar physical reactions of many at this same holy site.

Paula, like Egeria, was concerned with visiting and meeting holy people, though Jerome downplayed this concern in his account. She spent ten days on Cyprus visiting the monk Epiphanius. While there she made a tour of all the monasteries on the island "and left, so far as her means allowed, substantial relief for the brothers whom love of the holy man had brought thither from all parts of the world."[77] In Jerusalem, after her ecstatic experience, she once again visited monks and distributed money to them and to the poor.[78] The exchange of money, through donations to the monks, was another form of physical manifestation of the connection between Paula's spiritual experience and those of the monks. The money supported the spiritual exercises of the monks while also physically connecting Paula to the monks. The monetary donation also provided a tangible connection between the woman traveler and her monastic hosts.

Paula did not, however, end her travels in the Holy Land. Jerome wrote that she continued to Egypt, a province Egeria also visited. Her reasons for going to Egypt were obvious: to visit the monks, especially those of Nitria.[79] Paula visited every cell, according to Jerome, giving gifts to all. It was here that she wanted to settle, but although she was invited to do so by the monks, Jerome dissuaded her. Paula eventually settled in Bethlehem, Jerome's own home. Jerome plays up his influence on Paula, yet through his account we can also see her making her own decisions.

Jerome wrote that Paula gave all she possessed to her children and family members remaining in Rome, but he could not have meant all her wealth in every form, for during her travels she gave many gifts, both to monks

76. Egeria *Itin.* 37.111.

77. "Nam omnia illius regionis lustrans monasteria, prout potuit, refrigeria sumptuum fratribus dereliquit, quos amor sancti viri de toto illuc orbe conduxerat." Jerome *Ep.* 108.7.

78. Ibid., 108.10.

79. "Quod cum vidisset, occurrente sibi sancto et venerabili Episcopo Isidoro Confessore, et turbis innumerabilibus Monachoruum, ex quibus multos Sacerdotalis et Leviticus sublimabat gradus." Ibid., 108.14.

and to the poor.[80] Her wealth also aided in her establishment, not only of many monasteries in Bethlehem, but also a large guesthouse catering to the needs of travelers, so that "they might find the welcome which Mary and Joseph had missed."[81] As a frequent traveler herself, Paula realized the practical benefits of a guesthouse, and by its construction she was able to help other religious travelers coming through Bethlehem.

There is another source of information on Paula's attitude toward travel and toward the city of Jerusalem. In the vast collection of Jerome's letters, there is one written to Marcella, a Roman noblewoman, from Paula and Eustochium.[82] The letter urges Marcella to make the journey to Jerusalem and join with Paula and Eustochium. It describes the biblical history of the city and counters the assertion that it was cursed, since it was the site of the Crucifixion.[83] But Marcella's purpose in coming to the Holy Land, the letter stressed, was not primarily to see the places in which past biblical events occurred, but instead to connect with the present sanctity of the city, a sanctity manifested in its holy inhabitants. In Jerusalem Marcella would be surrounded by monks and virgins, and the letter ends with an emotional description of what the Paula and her daughter Eustochium would do once Marcella arrived in Jerusalem:

> Will the time never come when a breathless messenger shall bring the news that our dear Marcella has reached the shores of Palestine, and when every band of monks and every troop of virgins shall unite in a song of welcome? In our excitement we are already hurrying to meet you: without waiting for a vehicle, we hasten off

80. "Fateor, nulla sic amavit filios, quibus antequam proficisceretur: cuncta largita est: exhaeredans se in terra, ut haereditatem inveniret in coelo." Ibid., 108.6.

81. "donec exstrueret cellulas, ac monasteria, et diversorum peregrinorum juxta viam conderet mansiones, in qua Maria et Joseph hospitium non invenerant." Ibid., 108.14.

82. Ibid., 46, from Paula and Eustochium to Marcella. Though many have believed that this letter was written by Jerome himself on behalf of Paula and her daughter, there is no strong evidence for this. Peter Dronke believes the letter was written by Paula and Eustochium, not Jerome. He writes that some who believe that it was written by Jerome even state that the style and content contrast with his other letter. See Dronke, *Women Writers,* 17. Until new information comes to light, therefore, the letter should be considered as having been written by Paula and Eustochium, as it is labeled. Indeed, a comparison of this letter with Jerome's letter to Paulinus of Nola, Ep. 58, urging him not to travel to the Holy Land, further reinforces this view. Also see the discussion in Limor, "Reading Sacred Space," 6–7.

83. "Maledictam terram nominant, quod cruorem Domini hauserit." Paula and Eustochium [Jerome] *Ep.* 46.8.

at once on foot. . . . Will the day never come when we shall together enter the Saviour's cave, and together weep in the sepulchre of the Lord with His sister and with His mother? Then shall we touch with our lips the wood of the cross, and rise in prayer and resolve upon the Mount of Olives with the ascending Lord.[84]

Fabiola, mentioned briefly at the beginning of this book, was another Roman friend of Paula, Eustochium, and Jerome. She undertook her journey of monastic travel in direct response to her changing marital situation. Fabiola had divorced her first husband and remarried another man, a course of events that greatly upset Jerome. He did not criticize her for the divorce, as he described Fabiola's first husband as an "evil man," but he did disapprove of her remarriage. Only after her second husband died did Fabiola confess the error of her second marriage and make public penance in the Lateran Basilica in Rome. She then embarked on a new life of charity, kindness, and asceticism. In Rome she supported the poor, the sick, clergy, and of course monks, both male and female, with generous donations. "What monastery was there which her purse did not aid?"[85] Jerome asked rhetorically. Eventually Fabiola began a life of travel and monastic pursuits.

Predictably, Fabiola sailed to Jerusalem, though Jerome stated that this was "much to everyone's surprise."[86] She spent time with Jerome in Bethlehem, but while he looked for a suitable place for her to stay, she decided to return to Rome. Jerome had his own explanation for why she left, but in giving it he inadvertently revealed what may have been the underlying reason for her desire to continue traveling. He wrote that she lived out of her "traveling baggage and was a stranger (*peregrina*) in every land."[87] Fabiola was apparently traveling as a form of religious and ascetic expression, voluntarily living a religious life of homelessness and exile. She had not taken

---

84. "O quando tempus illud adveniet, cum anhelus nuntium viator apportet, Marcellam nostram ad Palaestinae littus appulsam: et toti Monachorum chori, tota virginum agmina concrepabunt? Obviam iam gestimus occurrere: et non expectato vehiculo, concitum pedibus ferre corpus. . . . Ergo ne erit illa dies, quando nobis liceat speluncam Salvatoris intrare? In sepulcro Domini flere (a) cum sorore, flere cum matre? Crucis deinde lignum lambere, et in Oliveti monte cum ascendente Domino, voto et animo sublevari?" Ibid., 46.12.

85. "Quod Monasterium non illius opibus sustentatum est?" Jerome *Ep.* 77.6.

86. "Unde repente et contra opinionem omnium." Ibid., 77.7.

87. "Illa, quae tota in sarcinis erat, et in omni urbe peregrina." Ibid., 77.8.

Jerome's advice to stay in Bethlehem, but had instead followed her own path, resuming her travels in 394, eventually returning to her home in Rome a few years later, where she remained until her death.

Fabiola represents a certain model of the female monastic wanderer—a widow with control over her life and wealth, beginning a religious life through travel and patronage, both in her home city of Rome and beyond. Eventually, like Egeria, she would return to her home after years of travel, bringing with her the fruits of her voyages. She was a *peregrina*, a stranger, a kind and generous stranger. This was not necessarily a life that Jerome and other church authorities approved of, but it was clearly a pattern of behavior, encompassing ascetic and monastic impulses, that responded to needs and pressures felt by women in particular situations.

It seems that Jerome willingly served as a node in the network of spiritual travelers, but other evidence reveals that his interest in Paula, Eustochium, and Fabiola centered on their permanent residence near his own home in the Holy Land, rather than in their leading lives of monastic travel and visiting. In a letter written in 411 to Rusticus, a young man who had just embarked on a monastic life, Jerome offered the following advice: "Do not imitate those who leave their own relatives and run after strange women. Their infamy is plain; for under the pretext of piety they really seek illicit intercourse."[88] In the same letter Jerome warned Rusticus to beware of women who sought his company for spiritual reasons: "I know some women of ripe age who in many cases take their pleasure with young freedmen, calling them their spiritual children, and gradually so far overcoming any sense of shame as to allow themselves under this pretense of motherhood all the license of marriage."[89] Jerome's criticism of women associating with monks and visiting holy people included an attack on Melania the Elder, of whom he had a very low opinion. In a letter to Furia, yet another Roman matron he corresponded with, he mentioned seeing an unnamed woman, perhaps Melania, traveling in the Holy Land with a disreputable entourage.[90] She was showy and held

---

88. "Nec aliorum imiteris exemplum, qui relinquunt suas et alienas appetunt, quorum dedecus in propatulo est sub nominibus pietatis quaerentium suspecta consortia." Ibid., 125.6, to Rusticus the monk.

89. "Novi ego quasdam iam maturioris aetatis et plerasque generis libertini adulescentibus delectari et filios quaerere spiritales paulatimque pudore superato per ficta matrum nomina erumpere in licentiam maritalem." Ibid.

90. At this time Jerome had had a major disagreement with Rufinus (Melania's spiritual adviser) and had severed his relationship with him.

"elaborate dinners" in high style, Jerome wrote, stingingly calling her "a fitting bride for Nero."[91]

Jerome attacked the very desire to travel to the Holy Land in a letter to Paulinus of Nola.[92] Paulinus had written to Jerome in the hopes of coming to the Holy Land. In 409 he wrote that "the principal motive which draws people to Jerusalem is the desire to see and touch the places where Christ was present in body, and as a consequence to recite, 'We will worship at the place where his feet stood [Ps. 132.7].'. . . Our religion prompts us to see the places to which Christ came."[93] Paulinus's interest in the Holy Land centered on the manner in which physical places and the objects could confirm what the Bible said: "These lifeless objects which can confirm the truths of long ago."[94] Paulinus's emphasis on the physicality of the holy and the inherent sanctity of a holy place must have irritated Jerome; far from encouraging Paulinus, as he had Paula, Eustochium, and Fabiola, Jerome attempted in every way to dissuade him from making the journey. He cited numerous reasons, including the urban dangers of crime, prostitution, and overcrowding, present even in the holy city of Jerusalem, as well as Paulinus's duty to his wife Therasia, with whom he lived in a chaste relationship.[95] Jerome also made the case that it was not necessary to travel to a holy place in order to lead a proper monastic life: "I assure you that nothing is lacking to your faith although you have not seen Jerusalem and that I am none the better for living where I do."[96] Jerome realized, however, that his argument was rather hypocritical: "In speaking thus I am not laying myself open to a charge of inconsistency or condemning the course which I have myself taken. It is not, I believe, for nothing that I, like Abraham, have left my home and people. But I do not presume to limit God's omnipotence or to restrict to a narrow strip of earth Him whom the heaven cannot contain."[97]

91. "Vidimus nuper ignominiosum per totum Orientem volitasse; et aetas et cultus et habitus et incessus, indiscreta societas, exquisitae epulae, regius apparatus Neronis et Sardanapalli nuptias loquebantur." Jerome Ep. 54.13.

92. Jerome Ep. 58, to Paulinus, written around 395.

93. Paulinus of Nola Ep. 49.

94. Ibid.

95. Jerome Ep. 58.4 and 6.

96. "Videlicet ne quidquam fidei tuae deesse putes, quia Jerosolymam non vidisti: nec nos idcirco meliores aestimes, quod huius loci habitaculo fruimur." Ibid., 58.4.

97. "Neque vero hoc dicens, memetipsum inconstantiae redarguo, damnoque quod facio: ut frustra videar ad exemplum Abraham, et meos et patriam reliquisse: sed non audeo Dei omnipotentiam angusto fine concludere, et coarctare parvo terrae loco, quem non capit coelum." Ibid., 58.3.

Although Jerome's argument concerning his own presence in the Holy Land appears rather weak, he does attack the notion of an inherent holiness of place. Jerome linked the holiness of a location to the holiness of those living and worshiping there, "the spots which witnessed the crucifixion and the resurrection profit only those who bear their several crosses, who day by day rise again with Christ, and who thus show themselves worthy of an abode so holy."[98] This association is similar to Egeria's notion that locations express sanctity through their holy inhabitants, the living *sancti* with whom she visited.

Jerome also emphasized that *locus* was unimportant when compared to the manner of one's life. The monastic life, which Paulinus and his wife had chosen for themselves, was the perfect life. Jerome provided a long list of monks, including Antony and Hilarion, who had never set foot in the physical city of Jerusalem.[99] Heavenly Jerusalem was the city that was to be sought by the perfect Christian: "What is praiseworthy is not to have been at Jerusalem but to have lived a good life while there. The city which we are to praise and to seek is not that which has slain the prophets and shed the blood of Christ, but that . . . in which he rejoices to have his citizenship with the righteous."[100] Jerome thus actively dissuaded Paulinus from making his own journey to the East. Jerome agreed that the monk should cut himself off from society and from his home, but he advocated creating one's own holy place, and not making the journey to Jerusalem. What is missing from Jerome's letter is any mention whatsoever of the many monasteries and monks in Jerusalem. In his portrayal of the city in his letter to Paulinus, he makes it appear as if no one was able to lead a monastic life there. There is no mention of Paula, Eustochium, or any of the other Roman women whom he had persuaded to travel to the East. Paulinus would have to be satisfied with the relic of the cross given to him by Melania the Elder.

Other evidence of Western women travelers to the East can be found in works by Eastern authors. Cyril of Scythopolis briefly mentioned a female stranger in the Holy Land who built monasteries. In his *Life of Theognius the Bishop*, Cyril described a woman named Flavia who, in 454, had established

98. "Et Crucis igitur et Resurrectionis loca prosunt his, qui portant crucem suam; et cum Christo resurgunt quotidie; qui dignos se tanto exhibent habitaculo." Ibid.

99. Ibid., 58.5.

100. "Non Jerosolymis fuisse, sed Jerosolymis bene vixisse, laudandum est. Illa expetenda, illa laudanda est civitas, non quae occidit Prophetas, et Christi sanguinem fudit; sed . . . in qua se municipatum cum justis laetatur habere." Ibid., 58.2.

a monastery on the Mount of Olives dedicated to the martyr Julian. Theognius entered this monastery after Flavia first "tested him for a considerable time and found him reliable and virtuous."[101] Flavia, with her obviously Latin name, perhaps came from Rome, as did so many other women traveling to Jerusalem at the time. She had come to the Holy Land to establish her monastery, but was forced to return to her homeland, "because of the needs of the church she had built."[102] She never returned to Jerusalem, and so Theognius was forced to take over the administration of the monastery, which turned out to be too much for the monk, who then fled into the desert.

In 412 Palladius, a pupil of Evagrius Ponticus, wrote an account of his travels and particularly of the holy people he met along the way.[103] His *Lausiac History,* so called due to its dedication to Lausus, a court official of Emperor Theodosius II, is an eyewitness account of a wide variety of monks, male and female. Women, in particular, both as travelers and as monks, play a special role in his work. Palladius began his account with a description of how he obtained his evidence. He wrote that he "traveled on foot and looked into every cave and cabin of the monks of the desert with all accuracy and pious motive. I wrote down some of the things I saw, and also some accounts I heard from the holy fathers. It is all in this book—the contests of the great men, and of the women, too, more like men in their nature than the name implies, thanks to their hope in Christ."[104] It is as if he himself was surprised by the number of holy women he had encountered and was obliged to include them in his account to Lausus. He accorded these holy women, whom he identified as "manly," the spiritual equals of holy men.

The *Lausiac History* not only reveals that Palladius was a religious traveler (he repeatedly emphasized his actual pious journey to the dwellings of the monks, revealing that he had "traversed 106 towns" during his lifetime) but also provides evidence of other monks who themselves lived itinerant lives. Lausus had requested an account of his travels, not so much of the places as of the people, "both male and female," whom Palladius had met.[105] The purpose of the book is to allow Lausus to travel through reading: "Each

101. Cyril of Scythopolis *Life of Our Father Theognius the Bishop* 241.20, in *Lives of the Monks of Palestine by Cyril of Scythopolis,* ed. R. M. Price (Kalamazoo, Mich., 1991), 269.

102. Ibid., 242, 269.

103. Meyer, "Palladius as Biographer and Autobiographer."

104. *HL,* Prol., 3. English translation from W. K. Lowther Clarke, trans., *The Lausiac History of Palladius* (New York, 1918), 40.

105. Ibid., Prol., 2.

day you will be expecting the departure of your soul."[106] Palladius includes two scriptural quotations about the spiritual departure of the soul and learning from one's elders.[107] These quotations act as justifications for Palladius's own "departure" and travels. To be with Christ was not necessarily to go to the places he walked through, but to travel, meet, and live with monks, his most holy earthly representatives: "I then, O man of God most eager to learn, following in part this precept, have been in contact with many of the saints."[108] Here is the justification of the journey; it is the physical contact with the holy men and women that he seeks. Palladius wanted Lausus to learn from and imitate the *Lausiac History*, but he also urged him to seek out actual meetings with holy men and women.[109] He repeatedly stressed that it was not just holy men, but holy women too who were worthy of encounter. One of the many women he mentioned in his work is Melania.[110]

Palladius frequently stressed the physical dangers of travel and of visiting monks, both those he himself experienced and those experienced by others, including the story of a woman traveler named Poemenia.[111] While Poemenia and her entourage were in Alexandria, a fight broke out between her servants and the townspeople that resulted in both a murder and the bishop of the city being thrown into the river.[112] Palladius was quite critical of Poemenia, but he had nothing but praise for Paula, even though he did not care for her spiritual guide, Jerome.[113]

---

106. *HL*, Prol., 3.

107. "It is good to depart and be with Christ." Phil. 1.23. "Prepare thy works for thy departure and be ready in thy field." Prov. 24.27. "Miss not the discourse of the aged, for they also learned of their fathers." Ecclus. 8.9. *HL*, Prol., 4.

108. *HL*, Prol., 5.

109. "But go near a bright window and seek encounters with holy men and women, in order that by their help you may be able to see clearly also your own heart as it were a closely-written book, being able by comparison to discern your own slackness or neglect." Ibid., Prol., 15.

110. Melania is briefly mentioned in ibid., 5.9; also 18.28, in which she receives a fleece from Macarius of Alexandria. Longer accounts of Melania can be found at *HL* 4.6.1–5 and 54.1–7.

111. His visit to John of Lycopolis was undertaken during the Nile's flood season; it took over eighteen days journeying both by foot and by boat, and Palladius became very ill during the journey. Ibid., 35.4.

112. Ibid., 35.15.

113. Palladius apparently learned about Jerome through words whispered in his ear by the monk Posidonius. He described him as, "a certain Jerome, a priest, distinguished Latin writer and cultivated scholar as he was, showed qualities of temper so disastrous that they threw into the shade his splendid achievements." Ibid., 36.6.

In the fifth century, Melania the Younger's life of travel became a model for the empress Eudocia, wife of Theodosius II, in her own journeys to the Holy Land. Eudocia, born Athenaïs, was the daughter of a pagan sophist named Leontius from Athens. There she received a good education and was known as a writer of poems and stories. She converted to Christianity and changed her name when selected, in 421, to be the wife of Theodosius II by his powerful older sister Pulcheria.[114] It was a difficult marriage, and Eudocia decided to make a trip to Jerusalem in 437 shortly after meeting Melania the Younger in Constantinople.[115] According to Gerontius, one of the reasons she went to the Holy Land was to visit with Melania the Younger.[116] Her contemporaries referred to her as the "New Helena," and perhaps her voyage, too, can in some ways be understood as one of imperial patronage. She visited various cities along the way, including Antioch, and she endowed many churches, including a church to St. Stephen in Jerusalem. Eudocia returned from Jerusalem with the powerful relics of St. Stephen, which would later cure her of an illness.

The empress's second visit to the Holy Land clearly had a different purpose. A rivalry between Eudocia and her sister-in-law came to a head in 442, when Pulcheria falsely convinced Theodosius II that Eudocia had been unfaithful to him.[117] For this she was exiled, an exile she decided to spend in the Holy Land. She became embroiled for some time in the Nestorian controversy through her association with Theodosius, the patriarch of Jerusalem.[118] She later shifted her allegiance, after coming under the influence of the monk Euthymius.[119] Most of her time was spent in Bethlehem, where she began to build monasteries, donate money to churches, and keep company with monks and clerics. Cyril of Scythopolis wrote the following about her charitable works: "Blessed Eudocia built a huge number of churches to Christ, and more monasteries and homes for the poor and elderly than I am able to count."[120] Eudocia passed the rest of her life in Bethlehem, dying in the year 460.

---

114. See Kenneth G. Holum, *Theodosian Empresses: Women and Imperial Dominion in Late Antiquity* (Berkeley and Los Angeles, 1982).

115. This was also the same year that her daughter Licinia Eudoxia was married off to the Western emperor Valentinian III, son of Galla Placidia, and moved from Constantinople to Rome.

116. Gerontius *Life of Melania*, chap. 57, pp. 70–71.

117. See Holum, *Theodosian Empresses.*

118. Cyril of Scythopolis *Life of Euthymius* 41, 20, in *Lives of the Monks*, 38.

119. Ibid., 49, 45.

120. Ibid., 53.5, 49.

Helena and Eudocia, because of their rank, cannot be easily placed within a framework of traditional Holy Land pilgrimage, nor within that of monastic wandering. They were powerful patrons, gift-givers, and founders of important churches. Though their voyages bear some similarity to the voyages of other late antique women, these similarities are superficial. They are perhaps better viewed as the precursors of someone like the powerful sixth-century Augusta Theodora, wife of the emperor Justinian. Theodora, patron of Monophysite monks, was frequently represented, verbally and visually, as being on an equal footing with her husband, such as in the famous mosaics at San Vitale in Ravenna, where she is depicted with an imperial retinue as she presents a golden chalice to the altar of San Vitale. The hem of her cloak is decorated with images of the three magi who strike a similar pose as they present their gifts. Gary Vikan has shown that representations of the magi can be understood as images of pilgrims *par excellence*.[121] The magi, like Helena, Eudocia, and Theodora, are gift-giving, regal pilgrims, who bestow magnificent gifts that hint at their vast riches. The fifth-century representation of the Adoration of the Magi from the triumphal arch of Santa Maria Maggiore seems to represent an imperial audience, with Mary dressed as an *augusta* and the Christ child seated on a huge jeweled throne.[122] Images of the magi are by far the most popular motif on *ampullae* and other pilgrimage *eulogiae*.[123] Less popular but nonetheless ubiquitous on holy land *ampullae* are scenes of the women approaching the tomb of Christ, and it is precisely this motif that seems more related to the women travelers of this chapter. In a sense the women at the tomb, a Resurrection motif, yet clearly also a symbol of religious travel, can be seen as a representation of women's experience of travel to the holy city. These women are witnesses to the Resurrection through their experience and interactions with Christ as a holy man. Egeria, Marthana, Paula, Eustochium, Fabiola, the Melanias, Mary, and Euphemia all traveled and experienced not only the *terra sancta* but actual holy people. If we consider the *ampullae* from the Monza treasury, which were originally gifts for the Ostrogothic queen Theodelinda, the *ampullae* could symbolize

121. Vikan specifically states that they were representations of overland travelers. Vikan, "Guided by Land and Sea," 80.

122. Beckwith, *Early Christian and Byzantine Art,* 38.

123. Vikan, "Guided by Land and Sea."

her own spiritual journey to the Holy Land through her possession of these special objects. Could these two typological representations of pilgrims, the holy women at the tomb and the adoration of the magi, speak to different sorts of religious travel? Was one more "female" and concerned more with experience while the other was imperial, more "male" and concerned with gift-giving and patronage? One way of getting at the answers to these questions is by looking at the impact women travelers had on Jerusalem, as well as the role of the experience of Jerusalem in their construction of their journeys.

WOMEN TRAVELERS AND THE CITY OF JERUSALEM

The emergence of Jerusalem as a Christian holy city was not inevitable, nor was "holiness" inherent in the city since the apostolic age. A conjunction of forces was necessary to create a Christian Jerusalem as a place to be physically experienced. Scholars have pointed to the role of Constantine's patronage expressed especially through a building campaign and by the efforts of Jerusalem's fourth- and fifth-century bishops in promoting the city as a special Christian site.[124] While these efforts at creating a holy place are not in dispute, the role of travelers, particularly women travelers, in shaping the city as a holy place to be venerated and visited, has not been addressed. The Christian sanctification of Jerusalem came about through a combination of forces. Beginning in the fourth century, travelers began to shape the city and holy places through their visits and by their patronage. This patronage sometimes involved providing funds for building new churches, but women visitors to Jerusalem and its surroundings primarily marked their visits through monastic patronage and by building monasteries. Women travelers also expressed their support of religious travel by building facilities, such as xenodochia, for future visitors. Both of these concerns, monasticism and travel, were central to these women's lives, and thus it is not surprising that these concerns were reflected in their activities in the Holy Land.

---

124. The city found an able advocate in its bishop, Cyril, who embellished the holy places and, like Constantine and Helena, encouraged monasticism within the city, thus furthering its sacrality and improving its status in comparison with that of Caesarea. Walker, "Eusebius, Cyril and the Holy Places."

Unlike pagans and Jews, early Christians did not consider *place* itself inherently sacred.[125] The gospels undermine the holiness of the Temple by stressing Jesus as temple and sacrifice. Some Christians rejected as Jewish the idea that a specific place contained within itself sacral qualities. Travel to holy places was also part of Jewish practice and had a cognate in the polytheistic Greco-Roman world in travel to oracles and healing sites. In early Christian eschatological beliefs, Jerusalem was not a physical place to be visited, but instead a manifestation of heaven. The holy city was the heavenly Jerusalem, an argument made forcefully in the third century by Origen.[126] Eusebius had originally followed in Origen's footsteps in his opinion of Jerusalem. His interpretation of Isaiah, concerning the eventual restoration of Jerusalem, was that the reference was not to the physical city, as the Jews believed, but rather to a "Jerusalem above which is the mother of us all."[127] Eusebius, however, would begin to change his position, from the time of his association with Constantine.[128]

Christianization of the city began at some distance from the ruined Temple Mount, the most prominent physical feature of Jerusalem.[129] Constantine's Holy Sepulcher complex, built on his orders between 325 and 335,

125. "In Christian eyes holiness was not inherent in place, it could nonetheless be achieved by Christian ritual and by regular worship. . . . for many Christians, space, the physical environment in which one lived, was itself neutral." Sabine MacCormack, "Loca Sancta: The Organization of Sacred Topography in Late Antiquity," in *The Blessings of Pilgrimage,* ed. Robert Ousterhout (Urbana, Ill., 1990), 17. For a discussion of pilgrimage in relation to holy space, see Dupront, *Du Sacré*; Bernard Valade, ed., *Saint Jacques de Compostelle: La Quête du Sacré* (Turnhout, 1985); and Frankfurter, *Pilgrimage and Holy Space.*

126. Combating Jewish interpretation, Origen promoted a spiritual and allegorical interpretation of scripture, especially in relation to the promise of the Holy Land and an earthly Jerusalem as a religious center. See Wilken, *The Land Called Holy,* 65–78.

127. Eusebius *Commentary on Isaiah* 2.16.15–16, quoted in Wilken, *The Land Called Holy,* 80.

128. On his changing position, see Walker, "Eusebius, Cyril and the Holy Places" and *Holy City, Holy Places.* See also Barnes, *Constantine and Eusebius.*

129. Hadrian had a religious structure built on the platform, the remnants of which the Bordeaux itinerant described, but Constantine did not build there, perhaps because of the strong Jewish presence in the city and the overtly Jewish identity of the platform. "Two statues of Hadrian" on the Temple Mount were possibly remnants from a temple to Capitoline Jupiter and the imperial cult temple of Hadrian. The space was not Christianized until the early twelfth century, long after the Muslims had built the Dome of the Rock and the al-Aqsa mosque, thus claiming the platform as an Islamic holy place. The Bordeaux itinerant also wrote that he saw "a pierced stone which the Jews come and anoint each year," revealing that even in the fourth century the Jews continued to venerate the holy site of the Temple. "Est et non longe de statuas lapis pertusus, ad quem veniunt Iudaei singulis annis et unguent eum." *Itin. Burd.* 591.

was located at the very center of the city. Constantine never visited the city but instead sent his mother Helena in his stead. Egeria refers to the basilica as being built by Constantine and decorated during Helena's visit, perhaps referring to Helena's bestowal of gifts to the complex.[130] Constantine's imperial patronage, through the establishment of new churches, began the first steps toward the physical Christianization of Jerusalem.[131]

The Holy Sepulcher complex was the premier location for Christian visitors, including women, to the city. Egeria supplies our best description of the complex and the liturgical organization of the space. Her realization that the dedication festival of the Holy Sepulcher occurred on the same date as both the finding of the True Cross and Solomon's dedication of the ancient Temple reinforced her conviction of the holiness of the place.[132] It revealed a temporal link of sanctity between the past and present within Jerusalem.[133] The Easter liturgy involved a procession not only within the huge Holy Sepulcher complex but also through the city.[134] In this way the Easter liturgy in Jerusalem united the entire city and claimed Christian holy space. The elaborate processions were led by the bishop and included monks, virgins, clergy, laity, and travelers like Egeria. During Easter week, after the celebration of Mass in the church, the congregation moved outdoors

130. Egeria *Itin.* 25.1. See the discussion in Pohlsander, *Helena*, 91.

131. In reference to Jerusalem as a center of Christian pilgrimage he writes, "The fourth-century Holy City that Constantine endowed was an invention from whole cloth, constructed to give visible topography to the legends, sacred books, and developing liturgy." Frankfurter, *Pilgrimage and Holy Space*, 15.

132. "Et ideo propter hoc ita ordinatum est, ut quando primum sanctae ecclesiae suprascriptae consecrabantur, ea dies esset, qua crux Domini fuerat inuenta, ut simul omni laetitia eadem die celebrarentur. Et hoc per scripturas sanctas inuenitur, quod ea dies sit enceniarum, qua et sanctus Salomon consummata domo Dei, quam edificauerat, steterit ante altarium Dei et orauerit, sicut scriptum est in libris Paralipomenon." Egeria *Itin.* 48.2. See also MacCormack, "Loca Sancta," 25. Significantly, perhaps, Egeria does not mention Helena in relation to the *invenio* of the True Cross, but Egeria rarely gives us names in her account. She does not name any of the bishops she meets with on her journey, for instance. Egeria is more interested in the fact of the finding of the True Cross and its veneration in the Holy Sepulcher complex.

133. Festivals and holy days could serve to define sanctity as powerfully as buildings could. Much discussion of festivals found in pilgrim guides and in the accounts of travelers to the city stressed the significance of the proper location *and* time of their celebration. The coincidence of proper time and place was crucial in establishing the sanctity of the event.

134. "Facta ergo missa in ecclesia maiore, id est ad Martyrium, deducitur episcopus cum omnis ad Anastase, et ibi completis quae consuetudo est." Egeria *Itin.* 30.3. On Egeria and her description of the Holy Sepulcher, see Pasquale Testini, "Egeria e il S. Sepolcro di Gerusalemme," in *Atti del Convegno Internazionale sulla Peregrinatio Egeriae, nel centenario della pubblicazione del Codex Aretinus 405 (già Aretinus VI, 3)*, 215–30 (Arezzo, 1990). On liturgical processions in Jerusalem, see Baldovin, *Urban Character of Christian Worship*.

through the interior atrium toward the Anastasis. On Good Friday, the bishop led a procession through the entire city, ending at the Holy Sepulcher complex. A throne for the bishop was set up in front of the rock of the Calvary, and the highlight of the ceremony occurred when attendants brought out the relic of the True Cross for all to venerate. The faithful, including the catechumens, each in turn kissed the holy relic.[135] Egeria movingly wrote about this event. "When the sixth hour is at hand, everyone goes before the Cross, regardless of whether it is raining or whether it is hot. This place has no roof, for it is a sort of very large and beautiful courtyard lying between the Cross and the Anastasis. The people are so clustered together there that it is impossible for anything to be opened."[136]

During Pentecost, processions linked Jerusalem to locations just outside its walls. Although the Mount of Olives was outside the city walls, it functioned as an extension of the religious topography of the city, especially during holy festivals. The Pentecost procession, according to Egeria, lasted all day and involved all the Christians of Jerusalem. At dawn, the people congregated at the Anastasis, the location of the tomb in the Holy Sepulcher complex. The bishop of the city read passages on the Resurrection, then the crowd shifted into the adjacent Martyrium, the basilica built by Constantine, for the liturgy. Singing hymns, the procession then moved to Mount Sion where they celebrated the Eucharist and listened to passages from Acts. After a short break for dinner, the congregation met together on the Mount of Olives, where they heard passages about the Ascension. They entered and exited the cave itself, all along singing hymns. Slowly, the crowd descended the hill and into the city. "Then all the people without exception come down from there singing hymns, everyone together with the bishop singing hymns and antiphons proper to the day itself. And in this fashion they make their way slowly and easily to the Martyrium. When they reach the city gate, it is already night, and around two hundred candles are brought out for the people."[137] The procession entered once more into the Anastasis, and again to the southwestern corner of the city, to Sion. By this time, as it was close to midnight, the crowd dispersed to their homes.

135. "Quia consuetudo est ut unus et unus omnis populus veniens, tam fideles quam cathecumini, acclinantes se ad mensam, osculentur sanctum lignum et pertranseant." Egeria *Itin.* 37.2.

136. "At ubi autem sexta hora se fecerit, sic itur ante Crucem, sive pluvia sive estus sit, quia ipse locus subdivanus est, id est quasi atrium valde grandem et pulchrum satis, quod est inter Cruce et Anastase. Ibi ergo omnis populus se colliget, ita ut nec aperiri possit." Ibid., 37.4.

137. Ibid., 43.6–7.

Egeria emphasized how the procession not only took the entire day, but it also made a circuit around the city and to the Mount of Olives. She wrote that the ceremonies exhausted many, but that it was the walking, combined with the reading and visiting the holy places, that created an aura of sanctity. Movement brought the holy places of the city together. With the aid of the reading of scripture, the congregation was able to commune, spiritually and physically, with the holy places. Liturgical processions not only united the Christian residents and visitors, but they also helped to claim holy space in the city. It was through the movements of people walking, praying, and remembering from site to site, that holy places were created.

Because of its collection of Christ-related relics, the early church of Holy Sion was an important point of the Jerusalem circuit even though it was situated outside the walls in the far southwestern corner of the city. It was in this church that travelers could have a "physical" encounter with Christ and his torment through touching the imprints of his hands and the stains of his blood on the column of the scourging.[138] Egeria often visited this church, which she associated with the apostles.[139] Though she did not specifically mention the column, later travelers mentioned seeing the imprints of Jesus' palms and fingers on the column: "And you can see the way he clung to it when he was being scourged as if the marks were in wax. His arm, hands, and fingers clove to it, it shows even today. Also he made on it the impression of his whole face, chin, nose, and eyes as if it had been wax."[141] Paula, too, had visited this church and had seen the column, "stained with the Lord's blood."[141] Beginning in the eighth century, this church would come to be associated with Mary and her death.[142]

138. The Bordeaux itinerant, traveling in 333, who saw "the column at which they fell on Christ and scourged him," was the first to mention this relic. "Et columna adhuc ibi est, in qua Christum flagellis ceciderunt." *Itin. Burd.* 592. In the later Middle Ages a column of the scourging was set up in Rome at the Church of Santa Prassede; it currently resides in the Chapel of Zeno in the same church.

139. Egeria *Itin.* 43.3.

140. Theodosius *De situ terrae sanctae* 7.

141. Jerome *Ep.* 108.9.4.

142. Epiphanius wrote in the eighth century that the church on Mount Sion was the site of the death of the Virgin Mary and contained the room in which the Last Supper took place. His work is based on an earlier, perhaps mid-seventh century, core of material. He wrote after the city was held by the Arabs, but does not mention the Dome of the Rock, though he does note a "hanging rock" in the center of the Temple platform, perhaps the same rock that the Bordeaux itinerant had mentioned. See Epiphanius 3, in Wilkinson, *Jerusalem Pilgrims,* 117. Huneberc also mentioned Sion as the location of the dormition of Mary. Huneberc of Heidenheim, *Vita Willibaldi Episcopi Eichstetensis* 98.1, ed. O. Holder-Egger, *MGH* 15 (1887). By the twelfth century,

The largest post-Constantinian building project in Jerusalem was the construction of the Church of St. Stephen the Protomartyr, built under the patronage of the empress Eudocia. In December of 415, a priest named Lucian claimed to have discovered the body of Stephen, just a few miles from Jerusalem. John, the bishop of Jerusalem immediately promoted the new cult, and the body was originally placed in Holy Sion. Eudocia aided in the foundation of the Church of St. Stephen in 438 during her first trip to Jerusalem.[143] This massive complex, located just to the north of St. Stephen's gate, was finally completed and dedicated in 460, when the tomb of Stephen was moved from Holy Sion. Like Helena and the True Cross, Eudocia's name would be forever associated with this church, which would eventually contain her tomb.

The greatest impact women travelers had on the landscape of Jerusalem was on the Mount of Olives, the traditional spot of the Ascension and the supposed future location of the Last Judgment.[144] The Mount of Olives, just outside the city walls, lies to the east of the Temple platform, with the valley of Kidron separating it from the city. It was a steep-sided hill, slightly higher than Jerusalem itself, with stairways instead of streets leading to the summit. The cave on the Mount associated both with the teaching of the disciples and with the Ascension was one of the earliest known Christian sites in Jerusalem, and throughout the city's history it remained one of the most important.[145] Constantine included the Mount of Olives as part of his Jerusalem building campaign. As early as 333, the Eleona Church was described as having been built on Constantine's command.[147] In the late

---

Christians associated Mount Sion with the Virgin Mary: "Sion ergo mons, ad meridiem extra muros civitatis ex maxima parte constitutus, ecclesiam dominae nostrae sanctae Mariae." Theoderich, *Guide to the Holy Land,* trans. Aubrey Stewart (New York, 1986), 22. Latin text from Baldi, *Enchiridion.* Recently the Church of the Dormition was located; see E. Eisenberg, "Jerusalem: The Church of the Dormition," *Excavations and Surveys in Israel* 3 (1984): 47.

143. Holum, *Theodosian Empresses,* 186.

144. Luke 24.50–51. Jesus' teaching of his disciples also occurred on the Mount of Olives. Matt. 24.1–22. The Mount is also mentioned by the tenth-century Hebrew pilgrimage guide as a Jewish festival location. "Ibi iudicaturus est Dominus iustos et peccatores. Et ibi est fluvius parvus qui ignem vomit in consummationem saeculi. Et ibi sunt duos basilicas ubi docebat Christus discipulos suos." *Breviarius de Hierosolyma,* ed. P. Geyer and O. Cuntz, in *Itineraria et alia geographica, CC* 175:109–12.

145. The river is probably the Kidron. The Lord would judge from the summit of the Mount of Olives, looking down into the valley of Kidron.

146. Wilkinson, "Jewish Holy Places," 43.

147. "Inde ascendis in montem Oliveti, ubi Dominus ante passionem apostolos docuit: ibi facta est basilica iussu Constantini." *Itin. Burd.* 595.

fourth century, the Church of the Ascension, also called the Imbomon, was built on the highest point of the Mount of Olives, just above the Constantinian church. It consisted of a rotunda, open to the sky, covering the rock from which Jesus was said to have ascended into heaven.[148] Cyril of Jerusalem emphasized the importance of visiting the Mount of Olives as a location analogous to Golgotha, the site of the crucifixion.[149]

Melania the Elder was among the first women to especially patronize the Mount of Olives. She established both monasteries and a *xenodochium* there. Melania's description of the place left a lasting impression on her friend, Paulinus of Nola, who was never able to visit the Holy Land himself. In a letter to Sulpicius Severus, Paulinus described the Church of the Ascension with an emphasis on the surviving footprints of Jesus.

> In the basilica commemorating the Ascension is the place from which He was taken into a cloud . . . [t]hat single place and no other is said to have been so hallowed with God's footsteps that it has always rejected a covering of marble or paving. The soil throws off in contempt whatever the human hand tries to set there in eagerness to adorn the place. So in the whole area of the basilica this is the sole spot retaining its natural green appearance of turf. The sand is both visible and accessible to worshippers, and preserves the adored imprint of the divine feet in that dust trodden by God, so that one can truly say: "We have adored in the place where His feet stood." [Psalm 131. 7][150]

He sent this overtly "physical" description to Sulpicius Severus along with a fragment of the True Cross, which Melania the Elder had given him.

---

148. J. W. Crowfoot, *Early Churches in Palestine* (London, 1941), 91. A letter on Jerusalem written by Eucherius, bishop of Lyons, to a priest named Faustus living at Lérins provides one of the most important fifth-century sources on the Mount of Olives. Eucherius *Epistola ad Faustum de locis sanctis*, CC 175:236–43. The letter dates from around 440.

149. In *Enchiridion Locorum Sanctorum: Documenta S. Evangelii Loca Respicientia*, ed. P. Donatus Baldi (Jerusalem, 1935), 487.

150. "Mirum vero inter haec quod in basilica Ascensionis locus ille tantum de quo in nube susceptus ascendit . . . ita sacratus divinis vestigiis dicitur, ut numquam tegi marmore aut paviri receperit, semper excussis solo respuente, quae manus adornandi studio tentavit apponere. Itaque in toto basilicae spatio solus in sui cespitis specie virens permanet; et impressam divinorum pedum venerationem calcati Deo pulveris perspicua simul et attigua venerantibus arena conservat, ut vere dici possit: adoravimus ubi steterunt pedes eius." Paulinus of Nola *Ep.* 31, to Sulpicius Severus, in *CSEL* 29. English translation in P. G. Walsh, ed., *Letters of St. Paulinus of Nola* (New York, 1967), 2:129–30.

The Mount of Olives had yet another Christian identity: in the fourth century, it became the principal *locus* of monastic activity in the city. Following Melania the Elder, female travelers to Jerusalem, such as Melania the Younger and Flavia, established monasteries there. Other female travelers made their homes on the mount, such as Pelagia. Both male and female travelers were drawn to the hill, such as Palladius in the fifth century and the so-called Piacenza Pilgrim in the sixth century. This traveler visited many monks in and around Jerusalem, especially those living in the many monasteries on the Mount of Olives.[151]

As a Christian city, Jerusalem reached its apex in the sixth century. The city's identity as a Christian city would be forever altered in the seventh century, first by the destructive Persian conquest of the city in 614, and then, in 638, by the passing of the city into Muslim hands, thus marking the beginning of a new process of constructing religious identity in Jerusalem. The best evidence concerning sixth-century Jerusalem and the impact, influence, and experience of women travelers comes from an anonymous Italian man known as the Piacenza Pilgrim, who undertook his Eastern journey in 570.[152]

The Piacenza Pilgrim's journey appears to have been one of religious wandering rather than Jerusalem-centered pilgrimage. His interests seem to center on meeting with holy people and collecting their stories as well as collecting souvenirs of his visit to bring back to Italy. Although he describes various healing sites and miracles, he does not seem to be personally concerned with them. For most of the voyage, he was instead primarily an observer; when he did take an active role at a particular place it was to seek a blessing, collect a souvenir, or to physically "mark" his visit, as when he inscribed his parents' names on the couch, offered a jug of wine to the altar, and washed in the spring in Cana.[153] The only time he directly experienced a miracle occurred when he was unable to leave Jerusalem because of an illness of which he was subsequently cured through a vision of Saint

---

151. "Nam respicientibus in valles illas et perambulantes monasteria multa, loca mirabiliorum, vidimus multitudinem inclausorum virorum ac mulierum in monte Oliveti. Et sursum in monte in loco, unde ascendit Dominus, vidimus mirabilia multa et cellula, ubi fuit inclausa vel iacet sancta Pelagia in corpore." *Itin. Plac.* 16.

152. *Itinerarium Placentini,* ed. P. Geyer and O. Cuntz, in *Itineraria et alia geographica,* CC 175:127–74. See page 6 of Geyer's introduction for information on dating. For comparison with Egeria's account, see G. F. M. Vermeer, *Observations sur le vocabulaire du pélerinage chez Egerie et chez Antonin de Plaisance* (Utrecht, 1965).

153. "Ubi ego indignus nomina parentum meorum scripsi." *Itin. Plac.* 4.

Antony and Saint Euphemia.[154] His choice of these two holy people, the Egyptian father of monasticism and a holy woman, shows the reverence he felt for Eastern monastic holy people.[155]

Through his eyes we can not only see the role played by holy women for a sixth-century male traveler, but we can also see the impact of two centuries of Christianization and Christian travel on the city of Jerusalem and its immediate surroundings. The Church of the Holy Sepulcher was the first place the Piacenza Pilgrim visited upon entering Jerusalem. His description supports the fact that the complex was richly patronized by many visitors, including imperial ones. In front of the tomb "there are ornaments in vast numbers, which hang from iron rods: armlets, bracelets, necklaces, rings, tiaras, plaited girdles, belts, emperors' crowns of gold and precious stones, and the insignia of an empress."[156] These were all gifts of previous pilgrims, each functioning as a tribute or alms and as a physical memento of the traveler's visit. He also wrote that he "took a blessing" from the Holy Sepulcher, apparently in the form of holy oil poured out from a bronze lamp that was placed at the location where Jesus' head had rested.[157] He comments on some visitors taking earth from the tomb with them, earth that had constantly to be replaced from the outside.[158]

The Piacenza Pilgrim's account refers to a multitude of monks, both male and female, living on the Mount of Olives, which by the sixth century had fully emerged as an important locus of monasticism, particularly female monasticism. He and his companion visited many of these monastic houses, which he described as "places full of remarkable things."[159] He also visited

154. "Evidenter oculata fide vidi beatam Euphemiam per visionem et beatum Antonium; quomodo venerunt, sanaverunt me." Ibid., 46.

155. It is not clear which "sancta" Euphemia the Piacenza Pilgrim claims to have seen. The editors of his account believe that it was Euphemia the early fourth-century Chalcedonian martyr, whose relics performed a miracle during the Council of Chalcedon in 451 and were later transferred to Constantinople. The ruins of the Church of St. Euphemia are located near the Hippodrome. It is possible that the Euphemia of his vision was the Euphemia mentioned earlier in this chapter, the Syrian holy woman who ran a guesthouse for travelers in Amida and who later traveled to Jerusalem to be with her sister Mary.

156. "Ornamenta infinita: in virgis ferreis pendentes brachialia, dextroceria, murenas, anuli, capitulares, cingella girata, balteos, coronas imperatorum ex auro vel gemmis et ornamenta de imperatricis." *Itin. Plac.* 18.

157. "Ex qua benedictionem tulimus." Ibid., 18.

158. "In quo monumento de foris terra mittitur et ingredientes exinde benedictionem tollent." Ibid., 18.

159. "Nam respicientibus in valles illas et perambulantes monasteria multa, loca mirabiliorum, vidimus multitudinem inclausorum virorum ac mulierum in monte Oliveti." Ibid., 16.

the tomb of the famous Pelagia of Antioch, a former actress and prostitute who, after converting to a monastic life, gave away all she had, left Antioch, and moved to Jerusalem.[160] According to her *vita*, once Pelagia arrived in the holy city, she disguised herself as a man and lived the rest of her life in a male monastery on the Mount of Olives.[161] The Piacenza Pilgrim heard a similar story from the many monks, both male and female, living near her tomb.

The Piacenza Pilgrim visited the tomb of Empress Eudocia, housed in the Church of St. Stephen.[162] He remarked on the manner in which the empresses Helena and Eudocia were remembered in the Holy Land. After almost two centuries, the memory of their imperial presence and largess lived on. Helena was remembered in the Holy Land, not for building churches, but for providing charity to the poor and, interestingly, to travelers.[163] It was Eudocia, he noted, who had built the walls around Jerusalem, as well as the Church of Saint Stephen, a fact repeated in the sixth-century travel guide, *De situ terrae sanctae*, written by a man named Theodosius (unrelated to the imperial family).[164]

Women travelers and female monks figure prominently in the Piacenza Pilgrim's account. At times, he and his companion sought out holy women in particular. In Elusa, the bishop of the city told him the history of a noble woman named Mary who, after her husband died on their wedding night, promptly freed her slaves and gave away her property to monasteries. She then disappeared and was said to have ventured out to the desert, where she "moves about in the region of Segor by the Salt Sea," apparently leading an ascetic life of wandering.[165] The Piacenza Pilgrim heard more about this

160. "Et sursum in monte in loco, unde ascendit Dominus, vidimus mirabilia multa et cellula, ubi fuit inclausa vel iacet sancta Pelagia in corpore." Ibid., 16.

161. *Pelagia of Antioch,* in Brock and Harvey, *Holy Women,* 40–62. On the phenomenon of female monastic cross-dressing, see John Anson, "The Female Transvestite in Early Monasticism: The Origin and Development of a Motif," *Viator* 5 (1974): 1–32, and Valerie R. Hotchkiss, *Clothes Make the Man: Female Cross-dressing in Medieval Europe* (New York, 1999).

162. "Nam et modo ipsa fons Siloa infra civitatem inclausa est, quia Eudoxia imperatrix ipsa addidit muros in civitate. Nam ipsa muniuit basilicam et sepulchrum sancti Stephani et ipsa sepulchrum habet iuxta sepulchrum sancti Stephani." *Itin. Plac.* 25.

163. "Ubi etiam et panes erogantur ad homines pauperes et peregrinos, quod deputavit Helena." Ibid., 27.

164. "Sanctus Stephanus foras porta Galilaeae lapidatus est; ibi et ecclesia eius est, quam fabricavit domna Eudocia uxor Theodosii imperatoris." Theodosius *De situ terrae sanctae* 8. Nearby in Um er-Rasas, Jordan, there was another St. Stephen church, see Michele Piccirillo, "Recenti scoperte di Archeologia Cristiana in Giordania," in *Actes du XIe Congrès International d'Archéologie Chrétienne* (Rome, 1989), 2:1697–735.

165. "De qua dicitur in heremo esse trans Iordanem inter calamita vel palmita ambulante in finis Segor circa mare salinarum." *Itin. Plac.* 34.

wandering holy woman when he visited a small monastic community of women living in a "desert place" outside the city of Elusa.[166] These women, who were supported by the Christians of Elusa, surprised the Piacenza Pilgrim with their choice of pets: a donkey and a lion who lived together on very friendly terms. One of his companions attempted to buy these animals from the holy women, and the Piacenza Pilgrim even helped in the negotiations, which lasted over two days. Though money, food, and clothing were offered, the negotiations met with no success. It was, however, during this time that the Piacenza Pilgrim had the opportunity to find out more about the wandering desert hermit, Mary; his interest no doubt stemmed from his own wandering life.[167]

The Piacenza Pilgrim seems genuinely amazed at the number of monks in the Holy Land, such as when he remarks on the hermits of the Jordan river valley and around the Dead Sea.[168] Some of these hermits were women, including seven virgins who lived in cells carved out of the rock near the bank of the Jordan river. The Piacenza Pilgrim tried to see these women but was unable to do so, though he and his companion were allowed to pray at the cave.[169] This site was sanctified by the presence of the seven holy women living there, rather than by its biblical connections.

His account reveals that many monks were actively engaged in the care of travelers. Near the Jordan river, the Piacenza Pilgrim mentioned a large monastery dedicated to John the Baptist containing not one but two guesthouses, where presumably he stayed the night.[170] Another guesthouse was mentioned in the city of Jericho, a house that conveniently had a biblical connection as the House of Rahab.[171] Recent archaeology has supported his account of monastic guesthouses with the discovery of a

166. "In quibus locis invenimus monasterium puellarum ultra XVI vel XVII in loco heremi." Ibid., 34.

167. "Nam sic dicebant, quia ipsum asellum ipse leo in pascua gubernaret. Quibus per me centum solidos offerebat ille christianissimus, cum quo fui, sed noluerunt accipere. Sed mittens in Hierusolima adduxit illis tunicas tricenas et ad cellarium legumina vel oleum ad luminaria, et ipsae nobis dixerunt de virtutis Mariae, quae ambulabat in heremo." Ibid., 34.

168. "In circuitu vallis illius multitudo heremitarum." Ibid., 9. "In quibus locis multi sunt heremitae." Ibid., 10.

169. "In illa ripa Iordanis est spelunca, in qua sunt cellulae cum septem virgines, quae ibi infantulae mittuntur, . . . In quo loco cum timore magno ingressi sumus ad orationem, faciem quidem nullius videntes." Ibid., 12.

170. "In quo sunt xenodochia duo." Ibid.

171. "Domus Raab stat, quae est xenodochium," Ibid., 13.

sixth-century monastery in Ma'aleh Adummim, east of Jerusalem, that contained a *xenodochium*.[172]

Like Constantine two hundred years before, the emperor Justinian also pursued an important building program for Jerusalem. Procopius devotes an entire book of his *Buildings* to chronicling all the structures Justinian built during his reign. His main project in Jerusalem was the building of the Church of the Mother of God (*Theotokos*), popularly known as the *Nea* church, the "new" church in the city.[173] The *Nea* church surpassed the Church of Saint Stephen in size and grandeur, growing so large that engineers had to construct artificial extensions to its hilltop site in order to support it.[174] According to the Piacenza Pilgrim this church was populated by a "great congregation of monks" who ran a huge guesthouse. This xenodochium, which like many also operated as a hospital, could accommodate three thousand guests.[175]

The religious life of the Piacenza Pilgrim had many aspects, but first and foremost, he was a traveler. He often mentioned water and drinking in his account. Though water had a spiritual significance—receiving a blessing or carrying home holy water, for example—the Piacenza Pilgrim's concern had a simpler origin. As any traveler to an arid region knows, obtaining good drinking water at regular intervals is a necessity and a constant concern. The Piacenza Pilgrim frequently described the water supply and water flow in the cities he visited.[176] It is apparent in his discussion of the spring

172. "A separated hostel (*xenodochium*) for pilgrims was attached in the North-East, including dormitories, chapel and stables." Yoram Tsafrir, "Christian Archaeology in Israel in Recent Years," in *Actes du XIe Congrès International d'Archéologie Chrétienne* (Rome, 1989), 2:1753.

173. Procopius gives a detailed description not only of what the church looked like, but also of how difficult it was to build because of the city's steep hills and narrow streets. Procopius of Caesarea, *Justinian's Buildings,* edited and translated by H. B. Dewing and G. Downey, Loeb Classical Library (Cambridge, Mass., 1961), 5.6, 16–26.

174. Ibid., 5.6, 6–9. Recent reconstruction of the church shows that it was similar in shape and form to Santo Stefano Rotondo in Rome. See Y. Magen, "The Church of Mary Theotokos on Mount Gerizim," in *Christian Archeology in the Holy Land, New Discoveries. Essays in Honour of Virgilio C. Corbo, OFM,* ed. G. C. Bottini, L. Di Segni, and E. Alliata (Jerusalem, 1990), 333–41. For recent discoveries of inscriptions from the *Nea* church, see Pau Figueras, "Découvertes récentes d'épigraphie Chrétienne en Israel," in *Actes du XIe Congrès International d'Archéologie Chrétienne* (Rome, 1989), 2:1771–85.

175. "Ubi est congregatio nimia monachorum, ubi sunt et xenodochia virorum ac mulierum, susceptio peregrinorum, mensas innumerabiles, lecta aegrotorum amplius tria milia." *Itin. Plac.* 23.

176. On the water supply in Jerusalem, see Avinoam Shalem, "Bi'r al-Waraqa: Legend and Truth. A Note on Medieval Sacred Geography," *Palestine Exploration Quarterly* 127, no. 1 (1995): 50–61.

located three miles outside Jerusalem, at the tomb of Rachel, for example, that he was taking water not to obtain a blessing, but to drink:

> On the way to Bethlehem, at the third milestone from Jerusalem, lies the body of Rachel, on the edge of the area called Ramah. There I saw standing water which came from a rock, of which you can take as much as you like up to seven pints. Every one has his fill, and the water does not become less or more. It is indescribably sweet to drink, and people say that Saint Mary became thirsty on the flight into Egypt, and that when she stopped here this water immediately flowed. Nowadays there is also a church building there.[177]

On the surface his discussion appears to deal with the miraculous, but what comes through was the sweetness of the rationed water. For the Piacenza Pilgrim even the Virgin Mary appeared simply as a traveler in need of water nourished by this spring. At another point he related some of the difficulties he had while traveling through the desert. He wrote, "Our camels carried our water, and each person was given a pint in the morning and a pint in the evening. When the water in the skins had turned bitter like gall we put sand in it, and this made it sweet."[178] A bright moment on this six-day journey through the desert occurred when the travelers were visited by Bedouin Arabs who "brought skins of cool water from the remotest parts of the desert and gave us some."[179] The Piacenza Pilgrim frequently noted how friendly other cities were to travelers; Gaza, for example, was apparently very welcoming to travelers.[180] He called the citizens of Alexandria "worthless," though they too were welcoming to travelers.[181] He received an especially

---

177. "Via, quae ducit Bethlem, ad tertium miliarium de Hierosolima iacet Rachel in corpore, in finis loci, qui vocatur Rama. In ipso loco vidi in media via de petra exire aquam inmobilem ad arbitratum usque ad sextarios septem, unde conplent omnes et neque minuitur neque ampliatur. Suavitudo ad bibendum innarrabilis, dicentes, eo quod sancta Maria fugiens in Aegyptum in ipso loco sedit et sitivit, et sic egressa esset ipsa aqua. Ibi et ecclesia modo facta est." *Itin. Plac.* 28.

178. "Cameli nobis aquam portantes, sextarium mane et sextarium sero per hominem accipiebamus. Amarescente aqua illa in utres in felle mittebamus in ea harenam et indulcabatur." Ibid., 36.

179. "Adducebant utres cum aqua frigida de interiore parte heremi et dabant." Ibid., 36.

180. The citizens of Gaza are called "amatores peregrinorum." Ibid., 33.

181. "Alexandria civitas splendida, populus levissimus, sed amatores peregrinorum; haereses multae." Ibid., 45.

warm welcome upon his entry into the city of Pharan in the Sinai: "The women with their children came to meet us, carrying palms in their hands, and flasks of radish oil, and they fell at our feet, anointed our soles and our heads, and sang this anthem in the Egyptian language."[182] His account reveals a holy land shaped by the many travelers who visited, but most prominently by women. The Piacenza Pilgrim was moved by the many monks, male and female, whom he visited with and interacted with. He would return to Italy with a storehouse of experiences, stories, and physical souvenirs of his visit. In this way, he was bringing a Holy Land shaped by women, through their promotion and activity in monasticism, patronage, and travel, home to the West.

Throughout the account, the Piacenza Pilgrim expressed great interest in three inter-related topics: monasticism, women, and provisions for travel. He is not simply concerned with visiting the holy sites. This interest is especially apparent when his account is compared to a later manuscript recension of his travels.[183] This second version makes mostly grammatical changes, yet there are a series of omissions concerning both the Piacenza Pilgrim's interest in women and in travel. Several times when a xenodochium is mentioned or travelers are mentioned, it is excised in the later version.[184] The story of the woman Mary who wandered through the Sinai desert is also shortened, and the reference to her wandering is cut.[185] The strange reference to the death of John of Piacenza is missing the identification that

---

182. "Et occurrentes mulieres cum infantibus, palmas in manibus portantes et ampullas cum rafanino oleo, prostratae pedibus nostris unguebant plantas nostras et capita nostra, lingua Aegyptiaca psallentes antifonam." Ibid., 40.

183. This version, the *Recensio Altera*, can be found in *Itineraria et Alia Geographica, CC* 175:155–74.

184. In the very first line of the account, the author uses the verb "peregrinare" to describe his journey; this is omitted in the later version where the verb is "egredi": "Praece-dente beato Antonino martyre, ex eo quod a civitate Placentina egressus sum, in quibus locis sum peregrinatus, id est sancta loca." *Itin. Plac.* 1. "Procedente beato Antonino martyre una cum collega suo, ex eo quod civiatatem Placentiam egressus est, in quibus locis per regnum conatus est ire, vestigia Christi sequentes et miracula sanctorum prophetarum providere coeperunt." *Itin. Plac., Rec. Alt.,* 1. The description of the Basilica of Saint Mary (known as the *Nea* church) in Jerusalem no longer mentions the two xenodochia, one for men and one for women, or the way in which the church "caters to travelers." *Itin. Plac.* 23. The xenodochium in Jericho is also omitted, as is the reference to "hiding spies." Ibid., 13. Omitted also is any ref-erence to the empress Helena's funding of bread distribution to travelers (*peregrinos*); the later version only mentions distribution of bread to the poor. Ibid., 27.

185. Mary no longer freed her slaves or gave her property to monasteries, and the word "ambulante" is omitted in the description of her disappearance into the desert. *Itin. Plac.* 34.

he was the husband of Thecla in the later version.[186] These changes were not random but appear instead to be an attempt to cleanse the account of its emphasis on wandering, travelers, and women and to replace them with an emphasis on holy sites, an emphasis that fit more easily with later notions of goal-centered religious travel, but obscures the qualities of the account that were central to the pattern of early female Christian travel.

A great many women traveled around the Mediterranean basin for religious purposes during late antiquity. In addition to their own spiritual well-being, they were interested in visiting holy men and women, bestowing largess, and in setting up *xenodochia*, a wholly late antique institution. Many of these women were in a place in their lives where they had more liberty—they were widows, consecrated virgins, or wealthy imperial and other noble women.

There was never another period in the ancient and medieval worlds where women would possess this ability and desire to travel. Clearly the story of religious travel, particularly by women between the fourth and sixth centuries, is a complicated one, and no single model of religious travel at this time serves to explain all women's journeys. Monastic wandering, imperial patronage, and *locus*-centered visits all had a place within the religious landscape of late antique women travelers. Some of these women spent their entire lives traveling, while others led a life of wandering for a few years and then settled. The journeys of these women often took them to the Holy Land and brought them into the company of living *sancti* as well as other travelers.

The importance of early women travelers is perhaps best seen in their impact on the city of Jerusalem. Just as the study of the changing religious topography of the city of Jerusalem is crucial for understanding the nature and consequences of women's religious travel during late antiquity, so the nature of early religious travel in general is best understood through an examination of a particular geographic region. The Iberian Peninsula, with its peculiar history and traditions, holds a unique position in the histories of monasticism and of religious travel, including pilgrimage. It should

---

186. The later version also specifies at John was fellow traveler of the Piacenza Pilgrim: "Ibi vero defunctus est collega noster Iohannes de Placentia." *Itin. Plac., Rec. Alt.,* 7. The earlier version states: "Nam et ibi mortuus est Iohannes de Placentia, maritus Teclae." *Itin. Plac.* 7.

come as no surprise, then, that the richest field for uncovering the patterns of pre-pilgrimage Christian travel should emerge from Iberia. It is therefore to the unique structure of early Spanish monasticism and travel and the Iberian monastic travelers that we now turn.

CHAPTER FIVE

TRAVEL AND MONASTICISM
ON THE IBERIAN PENINSULA

The fifth-century Spanish chronicler and bishop, Hydatius, who lived in
the far western region of Galicia, wrote frequently of his feelings of isolation.
Yet from this vantage point in the corner of the known world, his writings,
the *Chronica,* shed light on the tumultuous history of the invasions of the
peninsula.[1] Hydatius was a traveler; as a young boy he traveled to the Holy
Land, and as a bishop he traveled to Gaul, as an envoy to Aëtius, seeking
assistance against the raids of the Sueves.[2] His emphasis on his isolation
from the world did not mean, for him, that he did not see the world. His
travels should not surprise us; he was from the same region as both Egeria
and Orosius, who were discussed in Chapter 2. Spain was also the home of
the Bachiarius, the wandering Spanish monk who was forced to defend his
lifestyle to authorities. Clearly the Iberian Peninsula, a region often ignored
in studies of early monasticism, is a fruitful area of investigation for the
intersection of travel and monasticism from the fifth to the seventh centuries. There is a wealth of material from Spain, such as monastic rules,
hagiographies, and the varied writings of the Iberian fathers. Through an
examination of this material we are not only able to perceive a society in
constant communication with the eastern Mediterranean and North Africa,
but also one in which monasticism was greatly influenced by distant forces.
This is also a period in which the Iberian Peninsula experienced some of
the greatest upheavals in its history: fifth-century invasions by four different

---

1. Hydatius, *Chronica,* in *The Chronicle of Hydatius and the Consularia Constantinopolitana: Two Contemporary Accounts of the Final Years of the Roman Empire,* ed. R. W. Burgess,
Oxford Classical Monographs (Oxford, 1993). For a useful bibliography on Hydatius, see
Dominguez Del Val, *Estudios,* 191–94.
2. "Ob quorum depraedationem Ydatius episcopus ad Aetium ducem, qui expeditionem
agebat in Gallis, suscipit legationem." Hydatius *Chronica* 91.

tribes, the disintegration of Roman rule, and Justinian's attempted reconquest in the sixth century—all of which served to further strain the fabric of
Spanish society. The culture of movement, discussed at the beginning of this
book, in conjunction with the development of monasticism, can be seen in
microcosm in Spain.

Christianity had long had a stronghold in Spain; by the mid-fourth
century, organized Catholic Christianity was the dominant religion among
the urban Hispano-Roman population of Spain. Priscillianism was active
in the region in this period, but this heresy helped to consolidate the
diverse forces within the Spanish church.[3] Of the tribes that invaded in
409, the Vandals were Arian Christians, the Sueves were initially pagan,
and the religion of the Uralo-Altaic Alans is unknown.[4] The Sueves converted to Arian Christianity in 464, under the influence of Ajax, a missionary
sent by the Visigoths.[5] The Visigoths promoted many Arian bishops, mainly
fellow Goths, to sees in Spain.[6] Catholic belief, however, spread among the
Goths, and by the sixth century there is evidence of Gothic bishops holding
Catholic sees.[7] The Visigoths, under king Leovigild, tried reconciling Arian
and Catholic beliefs in an attempt to stimulate Catholic conversions to
Arianism in the 580s with limited success. Finally, in 587 under Leovigild's
son, Reccared, the Visigothic realm converted to Catholic Christianity.[8]

It must be remembered that the organization and nature of late antique
church varied throughout the Mediterranean; the church in Spain differed
in many respects from that in Italy and Asia Minor. There was a strong relationship between the Spanish church and the church in Africa; it may have

---

3. Henry Chadwick, *Priscillian of Avila: The Occult and the Charismatic in the Early Church*
(Oxford, 1976).

4. The Alans were non-Germanic nomads, probably from the Caucasus Black Sea Region.
Why or how they were so easily able to join with the Vandals and Sueves, both Western
Germanic tribes, in crossing the Rhine and the Pyrenees is also unknown.

5. On the mission of Ajax, see J. N. Hillgarth, "Popular Religion in Visigothic Spain," in
Visigothic Spain: New Approaches, ed. Edward James (Oxford, 1980), 3–60; E. A. Thompson,
The Goths in Spain (Oxford, 1969); W. Reinhart, *Historia General del Reino Hispanico de los
Suevos* (Madrid, 1952); and Domínguez del Val, *Leandro de Sevilla.*

6. For example, Leovigild's support of Sunna as Arian bishop of Mérida. *Vitas Sanctorum
Patrum Emeretensium* (henceforth *VPE*), ed. A. Maya Sanchez (Turnholt, 1992), 20; see also
the older edition, *The "Vitas Sanctorum Patrum Emeretensium": Text and Translation,* ed.
Joseph N. Garvin (Washington, D.C., 1946).

7. For example, John of Biclaro and Masona of Mérida, who were bishops in the sixth
century.

8. Hillgarth, "Popular Religion in Visigothic Spain."

been from Africa that Christianity originally moved into Spain.[9] The Spanish church often turned to Africa rather than to Rome for spiritual guidance and advice.[10] Connections with the African church remained stronger than those with the church in Rome throughout the period under discussion, except during the fifth century when we do find Spaniards turning to Rome after the ravages of the Vandal invasion of Africa in 429. The Visigothic church, however, continued its virtual independence from Rome even after the conversion of the Goths to Catholicism.[11]

Monasticism, too, had an early start in Iberia, though the evidence on this subject is scarce. The Council of Saragossa around the year 380 makes the first reference to a monk, *monachus,* on the peninsula.[12] The province of Tarraconensis probably had some of Spain's earliest monasteries, owing to the influence of John Cassian in southern Gaul. We know of monastic foundations in the south, in Baetica and Lusitania, during the mid-sixth century; African monks, fleeing Vandal hostility, established these monasteries.

Spanish monasticism in this period was heterogeneous and has eluded simple characterization. Though scholars have often emphasized the influence of continental monasticism, the traditions of African monasticism may have been even more important. There is a great deal of evidence for the existence of a type of monasticism comprised of small urban communities, perhaps of friends, similar to Augustine's early community in Africa. Augustine's letter reprimanding a community of women and then describing a proper mode of life for them sheds light on this connection.[13] We know that this letter and rule for nuns became well known during the sixth and seventh centuries in Spain and perhaps nowhere else.[14]

Much writing from Iberians still survives, and by focusing on these texts, we can gain a better understanding, not only of Iberian monasticism, but also of religious travel in the Mediterranean region in general. From

9. Collins, *Early Medieval Spain,* 59–61. For the later influence of the African church on Spain, see Roger Collins, "Mérida and Toledo: 550–585," in *Visigothic Spain: New Approaches,* ed. Edward James (Oxford, 1980), 206.

10. See, for example, letters of Cyprian of Carthage addressed to a priest, Felix, and a deacon, Aelius, and to the people of Legio, Asturica, and Emerita, in Collins, *Early Medieval Spain,* 59.

11. Peter Linehan, *History and the Historians of Medieval Spain* (Oxford, 1993), 63–65.

12. Mundó, "Il monachesimo."

13. Lawless, *Augustine of Hippo;* Augustine *Ep.* 211.

14. Lawless, *Augustine of Hippo,* 131. The letter has been assigned various dates, from 397 to 423, but the earlier date is more likely.

Hosius of Córdoba to Avitus of Braga, from Egeria to Orosius—Spaniards were frequently found among the visitors to the eastern Mediterranean, both in the great cities, such as Constantinople, and in the Holy Land. It should not be surprising to find travel and wandering as an element of early Spanish monasticism. Some, such as the fifth-century monk Bachiarius, were quite clear in their writings that travel was, indeed, an integral part of their monastic pursuit.[15] Others were not as explicit, and so an examination of the relationship between travel and monasticism in Spain should scrutinize a variety of evidence that might not, at first glace, appear significant.

One of the earliest Iberian travelers who left a record of his journey was the poet Prudentius, who lived in the late fourth century and was probably a contemporary of Egeria.[16] He was an educated man who left mostly poetic works, including the *Liber Peristephanon,* a series of hymns for the martyrs.[17] Prudentius gathered information for his work by traveling to the martyr shrines. He was one of the earliest popularizer of the cult of Eulalia of Mérida. The cult of Eulalia is central to understanding, not only the early church in Spain, but the Visigothic church as well.[18] Her cult was a powerful one throughout the Iberian Peninsula, especially in the city of Mérida. A girl of twelve from a noble family, Eulalia was martyred during the persecutions of Diocletian. Prudentius's hymn portrays her as the Christian embodiment of Mérida, "So will we venerate her bones and the altar placed over her bones, while she, set at the feet of God, views all our doings, our song wins her favor, and she cherishes her people."[19]

Prudentius also traveled outside Spain to gather information on a variety of local martyrs. On a trip to Rome he stopped at the shrine of the martyr Cassian in a small town in Northern Italy.[20] Above the shrine was a painting

15. Bachiarius *Libellus de Fide* and *De reparatione lapsi ad Januarium, PL* 20:1019–63. See Chapter 2 for a discussion of Bachiarius.

16. See the annotated bibliography in Dominguez Del Val, *Estudios,* 132–67.

17. For a brief description of Prudentius and his work, see Marique, *Leaders of Iberean Christianity.*

18. For the cult of Eulalia in Mérida, see Javier Arce, "The City of Mérida (Emerita) in the *Vitas Patrum Emeritensium* (VIth century A.D.)," in *East and West: Modes of Communication. Proceedings of the First Plenary Conference at Mérida,* ed. Evangelos Chrysos and Ian Wood (Leiden, 1999), 1–14.

19. "Sic venerarier ossa libet ossibus altar et inpositum: illa Dei sita sub pedibus prospicit haec populosque suos carmine propitiata fovet." Prudentius *Peristephanon Liber* 3, in *Prudentius,* ed. H. J. Thomson, vol. 2 (Cambridge, Mass., 1949). On these poems, see Michael J. Roberts, *Poetry and the Cult of the Martyrs: The "Liber Peristephanon" of Prudentius* (Ann Arbor, Mich., 1993).

20. Prudentius *Peristephanon Liber* 9.

that depicted the brutal story of Cassian's martyrdom: he, a schoolteacher, was stabbed to death by his students' styluses. Prudentius was unclear as to the meaning of the picture and so asked the attendant, who related the details of the story. Prudentius ended his hymn to Cassian by noting that the martyr had answered his prayers: "I was heard. I visited Rome, and found all things issue happily. I returned home and now proclaim the praise of Cassian."[21] It was his prayers to the martyr Cassian that aided him on his travels.

In the city of Rome, Prudentius visited other martyr shrines: "Countless are the graves of saints I have seen in the city of Romulus."[22] Dramatic paintings of martyrdoms decorated many of the tombs; viewing the paintings was an important part of Prudentius's experience at each shrine. He expressed this with the words he attributed to the attendant: "What you are looking at, stranger, is no vain old wife's tale. The picture tells the story of what happened; it is recorded in books and displays the honest assurance of the olden time."[23] The paintings, combined with the inscriptions, oral testimony of the attendant, and the antique look of the shrine, served to prove the truth of the martyrdoms. Prudentius's poems not only brought to life these martyr stories, they also served as miniature journeys.

Prudentius's interest in the didactic and emotive qualities of paintings led him to prepare a series of descriptive verses to accompany a now-lost cycle of paintings on biblical events.[24] There were forty-eight paintings, one-half on Old Testament scenes and the other on the New Testament.[25] Knowledge of the actual holy places in Jerusalem, rather than information gleaned from biblical accounts, influenced Prudentius's description of at least two of the scenes: that of the scourging of Christ on the column, and the description of the church on the Mount of Olives containing Jesus' footprints.[26] Here

21. "Audior, urbem adeo, dextris successibus utor: domum revertor, Cassianum praedico." Ibid., 9.105–6. Herbert Kessler states that Prudentius is imitating Virgil's description of Aeneas viewing scenes of the Trojan war depicted in the temple of Juno, see Herbert L. Kessler, "Pictures as Scripture in Fifth-century Churches," in *Studies in Pictorial Narrative* (London, 1994), 363 n. 45.

22. "Innumeros cineres sanctorum Romula in urbe vidimus." Prudentius *Peristephanon Liber* 11.1–2.

23. "Quod prospicis, hospes, non est inanis aut anilis fabula; historiam pictura refert, quae tradita libris veram vetusti temporis monstrat fidem." Ibid., 9.17–20.

24. Prudentius *Tituli historiarum (Dittochaeon)*, in Thomson, *Prudentius*, 2:346–71.

25. One verse, number 43 on the Holy Sepulcher, was a later interpolation, bringing the number of verses in Thomson's edition to forty-nine.

26. It is unclear whether it was Prudentius or the artist of the painting who was influenced by stories of the holy places in Jerusalem. If it was the artist, it is strange that he or she

again these verses could bring the reader, as the paintings did, into Jerusalem and its sacred topography.

Historians often refer to Galicia, a province in the northwestern corner of the Iberian Peninsula, as remote and isolated, not only from the rest of Spain but also from the Mediterranean world as a whole.[27] This has led many to speak of "Galician particularism," and of monastic developments there as the result of isolation.[28] Much evidence, however, points to a surprising amount of contact between Galicia and the rest of Spain and the Mediterranean provinces.[29] We find contact not only through letters and intellectual activity, but *physical* contact, the journeys of people from the region to distant lands, and the journey of people from elsewhere to Galicia. Monastic ideas from throughout the Mediterranean influenced monastic practices in this part of Spain.

Galicia's monastic roots are traceable to the fourth century, with Egeria's voyage and her monastic community of sisters. Hydatius also traveled to the Holy Land and even met with the elderly Jerome in Bethlehem around the year 410. It is unclear from his description exactly what sort of a voyage this was; nothing suggests that it was a pilgrimage. Hydatius was probably traveling with his parents on official business.[30] His meeting with Jerome left a deep impression on the young boy. He pursued a religious life, eventually becoming a bishop, and he began writing a historical chronicle, which he intended to serve as a continuation of the ecclesiastical histories

---

painted the holy sepulcher as part of the cycle. Bethlehem is also emphasized over Jerusalem as a holy city.

27. On Galicia as the end of the world, see R. A. Fletcher, *Saint James's Catapult: The Life and Times of Diego Gelmírez of Santiago de Compostela* (Oxford, 1984), 1. See also Manuel C. Díaz y Díaz, *Visiones del más alla en Galicia durante la alta edad media* (Santiago de Compostela, 1985).

28. See the work of Charles Julian Bishko, such as "Spanish Abbots and the Visigothic Councils of Toledo," in *Spanish and Portuguese Monastic History, 600–1300,* ed. Charles Julian Bishko (London, 1984), 139–52; "The Date and Nature of the Spanish *Consensoria Monachorum,*" *American Journal of Philology* 69, also in Variorum Reprints (1948): 377–95; and "Gallegan Pactual Monasticism in the Repopulation of Castile," in *Variorum Reprints,* 513–36A (London, 1951).

29. R. A. Fletcher agrees that in the late antique and early medieval periods, Galicia was more connected to the rest of the Mediterranean world, though this changes, and the province is isolated in the eleventh century. Thompson, on the other hand, stresses the isolation of the province throughout its history. Fletcher, *Saint James's Catapult,* 20–21; Thompson, "End of Roman Spain," pt. 1.

30. R. W. Burgess, the translator and editor of Hydatius's *Chronicle,* uses the word "pilgrimage" to describe this journey. "Quem quodam tempore propriae peregrinationis in

of Eusebius and Jerome.[31] Living in a chaotic time, he filled his chronicle with accounts of raids, invasions, evil portents, and the decay of traditional Roman authority in the West. One of the events he described was the entry of the Visigoths into Spain under Theoderic and their battles with the Sueves. Hydatius described in great detail the sack of the city of Braga in Galicia by Theoderic and his Visigothic army.

> And on Sunday, 28 October he sacked it, an action which, although accomplished without bloodshed, was nevertheless tragic and lamentable enough. A great many Romans were taken captives; the basilicas of the saints stormed; altars thrown down and broken up; virgins of God abducted from the city, but not violated; the clergy stripped right down to the shame of their nakedness; the whole population regardless of sex along with little children dragged from the holy places of sanctuary; the sacred place filled with the sacrilegious presence of mules, cattle, and camels. This sack partially revived the examples of heavenly wrath written about Jerusalem.[32]

In this vivid paragraph, Hydatius reveals the destruction wrought on monastic culture, the clergy, and the holy places, casting it in the language of biblical metaphor, where Braga becomes Jerusalem, and the Visigoths the wrath of God.

Hydatius based his history on his own experiences as well as on the evidence he could gather, including statements from informants.[33] One of these informants was a priest named Germanus from Arabia, who was traveling through Galicia; he also spoke with Greeks traveling in Galicia.[34] Although Hydatius frequently bemoaned the isolation of his homeland at the "end of the earth," he did have quite a few opportunities to associate with the rest of the Mediterranean world.[35]

---

supradictis regionibus adhuc infantulus videsse me certus sum." Hydatius *Chronica,* in *The Chronicle of Hydatius,* 73.

31. Ibid., 71–73.

32. Ibid., 107.

33. Ibid., 75.

34. "Germani presbiteri Arabicae regionis exinde ad Calleciam venientis et aliquorum Grecorum relatione comperimus." Ibid., 93.

35. In the late sixth century, Iberia produced another bishop who spent part of his youth in the East and wrote a chronicle, John of Biclar, a Goth. Isidore of Seville wrote in his *De viris illustribus* that John left Spain for Constantinople in 558 and there received an education

The most important figure for early Galician monasticism was Martin of Braga. Martin was born in Pannonia, in 520.[36] He received a Greek as well as Latin education and traveled throughout the eastern Mediterranean and eventually, in 550, made his way to Galicia in northwestern Spain and settled there. Martin is most famous as the converter of the Sueves, but emphasis on his missionary work has eclipsed other significant aspects of his life. Martin's roles as abbot, as bishop, and finally as a traveler are the key to understanding his contribution to the religious landscape of late antique Iberia.

The story of Martin's place in the conversion of the Sueves to Catholicism comes to us from Gregory of Tours's *De virtutibus sancti Martini*, which is of course about Martin of Tours, not Martin of Braga.[37] According to Gregory, the son of the Arian king Chararich was stricken with leprosy. After hearing of the miraculous healing power of the Catholic Martin of Tours, the king vowed to convert and to build a church dedicated to the saint. He then sent emissaries with gifts to the shrine in Tours in order to effect a cure for his son's illness. The messengers prayed at the shrine and placed a silken cloth over Martin's tomb. These actions resulted in the miraculous cure of the king's son. The messengers returned to Galicia with

---

Greek and Latin letters. After seventeen years he returned to Spain, entered a monastery, and sometime between 590 and 591 became bishop of Gerona. Isidore tells us that he, too, wrote a monastic rule, but it does not survive. Eastern monasticism probably influenced this rule, given John's intimate knowledge of and interest in the Greek East. Some Spanish scholars have tried to attribute the *Regula Magistri* and even the *Regula Macharii* to him. See Dominguez Del Val, *Estudios*, 196. What does survive from John's pen is *Chronicon*, presumably written in the last decade of the sixth century, a brief chronicle of historical and ecclesiastical events in the Mediterranean from 567 to about 590. Though the work concentrates on Spain and the rest of the West, John includes a great deal of material about the East. Isidore of Seville, *De viris illustribus*, in Julio Campos, *Juan de Biclaro, Obispo de Gerona: Su Vida y Su Obra* (Madrid, 1960); Linehan, *History and the Historians*, 23.

36. The standard edition of the works of Martin of Braga is C. W. Barlow, ed., *Martini Episcopi Bracarensis: Opera omnia* (New Haven, Conn., 1950); see also the new Spanish edition, *Martin de Braga: Obras Completas*, ed. Ursicino Domínguez del Val (Madrid, 1990). An English translation of the works of Martin of Braga can be found in C. W. Barlow, trans., *Iberian Fathers, volume 1: Martin of Braga, Paschasius of Dumium, Leander of Seville* (Washington, D.C., 1969). For an overview of Martin of Braga's life, see Marique, *Leaders of Iberean Christianity*. See also Maria João Violante-Branco, "St. Martin of Braga, the Sueves and Gallaecia," in Ferreiro, *The Visigoths: Studies in Culture and Society*, 63–97. Alberto Ferreiro, "The Cult of Saints and Divine Patronage in Gallaecia before Santiago," in *The Pilgrimage to Compostela in the Middle Ages: A Book of Essays*, ed. Maryjane Dunn and Linda Kay Davidson (New York, 1996), 3–22. A bibliography on Martin of Braga can be found on pages 555–69 in Alberto Ferreiro, *The Visigoths in Gaul and Spain, A.D. 418–711* (Leiden, 1988).

37. Gregory of Tours *De virtutibus s. Martini*, liber 1.11, *De Gallis Suavis conversis*. In Martin of Braga *Martini Episcopi Bracarensis*, appendix 5, 298–300.

the silk cloth, now a powerful healing relic. Gregory linked this story with the arrival of Martin of Braga:

> Then the blessed Martin [of Braga], who is now bishop there, was advised by God and came from a distant region. I do not think that this happened without divine providence, because he traveled from his homeland on the day when the blessed relics were brought from that spot, and so he entered the port in Galicia simultaneously with those relics. . . . Then the blessed Martin accepted the sovereignty of Episcopal grace. The king confessed the unity of the Father and Son and the Holy Spirit and was baptized along with his entire household.[38]

Gregory thus promoted Martin of Braga as the converter of the Sueves; he was a man in the mold of the fourth-century Martin of Tours, who also came from the East and converted a great many people. Gregory later repeated the story in his *History of the Franks*.[39] Isidore of Seville continued this tradition in his *De viris illustribus,* when he wrote of Martin as the "missionary to the Sueves."[40]

Martin's role in the conversion of the Sueves from Arianism overshadows his own goals and his own view of his activities in Galicia. Something compelled Martin to travel to the West. According to the epitaph he apparently wrote for himself, he was moved by a "divine calling" to travel to the far-off Iberian Peninsula.[41] This calling was apparently a monastic one: Martin wanted to bring monasticism, particularly Eastern monasticism, to Galicia. He arrived prepared for this mission; he brought with him his

---

38. "Tunc commonitus a Deo beatus Martinus de regione longinqua, qui ibidem nunc sacerdos habetur, advenit. Sed nec hoc credo sine divina fuisse providentia, quod ea die se commoveret de patria, qua beatae reliquiae de loco levatae sunt, et sic simul cum ipsis pignoribus Galliciae portum ingressus sit. . . . Beatus autem Martinus sacerdotalis gratiae accepit principatum. Rex unitatem Patris et Filii et Spiritus sancti confessus, cum omni domo suo crysmatus est." Gregory of Tours *De virtutibus s. Martini, MGM SRM* 1 (Hanover, 1885); the English translation is from R. Van Dam, *Saints and Their Miracles in Late Antique Gaul* (Princeton, N.J., 1993), 213.

39. Gregory of Tours *Historia Francorum* 5.37, in Martin of Braga *Martini Episcopi Bracarensis,* appendix 6.

40. "Ibique conversis ab Ariana impietate ad fidem Catholicam Suevorum populis." Isidore of Seville *De viris illustribus* 35, in Martin of Braga *Martini Episcopi Bracarensis,* appendix 8, 301.

41. "Pannonis genitus, transcendens aequora vasta, Galliciae in gremium divinis nutibus actus." Martin of Braga *Martini Episcopi Bracarensis* 283.

personal experience of Egyptian monasticism. He also brought Greek and perhaps Latin manuscripts. The Greek works included the *Apophthegmata Patrum* and a copy of the canons of the fourth-century councils of the Eastern Church.[42] These treasured copies were to play an important role in Martin's religious work in Spain.

His first actions in Galicia were telling: he established a monastery at Dumio and began to teach Greek to one of his young followers, Paschasius, who would later translate much of the *Apophthegmata* at Martin's request. Martin himself translated some of the sayings of the Desert Fathers. We know he began these activities quite soon after his arrival, for Paschasius's preface to his translation refers to Martin as a "priest and abbot,"[43] not as a bishop, a position he held from 556. These monastic accomplishments did not go unnoticed. Isidore, in his *De viris illustribus,* mentioned Martin's founding of monasteries and his authorship of a monastic rule.[44] Although the model of Martin of Tours suggested by Gregory took hold and became widely accepted, a more appropriate model for Martin's mission is that of John Cassian.[45] Like Cassian, Martin of Braga traveled in the East and brought Eastern monasticism to the West. Like Cassian, he founded monasteries, and like Cassian, he made the Egyptian desert accessible to the West.

It is impossible to know the exact number or kind of monastic institutions Martin encountered when he arrived in Galicia. One of the least romanized provinces in the empire, Galicia was the birthplace of Priscillianism, an "ascetic" heresy.[46] The traveler Egeria and her sisters may have been from Galicia.[47] The onset of the Suevic invasions in the early fifth century must have altered the religious landscape. By the end of the fifth century, there is very little evidence of an active monastic culture in Galicia.

---

42. I assume this, since these are the works that Martin translates or has translated while he is in Galicia. There is a chance that Braga's library could have already possessed copies, but it is doubtful. It seems more likely that Martin brought these with him to Iberia from the East.

43. "Domino venerabili patri Martino presbytero et abbati Paschasius." Prologue of Paschasius's *Vitae Patrum,* in Martin of Braga *Martini Episcopi Bracarensis,* appendix 3, 293–94.

44. "Regulam fidei et sanctae religionis constituit, ecclesias confirmavit, monasteria condidit, copiosaque praecepta piae instituionis composuit." Isidore of Seville *De viris illustribus* 35, in Martin of Braga *Martini Episcopi Bracarensis,* appendix 8, 301.

45. On John Cassian, see Rousseau, *Ascetics, Authority, and the Church,* and Owen Chadwick, *John Cassian* (London, 1968).

46. Priscillian preached a rigid ascetic doctrine in Spain, ca. 370–75. The doctrine was condemned in 380 at the Council of Saragossa. The movement was active in Spain for much of the fifth century. See Virginia Burrus, *The Making of a Heretic: Gender, Authority, and the Priscillianist Controversy* (Berkeley and Los Angeles, 1995).

47. For the travel diary of Egeria, see Maraval, *Égérie;* see also my Chapter 2.

The sixth century brought a golden age of monasticism in the West, which witnessed the writing of the *Regula Magistri*, the *Regula Benedictina*, and the rule of Caesarius of Arles among others.[48] The rule Isidore claimed Martin wrote does not survive, yet the monks of Dumio must have followed some form of rule, or perhaps they needed none: the translated *Sayings*, accompanied by Martin's firm guidance as abbot, could have served quite well to regulate life at the monastery.[49]

There was another side to Martin's life: he was advanced to the bishopric in the year 556. Little evidence survives about this event, but it appears that Martin was able to retain his leadership of the monastery at Dumio, which suggests that the ecclesiastical leadership made certain concessions in order to convince the Pannonian abbot to assume this position of authority in the church. Martin could now have looked toward the model of Augustine, rather than that of Cassian, in his transition to episcopal power. One can imagine that it was with some initial reluctance that the abbot took the position, a reluctance similar to Augustine's in assuming the bishopric at Hippo.

Martin, like his model, quickly excelled at the position, and was active not only at the councils of Braga in 561 and 572, presiding over the latter as metropolitan, but also in writing moral treatises at the request of fellow bishops. One of these, the *De correctione rusticorum*, he ostensibly wrote for Polemius, bishop of Astorga, who wanted to know how to preach to local peasants concerning their continuation of pagan practices. Scholars have employed this work to reveal actual religious practices in the country-side, but it is clear that Martin was borrowing heavily from Augustine's *De*

---

48. On this flowering of monasticism and monastic rules in the West, see Adalbert de Vogüé, *Histoire Littéraire du Mouvement Monastique dans L'Antiquité: Première Partie: Le monachisme Latin de la mort d'Antoine à la fin du séjour de Jérôme à Rome (356–385)* (Paris, 1991); idem, *Les Règles Monastiques Anciennes;* G. Penco, "S. Benedetto nella storia della Cristianità occidentale," in *Medievo Monastico*, ed. P. G. Farnedi (Rome, 1988), 61–80; idem, *Il monachesimo fra spiritualità e cultura* (Milan, 1991); F. Prinz, *Frühes Mönchtum im Frankenreich: Kultur und Gesellschaft in Gallien, den Rheinlanden und Bayern am Beispiel der monastischen Entwicklung (4. bis 8. Jahrhundert)* (Munich, 1965); and idem, *Askese und Kultur: Vor- und frühbenediktinisches Mönchtum an der Wiege Europas* (Munich, 1980). For Caesarius of Arles, see W. Klingshirn, "Caesarius's Monastery for Women in Arles and the Composition and Function of the *Vita Caesarii*," *Revue Bénédictine* 100, no. 4 (1990): 441–81, and Vogüé, "Cesáreo de Arlés y los orígenes de la clausura de las monjas." For early monasticism in Spain, see A. Linage Conde, "El monacato visigotico, hacia la Benedictinizacion," in *Los Visigodos: Historia y Civilizacion* (Murcia, 1986), 235–59, and Mundó, "Il monachesimo."

49. A. Ferreiro, "The Missionary Labors of St. Martin of Braga in Sixth-century Galicia," *Studia Monastica* 23 (1981): 11–26; see also idem, "The Westward Journey of St. Martin of Braga," *Studia Monastica* 22 (1980): 243–51.

catechizandis rudibus.[50] His interest in Augustine is also revealed in his correspondence with Venantius Fortunatus. Although Martin's letters do not survive, a letter of his friend and correspondent Venantius shows that Martin had written inquiring about Augustine.[51]

In addition to being a monk, abbot, and bishop, Martin was a traveler. He spent his early life traveling in the eastern Mediterranean, visiting the holy places, and probably going to Egypt and visiting the monks and ascetics. He may have traveled to Gaul, possibly meeting his friend and correspondent Venantius. He made it a point to keep abreast of church activities throughout the Mediterranean. In Martin's view, there was no reason for the church in Galicia to be different from any other. This is evident in his *De trina mersione,* where in responding to accusations leveled by a foreign bishop, Boniface, Martin argued for the method of baptism used throughout the Mediterranean. He believed it would be a mistake to change simply to avoid the appearance of Arianism.[52] Among the evidence he used to support his view was a letter received in Braga in 538 from Pope Vigilius concerning baptism, and a personal account given to him by delegates of the Suevic king who had been sent to Constantinople, of the baptisms they witnessed. He concluded that it would be wrong to change to single immersion baptism: "The Arians make use of the Psalms, the Apostle, the Gospels, and many other things, just as the Catholics do—do we, for that reason, reject all these things in order not to approach their error?"[53] Martin's view, however, was not to prevail, and by the end of the sixth century single immersion was the norm in Spain.[54]

Because of his travels, Martin had a wider outlook, one that transcended the borders of the Iberian Peninsula. The role of travel was not only to inform Martin's views on doctrinal matters. He also promoted travel to sacred places as a religious act in itself. In the *De correctione rusticorum,* he exhorted his parishioners to go often to holy places to pray. In fact, he

50. For example, McKenna, *Paganism and Pagan Survivals in Spain.*
51. Venantius Fortunatus, *Carminum libri,* ed. F. Leo, *MGH AA* 4 (Berlin 1881), 101–6. Also in Martin of Braga *Martini Episcopi Bracarensis,* appendix 4.
52. Martin of Braga *De trina mersione,* in *Martini Episcopi Bracarensis,* 256–58.
53. "Numquid quia Ariani Psalmum, Apotolum, Evangelia, et alia multa ita ut Catholici celebrant, nos errorum vicinitatem fugiendo haec sumus omnia reiecturi?" Martin of Braga *De trina mersione,* in *Martini Episcopi Bracarensis,* 258.
54. In 591, Pope Gregory the Great wrote to Leander of Seville allowing Spain to use single immersion because of the fear of Arianism. This was later confirmed in Spanish church councils.

wrote that journeying to holy places was one of the few forms of travel that one should undertake on a Sunday.[55]

Another important figure in the Spanish church of the sixth century was Leander of Seville, the older brother of Isidore, who was born in Cartagena.[56] Leander and Isidore, however, were not the only religiously minded members of their family.[57] Their sister, Florentina, was a virgin dedicated to God. Leander's most popular work was his monastic rule for women, which he wrote for Florentina and her companions, known as the *De institutione virginum et contemptu mundi*. Leander outlined a religious life of reading, study, and prayer. The model of virginity they were to follow was that of the Virgin Mary. One of the first precepts of the rule concerns the importance of the avoidance of holy men, no matter how holy.[58] Similar to Jerome's injunctions to Eustochium, the precept suggests that there were holy men in Spain who kept company with monastic women, and it implicitly criticizes those who did, such as the hermit Nanctus in Mérida.[59] Leander also criticized virgins who lived in cells in the city, revealing some diversity of female monastic behavior. He makes the connection between the monastic vocation and that of the traveler, but on a purely metaphorical level; "Know that you are a sojourner in the world, that your country is not here, but in heaven."[60] Actual travel was out of the question for Leander's holy women, as he stressed the importance of remaining in the monastery.

Leander illustrates the model of the sojourner for his sister with a reference to their own mother, who was forced to leave her native city in southern

55. "Frequentate ad deprecandum deum in ecclesia vel per loca sanctorum." Martin of Braga *De correctione rustiorum* 18.10. "Et in locis proximis licet viam die domino facere, non tamen pro occasionibus malis, sed magis pro bonis, id est aut ad loca sancta ambulare, aut fratrem vel amicum visitare, vel infirmum consolare, aut tribulanti consilium vel adiutorium pro bona causa portare." Martin of Braga *De correctione rustiorum* 18.17, in *Martini Episcopi Bracarensis*, 202.

56. See Ursicino Dominguez Del Val, "Algunos temas monásticos de San Leandro de Sevilla," *Studia Patristica* 16, no. 3 (1985): 1–14; Barlow, *Iberian Fathers*, vol. 1. For an annotated bibliography, see Dominguez Del Val, *Estudios*, 226–33.

57. There are similarities between this family and that of Macrina and Basil in the fourth century. The notion of a family of ascetics is discussed in Elm, *Virgins of God*.

58. "Iam quali fuga viros fugias soror, tu iudica, si tam sollicite feminas saeculi declinabis. Quisquam vir, si sanctus est, nullam tecum gerat familiaritatem, ne virili iugitate aut infametur utriusque sanctitas aut pereat." Leander of Seville *De institutione virginum et contemptu mundi* 2.1.

59. *VPE* 3.3–8; see discussion later in this chapter.

60. "Peregrinari te in mundo discito, nec hic habere patriam, sed in caelo." Leander of Seville *De institutione virginum et contemptu mundi* 21.4.

Spain. He used the metaphor of "refugee" and "exile" in explaining the life Florentina had chosen. Their mother, a physical exile, thus became a model for spiritual exile. Leander writes that he repeatedly asked his mother whether she ever wished to return to her home and that "she knew that she had been removed for her own safety by the will of God, and she used to swear a solemn oath that she never wanted to see and never would see her country again and with many tears she would add: 'My sojourn has given me to know God; I shall die a sojourner (*peregrina*), and I shall have my tomb where I found the knowledge of God.'"[61] In late sixth-century Spain, then, we find notions of religious women as holy wanderers, but on a metaphorical level rather than as an actual religious expression.

Leander played a pivotal role in the conversion of the Visigoths to Catholicism, a conversion with strong political overtones, which brought many dangers to his life. Gregory of Tours wrote of him as the apostle to the Visigoths. His involvement in Hermanigild's conversion and, perhaps, even in his revolt against his father brought Leander into conflict with the powerful Visigothic king, Leovigild. Though first a monk, he became bishop of Seville by 579, and was involved in the effort to convert the Visigothic rulers of Spain from Arianism. In the 580s Leander was forced to flee to Constantinople to escape religious persecution by Leovigild. During this time of exile he wrote various anti-Arian treatises and met Pope Gregory the Great. Leovigild later permitted Leander to return; and when Reccared took the throne in 587, Spain officially became Catholic.

One of the most illuminating works written in the seventh century is the *Vitas sanctorum patrum Emeritensium* (*VPE*).[62] This work, written in Mérida around the 630s, contains miracle stories along with an account of the lives of five of the city's bishops from the late sixth century.[63] The anonymous author was probably associated with the Church of Saint

61. "Nosse cupiens si vellet reverti ad atriam, illa autem, quae se noverat Dei voluntate causa inde salutis exiisse, sub divina obtestatione dicebat nec velle se videre nec unquam visuram patriam illam esse; et cum magnis dicebat fletibus: 'Peregrinatio me Deum fecit agnoscere, peregrina moriar; et ibi sepulturam habeam, ubi Domini cognitionem accepi.'" Ibid., 31.3.

62. For a warning against overly trusting the historic content of the *VPE*, see Arce, "City of Mérida." For a recent discussion of the *VPE*, see Santiago Castellanos, "The Significance of Social Unanimity in a Visigothic Hagiography: Keys to an Ideological Screen," *Journal of Early Christian Studies* 11, no. 3 (2003): 387–419.

63. Collins, "Mérida and Toledo."

Eulalia, which plays an important role throughout the account.[64] Although he modeled his work on the *Dialogues* of Gregory the Great, the *VPE* is far more biographical than a collection of miracle stories.[65] The *VPE* sheds light on urban life in Mérida in the sixth century, especially in terms of episcopal-secular power relations and the role of travel and monasticism. The cult of the martyr Eulalia is the only unifying element in the account. The shrine of Eulalia was the site of miraculous healings, and it attracted people to Mérida, such as the African holy man Nanctus. Nanctus had come to the province in the mid-sixth century and served as an abbot in a Lusitanian monastery.[66] Eventually the "holy virgin Eulalia" induced him to enter her basilica in Mérida.[67] Although he spent much time in the basilica of the martyr, Nanctus also walked around the city in the company of other monks, always actively avoiding women in order not to face temptation. The city, however, was also home to at least one "noble and holy widow," Eusebia, who wished to visit with the wandering monk.[68] Nanctus's inability to remain apart from the women of Mérida caused him to flee and to build for himself and a few companions a small monastery outside the city.[69] The account states that he became so popular that even the Arian Leovigild, king of the Visigoths, donated the revenue from some of his lands to the holy monk. The men who worked on the land later brutally murdered Nanctus in the woods, while he was tending his sheep.[70] The characterization of Nanctus in the *VPE* is rather odd and departs from traditional hagiographic conventions. He is a holy man with flaws, particularly in his relations with women. The author of the *VPE* also emphasized his great popularity, yet never explains his brutal murder.

The lives of the diverse group of men, which included Hispano-Romans, Greeks, and Goths, who held the bishopric of Mérida, occupies

---

64. "Quamobrem ego indignus et omnium peccatorum primus, levita Christi, quemadmodum narravit scribere malui." *VPE* 1.22.

65. Collins, "Mérida and Toledo," 193.

66. "Narrant itaque plurimi ante multa iam curricula annorum temporibus Leuvigildi Visegothorum regis ab Africanis regionibus in porvinciam Lusitaniae Nanctus nomine advenisse abbatem." *VPE* 3.2.

67. *VPE* 3.2.

68. "Quaedam nobilissima et sanctissima vidua nomine Eusebia omni desiderio eum videre cupiebat." *VPE* 3.5.

69. "Posthaec denique statim inde egressus ad eremi loca paucis cum fratribus pervenit ibique sibi vilissimum habitaculum construxit." *VPE* 3.8.

70. *VPE* 3.11–12.

the greater part of the *VPE*. The first to appear was a Greek named Paul, another "holy man" who had arrived in the city, almost like a Lusitanian version of Martin of Braga.[71] The *VPE* never states that he was a monk, but it does describe him as "abounding in sanctity and many virtues and sur- passing everyone in humility and kindness."[72]

Paul was also a trained doctor, and even after he became bishop of the city, he sometimes had recourse to his surgical skills, though only in dire circumstances. Once, with the aid of the martyr Eulalia, Paul surgically removed a dead fetus from the womb of a prominent noblewoman of Mérida.[73] He was apparently coerced by her husband, a "senator" of the city, to perform the operation. The woman recovered, and in return for Paul's help, she and her husband immediately donated half their estate to the bishop, with the other half to follow upon their deaths. According to the *VPE,* the couple were among the wealthiest people in Lusitania.[74] When they did die, a short time later, Paul, a foreigner in Mérida, found himself in the strange position of being one of the richest individuals in the city, while also serving as its bishop.[75] The account emphasizes the tension this created, stressing that Paul was not only a relative newcomer to Mérida, but also that he was neither a Goth nor a Hispano-Roman. Though the account of the Bishop Paul in the *VPE* generally casts him in a positive light, it also reveals a high level of suspicion surrounding him.

As bishop, he had close relations with certain powerful nobles in the city, and he was enriched through their patronage. Yet Paul was clearly vulnerable to the accusations and jealousy of other nobles in Mérida. One sign of Paul's authority was his power to name his nephew as his successor

71. *VPE* 4.1.1. The *VPE* is the only place where this bishop Paul of Mérida is mentioned. See commentary in Garvin, *The "Vitas Sanctorum Patrum Emeretensium,"* 356.

72. "Qui cum multo tempore ibidem degens sanctitate et virtutibus multis polleret et humilitate atque benignitate cunctos superaret." *VPE* 4.1.2.

73. "Qui mox inibi oraculo divino est commonitus statimque consurgens ad mulieris aegrae domum incunctanter perrexit ac festinus properavit, orationem fudit, manus in nomine Domini super infirmam imposuit, in spe Dei mira subtilitate incisionem subtilissimam subtili cum ferramento fecit atque ipsum infantulum iam putridum membratim compadiatimque abstraxit." *VPE* 4.2.9–12.

74. "Tanta namque illis inerat copia rerum ut nullus senatorum in provincia Lusitaniae illis reperiretur locupletior." *VPE* 4.2.15.

75. "Quibus defunctis, omne eorum patrimonium sanctissimus Paulus episcopus accipere promeruit et qui peregrinus nihilque habens advenerat factus est cunctis potentibus potentior intantum ut omnis facultas ecclesiae ad comparationem bonorum illius pro nihilo putarentur." *VPE* 4.2.18.

to the bishopric. Fidelis, who was also a Greek, arrived in Mérida on a merchant ship, on which he served as part of the crew.[76] These seamen, perhaps like other visitors to the city, were accustomed to pay their respects to the bishop with the presentation of a gift.[77] Paul was surprised when he realized that the bearer of the gift was his own nephew. Paul then had to bribe the merchants to turn the boy over to him, for he believed Fidelis had been sent to him as a divine sign, and he told the merchants to tell his sister, the mother of Fidelis, that he had "kept her son with me to console me in my exile."[78] Like Martin of Braga, Paul was far from home and so sought connections to his homeland. With his wealth he was able to obtain his nephew from the merchants, while as bishop, he was able to appoint Fidelis as his successor.

The precariousness of the relationship between the Greek bishop and Mérida's nobles revealed itself in the opposition Fidelis faced in assuming the episcopacy after his uncle's death. Fidelis, in addition to the bishopric, had also inherited his uncle's great wealth, which stirred some of the nobles against him. They plotted to overthrow and exile him.[79] In return for being allowed to remain bishop, Fidelis promised to bequeath his wealth to the church, which would make it the wealthiest in Spain. As bishop, he used his wealth to rebuild both the bishop's palace and the basilica of Saint Eulalia.[80] Marble decorated the walls of the palace, and "ornate columns" supported the "marvelous roof."[81] Fidelis also added towers to the new basilica. He provided charity to the poor and to "captives," possibly refugees, prisoners, or exiles.[82] His great wealth also made it possible for him to make loans to the people of Mérida. On his deathbed he returned his portion of the promissory chirographs and canceled all outstanding loans.[83] Not everyone, however, received their notes in a timely manner.

---

76. *VPE* 4.3.3.

77. "Ad eum munusculum miserunt pro gratiarum actione." *VPE* 4.3.3.

78. "Renunciantes sorori meae quia filium eius ob consolationem captivitatis meae penes me retinui." *VPE* 4.3.11.

79. *VPE* 4.5.1.

80. "Quod ita factum est, ut eo tempore tantum ecclesia illa locupletata est ut illi in Hispaniae finibus nulla ecclesia esset opulentior." *VPE* 4.5.3.

81. "Ita nimirum ipsius aedificiii spatia longe lateque altis culminimbus erigens pretiosaque atria columnarum ornatibus suspendens ac pavimentum omne vel parietes cunctos nitidis marmoribus vestiens, miranda desuper tecta contexuit." *VPE* 4.4.7.

82. "Deinde multis captivis et egenis multam largitus est stipem." *VPE* 4.10.2.

83. "Ad ultimum redditis chirographis cunctorum debita relaxavit." *VPE* 4.10.2.

The author of the *VPE* related how the crowd surrounding the bishop was so large that one widow was unable to get her note from him. A miraculous vision of the martyrs Cyprian and Lawrence and the widow's subsequent prayer at their basilica were required before she could finally obtain the note from Fidelis.[84]

The account of the bishop Fidelis sheds light on the religious topography of Mérida and the spiritual importance of making the rounds of the many basilicas.[85] Twice the author mentions visions that people had of Fidelis, in the company of saints and martyrs, on a circuit of all the basilicas in the city.[86] A later successor to Fidelis, the bishop Innocent, along with the faithful of Mérida, undertook a procession around the city's churches in an attempt to alleviate a drought.[87] Most of the basilicas were dedicated to the Spanish martyrs mentioned by Prudentius in his *Peristephanon.*[88] Although this points to the local nature of the cult sites in Mérida, it also suggests the importance of the connection to the early African church. Eulalia's was the most important site, and although she was the patron saint of Mérida, her shrine was the most popular martyr shrine in the entire peninsula. Possibly the oldest church in the city, and the cathedral church, was the Church of Saint Mary, which housed the baptistery of Saint John.[89] The author of the *VPE* says that this church was called "Holy Jerusalem" in his time, and he refers to it as such in other sections of the account.[90] The acts of the Council of Mérida, which was held at this church in 666, also

---

84. *VPE* 411.3–7.

85. See Xavier Barral I Altet, "L'Image Littèraire de la ville dans la Péninsule Ibèrique pendant l'antiquité tardive," in *Actes du XIe Congrès International d'Archéologie Chrétienne* (Rome, 1989), 2:1393–1400.

86. "Alia quoque vice similiter eum quidam religiosus cum multitudine sanctorum quadam nocte de ecclesia sanctae Eulaliae egredientem et per basilicas martyrum euntem vidit, sed incaute agens multis statim indicavit." *VPE* 4.7.5–10 and *VPE* 4.8.1–4.

87. "Collecti in unum cives urbis illius cum eodem per basilicas sanctorum precibus Dominum exorantes pergebant." *VPE* 5.14.2. Garvin states, however, that this incident was one of the few times that the anonymous author of the *VPE* actually borrowed from Gregory the Great. See *Dialogues* 3.15. Garvin, *The "Vitas Sanctorum Patrum Emeretensium,"* 528.

88. These include St. Fautus, one mile outside the city, St. Lucretia, and St. Eulalia. There were also basilicas dedicated to Cyprian, an African, and Lawrence, a Roman martyr but considered a Spaniard in early Spanish sources. *VPE* 4.11.4. See Garvin, *The "Vitas Sanctorum Patrum Emeretensium,"* 400–402 and 422–24. Prudentius wrote hymns about both Lawrence and Cyprian. See *Peristephanon* 2 and 13.

89. It is mentioned as being older than the basilica of St. Eulalia. *VPE* 5.6.14.

90. "Atubi ingressus est ecclesiam sanctae Mariae quae sancta Iherusalem nunc usque vocatur." *VPE* 4.9.3. See also *VPE* 4.6.14. The name "Holy Jerusalem" also echoes Constantine's "Jerusalem" church, now called Santa Croce, in Rome.

preserves the same name.[91] It is unclear why the name changed, but there is evidence for contemporary churches in Seville, Toledo, and Tarragona also being called "Holy Jerusalem."[92] Perhaps these churches held relics from the Holy Land. The change may also relate to the practice, evidenced in the *VPE*, of making the rounds of the basilicas as a type of pilgrimage activity. Anyone could easily undertake a journey to both the spiritual and the physical Jerusalem within the confines of Mérida, eliminating the need for extended foreign travel.

The longest account in the *VPE* is that devoted to Bishop Masona. His name also appears in the proceedings of the Third Council of Toledo in 589.[93] He became bishop of Mérida around 573, and he also appears in John of Biclar's *Chronicle* as one "held in high esteem as an exponent of our [Catholic] doctrine."[94] Masona was a Goth, possibly a convert from Arianism, and the account focuses on his battles with Leovigild and Sunna, a fellow Goth and the Arian bishop of Mérida. The rivalry between Masona and Sunna was intense; they even debated each other in public. Leovigild eventually summoned Masona to Toledo, and requested that he hand over the holy tunic of the martyr Eulalia, but Masona, who traveled to Toledo with the tunic secretly hidden on his own body, refused the king's request. When threatened with exile, Masona responded, "I do not fear your threats nor am I afraid of exile and therefore I beg of you that if you know of any place where God is not present, you have me exiled there."[95] Leovigild exiled Masona to a monastery, where he spent three years with only three servants.[96] The author of the *VPE* called this period of exile a *peregrinatio,* which was the "cause of immense happiness" for Masona.[97] During his exile in the monastery he felt free from "the storms and troubles of the

---

91. See Garvin, *The "Vitas Sanctorum Patrum Emeretensium,"* 408. For the Council of Mérida, see *PL* 84:615.

92. See Garvin, *The "Vitas Sanctorum Patrum Emeretensium,"*408.

93. For Masona, see ibid., 426–29.

94. "Mausona Emeritensis ecclesiae episcopus in nostro dogmate clarus habetur." John of Biclaro, *Chronica,* 573, 8, quoted from Garvin, *The "Vitas Sanctorum Patrum Emeretensium,"* 426. English translation in Kenneth Baxter Wolf, ed., *Conquerors and Chroniclers of Early Medieval Spain* (Liverpool, 1990), 61–80.

95. "Minas tuas non pertimesco et exilium nullatenus pavesco, et ideo obsecro te ut si nosti aliquam regionem ubi Deus non est illic me exilio tradi iubeas." *VPE* 5.6.17.

96. For monasticism and liturgical processions, see Diaz, "Monasticism and Liturgy in Visigothic Spain," in Ferreiro, *The Visigoths: Studies in Culture and Society.*

97. "Cuius religatio fuit summa sublimitas, contumelium perspicua sanctitas, peregrinatio immensa felicitas." *VPE* 5.6.28.

world," and although Masona experienced difficulties during this time, his isolation was portrayed in a positive light.[98] The Catholics in the surrounding area supported him by sending supplies.[99] Eventually Masona ended his own exile when Eulalia herself visited him in a vision and told him that it was time to return to Mérida, for Leovigild had died. Masona made a triumphal entrance into the city. The Arian bishop Sunna attempted to have him killed and sent young Arian Gothic nobles to do the job. Masona, however, was under the able protection of the duke of Mérida, Claudius, a Hispano-Roman held in high esteem by the author of the *VPE*. "Claudius was sprung of noble stock, the son of Roman parents. He was staunchly Catholic in faith and strongly bound by the bonds of religion, strenuous in war, most responsive in the fear of the Lord, trained for the pursuits of war, and also experienced in the deeds of war."[100] Masona, though a Goth, had close ties to the Hispano-Roman nobility of Mérida. Sunna's plan was thwarted; and after refusing to convert to Catholic belief, he fled with his supporters to Africa.[101]

The *VPE* has great praise for Masona, who, before he became bishop, served the basilica of Eulalia as a deacon or priest, as did the anonymous author of the account. As bishop, Masona founded monasteries outside the city and built a xenodochium for travelers and the sick, which he very richly endowed.[102] Mérida, situated on the Guadiana river, was an important center of trade in Spain. Travelers frequently came to the city and some, such as Nanctus, Paul, and Fidelis, decided to stay. This gave Mérida a diverse population of Goths, Hispano-Romans, Africans, Greeks, and other foreigners. It was also a religiously mixed society with Catholics, Arians, Jews, and Gentiles.[103]

---

98. "Ad turbines et procellas mundiales." *VPE* 5.8.2.

99. "Antes fores monasterii reperti sunt ducenti asini onusti stantes qui missi cum diversis alimoniis ad eumdem virum a diversis viris catholicis fuerant." *VPE* 5.7.7.

100. "Idem vero Claudius nobili genere ortus Romanis fuit parentibus progenitus. Existebat prorsus fide catholicus et religionis vinculis fortiter astrictus, in praeliis strenuus, in timore Dei valde promptissimus, in bellica studia eruditus, in causis bellicis nihilominus exercitatus." *VPE* 5.10.7.

101. *VPE* 5.11.13–15. Sunna, his revolt, and his exile are also mentioned by John of Biclar, *Chronica* 88, in Wolf, *Conquerors and Chroniclers*.

102. "Statim in exordio episcopatus sui monasteria multa fundavit, praediis magnis locupletavit." *VPE* 5.3.3. "Deinde xenodochium fabricavit magnisque patrimoniis ditavit constitutisque ministris vel medicis, peregrinorum et aegrotantium usibus deservire praecepit." *VPE* 5.3.4.

103. Jews and non-Christians were admitted to the xenodochium, and both of these populations were supporters of Masona. *VPE* 5.2.7.

The last bishop discussed in the *VPE* was, like Masona, a Goth named Renovatus. Unlike his Gothic predecessor, Renovatus was the abbot of the monastery of Cauliana, just eight miles outside the city on the banks of the Guadiana.[104] Renovatus appears both in the beginning of the account in a story about one of the monks of his monastery who reforms his ways, and at the end as the bishop of Mérida, apparently recently deceased. In the second instance, the author of the *VPE* provides a detailed description of the bishop's appearance: "tall of body, remarkably handsome, of graceful build, pleasing to look upon, of attractive face, comely countenance, and exceedingly admirable to behold."[105] This description, combined with high praise for Renovatus's skill at teaching and training students and his position at the beginning and the end of the account may suggest that the author of the *VPE* was one of Renovatus's former students.[106]

The *VPE*, though hagiographic in nature, breaks away from many of the standard approaches and use of *topoi* present in most works of hagiography. By telling the story of a group of religious men, mostly bishops, and using their relation to the cult of Eulalia as a common thread, the *VPE* provides fascinating insight into the social, episcopal, and monastic world of Mérida. It was a city full of foreigners, travelers, and exiles of different nationalities and religious loyalties. The work also reveals the diverse backgrounds of the city's bishops and how the position of the bishop gradually came to be held by Catholic Goths.[107] There was a close relationship between the bishop, the relics of St. Eulalia, and the monasteries surrounding the city.

---

104. *VPE* 2.2. Garvin states that this monastery was identified in the nineteenth century as the hilltop monastery of Santa Maria de Cubillana, which is next to the Guadiana river. Garvin, *The "Vitas Sanctorum Patrum Emeretensium,"* 312.

105. "Erat enim procerus corpore, forma prespicuus, statura decorus, obtutu gratus, venusto vultu, decora facie nimiumque admirablilis aspectu." *VPE* 5.14.4.

106. This is the only source that mentions Renovatus as a bishop of Mérida. Garvin refers to other scholars who believe that the author of the *VPE* had studied under Renovatus. Garvin, *The "Vitas Sanctorum Patrum Emeretensium,"* 529.

107. Mérida was not the only city where Goths served as bishops in the seventh century: the Goth Ildefonsus became bishop of Toledo in 657. Ildefonsus himself wrote several theological works, including *De cognitione baptismi, De itinere deserti, De virginitate perpetua Sanctae Mariae,* and a continuation of Isidore of Seville's *De viris illustribus. De itinere deserti* compares the life of the newly baptized Christian to a spiritual journey through the desert, purposefully alluding to the Desert Fathers. This was a journey through the desert meant not just for monks, but for all Christians. The desert was a place of spiritual warfare and a focus of symbolic meanings. The *De cognitione baptismi, De itinere deserti,* and *De virginitate perpetua Sanctae Mariae* can be found in Vicente Blanco Garcia and Julio Campos Ruiz, eds. *Santos Padres Españoles,* vol. 1, *San Ildefonso de Toledo* (Madrid, 1971). *De viris illustribus* can be found

The most famous Hispano-gothic holy man was Fructuosus of Braga.[108] Though Fructuosus became a bishop, he was first and foremost a monk. His monasticism was clearly a product of a Visigothic world. Although our evidence for Fructuosus's life is rather full for a seventh-century figure, we are certain of only one date in his life, December 1, 656, when he became the metropolitan of Braga.[109] He was probably born around the year 600 and began his life of monastic wandering around 625. Our most detailed and interesting information on Fructuosus comes from the anonymous *Vita sancti Fructuosi,* written soon after his death, which may have occurred in 665.[110]

According to the *vita,* Fructuosus's father was a military leader.[111] As in many hagiographic texts, the future greatness of the saintly protagonist is foreshadowed in childhood, yet the *vita* varies from traditional hagiographic conventions in many other ways. The *vita* begins with the story of Fructuosus's father taking him as a young boy, *puerulus,* to the mountains around Bierzo in order to meet with shepherds and inquire as to the condition of his flocks. While his father was busy, Fructuosus was secretly surveying the area as to its suitability for monasteries.[112] The author emphasizes Fructuosus's monastic destiny rather than his rise to episcopal power. Upon the death of his parents Fructuosus became a monk, literally putting off his secular clothing

in Carmen Codoñer Merino, ed., *El "De viris illustribus" de Ildefonso de Toledo: Estudio y Edicion critica* (Salamanca, 1972). On Ildefonsus, see Juan Francisco Rivera Recio, *San Ildefonso de Toledo: Biografía, época y posteridad* (Madrid, 1985), and Sister Athanasius Braegelmann, *The Life and Writings of Saint Ildefonsus of Toledo* (Washington, D.C., 1942), 5. For an annotated bibliography, see Dominguez Del Val, *Estudios,* 347–57.

108. Dominguez Del Val, *Estudios,* 234–44.

109. We have a near contemporary *vita* as well as two monastic rules and a couple letters attributed to him, plus mentions of him in other writers, Valerius of Bierzo, and in the acts of the tenth council of Toledo.

110. See Claude Barlow, ed., *Iberian Fathers, volume 2: Braulio of Saragossa, Fructuosus of Braga* (Washington, D.C., 1969); Charles Julian Bishko, "The Pactual Tradition in Hispanic Monasticism," in *Spanish and Portuguese Monastic History, 600–1300,* ed. Charles Julian Bishko (London, 1984) 1–43; Manuel C. Díaz y Díaz, *La Vida de San Fructuoso de Braga* (Braga, 1974); Antonio Linage, "San Benito y las Fuentes Literarias de la Obra Monastica de Fructuoso De Braga," *Studia Patristica* 20 (1989): 264–73; and *The Vita Sancti Fructuosi: Text with a Translation, Introduction, and Commentary* (henceforth VSF), trans. Sister Frances Clare Nock (Washington, D.C., 1946). Some have attributed the life to Valerius of Bierzo, but there is much opposition to this notion. Valerius does however mention Fructuosus in his writing and was the abbot of one of his monastic foundations.

111. "Ducis exercitus Spaniae proles." *VSF* 11.89.

112. "Hic vero puerulus, inspirante Domino, pro aedificatione monasterii apta loca pensabat; et intra semetipsum retinens nemini manifestabat." *VSF* 2.89.

and receiving the tonsure.[113] At this point the author writes that Fructuosus placed himself not in a monastery but under the spiritual guidance of a bishop, Conantius, possibly the seventh-century bishop of Palencia. This relationship continued for a period and ended abruptly. The *vita* contains a strange story surrounding Fructuosus's taking possession of some sort of dwelling, *habitaculus,* belonging to the church. Due to a misunderstanding, a nameless enemy challenged him and summarily expelled Fructuosus from his new home along with all his baggage. The enemy, full of pride and envy of Fructuosus, took over the dwelling for himself.[114] Fructuosus remained silent about this injustice, one that is never resolved in the account. This was the time that Fructuosus returned to the place he had thought suitable for a monastery, in the hills around Bierzo, and there established the monastery of Compludo.[115]

This strange story reveals a tension between the ecclesiastical hierarchy of the region and the ambitions of the young monk. Never again is his relationship with Conantius mentioned. Clearly there had been trouble during his stay under Conantius. But what sort of trouble? The description of the foundation of Compludo provides an indication. Fructuosus used his own funds, his inheritance, to create the monastery, and he was able to fill it quickly with monks, many from his own family, perhaps ex-slaves, and others from distant regions in Spain. Once again a problem quickly developed. Fructuosus's use of the inheritance angered his sister and her husband. The couple subsequently took their case to the king (it is unclear which one), who ordered Fructuosus to give up part of his endowment of the monastery and return it to his sister and brother-in-law. The author of the *vita* clearly shares what must have been Fructuosus's own indignation at this order to part with the monastery's patrimony. He writes that the young monk immediately went into mourning for himself and his monastery, a state which included fasts, lamentations, prayer vigils, and draping the entire monastery in somber sack-clothes. According to the *vita,* Fructuosus then wrote an angry letter warning of divine retribution, and his nameless brother-in-law soon died before his time. Once again with this odd account of conflict between Fructuosus and his sister, resulting in the holy man losing

---

113. "Abiecto saeculari habitu tonsoque capite." *VSF* 2.89.

114. *VSF* 2.91.

115. The author does states that a mysterious fire of divine origin later broke out and burned down the dwelling.

his case and his property, and apparently in his seeking revenge by causing the death of his brother-in-law, we see a *vita* very different from the traditional models of hagiography.

The monastery survived, but Fructuosus quickly left, after writing a rule, between 630 and 635, and appointing a leader, a *pater* for the community.[116] The author attributes Fructuosus's departure to the growing fame of his sanctity and the disruption this fame was causing in his life. It was at this point that Fructuosus began to wander. Barefoot and wearing goat skins, he traveled deep into the forests, valleys, and caves surrounding Bierzo and Astorga. He was so enveloped by the wilderness, according to the *vita,* that at one time a hunter mistook him for a wild animal and only divine intervention prevented from him firing an arrow at the holy man.[117] Once again, Fructuosus felt compelled to establish monasteries, and the *vita* intersperses the accounts of his many foundations with additional anecdotes revealing his holiness. He established the monastery of Rufianense in the mountains, and there he stayed alone until his monks at Compludo "lovingly" forced him to return to them.[118] Even on his return journey, he set up another foundation, the monastery of Visonia. Later he established another monastery on a remote island off the coast of Galicia, which he called Peonense. This location was chosen, according to the hagiographer, because of his fondness for navigation. In fact, at one point he plunged into the churning seas in order to swim to a poorly moored boat that was cast adrift.

Although the author of the *vita* stresses that Fructuosus's establishment of these monasteries was a feat accomplished alone, in all four cases discussed thus far, his community of monks was not far off. They act like a chorus cheering and supporting each foundation. In opposition to this choir of supportive monks stand the ever nameless enemies who try to thwart his intentions. These enemies, always described as either wicked, *iniqui,* or jealous, *invidi,* or proud, always try to hinder his monastic endeavors. Near the end of the *vita* another monastery is named, Nono, nine miles from the seashore, probably near Cadiz.[119] This monastery housed communities of both men and women. This is the first time that the author of the *vita* mentions women, and the origins of this double monastery will be examined later in this chapter.

116. *VSF* 4. The rule still survives.
117. *VSF* 5.
118. *VSF* 6.
119. *VSF* 14.

The *vita* also recounts a visit Fructuosus made to the shrine of the martyr Eulalia in Mérida, in the province of Lusitania to the south. Fructuosus made his journey to the Eulalia shrine as a stop along the way to an island off Cadiz. Our author notes that Fructuosus was in the company of fellow monks during this journey, but when he became separated from the rest, another case of mistaken identity occurred.[120] His companions had gone ahead, and Fructuosus stopped in a forest to say a short prayer. He threw himself to the ground.[121] A madman, according to the hagiographer, spotted him and because of his location, actions, and attire (he was once again barefoot and clad in goat skins and a coarse cloak) mistook him for a fugitive, *fugitivus,* and began to hurl insults at the prostrate monk. Fructuosus answered, "Clearly I am not a fugitive."[122] The madman, now referred to as a *rusticus,* became angry at Fructuosus's statement and, according to our author, "insisted that he was in every way a fugitive."[123] After this exchange of words between Fructuosus and his accuser, there was violence: the rustic began to beat Fructuosus repeatedly with his staff. Fructuosus then made the sign of the cross, and according to the *vita,* a demon appeared, who immediately began to do great violence to the rustic. Eventually the holy man prayed and healed the rustic, and the strange episode ended.

Fructuosus wore the tonsure, but he repeatedly had difficulty being recognized as a monk. Was this because he was not in a monastery and instead wandering the wilderness? Or is the hagiographer alluding to the problem Fructuosus had with his nameless enemies? Did his enemies fail to recognize him as a monk? Were his activities and the legitimacy of his monasteries questioned by the authorities? The *vita* often mentions Fructuosus's attire, animal skins, bare feet, coarse clothing, and how people, such as the hunter, the nameless man who ordered him out of the *habitaculus,* and the rustic madman in the woods who thought he was a fugitive, seem to mistake him for someone or something else. He was a wandering monk and clearly not alone in his endeavor. Others usually accompanied him, including the monk Benenatus, who provided our anonymous hagiographer with eyewitness accounts of miracles performed by Fructuosus, which the hagiographer inserted into the *vita* in the first person. Benenatus, who was also a priest, traveled with Fructuosus to Baetica from Lusitania.

120. "Cum ceteris comitibus." *VSF* ii.
121. "Qui dum humo prostratus iaceret." *VSF* ii.
122. "Plane fugitivus non sum." *VSF* ii.
123. *VSF* ii.

Women were a part of his monastic establishments, and some of these women also practiced a form of wandering asceticism. Near the end of the *vita,* the author gives an account of the life of a woman named Benedicta. Benedicta is portrayed in many ways as a female version of Fructuosus. She too came from an important family and had been engaged to a Visigothic military commander who was close to the king. She escaped this union by fleeing her family and home and setting out on a monastic life of wandering. The hagiographer writes: "Secretly fleeing from her parents [she] went to diverse places of the desert, and wandering thus through pathless and unknown spots at length under the guidance of the Lord," she eventually came upon Fructuosus's monastic establishment called Nono, and, by means of secret messages, asked Fructuosus for help.[124] His monastery supported her with food and shelter in her own private hermitage. Soon other women, hearing of her holiness, attempted to join her. When over eighty women had joined her, she, like Fructuosus before her, established her own monastery. The author of the *vita* writes: "For these [the other women] in another solitude she, in the accustomed manner, constructed a monastery."[125] This "accustomed manner" appears to be the manner of Fructuosus, a link our hagiographer makes clear. But the similarity did not end there. Benedicta too had her unnamed enemies, including her jilted fiancé, who "because of his great grief and pain" went to the king to denounce her. The king was sympathetic to his military official and sent a judge to the monastery to conduct an investigation. The judge, moved by her holy life, decided against her suitor, telling him to "leave her to serve the Lord and seek for yourself another wife."[126] Her monastery of women flourished and grew in stature alongside that of Fructuosus.

Fructuosus and Benedicta led monastic lives devoted to travel, wandering, and the establishment of monasteries. Their travel does not seem to have been continuous, but rather a stage, though often a recurring one. Fructuosus used travel as a part of his own monastic vocation and as a method for spreading monasticism as a way of life. It was a way of life that many did not approve of, and he often faced opposition, as did Benedicta. So how and why did Fructuosus become a bishop? Near the end of the *vita,* Fructuosus

124. "Suis occulte fugiens parentibus, sola ingressa est diversa eremi loca et sic per invia et ignota errando loca, tandem, duce Domino." *VSF* 15.
125. "Quibus in alia solitudine, more solito, construit monasterium." *VSF* 15.
126. "Dimitte eam Domino servire et quaere tibi aliam uxorem." *VSF* 15.

was finally overcome, around the year 650, by the desire to "undertake a new pilgrimage to visit the East."[127] He was ready to leave Spain and continue his wandering to the eastern parts of the Mediterranean, to Egypt, the birthplace of monasticism, and to the holy places in Palestine. After selecting companions to make the journey with him and secretly preparing to embark, he once again encountered royal opposition and was suddenly arrested on orders from the king. The hagiographer explained that the king and his advisers did not want to let "such a shining light" leave Spain.[128] Yet Fructuosus was still put into a prison cell and eventually brought before the king in chains.

After Fructuosus's arrest he was forced to become bishop of Braga, thus eliminating the possibility of a journey to the East and also ending his wandering ways. Our hagiographer is quick to point out that Fructuosus did not change his attire or his style of living, and that he continued to establish monasteries, although he does not name them. Leaving his many monasteries under the control of fathers or abbots and ensconced in a bishopric, Fructuosus was thus conveniently assimilated into the ecclesiastical power structure. Evidence of his rise to the episcopacy also exists in the acts of the tenth Council of Toledo, held in 656, where he was given metropolitan status in Braga by a unanimous vote, replacing the scandal-ridden episcopacy of Potamius.

The statement of elevation claimed that Fructuosus was already bishop of Dumio, a fact not mentioned by the hagiographer. Dumio was recognized as a see by 580 and is one of thirteen episcopal sees in Galicia listed in the Suevic parochial document.[129] The *vita* referred to Dumio as the location of one of Fructuosus's monastic foundations as well as the location of his sepulcher, now called São Frutuoso de Montelios, which still stands outside Braga.[130] The building is similar in size and shape to the mausoleum of Galla Placidia in Ravenna. Perhaps he was an abbot and a bishop, a bishop under the influence of the rule, as suggested by his monastic writings. Martin of Braga too had founded a monastery at Dumio, though once again this was not mentioned in the *vita*.

---

127. "Ut partem occupans orientis novam arriperet peregrinationem." *VSF* 17.
128. "Ne talis lux Spaniam desereret." *VSF* 17.
129. See Fletcher, *St. James's Catapult*, 26–27.
130. Jerrilyn D. Dodds, *Architecture and Ideology in Early Medieval Spain* (University Park, Pa., 1990), 12.

We know of two monastic rules that come from Fructuosus's monasteries, possibly written by Fructuosus himself. Both of these are rooted in Eastern asceticism and the *Sayings of the Desert Fathers,* as well as in Augustine's rule and Cassian's monastic writings. In a surviving letter of Fructuosus, he thanks Braulio, the bishop of Saragossa, for sending him a copy of Cassian's *Conferences.*[131] The *Regula Monachorum Complutensis,* written around 630–35 for the monks of the monastery of Compludo, is on the surface a very severe rule, obsessed with proper behavior, perhaps indicating a discipline problem at Compludo.[132] The other rule, *Regula Monastica Communis,* written in 660, is a general rule that contains some very curious precepts condemning the creation of monasteries by the laity or secular priests without the permission of the local bishop.[133] The rule also reveals a fully monastic society, even placing the bishop under the monastic system. There are provisions for the entry of entire families, husband, wife, and children, into the monastery. There is evidence of kind treatment of strangers and travelers who come to the monastery.[134] The rule specifies that the brethren should not appear suspicious of any guests and to attempt to heal those who arrive ill at the monastery. The last precept of the *Regula Monastica Communis* concerns any monk who flees from his monastery, who if caught "must be brought back to his own abbot with his hands tied behind his back."[135] If, however, the monk has "returned to the world," the church and the entire lay community must banish him. A provision for the return of such fallen monks is made in the following closing sentence of the rule: "If the apostates are driven away by all, and wander here and there unsettled and constantly on the move, and from sheer necessity desire to return to their monastery, they shall be brought to an assembly of the elders and tried like potter's vases in the furnace, and when proved, they may be taken back to their monastery, but must sit in the lowest rank, not the highest."[136]

131. Fructuosus of Braga to Bishop Braulio of Saragossa, letter 43, in Braulio of Saragossa *Epistulae* (henceforth *Ep.*), *PL* 80; an English translation can be found in *Iberian Fathers, volume 2: Braulio of Saragossa, Fructuosus of Braga,* ed. Claude W. Barlow (Washington, D.C., 1969).

132. *Regula Monachorum Complutensis,* translated in Barlow, *Iberian Fathers volume 2,* 155–75.

133. *Regula Monastica Communis* 1–2, translated in Barlow, *Iberian Fathers volume 2,* 176–206.

134. See Antonio Viñayo González, "La Hospitalidad Monástica en las Reglas de San Isidoro de Sevilla y de San Fructuoso del Bierzo," in *El Camino de Santiago, la hospitalidad monástica y las peregrinaciones,* ed. Horacio Santiago-Otero (Salamanca, 1992), 39–51.

135. *Regula Monastica Communis* 20.

136. Ibid.

On the one hand, this rule is clearly a response not only to monastic wandering but also to increasing regional turmoil. The invasions and battles between the Germanic tribes caused the dislocation of many, and in this unstable environment people sought refuge in monasteries, sometimes only claiming to lead religious lives. On the other hand, we may understand the strictures of the rule as a commentary on the monastic life of genuine monks in this unstable time, a time when all confidence in the order of daily life was removed. It must have seemed to many as if the world were coming to an end. As was apparently the case for Fructuosus, monastic expression through wandering, focusing on the homelessness of the Christian, may have seemed the only coherent religious way of life under such circumstances.

Fructuosus of Braga's monasticism, as evidenced by the *vita* and by his own monastic rules, only seems strange if one is using the Benedictine Rule as a guide in interpreting proper monastic behavior. The importance of wandering and the foundation of monasteries are actually quite in tune with the forms of monasticism we find not only on the Iberian Peninsula but elsewhere in the West. Fructuosus, Benedicta, Benenatus, and the other monks of these seventh-century monasteries were part of a diverse monastic world—a world in which competing monastic practices and episcopal opposition could easily be represented in a *vita* or monastic rule as envious "enemies," confused madmen, or ignorant rustics. Such language in a monastic rule indicates a tumultuous and insecure environment, the kind that we would expect to give rise not only to a diverse set of monastic practices but also to severe efforts to control them.

It is not surprising that notions of travel as a form of monastic asceticism continued at Compludo after the death of Fructuosus. These ideas had a profound influence on Valerius of Bierzo, a monk, and later abbot, at Compludo in the late seventh century. Valerius is best known for supplying the name Egeria to the previously anonymous text of her journeys in the East.[137] Egeria, whom he called a *sanctimonialis,* and her journey to the Holy Land had impressed Valerius.[138] His ability to recognize Egeria as a nun reveals that, at least in the seventh century, a Spanish monk did not see

---

137. Valerius of Bierzo *Epistola.* For an annotated bibliography on Valerius, see Dominguez Del Val, *Estudios,* 245–48.

138. Valerius of Bierzo *Epistola* 1. The connection between the letter of Valerius and the text of Egeria's voyage was first made by M. Férotin, "Le Véritable auteur de la *Peregrinatio Silviae.*"

any inconsistency between a relatively itinerant lifestyle and a monastic profession. Valerius himself was probably more of a wanderer than a stationary monk. In his *Ordo Querimoniae,* a unique autobiographical source, he describes how he literally fled from the world to Compludo and later to "a desert hermitage" outside the city of Astorga in Spain. The theme of a monastic desire for travel, flight, and pilgrimage is present in many of Valerius of Bierzo's other works.[139]

Braulio of Saragossa, who corresponded with Fructuosus, is another central figure in understanding the monastic landscape of the Iberian Peninsula. Like Leander and Isidore, he came from a family of monks and bishops.[140] His father, Gregory, was a bishop, as was his older brother John, who was bishop of Saragossa from 619 to 631.[141] Another brother served as abbot of the monastery of Saint Emilian in the Rioja, the upper Ebro valley. Braulio wrote the life of Saint Emilian for his brother, Fronimian. His sister Pomponia was also a monastic leader in the Rioja, and Braulio tells us that she was an abbess.[142] Braulio, bishop of Saragossa from 631 to 651, was present at the fourth Council of Toledo, in 633, which sought unification of the Spanish church through a standard liturgy.[143] The other bishops chose him to write a letter to Pope Honorius expressing the opinion of the Spanish church concerning converted Jews who had lapsed to their previous beliefs.[144]

The surviving collection of Braulio's letters gives a detailed view of seventh-century ecclesiastical Spain, including references to several journeys within Spain. Braulio often wrote to Isidore of Seville asking for copies of various works, revealing some of the more troubling aspects of seventh-century Iberian life, including famine, sickness, and Basque raiding parties. In one letter, Braulio responds to questions concerning the Resurrection posed to

---

139. In his *De Genere monachorum,* in addition to describing genuine monks, he discusses the behavior of various false and "bad" monks. His other works, such as *De Maximo monacho, De Bonello monacho,* and *De Caelesti revelatione,* deal with monastic visions of heaven and hell, see Díaz y Díaz, *Visiones.* Roger Collins, "The 'Autobiographical' Works of Valerius of Bierzo: Their Structure and Purpose," in *Los Visigodos: Historia y Civilización* (Murcia, 1986), 425–42; Aherne, *Valerio of Bierzo;* and Antonio Viñayo González, "San Fructuoso y San Valerio: Dos archiveros Bercianos del siglo VI," in *Memoria Ecclesiae II: Las raices visigoticas de la iglesia en España: en torno al concilio III de Toledo* (Oviedo, 1991), 57–62.

140. On Braulio, see Linehan, *History and the Historians,* 47–50. For an annotated bibliography on Braulio, see Dominguez Del Val, *Estudios,* 331–37.

141. Collins, *Early Medieval Spain,* 68–70.

142. Barlow, *Iberian Fathers volume 2,* 3.

143. He also attended the fifth and sixth councils of Toledo. Linehan, *History and the Historians,* 47.

144. Braulio *Ep.* 12, to Pope Honorius.

him by the abbot Tajo, who around 650 had just returned from a long trip to Rome. Braulio was excited about the copies of works by Gregory the Great that Tajo had brought back to Spain: "Please send me quickly to be copied the books of the holy Pope Gregory which previously did not exist in Spain, but which have been brought here from Rome by your zeal and effort."[145] He made the request in the name of his brother Fronimian, and specified that he would quickly return the copies to Tajo. Tajo, as an abbot, was apparently able to travel away from his monastery, but this appears to have been out of the ordinary. Tajo not only collected works to bring back to Spain, but he also visited many churches during his journey, for it was his discovery that some contained relics of the blood of the Lord that caused his worry about the Resurrection.[146]

Fructuosus likewise expressed dismay, in a letter to Braulio, at the unavailability of important monastic writings, such as Cassian's *Conferences,* in Spain. He therefore also requested various Gallic *vitae,* as well as Braulio's own recently published *Life of Emilian.*[147] For Fructuosus, Braulio provided a link to the greater monastic world. Braulio's reply to Fructuosus contains a digression on the beauty of monastic life as opposed to the life of a worldly bishop. His emotional words echoed the idea of the monk as a pilgrim and exile, and a rightful future inhabitant of the heavenly Jerusalem. "How happy you are for having abandoned the business of this world and chosen in advance the holy leisure! . . . How blessed is that desert and vast solitude which recently knew only wild beasts and is now filled with the habitations of monks, congregated by you and singing praises of God; of pilgrims of the world, citizens of God, captives from Babylon, predestined to Jerusalem."[148] Braulio also warned Fructuosus to continue to be wary of Priscillianism in Galicia. He even accused Orosius of Priscillianist beliefs, beliefs that he only discarded under the influence of Augustine.[149]

Braulio is the author of the *Life of Saint Emilian,* a monk of the sixth century. He wrote the *vita* at the request of his brothers, the bishop of

145. Braulio *Ep.* 42, to Tajo, in Barlow, *Iberian Fathers volume 2,* 95.
146. Tajo, fragment of a letter to Braulio, in Barlow, *Iberian Fathers volume 2,* 88.
147. Fructuosus to Braulio, in Braulio *Ep.* 43.
148. "Felix tu qui, huius mundi contemnens negotia, praeelegisti otia sancta. . . . Felix illa eremus, et vasta solitudo, quae dudum tantum ferarum conscia, nunc monachorum per te congregatorum laudes Deo praecinentium habitaculis est referta, peregrinorum mundi, civium Dei, Babylonia captivorum, Jerusalem praedestinatorum." Braulio *Ep.* 44, to Fructuosus, *PL* 80:693.
149. Ibid.

Saragossa, John, and the abbot, Fronimian. John had already built a basilica to honor Emilian and wanted his talented brother to write a *vita* to accompany the building of the church. Owing to various administrative duties, Braulio was unable to compose the life before Bishop John's death, but the guilt of receiving the request and not acting on it sooner, coupled with a new request from his other brother, encouraged Braulio to set down in words the story of Emilian. "But because my notes on his virtues were interrupted almost as soon as I began them by inattention, due to a large amount of administrative work, I soon became busy with various ensuing misfortunes and with the troubles of uncertain times, until I lost even the desire to write and could not give my attention to it although you yourself strongly urged it."[150]

Braulio identifies Emilian as the patron of his own religious family. He draws his evidence from the written testimony of the deceased Abbot Citonatus and the "holy woman" Potamia, as well as from the living memory of two priests, Sofronius and Gerontius.[151] Potamia may have been one of the holy virgins with whom Emilian lived at the end of his life.[152] The holy man had moved in with the virgins of Christ when he was eighty years old and suffering from many illnesses. He had been a shepherd, and while herding his flock had decided to flee his homeland: "He meditated on the celestial life and left that country and hastened to a desert region."[153] Like Antony, he became the follower of a hermit named Felix. When he had learned the ways of a hermit, he left Felix, returning to his homeland and settling in a remote place on a mountain outside his old village, where he remained for forty years. His isolated home aroused the interest of the local population, and soon the stream of visitors began to concern the local bishop, Didymus.

Didymus dealt with the holy man by forcing him to become a priest, a fate Emilian did not desire.[154] This change from "the contemplative to the active life," brought on a series of new troubles for the holy man. Jealousy raged among his fellow clerics, who plotted to discredit him before the bishop. Believing Emilian guilty of ruining church property, the bishop stripped him of his priesthood.[155] Emilian then appears to have settled

---

150. Braulio, *Life of St. Emilian*, preface; Braulio *Ep.* 44, to Fructuosus.
151. Braulio, *Life of St. Emilian*, preface.
152. Ibid., 23.
153. Ibid., 1.
154. Ibid., 5.
155. Ibid., 6.

nearby, and become even more popular, through the performance of miracles, than he had been before. The populace supported him, as did some of the nobility, such as the senator Honorius, whose household Emilian had freed of demons. Honorius sent the holy man wagons loaded with food and provisions.[156] In turn Emilian provided charity, miraculous cures, and exorcisms for the surrounding population. Hospitality was one of his principal precepts. He often invited many of those who came to visit him to stay as guests in his monastery, but he also traveled. One of Braulio's stories revealing the dangers of travel concerned Emilian: while on a journey, the devil approached him and challenged him to a wrestling match on the road. Emilian, aided by prayer, was able to overcome the demon.

Despite opposition, the holy man Emilian, whom Braulio compared to Antony and Martin, went his own way.[157] With some supporters from local nobility and aided by the holy virgins whom he lived with for twenty years (not without criticism), Emilian became an important force in the community.[158] Though Braulio states that Emilian died during the reign of Leovigild, he never alludes to the possible Arianism of the clergy in sixth-century Rioja. Nor does he account for the fact that although the holy man prophesized the end of Cantabria, and the rule of the nobles, the same nobles, who allegedly "all reverently paid attention to him," did not heed his advice and perform penance for their sins. They were killed by Leovigild, or so Braulio informs us.

With the *Life of Emilian,* Braulio and his brothers sought to associate themselves with a popular holy man and with the growth of monasticism in the Rioja. When seen in light of Braulio's letter to Fructuosus praising the monastic pursuit, Braulio's elevation of monasticism over the life of the secular clergy becomes understandable. Braulio and his brother John, though bishops, were eager to make connections with a wider circle of nobles, and it was through the holy man Emilian and their support of monasticism that this would be achieved. Braulio's family was already an important one in the area, probably of noble status. His father had been a local bishop, and one of Braulio's sisters, Basilla, was married to a wealthy noble. After her

---

156. Ibid., 17 and 22.

157. Ibid., 5. The priest Asellus, who was with Emilian at his death, is the only priest mentioned in a positive light. He is called "a most holy priest." Ibid., 27.

158. Braulio, *Life of St. Emilian,* mentions the following nobles: Senator Sicorius, 11, Count Eugene, 14, Senator Nepotianus and wife Proseria, 15, Curial Maximus, 16, Senator Honorius, 17 and 22, and Senator Abundantius, 26. On living with the virgins, see p. 23.

husband's death, she seems to have supported monks and nuns, and she may have even founded a guesthouse for travelers.[159] Association with the cult of Emilian strengthened Braulio's family's position. His generation produced an array of episcopal and monastic leaders.

On the Iberian Peninsula we find the continuity of non-Benedictine forms of monasticism until the Islamic invasion of the early eighth century. The Benedictine Rule came into Spain only after the conquest, and even later in a form adapted for women. The earliest evidence of the Benedictine Rule in Spain is from 822, in the Spanish March.[160] Penetration came from France and via Frankish influence. The earliest Benedictine houses were in Catalonia, founded or restored in the ninth and tenth centuries.[161]

The monastic practices of Egeria, Orosius, and the other travelers were very different from the precepts set out in the *Regula Benedictina*. It was a slow process by which Benedictine monasticism grew to dominance in Western Europe and overwhelmed the variety of practices that had prevailed. By the twelfth century the new Cistercian and Carthusian reform movements, both based on stricter observance of the Benedictine Rule, served to further strengthen the hold of Benedictine monasticism. This dominant position was eventually challenged in the thirteenth century with the advent of two new movements, the Franciscan and the Dominican, mendicant movements that stressed travel and preaching and downplayed the importance of a permanent and stationary monastery. Perhaps it was this challenge from a new mobile and very successful monasticism that finally effaced the memory of the variety of early Western monastic practices, a variety that had travel and exile at its heart.

159. Braulio *Ep.* 18, to Pomponia. This letter was written to his sister Pomponia, an abbess, in order to console her on the death of their sister Basilla. In the letter, Braulio compares Basilla to the also recently deceased bishop of Gerona, Nunnitus, calling them both protectors of monks and nuns and providers of hospitality for travelers.

160. Linage Conde, "El monacato visigotico," 241; see also volume 1, *El monacato Hispano prebenedictino*, of Linage Conde, *Los Origenes.*

161. Collins, *Early Medieval Spain*, 259–60.

CHAPTER SIX

CHRISTIAN TRAVEL IN THE EARLY ISLAMIC PERIOD

Religiously motivated travel continued to exist within a monastic context as late as the seventh and eighth centuries. Initially, the Islamic conquest did not have a major impact, as some have believed, on the ability of Christians to travel to the Holy Land. What did have a greater effect on religious travel were both the growing influence in Western Europe of Benedictine monasticism, with its provisions for physical stability, and the dramatic transformations within the city of Jerusalem beginning in the seventh century. It is to the fate of Jerusalem as a holy destination, as well as to the changes in Western monastic practices and their effects on travel, that we will now turn to.

Jerusalem experienced massive destruction in the early seventh century, but not at the hands of the Muslims. A generation before its surrender to the Muslims, Jerusalem fell to the Persians during an invasion that brought much devastation and bloodshed. In 614 Persian invaders breached the walls of the city, causing its inhabitants to seek refuge in churches, cisterns, caves, and even aqueducts.[1] The Persians burned many buildings, including churches, and killed approximately forty thousand people. Sophronius, the future patriarch of Jerusalem, wrote that the Anastasis, the Martyrium, the basilicas on the Mount of Olives, and all the city's monasteries were burned and completely destroyed.[2] The surviving inhabitants of Jerusalem were

---

1. See "Antiochus Strategos' Account of the Sack of Jerusalem in A.D. 614," trans. F. C. Conybeare, *English Historical Review* 25 (1910): 502–17, and Michel Join-Lambert, *Jerusalem,* trans. Charlotte Haldane (London, 1958), 140–43.

2. Sophronius, *Anacreonticon* 14, in *Soprhonii Anacreontica,* ed. M. Gigante (Rome, 1957), 102–7, 171–73. See also Hugh Kennedy, *The Prophet and the Age of the Caliphates: The Islamic Near East from the Sixth to the Eleventh Century* (New York, 1986).

taken prisoner and sent into Persia, including the Patriarch Zachariah. Perhaps the greatest insult to the city was that the Persians removed the relic of the True Cross and took it to their capital. Antiochus Strategos, in an eyewitness account of this event, implausibly implicated the Jewish population of Jerusalem as co-conspirators in the invasion.

> Thereupon the Jews, enemies of the truth and haters of Christ, when they perceived that the Christians were given over into the hands of the enemy, rejoiced exceedingly because they detested the Christians; and they conceived an evil plan in keeping with their vileness about the people. For in the eyes of the Persians their importance was great because they were betrayers of the Christians. . . . [the Jews] imagined another plot . . . they purchased Christians out of the reservoir; for they gave the Persians silver and they bought a Christian and slew him like a sheep. . . . When the people were carried into Persia, and the Jews were left in Jerusalem, they began with their own hands to demolish and burn such of the holy churches as were left standing.[3]

According to Antiochus Strategos, the Jews remained in Jerusalem and "in control" for only three years, after which the Persians decided to expel them from the city.[4] It is important to state here that Antiochus Strategos provides the only evidence for the collusion of the Jews with the Persian invaders, and it is very unlikely that such an event took place. There is no evidence showing Jewish support of the Persian raiders in any other city in the Byzantine Empire. In fact, when Sardis in Asia Minor fell to the Persians, the large synagogue was destroyed along with the rest of the city.[5]

The emperor Heraclius soon began a campaign of reconquest, eventually liberating Jerusalem from Persian control and bringing back the relic of the True Cross. After nearly twenty years, the exiles in Persia came back to Jerusalem, where the rebuilding had already begun. The Church of the Holy Sepulcher was repaired but significantly altered in terms of its overall plan. Other churches, such as the Eleona, St. Sophia, and St. Stephen (the location of the empress Eudocia's tomb) were never rebuilt. The Persian

---

3. "Antiochus Strategos' Account," 508.
4. F. E. Peters, *Jerusalem: The Holy City in the Eyes of Chroniclers, Visitors, Pilgrims, and Prophets from the Days of Abraham to the Beginnings of Modern Times* (Princeton, N.J., 1985), 173.
5. Clive Foss, *Byzantine and Turkish Sardis* (Cambridge, Mass., 1976), 41–42 and 55–56.

conquest had changed the physical and religious geography and identity of Jerusalem for all time.

Only a few years later, in 638, new invaders, this time the Muslim Arabs, were again at Jerusalem's walls. The Arabs laid siege to the city until the Patriarch Sophronius decided to avoid destruction by opening the gates and surrendering Jerusalem to the Arabs. In return, the Arab invaders agreed to respect Christian churches and holy places. Sophronius then led the conquering Caliph Umar on a tour of the city and its holy places.[6] The first place the patriarch showed Umar was the Holy Sepulcher. Umar, however, was eager to see the Temple Mount, known to the Muslims as the Haram-as-Sharif, "the Noble Sanctuary."[7] When they finally arrived at the platform the caliph found it covered in filth, and immediately began clearing the debris. A Jewish convert to Islam, Ka'b al-Ahbar, was said to have shown Umar the sacred rock.[8] Umar, a man who avoided luxury, built a simple mosque there on the Temple Mount. This was probably the mosque mentioned by Arculf, a bishop from Gaul, who traveled to Jerusalem shortly after the conquest: "Moreover near the wall on the East, in that famous place where once there stood the magnificent Temple, the Saracens have now built an oblong house of prayer, which they pieced together with upright planks and large beams over some ruined remains. This they attend, and it is said that this building can hold three thousand people."[9]

Holy space within Jerusalem and the Holy Land was to be shared among Judaism, Christianity, and Islam, now competing monotheistic religions.[10] In 692 Caliph Abd al-Malik built an architecturally unique building over the rocky protrusion on the Temple Mount that Jewish tradition considered to be the "foundation stone" of the great Temple.[11] The Dome of the Rock was an octagonal building with a large rotunda over the bare rock. Elaborate mosaics, probably created by Byzantine artisans, decorated the interior. The

6. Join-Lambert, *Jerusalem*, 165.

7. Ibid.

8. Peters, *Jerusalem*, 191.

9. Adomnán *De locis sanctis* 1.14, in *Itineraria et Alia Geographica*, ed. P. Geyer, *CC* 175:175–234 (Turnholt, 1965); English translation from Denis Meehan, ed., *Adamnan. De locis sanctis* (Dublin, 1958).

10. It is interesting to note that though ideas of "holy cities" existed in each of these religions, only Islam would formalize the notion of adherents making a pilgrimage, the *Hajj*, at least once in their lives to the holy city of Mecca. See F. E. Peters, *Jerusalem and Mecca: The Typology of the Holy City in the Near East* (New York, 1986), and idem, *Jerusalem*.

11. Oleg Grabar makes a strong case for Caliph Mu'awiyah as the true man behind the planning and building of the Dome of the Rock. See Oleg Grabar, "The Meaning of the

Dome of the Rock dominated Jerusalem's skyline. It was unique among early Islamic architecture in design and function; it appears to have been built in response to the Church of the Ascension on the nearby Mount of Olives. Oil lamps illuminated both buildings, the Church of the Ascension and the Dome of the Rock, at night with the dark valley of Kidron in between them.[12] The two glowing domes must have been an impressive sight from the valleys surrounding Jerusalem, lending an otherworldly quality to the city.

The construction of the Dome of the Rock created a major change in Jerusalem's religious topography, surpassing even that caused by the building of the early mosque on the Temple Mount. The focus of the city was once again on the Temple Mount. The building itself, with its round shape and important relic, the rock from which Mohammed ascended into the seven heavens on his night journey, served as a destination for Muslim pilgrimage. Pilgrims would have ascended onto the Temple Mount, entered the Dome of the Rock, and circled the building. The Dome of the Rock legitimized Jerusalem as a goal for Islamic pilgrimage: Jerusalem became the third holy city after Mecca and Medina. A new religious group, the Muslims, who had at the center of their religion the necessity of pilgrimage, now shared the city's religious sites.[13]

Muslim Arabs, of course, now saw themselves as the proper heirs to this holy Jewish and Christian city. The city had a connection to Mohammed, and although he never actually traveled to it, his spiritual night journey to Jerusalem left a physical mark: the imprint of his feet on the rock on the Temple Mount. Muslim pilgrimage helped to define an Islamic Jerusalem in a city still populated primarily by Christians and Jews. Yet in 750 the Umayyad rulers were ousted, and the Abbasids took over control of Jerusalem and the Muslim empire. They moved their capital from Damascus to Baghdad, thus retreating from the boundaries of the Mediterranean world.

WESTERN TRAVELERS TO ISLAMIC JERUSALEM

Traditionally, scholars have believed that the seventh-century Islamic conquest radically transformed the relationship, communications, and travel in the

---

Dome of the Rock," in *The Medieval Mediterranean: Cross-Cultural Contacts,* ed. Marilyn J. Chiat and Kathryn L. Reyerson (St. Cloud, Minn., 1988), 1–10.

12. Adomnán wrote that eight lamps burned around the Church of the Ascension every night. Adomnán *De locis sanctis* 23.20.

13. Elad, "Pilgrims and Pilgrimage."

Mediterranean basin. Interestingly, however, the Arab conquest did not have a significant initial impact on the steady tide of Christian visitors to Jerusalem. Concern in the West about the proper upkeep of the Holy Sepulcher complex in fact intensified once Jerusalem had come under Muslim control. An early ninth-century account of the churches and monasteries in Palestine, written for Charlemagne, gives the following list of personnel at the Holy Sepulcher complex in Jerusalem:

> First at the Holy Sepulcher of the Lord: nine priests, fourteen deacons, six subdeacons, twenty-three canonical clergy, thirteen guardians called *fragelites,* forty-one monks, twelve attendants who carry candles before the patriarch, seventeen servants of the patriarch, two superiors, two treasurers, two scribes, two guardians. The priests who look after the Lord's Sepulcher: one for Holy Calvary, two for the Lord's Chalice, two for the Holy Cross and the Headcloth, and one deacon. One secretary who orders everything after the patriarch, two cellarers, one treasurer, one guardian of the springs, nine porters. There are 150 people in all, not counting the three guestmasters.[14]

The Holy Sepulcher complex was the most important Christian shrine in the East, and such an extensive retinue of attendants would not have been found at other churches. One interesting aspect of this list is the mention of "three guestmasters," implying that visitors continued to come to Jerusalem. Such a large complement of attendants had a high price. The document concludes with a financial summary of the patriarch's annual expenses; out of an annual budget of 2,190 gold solidi, over 25 percent of the budget, 580 gold solidi, was paid to the Arab rulers.[15]

Most of the surviving sources show that Western travelers continued to travel to Jerusalem and had full access to Christian sites in the city. The best surviving accounts of Western travelers visiting the newly Muslim-controlled East are those of the Gallic bishop Arculf and Anglo-Saxon monk Willibald, each of whom journeyed to the Holy Land between 679 and 750. Though these travelers themselves left no written account of their journeys, each

---

14. *Commemoratorium,* in Baldi, ed., *Enchiridion,* English translation from Peters, *Jerusalem,* 219.

15. Ibid., 220.

told of his adventures to others who preserved them. Arculf related his story to the Irish abbot of Iona, Adomnán; and nearly a century later, the Anglo-Saxon Willibald, then bishop of Eichstätt, told of his to a nun of Heidenheim, Huneberc. These travelers' accounts reveal a remarkable continuity with the previous generation of travelers in terms of their monastic experience of the Holy Land.

It is no coincidence that Adomnán was Irish and Huneberc was an Anglo-Saxon. In the seventh and eighth centuries the primary monastic travelers were from the British Isles. As with late antique Spain, Ireland and England were home to a wide variety of monastic practices, including itinerant spirituality, and witnessed the relatively late arrival of the Benedictine Rule.[16] In sixth- and seventh-century Ireland in particular, there is evidence of a form of monastic wandering and an asceticism of perpetual pilgrimage that especially emphasized missionary activity and penance.[17] These practices clearly did not arise out of Benedictine-styled monasticism but from a native tradition of religious travel, which is probably traceable as far back as Saint Patrick's mission. Evidence also suggests strong interactions between Ireland and Spain during the sixth and seventh centuries, and there may have been reciprocal influence between their traditions of itinerant spirituality in spite of their distinct origins.[18]

Unlike every other region within the scope of this study, Ireland was never part of the Roman Empire. This difference had a tremendous impact on the process of Christianization that the island underwent in the fifth century. It was the Christian Briton Patrick who is credited with bringing Christianity to Ireland.[19] He brought a Christianity with a decidedly monastic emphasis; in many ways, Ireland, with its absence of cities, isolated expanses and deserted coastal islands, was a land supremely suited to monasticism.[20] Exile and wandering were important elements of pre-Christian Celtic culture and also served to determine the type of monasticism that would prove

16. Dunn, *Emergence of Monasticism,* especially 138–208.
17. Thomas Charles-Edwards, "The Social Background of Irish *Peregrinatio,*" *Celtica* 11 (1976): 43–59, and Hughes, "Changing Theory and Practice of Irish Pilgrimage."
18. Hillgarth, "Visigothic Spain and Early Christian Ireland."
19. See Wood, *Missionary Life,* 26–28. On the earlier Palladian mission to Ireland, see Dunn, *Emergence of Monasticism,* 142–43.
20. Lisa M. Bitel, *Isle of the Saints: Monastic Settlement and Christian Community in Early Ireland* (Ithaca, N.Y., 1990).

popular with the Irish.[21] Travel and wandering seem to emerge naturally as important elements within early Irish monasticism.[22]

The career of the Irish monk Columba provides evidence for this in his travels and in his pursuit of monastic perfection. Columba, originally called Colum Cille, came from a noble Irish family, probably a northern branch of the powerful Uí Néill family; when he was forty-one years old, he embarked on a monastic life.[23] He established monasteries at Derry and Durrow, but in 563 he left Ireland for the sea, finally settling at Iona, an island of the Inner Hebrides, just off the coast of Argyll, Scotland. Bede viewed him as a missionary, calling him the apostle of the Picts;[24] and although missionary activity is featured in his *vita* written by Adomnán, one of his successors as abbot of Iona, Columba was also a monastic wanderer.[25] Most of the miracles mentioned in the *vita* concern the sea; Columba is constantly calming the sea and bringing about fair winds to aid the sea traveler, sometimes himself, sometimes others.[26] He frequently visits other monks and is visited by monks, which also appears to match the practice of the other monastic wanderers we have studied.

But there is another element to Columba's travel and to Irish monastic wandering in general, that of the penitential nature of Irish notions of *peregrinatio*. Some have pointed to Columba's departure for Iona as a result of his excommunication at the Synod of Teltown and that his *peregrinatio* was a form of penance.[27] Penitential pilgrimage seems to have been an Irish invention, which later spread to the Continent through the voyages of Irish

21. For the theme of exile and *peregrinatio* in early Anglo-Saxon poetry, see Dorothy Whitelock, "The Interpretation of the Seafarer," in *The Early Cultures of North-West Europe,* ed. Sir Cyril Fox and Bruce Dickins (Cambridge, 1950), 261–72.

22. Although the *Voyage of St. Brendan* was probably written in the ninth or tenth century, it purports to be about a sixth-century Irish monk who spent most of his life on the sea in the company of a few fellow monks. *Navigatio S. Brendani Abbatis,* ed. C. Selmer (Notre Dame, Ind., 1959).

23. Máire Herbert, *Iona, Kells and Derry: The History and Hagiography of the Monastic Familia of Columba* (Dublin, 1996).

24. Bede *Historia Ecclesiastica* 3.4.

25. For a discussion on Adomnán, see Herbert, *Iona, Kells and Derry,* 47–56, 134–50.

26. The earliest mention of the Loch Ness monster occurs in the *vita* when Columba orders the monster not to attack the young monk he had sent in the river to swim to the boat of a man who had just been devoured by the monster. Adomnán *Vita S. Columbae* 2.27.

27. See the discussion by Sharpe in the introduction to his *Adomnán of Iona, Life of St. Columba,* 13–15.

monks such as Columbanus, who traveled to Gaul in the 590s.[28] Both penitential pilgrimage and monastic travel are evident in the early Irish monastic rules as well.[29] The travels of Columbanus and his Continental foundations of Bobbio and Luxeuil brought Irish ideas of combining monastic life with travel into an increasing Benedictine world.[30] Many have noted a missionary impetus to Columbanus's travels; yet recently Ian Wood has shown that it was his hagiographer, Jonas, who attempted to place the Irishman's wandering life within an acceptable missionary framework. Columbanus, according to Wood, was a *peregrinus pro Christo*.[31]

It is no wonder that Adomnán, author of the *Life of Columba,* would take a great interest in the journey of Arculf. Adomnán was abbot of Iona from 679 to 704 and was probably a distant relative of Columba. At some point during Adomnán's tenure as abbot a bishop from Gaul named Arculf was shipwrecked and stranded at the island monastery. Arculf recounted to Adomnán a journey he had made to the East between the years 679 and 688, at a time when the region was firmly under Muslim control. Adomnán was very careful in setting down Arculf's words and repeatedly stressed the accuracy of his text. Adomnán interviewed Arculf and wrote his responses on wax tablets, which he then used to assemble a succinct account on vellum.[32] Adomnán also made simple drawings based on Arculf's descriptions of the principal churches he visited. This account differs from other travelers' accounts in that the Irish abbot served as a filter, editing out items he deemed useless or unnecessary. At the very beginning of the work Adomnán admitted to playing this role: "I now propose to write a little of what the holy Arculf

28. Ludwig Bieler, *The Irish Penitentials* (Dublin, 1963); Dunn, *Emergence of Monasticism,* 146.

29. Adalbert de Vogüé, ed., *Regles et penitentiels monastiques* (Begrolles-en-Mauges, 1989); *The Celtic Monk: Rules and Writings of Early Irish Monks,* ed. Uinseann Ó Maidín (Kalamazoo, Mich., 1996).

30. His own rule would often be used in combination with the Benedictine Rule. See Pierre Riché, "Columbanus, His Followers and the Merovingian Church," in *Columbanus and Merovingian Monasticism,* ed. H. B. Clarke and Mary Brennan (London, 1981), 59–72, and Friedrich Prinz, "Columbanus, the Frankish Nobility and the Territories East of the Rhine," in *Columbanus and Merovingian Monasticism,* ed. H. B. Clarke and Mary Brennan (London, 1981), 73–87.

31. Wood, *Missionary Life,* 34; see also Riché, "Columbanus, His Followers and the Merovingian Church."

32. "Mihi Adomnano haec universa quae infra craxanda sunt experimenta diligentius percunctanti et primo in tabulis describenti fideli et indubitabili narratione dictavit; quae nunc in membranis brevi textu scribuntur." Adomnán *De locis sanctis* prologue.

told me concerning the site of Jerusalem, omitting the matter that is contained in the books of others about the position of the city."[33]

The resulting account has an emphasis on the physical structure of the city and holy places rather than on the people that populated these places, especially when compared to the accounts of Egeria, Theodosius, and the Piacenza Pilgrim. For example, Adomnán related how on September 12, a great festival took place in Jerusalem, and the city was filled with people. Rather than narrate the events of the festival, he preferred to relate how the city soon abounded with animal waste, producing a horrible stench. He then described how, owing to the city's topography, the streets were cleansed by the subsequent downpour, a "flood of heavenly waters," that washed the waste down the steeply inclined streets.[34]

One of the main changes that had taken place in the city by the time of Arculf's visit was that it had fallen under Islamic control. Adomnán's only notice of this was in his description of the Temple Mount, which had a "quadrangular prayer house" on it that could hold three thousand people.[35] The Arab presence in the city was also referred to in an interesting story that Arculf told about the origins of the holy shroud. The shroud had been kept by a Jewish family for many generations, and only three years prior to Arculf's visit, a dispute had arisen between the Jews and Christians of Jerusalem concerning the ownership of the shroud. The dispute was settled by the Muslim caliph at the time, Mu'awiya, called Mavias, *rex Saracinorum* by Adomnán.[36] Arculf noted that Damascus served as the capital and that the king resided there.[37]

Religious space in Muslim-controlled Jerusalem was shared with both Christians and Jews. In the tenth century an anonymous Hebrew writer

33. "De situ Hierusalem nunc quaedam scribenda sunt pauca ex his quae mihi sanctus dictavit Arculfus; ea vero quae in aliorum libris de eiusdem civitatis positione repperiuntur a nobis pretermittenda sunt." Ibid., 1.1.1.

34. "Quae scilicet caelestium aquarum inundatio per orientales influiens portas et omnia secum stercuralia auferens abhominamenta vallem Iosaphat intrans torrentem Cedron auget, et post talem Hierusolimitanam baptizationem continuatim eadem pluvialis exuberatio cessat." Ibid., 1.1.12.

35. "Ceterum in illo famoso loco ubi quondam templum magnifice constructum fuerat in vicinia muri ab oriente locatum nunc Saracini quadrangulam orationis domum, quam subrectis tabulis et magnis trabibus super quasdam ruinarum reliquias construentes vili fabricati sunt opere, ipsi frequentant; quae utique domus tria hominum milia, ut fertur, capere potest." Ibid., 1.1.14.

36. Ibid., 1.9.11.

37. "In qua [Damascus] Saracinorum rex adeptus eius principatum regnat." Ibid., 2.28.1–2.

produced a guide to the various holy sites in and around Jerusalem, perhaps for Jewish pilgrims. All that remains of this work are two small leaves of papyrus discovered in the Cairo Geniza, but it is the earliest of the pilgrim genre that survives in Hebrew.[38] This text bears striking similarities to Christian accounts of the city and its holy places. The guide's importance lies not only in its discussion of Jerusalem as a holy city for three distinct religions, but in the apparent necessity its author felt to define and stake a claim to religious locations. These guides, whether Jewish, Christian, or Muslim, defined sacred space for the travelers and pilgrims, who in turn by their own patronage of the sites claimed the space for their own religion.

The surviving fragments of the guide shed light on the condition of the holy spaces around the gates of the Temple Mount, the valley of Kidron, and the Mount of Olives. Judging from what remains, it appears that the author intended the guide as a descriptive list of all holy places in Jerusalem, not simply Jewish locations. It lists the Hebrew and Arabic names for most of the places mentioned, as well as scriptural or Talmudic quotations as evidence for the sites' importance and authenticity.

Although the Muslims clearly controlled the Temple Mount, the guide suggested that Jews were permitted to pray at some of its gates. The guide discusses Christian sites, including religious buildings said to have been built by King Solomon, and seven interconnected "houses," possibly cells of monks, in the Kidron valley. The guide also refers to the "Church of James the brother of the Messiah," probably the location of the tomb of James in the valley of Kidron.[39]

In addition to the Temple Mount, Arculf also visited the Mount of Olives and provided a long and elaborate description to Adomnán, one with similarities to Paulinus of Nola's early fifth-century account:

> Nowhere on the whole Mount of Olives does one find a higher place than the one from which it is said that the Lord ascended into the heavens. A great round church stands there, which has round it three porticoes with vaulted roofs. But there is no vault or roof over the central part; it is out of doors and open to the sky. At the east of it has been built an altar with a small roof over it. The

---

38. J. Braslavi, "Le plus ancien guide juif de Jerusalem, Der älteste Jüdische Jerusalem-Führer," in *Jerusalem: Texte—Bilder—Steine,* ed. Max Küchler and Christoph Uehlinger (Freiburg, 1987), 37–81.

39. Braslavi, "Le plus ancien guide juif de Jerusalem," 66.

reason why there is no roof over the inner part of this building is so as not to hinder those who pray there from seeing the way from the last place where the Lord's feet were standing, when he was taken up to heaven in a cloud.[40]

The Mount of Olives was no longer mentioned as a location of monasteries, especially communities of women. By the tenth century the Mount of Olives also appears to have been the location of the place of prayer and of public reunion for the Jewish festival of Hoshana Rabba.[41] Judging from the evidence of the tenth-century Jewish guidebook, it seems that the Jews might have taken over the site of the Church of the Ascension. The text gives the measurements of a large stone on the Mount of Olives, and then relates its location to that where God stood after having risen from the center of the city when the Temple was destroyed.[42] Many travelers noted the impressive view of the Temple platform from this site, and the Jews on the Mount of Olives may have prayed facing the Temple Mount.[43]

Other travelers were mentioned only once in the Arculf's account, and in a rather morbid way. The field known as Aceldama, which was described by the Piacenza Pilgrim as being full of monks, had been turned into a graveyard for travelers and pilgrims by the time of Arculf's visit. Many of the bodies were not fully buried, but instead lay exposed and rotting on the surface.[44] Adomnán referred to monks or monasteries only three times in his account of Arculf's journey, though monks were quite numerous in this region.[45] Only one monk was specified by name, the hermit Peter, whom he described as a soldier of Christ.[46] Peter, originally from Burgundy, served as Arculf's sometimes pushy guide. He was not a temporary visitor to the Holy Land like Arculf, having evidently lived there long enough to act as a guide. Peter first appeared in Adomnán's work as Arculf's guide through the city of Nazareth. Unfortunately for our purposes, Adomnán

40. Adomnán *De locis sanctis* 23.1–3.
41. Braslavi, "Le plus ancien guide juif de Jerusalem," 56, 78–81.
42. Ibid., 68–69.
43. This is Braslavi's opinion.
44. "In quo diligentius plurimi humantur peregrini. Alii vero ex ipsis aut pannis aut pelliculis tecti neglegentius relinguuntur inhumati super terrae faciem putrefacti iacentes." Adomnán *De locis sanctis* 1.19.1.
45. Great monasteries are mentioned at Bethany and at the site of Jesus' baptism on the Jordan river. The other monastery mentioned was on the summit of Mount Thabor. Ibid., 1.25.1, 2.16.8, 2.27.4–5.
46. "Christi miles." Ibid., 2.26.5.

was uninterested in Peter, and his brief notice of him was of a disapproving nature. Peter forced Arculf to keep moving and did not allow him to stay longer than one night at a particular location. Perhaps he was attempting to follow a rule that guarded against the abuse of hospitality. We cannot be sure how long Peter served as Arculf's guide, but Adomnán did write that after giving this "tour," he returned to his solitary life in the desert.[47] This brief account of this Gallic wandering monk who finally settled in the Holy Land and worked as a guide provides us with tantalizing evidence of Western traveling monks in the East. One wishes to know more about this Peter and whether or not there were others like him in seventh-century Jerusalem.

Adomnán's account centered on the holy sites of Jerusalem, especially on the Church of the Holy Sepulcher. Like the Piacenza Pilgrim, Arculf took a "measure," with his hands, of the length of the Sepulcher.[48] Arculf's voyage, however, covered much more territory than simply Jerusalem. He traveled to Syria and Egypt, then took a boat from Alexandria to Constantinople, spending time in Crete along the way. He again traveled by sea from Constantinople to Sicily. Adomnán provides no further details about Arculf's westward journey. According to Bede, who used Adomnán's account for his own work on the holy places, Arculf, after his wanderings in the East, was caught in a terrible storm and shipwrecked on the west coast of Britain.[49] It is curious that Arculf would be shipwrecked in Britain on his way from Sicily to Gaul. Either he traveled around the Iberian Peninsula to the Atlantic, or perhaps this shipwreck occurred while he was on another journey. It is also odd that a man described as a bishop by both Adomnán and Bede spent so much time traveling.[50] Perhaps Arculf had more in common with his guide Peter than simply a shared homeland; Adomnán's account seems to suggest that Arculf was traveling as part of his religious vocation.

The Islamic conquest of Jerusalem and most of the eastern Mediterranean did not stop Western Christians from traveling to the East. About a hundred years after Arculf's journey, Willibald, an Anglo-Saxon and the future bishop of Eichstätt in Germany, undertook a similar long-distance

47. "Petrus nomine, qui post eundem circuitum ad illum in quo prius est commoratus reversus est solitarium locum." Ibid.

48. "Cuius longitudinem Arculfus in septem pedum mensura mensus est manu." Ibid., 1.2.10.

49. "Patriamque navigio revertens, vi tempestatis in occidentalia Brittaniae littora delatus est." Bede *Historia Ecclesiastica* 5.15.

50. We know from Adomnán that Arculf spent at least nine months in Jerusalem alone. Adomnán *De locis sanctis,* prologue.

journey. Willibald traveled from England to Rome, Constantinople, Jerusalem, and other Eastern cities, then back to Rome and later into Germany.[51] As with Arculf's journey, it was another writer who interviewed Willibald about his travels and preserved the story. This account, called the *Hodoeporicon,* was written by Huneberc, a nun who was a member of Willibald's family and, like him, had come to Bavaria from England.[52]

Willibald and his brother, Wynnebald, together with their father, decided to undertake a journey to Rome from their homeland of England.[53] Their father died on the journey before reaching Rome and was buried by his sons in the Italian city of Lucca. Willibald and Wynnebald arrived at Rome and lived there as monks for several years. Soon Willibald decided that it was time to travel again. This time his brother did not accompany him, but Willibald was able to convince two friends, one of whom was named Tidbercht, to join him on a journey to Jerusalem.[54] Huneberc provides a detailed account of this journey, discussing every stop along the way. Willibald and his companions traveled south from Rome to Naples, where they embarked on a sea journey to Asia Minor via Sicily and Greece, finally landing in Ephesus. In Ephesus they visited both the cave of the Seven Sleepers and the Basilica of St. John the Evangelist.

Willibald, however, soon encountered some difficulty on his journey eastward. Entering Syria, which was under Muslim control, he and his companions, who numbered seven at the time, were arrested.[55] The group was questioned by an elder who recognized them at once as harmless Christian travelers from the West. Huneberc recorded the old man's statement: "I have often seen men coming from those parts of the world, fellow-countrymen of

51. This is not the same Willibald who authored the *Life of St. Boniface.*

52. Ian Wood calls her "Hygeburg" in his *Missionary Life,* 64–65, and she is called "Hugeburc" in the *MGH.* Hugeburc *Vita Willibaldi Episcopi Eichstetensis* 87.20–23, ed. O. Holder-Egger, *MGH* 15:86–106 (Hanover, 1887). An English translation, "The Hodoeporicon of St. Willibald by Huneberc of Heidenheim," can be found in C. H. Talbot, ed., *The Anglo-Saxon Missionaries in Germany* (New York, 1954), 153–77. This translation was reprinted and the prologue revised as "The *Hodoeporicon* of Saint Willibald," in *Soldiers of Christ,* ed. T. F. X. Noble and T. Head (University Park, Pa., 1995), 141–64. Jerome describes Paula's wanderings as *hodoeporicon* as well. See Jerome *Ep.* 108.8, and Chap. 4, note 74 herein. See the recent discussion and useful map of Willibald's journey in McCormick, *Origins of the European Economy,* 129–34.

53. Hugeburc *Vita Willibaldi* 91.1–3.

54. Ibid., 92.27. We only learn Tidbercht's name near the end of the account when he and Willibald return to Rome. Ibid., 102.19. The other companion is not directly mentioned again in the account.

55. "Confestimque illi pagani Sarracini repperientes, quod adveni et ignoti homines lillic venti fuerunt, tulerunt eos et captivos habebant." Ibid., 94.14–16.

theirs; they cause no mischief and are merely anxious to fulfill their law."[56] It is not apparent whether he meant that they were pilgrims on their quest to Jerusalem, or traveling monks following their rule of life. The old man recognized them as religious travelers, or at least this was what Huneberc wanted to show. Repeatedly she emphasized how Willibald's journey was recognized as a religious one by people he met. Or perhaps the old man actually used the equivalent of the word *lex,* which showed a familiarity with Jewish and Islamic law, both of which required pilgrimage to Jerusalem. Either way, the old man's judgment on their behalf did not aid the travelers, who were promptly thrown in prison. In prison they were assisted by two different strangers, one a Christian merchant who paid for their meals and took them to church and to the public baths, and the other a Spaniard, perhaps a Muslim, whose brother was an official at the caliph's court.[57] It was due to the Spaniard's efforts that Willibald and his companions were eventually freed.

Willibald's experience in prison did not prevent him from returning to Syria on another occasion after he had been living and traveling around the Holy Land for some time. This time he and his companions went to considerable lengths to obtain letters of safe conduct from Muslim officials. In the end, they were only given letters for travel in pairs, rather than for the entire group. Huneberc attributes this to the difficulty of obtaining food for more than two people at a time while traveling.[58] It is unclear whether this was the reason given by the officials, by Willibald, or by Huneberc herself.

Willibald, however, was arrested again, in Tyre, when a Muslim official suspected that he was carrying contraband. Surprisingly, Huneberc tells us that the holy man was indeed smuggling balsam, which he had purchased in Jerusalem and very carefully concealed in a hollowed-out gourd, fortunately for Willibald the customs official never found it.[59] Though the penalty for such an offense was death, according to Huneberc, Willibald had apparently been willing to defy the law.

---

56. "Frequenter hic venientes vidi homines de illis terre partibus istorum contribulos; non querunt mala, sed legem eorum adimplere cupiunt." Ibid., 94.19–20.

57. The Spaniard was probably not a Christian, since unlike the friendly merchant, he is not identified. He was probably a Muslim or perhaps a Jew, considering his family connections to the caliph's court. Clearly he spoke some form of Latin or early Romance language in order to communicate with Willibald.

58. Hugeburc *Vita Willibaldi* 100.11–12.

59. She provides quite a detailed account of how Willibald concealed the balsam from the officials. Ibid., 101.5–16.

Like the other travelers we have discussed, Willibald visited a variety of places and took his time on his journey. He often encountered monks; the first monks described were two stylites living on columns in the city of Miletus in Asia Minor.[60] Willibald and his companions stayed on Mount Thabor at a monastery.[61] In Caesarea, they stayed at a small monastery of about twenty monks, dedicated to John the Baptist.[62] Between Jerusalem and Jericho, they visited a monastery Huneberc called "the monastery of St. Eustochium."[63] The largest and most important monastery they visited was the Great Laura of St. Sabas, outside Jerusalem in the valley of Kidron.[64] The Laura impressed Willibald, and he gave a detailed description of it to Huneberc. Willibald also referred to visiting churches built by the empress Helena and by Constantine.[65]

Willibald fell ill on a few occasions during his journey. While in Gaza, he suddenly went blind while attending Mass, only regaining his sight upon entering the Holy Sepulcher in Jerusalem two months later. Huneberc did not, however, attribute the cure to a miracle, nor did she attempt to cast Willibald's return to Jerusalem and entry into the church as a search for a cure for his blindness.[66] In fact, during those two months of blindness, Willibald continued to travel and even visited the Tomb of the Patriarchs in Hebron. Illness again befell Willibald on his second journey into Syria. Huneberc

60. "Ibi sedebant duo solitarii in stulice." Ibid., 93.23.

61. "Ibi est nunc monasterium monachorum." Ibid., 95.29.

62. "Iterum pergebant ad monasterio Sancti Iohannis baptiste; et ibi erant fere 20 monachorum; unam noctem ibi manebant." Ibid., 96.15–16.

63. "Monasterium Sancti Eustochii." Ibid., 97.9. This reference has been thought to be a mistake for either Eusthochius or Eustachium, according to the editor Holder-Egger; Talbot calls it Eustochium or Euthymius, according to Wilkinson. It is a male saint, unless Huneberc confused this monastery with the monasteries founded by Paula and Eustochium in the early fifth century as mentioned by Jerome in *Ep.* 108.14.4.

64. "Et tunc venit inde in valle Laura; ibi est monasterium magnum, et ibi sedit abbas ad aecclesia et ille ianuarius aecclesiae; alii monachi multi, qui ibi sunt in ipso monasterio, et sedent circa vallem in oneo rupis montis et habent illis excisum in saxosa rupe montis parvas receptaculas ubi et ubi. Ille mons est in giro circa vallem et monasterium aedificatum in valle; et ibi requiescit sanctus Saba." Hugeburc *Vita Willibaldi* 99.3–8. For a recent discussion of this monastery, see Yizhar Hirschfeld, *The Judean Desert Monasteries in the Byzantine Period* (New Haven, Conn., 1992); Meinardus, *Monks and Monasteries;* and Chitty, *The Desert a City.*

65. In Emesa, Syria, he visited a church dedicated to John the Baptist founded by Helena. Hugeburc *Vita Willibaldi* 94.12. In Jerusalem Willibald visited the Church of Holy Sepulcher. Huneberc mentions the connection with Helena and the True Cross. Ibid., 97.12.

66. "Cumque sacra missarum sollemnia ibi fuerant celebrata, episcopus noster Willibaldus stans ibi ad missam lumen oculorum amisit et cecus fuit duos menses . . . [discussion of visit to Hebron] . . . Et inde venit iterum in Hierusalem, et introiens in aecclesiam ubi sancta crux Domini inventa fuerat, aperti sunt oculi eius, et visionem recipit." Ibid., 99.11–16.

discusses neither the nature of the illness nor the resolution, indicating only that it prevented him from traveling for almost two months.[67]

It is instructive to compare the absence of miraculous intervention in the curing of Willibald's illness with Huneberc's account of his encounter with a lion. While on his way to the seaside town of Ptolemais, Willibald and his companions traveled with an Ethiopian man guiding a woman traveler.[68] As they passed through a grove of olive trees, a lion suddenly appeared and began to menace them. Huneberc wrote that all were terrified with the exception of the Ethiopian, who encouraged them to continue. Huneberc wrote, "So without hesitation they proceeded on their way and as they approached the lion it turned aside and, through the help of Almighty God, left the way open for them to continue their journey."[69] After they had passed, the lion continued to terrorize others who traveled through the grove. Huneberc thought this was miraculous, and she linked the incident with Willibald's desire to travel. The lion prevented him from traveling, while the miracle permitted him to move on. This incident was important enough for Huneberc to include in her account of Willibald's religious need for movement. One might think that a miraculous cure at a holy place would merit similar attention for Huneberc, but it did not. Religious travel itself was, for Huneberc, apparently of paramount importance in the story of Willibald.

Throughout her account, Huneberc repeatedly emphasized how Willibald always followed his monastic rule. She began the story with Willibald's parents giving him to a monastery as an offering to God for having saved his life when he was stricken with a grave disease. At the age of five Willibald entered the monastery of Waldheim in England as a novice. While there, according to Huneberc, he began to strive for monastic perfection: "Night and day he pondered anxiously on the means of monastic perfection and the importance of community life, wondering how he might become a

---

67. "Et ibi erat ille totum quadragensimi tempus, quia infirmus fuit et non poterat pergere." Ibid., 100.3–4.

68. "Et pergit cum illis unus Ethiops cum duobus camellis et uno mulo ducebat ducebat unam mulierem per silvam." Ibid., 100.22–23. It seems clear from Huneberc's description that Willibald did not consider them to be husband and wife. The text clearly states that there was one Ethiopian man guiding one woman on a mule. The Ethiopian's subsequent conduct with the lion further emphasizes his role as a guide and the woman as his customer. So here again we have evidence of a woman traveling alone, yet also that it was common for travelers to join together.

69. "Statimque illi pergentes, adpropinquaverunt ad illo, ast ille cito omnipotentis altithroni Dei adminiculo in aliam partem devertit et latabat illis viam, ut pergerent." Ibid., 100.26–27.

member of that chaste fellowship and share in the joys of their common discipline."[70] The young Willibald surprised even his fellow monks with his strict observance of the rule, yet, as we will see, in the end this obedience was compatible with religious travel.

As he followed the discipline of the monastery, he decided that he wanted to pursue a harder life, a life more fully isolated and separated from society. The young Willibald felt that this could only be achieved by leaving the monastery and all he knew. "Next he began to inquire how he could put these ideas into effect so that he could despise and renounce the fleeting pleasures of this world and forsake not merely the temporal riches of his earthly inheritance but also his country, parents, and relatives. He began also to devise means of setting out on pilgrimage and traveling to foreign countries that were unknown to him."[71]

Travel for Willibald was a form of perfecting his monastic life. It was not necessarily travel to the holy city of Jerusalem that accomplished this perfection, though he did eventually visit the city three times; it was the travel itself, and meeting other holy people and coming to know their lives. The central point of her account was Willibald's yearning for a stricter life, but this strictness took a peculiar form: a life in which he gave up his homeland and family for almost constant travel. Willibald's journey in the East had taken eight years, and that was after he had already spent over two years in Rome. He spent considerable time at some of the cities he visited, indeed at least two years each in Rome and Constantinople.[72]

Willibald finally returned to Rome, though Huneberc never gives the reason, instead emphasizing how he traveled from city to city in Italy and was eventually sent to Monte Cassino by the bishop of Teano.[73] At Monte

70. "Magna mentis diuturna meditatione tractando monasteriale moderationis instrumenta monachicalisque vitae monarchiam in abditu mentis quietudine die noctuque sollicite volutabat, quomodo illorum se intercopularet casta monachorum clientello, aut qualiter illorum faustis interfore possit familiaris vitae disciplinis." Ibid., 89.25–29.

71. "Cumque ista sedule intus intra mentis volubilitate volvans tractare cepit, qualiter ista cogitatio depromeri proferrique poterit in effectum, ut caduca cuncta cosmi istius contemnere sive derelinquere quearet et non solum temporales terrenarum divitias, set et patriam et parentes atque propinquos deserere peregrinationisque temptare telluram et ignotas externarum requirere ruras." Ibid., 89.29–33.

72. For Rome, see Hugeburc *Vita Willibaldi* 102.17, and for Constantinople, see 101.21.

73. "Et inde navigantes, venerunt ad urbem que vocatur Neapule; ibi esset multos dies. Ibi est sedis archiepiscopi, et magna dignitas eius illic habetur. Et ibi est prope castella, ubi requiescit sanctus Severinus. Et inde venit ad urbe Capua; et ille archiepiscopus misit eum ad alio urbe ad illo episcopo, et ille episcopus misit illum ad urbe Tiana ad illum episcopum, et ille episcopo misit illum ad Sanctum Benedictum." Ibid., 102.11–16.

Cassino Willibald decided to join the Benedictine community. Huneberc emphasized that the community suited him perfectly. Although he learned much from his brothers, he was also able to teach them. Huneberc stressed that his character was well suited to the Benedictine constitution, since he was disciplined and obedient.[74]

Willibald spent a total of ten years as a Benedictine monk, during which time he held important offices, his final eight years as the porter, both at Monte Cassino and at a daughter house two miles away. The position of porter was probably the best suited to Willibald. As porter he was the first to meet, greet, and assess the many visitors to the monastery. It was the office that was the closest to the outside world. Huneberc did hint that Willibald traveled from the monastery when she wrote that he personally brought many new brothers to the community "over long distances by foot and by sea,"[75] and mentioned one specific occasion when a priest visiting the monastery from Spain wanted to travel to Rome and needed a companion. The abbot asked Willibald to accompany him, to which Willibald quickly assented and was once again on the road.[76]

In Rome, Willibald met Pope Gregory III, a meeting that Huneberc related with much flourish. The pope, who had sent for Willibald when he heard he was in Rome, prostrated himself when the wandering holy man entered the room. The first words uttered by the pope were a series of questions about Willibald's travels.[77] This extreme display of deference on the part of the pontiff and his great interest in Willibald's travels once again reveals the importance Huneberc herself, as the author of this account, placed on Willibald's itinerancy. Huneberc repeatedly emphasized Willibald's travels as the central aspect of his monastic life, but nothing about the account hints at the familiar model of pilgrimage and return. She also used the opportunity of the meeting with the pope to explain how Willibald eventually left

74. "Et recte constitutionis formam et cenobialis vitae normam in semet ipso ostendendo prebebat . . . venerandus ille vir Willibaldus sacram sancti Benedicti regularis vitae institutionem." Ibid., 102.21–34.

75. "Super longa locorum stadia et super vastas barginum vias . . . perducebat." Ibid., 102.32–35.

76. "Et ille statim petitionibus eius consensum seu effectum promittebat." Ibid., 103.3.

77. "Cumque illic veniebat ad sanctum summae sacerdotalis pontifice, statim prono vultu in terram se vergebat et illum salutabat. Protinusque ille pius populorum speculator piis verborum vicissitudinis iteneris sui ordinem investigare coepit ab illo, quomodo septuplum annorum calculum in externis terminarum telluris probando peragraret, aut quomodo multa temporum spatia perniciosas paganorum pravitates penetrando evaseret, diligenter ab illo sciscitabat." Ibid., 103.7–12.

his Benedictine community. The pope, after hearing about Willibald's journeys, informed him that Boniface wanted Willibald to join him in his mission in Bavaria.[78] Huneberc then described in great detail how Willibald, bound by the strict rules of his community, agreed to the request with great hesitation and under the condition that he first ask permission from his abbot, as the Rule prescribed.[79] Throughout her account of Willibald, Huneberc strives to portray him as the perfect monk, even the model Benedictine monk, but at the same time she told the unmistakable story of a holy wanderer. Somehow Willibald, or perhaps Huneberc, was able to reconcile strict obedience and Benedictine *stabilitas* with a life of travel and living according to his own precepts, a life which might have appeared to some as that of the *gyrovague*. Huneberc's *Life of Willibald* served to justify a monastic pursuit very different from the Benedictine one, yet without directly challenging the Benedictine Rule.

Interestingly, the pope did not grant Willibald's request that he obtain permission from his abbot before leaving for Bavaria. The pope, according to Huneberc, stated, "If I am free to transfer the abbot Petronax himself to any other place, then certainly he has no permission or power to oppose my wishes."[80] With these strong words, Willibald withdrew his request and obeyed the pope's commands. The space Huneberc devoted to this incident and her inclusion of the papal orders for Willibald to leave his monastery seem to be an attempt to justify the unusual circumstances of his departure from his community without the permission of his abbot. Benedictine monks lived under the almost absolute control of their abbot. Huneberc may have been responding to criticism Willibald received over his departure. She also had to fit this apparent violation of Benedictine precepts with the image of Willibald as the model monk. Willibald broke his vows only because he was compelled to obey the greater authority of the pope.

Setting off toward the north, for the first time in his many journeys, Willibald traveled without his constant companion Tidbercht, who returned to the monastery near Monte Cassino. Willibald's journey to Bavaria was

---

78. Boniface, the Anglo-Saxon martyr and German missionary.

79. "Tunc ille inclitus Christi anthletus Willibaldus petitionibus pontificis simulque iussionibus se sollerter subsummatim effectum seuque oboedientiam perficere promittebat, si secundum reǵularis vitae disciplinam licentiam illo ad suo postularet abbate." Hugeburc *Vita Willibaldi* 104.16–19.

80. "Qui si illum ipsum abbatem Petronacem uspiam transmittere me libet, certe contradicere mihi licentiam non habet nec potestatem." Ibid., 104.21–22.

punctuated with many stops along the way, including a visit to his father's tomb in Lucca.[81] Willibald eventually reached Boniface, who gave him land in Eichstätt on which to build a monastery. His religious life then took a sharp turn when Boniface ordained him, first as a priest, and one year later as bishop of Eichstätt.[82] Even though Willibald became a bishop, Huneberc continued to emphasize his monastic activities and the role his travel played in these activities: "Then he was consecrated bishop. Afterwards he began to build a monastery in the place called Eichstätt, and he shortly afterwards practiced the monastic life there according to the observance which he had seen at St. Benedict's, and not merely there, but also in many other monastic houses, which he had examined with his experienced eye as he traveled through various lands. This observance he taught to others by the example of his own life."[83]

To make her case clear, Huneberc compared Willibald to a "busy bee" who flies from flower to flower bringing back to his hive only the sweetest nectar. His travels, far from threatening his monastic pursuit, actually enhanced his monasticism. Huneberc ended her account of his life by relating how popular his monastic foundation in Bavaria became, especially to those who came from afar.[84] Willibald died in Bavaria, never having returned to his English homeland.

Here was a monk who was committed to monastic perfection through a variety of means: through life in a monastery, through pious travel, through meeting other monks and using them as examples, and finally, through missionary work in hostile lands. Willibald's life fulfilled the central goal of the wandering monk, a life of perpetual pilgrimage in imitation of the homelessness of the Christian in this world. Huneberc understood this, and this is what she attempted to convey in her account.

Some scholars have commented that Huneberc's account was not the saints' life she stated in her preface she intended to write. These scholars

81. "Et veniebat ad Lucam, ubi pater eius requiescebat." Ibid., 104.28.
82. Ibid., 104.40 and 105.6.
83. "Sacri episcopatus gradum accepit, et in loco que dicitur Eihstat monasterium construere incipiebat atque oceo ibidem sacram monasterialis vitae disciplinam in usum prioris vitae, quod videndo ad Sanctum Benedictum, et non solum ibi, sed in aliis multis monachorum mansionibus, quas ipse solers et sophyrus vaste per ruras rimando explorabat, ast illorum cata normam venerandis vitae conversationem in semet ipso ostendendo exercebat." Ibid., 105.19–24. The "cata" in this passage is a transliteration of the Greek "kata."
84. "Statim undique de illis regionum provinciis et nihilominus de aliis longinquum limis ad saluberrimam eius sapientiae dogmam confluere ceperunt." Ibid., 106.5–6.

have rightly pointed out that the *Hodoeporicon* more closely resembles the travel accounts written by Adomnán and the Piacenza Pilgrim than it does traditional hagiography.[85] In her preface, Huneberc wrote that she would relate the life of Willibald, yet her focus was on his traveling rather than on his monastic, Benedictine, episcopal, or missionary activities. Perhaps this assessment reflects not Huneberc's misstatement of her intentions, but our overly narrow and misguided categories. Huneberc was not simply indulging in the colorful details of his travels, but rather purposely included his travels and in fact made them central to her account of his life because they were the central fact of his life.

We know very little about Huneberc as a woman or as a hagiographer. Some scholars do not even consider her an author and have discounted any creative influence she had over the *vita,* assuming instead that it is merely a transcription of the words spoken by Willibald.[86] But the *vita* was Huneberc's creation, and one that sheds light on who she was. Huneberc, like Willibald, was an Anglo-Saxon who had traveled to Bavaria and became a nun at the double monastery of Heidenheim, which had been founded by Wynnebald, Willibald's brother, and run by Walpurgis, their sister.[87] She likely wrote the life of Willibald not so much because he was a countryman and possibly a relative, but because he was her exemplar. She too had left the comforts of her homeland, to go to the monastery of her mentor Willibald, where she heard his stories in person.[88] Huneberc was concerned that some would question the veracity of her rendering of Willibald's *vita.* She did not have a personal knowledge of Rome, Jerusalem, or any of the other places Willibald visited, but she may have read earlier accounts of them. Some parts of the *Hodoeporicon,* such as the description of the formation of the river Jordan from the springs named Jor and Dan, appear to

85. In fact the name she gives her account means a relation of a journey. See the preface to "The *Hodoeporicon* of Saint Willibald," in Noble and Head, *Soldiers of Christ,* 141. It was later copiers and editors who called her work the *Vita Willibaldi.*

86. For example, see the opinion of her first translator into English, C. H. Talbot, ed., *The Anglo-Saxon Missionaries in Germany* (New York, 1954). See also McCormick, *Origins of the European Economy,* 129; and the short discussion of Huneberc in Prinz, *Frühes Mönchtum im Frankenreich,* 254–56.

87. Walpurgis was called to Bavaria by Willibald and Boniface and traveled there with fellow nuns. It seems likely that Huneberc accompanied her on this journey. It is unclear when this journey took place.

88. She mentions this fact twice in her account. Hugeburc *Vita Willibaldi* 87.20–23 and 105.15.

have been lifted from other accounts.[89] Perhaps her "slip of the pen" when she wrote in the first person plural rather than in the third person was not so much an indication of her use of a dictated text, but of her longing to have been there also and to have lived the experience with all its trials; to have herself received sour milk, as occurred in the incident.[90] With the spread of Benedictine monasticism and the further isolation of female monastics, Huneberc might have found the idea of a life of utter separation and exploration offered by itinerant spirituality very appealing indeed.

Willibald and his brother Wynnebald's journey to Rome and their monastic hiatus there presents us once again with the issue of pilgrimage to the city. Pilgrimage to late antique Rome was primarily local in nature and focused on the martyr shrines that ringed the city walls. Yet beginning in the early eighth century, a number of mainly English long-distance travelers made the long journey to Rome.[91] These English pilgrims were not drawn to Rome to see the martyr tombs as much as to visit with the pope, often in an official capacity. The Anglo-Saxons had been converted by a Roman monk, Augustine of Canterbury, whom Pope Gregory the Great had sent to them as a missionary in 596. The Anglo-Saxon church thus retained a special connection to the city of Rome in the early medieval period. Rome, to the Anglo-Saxons, was the city of the papacy. These primarily male travelers from England brought gifts to the popes, received their pallia from the pope, or collected manuscripts to bring back to England.[92] Bede, living in Northumbria, had intimate access to the latest additions to the *Liber Pontificalis* concerning Pope Gregory II, which could have only come from a copy of work being brought back to England.[93] Benedict Biscop

---

89. "Ubi duos fontes de terra emanant Ior et Dan, et tunc venientes de monte deorsum, in unum collecti faciunt Iordanem." Ibid., 96.8–9.

90. "Ibi morabant unam noctem inter duabus fontibus, et pastores dabant nobis acrum lac bebere." Ibid., 96.9–10.

91. Kings Ine (726) and Alfred, Benedict Biscop (650s–660s), Boniface (719, 726), Abbot Ceolfrid, and the brothers Willibald and Wynnebald (722), for example. The *Liber Pontificalis* states that during the reign of Pope Constantine, 708–15, "two kings of the Saxons came with many others to pray to the apostles; just as they were hoping, their lives quickly came to an end." *LP* 90.

92. Ceolfrid died on his journey to Rome, undertaken in order to give the pope the Codex Amiatinus.

93. Raymond Davis, ed., *The Lives of the Eighth-Century Popes (Liber Pontificalis). The Ancient Biographies of Nine Popes from A.D. 715 to A.D. 817* (Liverpool, 1992), 2. Kessler states that Bede probably had replicas of the fifth-century Roman mosaic cycles that he used when commissioning the art on the nave walls of the Church of St. Peter at Wearmouth. Kessler, "Pictures as Scripture," 378.

collected monastic rules and manuscripts during his five trips to Rome in the late seventh century.

Huneberc's eighth-century account of the journey of two Anglo-Saxon brothers, Willibald and Wynnebald, makes no mention of their visiting any martyr tombs in Rome. Their visit appears to have had the dual purpose of meeting with the pope and joining a Roman monastic community. Though they may have visited the famous churches and catacombs of Rome, it appears that such visits were not the primary reason for their journey. These Anglo-Saxon travelers were not pilgrims in the traditional sense of the word. Although their journeys did have a religious nature, it was one associated with the papacy rather than with the holy sights and the martyrs of Rome. By the eighth century, foreign visitors, beginning with the English, established hostels and monastic communities in the city of Rome, mostly in the neighborhood of St. Peter's.[94]

Huneberc's account of the life of Willibald reveals the tension between the growing Benedictine monasticism, which emphasized both physical and spiritual stability, and a monastic life based on religious travel. Willibald had lived both these forms of religious life, but eventually he left his Benedictine house outside Rome. Huneberc's account reveals the somewhat unusual and even suspect circumstances of his departure, as well as showing Willibald's obedience to the pope's request that he assist his countryman Boniface in Germany. It also reveals how Willibald's desire for a religious life of wandering was channeled to a new purpose—that of missionary activity. Missionary travel, as we have seen, was one of the ways that wandering was legitimized as the dominance of stability-based, Benedictine monasticism steadily grew.[95]

Willibald's life can thus be seen as a microcosm of the larger movements in Christianity in which it took place, illustrating the way in which monastic wandering was transformed into missionary travel on the one hand and Benedictine monasticism on the other. The role that the papacy played in the promotion of missionary activity was also connected to the role it played in the promotion of the Benedictine form of monasticism. It was no coincidence that Gregory the Great was famous for both reaching out to the Anglo-Saxons through an organized missionary effort and promoting the Benedictine Rule through his personal composition of a life of Benedict

---

94. For the Saxon community of the Borgo, see Llewellyn, *Rome in the Dark Ages,* 179, 193.
95. Wood, *Missionary Life.*

of Nursia in book 2 of his *Dialogues*.[96] Gregory was a wealthy native of Rome who began his religious life as a monk in the monastery he built on his family estate on the Caelian hill. He apparently knew the Benedictine Rule, praised it, and attempted to have it implemented, though there is not much evidence that it was very much in use in Rome at the time.[97] He also made the English and their conversion his own personal project.[98] It was a project that created strong ties between England and Rome and caused a steady flow of Anglo-Saxon visitors to the papal city.

The advent and spread of Islam in the seventh and eighth centuries had a profound impact on the world of the Mediterranean basin in terms of language, culture, and political organization. It did not, however, bring an end to the steady stream of Western travelers to the Eastern Mediterranean and the Holy Land. The Muslims did not shut off access to Christian holy places in and around Jerusalem. Monastic travel, as we have seen, continued to exist, even with the increasing dominance of the Benedictine Rule with its emphasis on physical stability. Arculf, though a bishop, traveled for years; and monks, such as Willibald, found ways to reconcile their monastic travel with the constraints of the Rule.

96. See discussion in Dunn, *Emergence of Monasticism*, 131–36, and Conrad Leyser, "St. Benedict and Gregory the Great: Another Dialogue," in *Sicilia e Italia suburbicaria tra IV e VIII secolo. Atti del Convegno di Studi (Catania, 24–27 ottobre 1989)*, ed. Salvatore Pricoco, Francesca Rizzo Nervo, and Teresa Sardella (Soveria Mannelli, 1991), 21–43.

97. For early monasticism in Rome, see Guy Ferrari, *Early Roman Monasteries. Notes for the History of the Monasteries and Convents at Rome from the V Through the X century* (Vatican City, 1957), and Georg Jenal, *Italia ascetica atque monastica. Das Asketen- und Mönchtum in Italien von den Anfängen bis zur Zeit der Langobarden (ca. 150/250–604)*, 2 vols. (Stuttgart, 1995).

98. Friedrich Prinz, "Papa Gregorio Magno, il monachesimo siciliano e dell'Italia meridionale e gli inizi della vita monastica presso gli anglosassoni," in *Sicilia e Italia suburbicaria tra IV e VIII secolo, Atti del Convegno di Studi (Catania, 24–27 ottobre 1989)*, ed. Salvatore Pricoco, Francesca Rizzo Nervo, and Teresa Sardella (Soveria Mannelli, 1991), 7–20; P. A. B. Llewellyn, "The Roman Church in the Seventh Century: The Legacy of Gregory I," *Journal of Ecclesiastical History* 25, no. 4 (1974): 363–80.

EPILOGUE

Even with all of the opposition to Christian pilgrimage and monastic wandering, the most powerful force leading to the elimination of monastic travel and wandering as a legitimate form of religious life was the growth and spread of the Benedictine Rule. The Benedictine Rule, which was adapted from the much longer Rule of the Master, is a sort of universal rule easily modified to different circumstances.[1] After its creation in the late sixth century, probably in Italy, the Rule began to slowly disseminate. It would not be until the reign of Louis the Pious, through the influence of Benedict of Aniane, that the Benedictine Rule alone would begin to be promoted as the ideal and the only legitimate form of monasticism.[2] It would take, however, the Cluniac reform movement of the tenth century to truly make the Benedictine Rule normative for Western monasticism.[3]

1. Marilyn Dunn disagrees with the primacy of the *Regula Magistri,* as she has argued in her excellent study, *Emergence of Monasticism,* 128–29, and in her thought-provoking article, "Mastering Benedict." As for the *Regula Magistri,* Dunn associates it with the rule mentioned by Pope Theodore in 643 as being in use at the northern Italian monastery of Bobbio, a monastery established by the Irish Columbanus. *Emergence of Monasticism,* 182–86. It seems odd to me that such an attack on monastic wandering and travel would be produced and used in a Columbanian monastery; see my discussion of the *Regula Magistri* in Chapter 3.

2. Imperial legislation of 816/17. See John Van Engen, "The 'Crisis of Cenobitism' Reconsidered: Benedictine Monasticism in the Years 1050–1150," *Speculum* 61, no. 2 (1986): 275, and J. M. Wallace-Hadrill, *The Frankish Church* (Oxford, 1983). See Mayke de Jong, "Carolingian Monasticism: The Power of Prayer," in *The New Cambridge Medieval History, Volume II, c. 700–c. 900,* ed. Rosamond McKitterick (Cambridge, 1996), 622–53, and Lowrie J. Daly, *Benedictine Monasticism: Its Foundation and Development Through the Twelfth Century* (New York, 1965).

3. See this argument in Phyllis G. Jestice, *Wayward Monks and the Religious Revolution of the Eleventh Century* (Leiden, 1997); see also Raffaello Morghen, "Monastic Reform and Cluniac Spirituality," in *Cluniac Monasticism in the Central Middle Ages,* ed. Noreen Hunt (London, 1971), 11–28.

The monastery of Cluny was established in 910, not by wandering Irish monks or papal missionaries, but by the efforts of the powerful Duke William of Aquitaine. The charter of Cluny reveals that it was established as an institution entirely free from secular or episcopal control; it governed itself, using the Benedictine Rule, and it was subordinate only to the papacy.[4] Cluniac monks were strict observers of the Benedictine Rule, and with their strong abbots and their independence they won new members and many wealthy patrons. The order expanded rapidly throughout France and into Spain and Germany. Through the process of filiation by both the establishment of new daughter houses and the conversion of preexisting monasteries into Cluniac houses, the Order grew to hundreds of monasteries by the end of the eleventh century. It was through the spread and popularity of Cluniac monasticism that the West would finally witness the almost complete dominance of the Benedictine Rule.

The Benedictine Rule was slow in entering Spain, where the monastic tradition was based on Eastern models or on the traditions of the communities founded by Augustine and Cassian.[5] The Islamic conquest of the peninsula in the early eighth century also had an impact on the spread of monasticism in the region. Initially, Cluny did not have a direct effect on Spanish monasticism, but by the eleventh century Cluniac monasticism was making inroads in Spain, first in the region of the Pyrenees, and then along the northern Asturian coast.[6]

Northern Spain, specifically Galicia, was also the birthplace of the quintessentially medieval pilgrimage site: Santiago de Compostela. Site-specific, long-distance pilgrimage within Europe developed by the tenth century, primarily in the form of travel to Santiago de Compostela. Pilgrimage to Santiago de Compostela appealed to the Spanish nobles of the *Reconquista*. Spanish nobles increasingly viewed their attempt to recapture the lands lost to the Muslims in decisively religious terms. Santiago, or Saint James the Greater, was given the nickname *Matamoros,* the Moor-slayer. The *Reconquista* was a holy war, and Santiago was its leader. As the eleventh century progressed, the powerful monastery of Cluny and its dependents began to

4. See Barbara Rosenwein, *Rhinoceros Bound: Cluny in the Tenth Century* (Philadelphia, 1982); Noreen Hunt, "Cluniac Monasticism," in *Cluniac Monasticism in the Central Middle Ages,* ed. Noreen Hunt (London, 1971), 1–10; and Van Engen, "The 'Crisis of Cenobitism' Reconsidered."

5. Anscari M. Mundó, "Monastic Movements in the East Pyrenees," in *Cluniac Monasticism in the Central Middle Ages,* ed. Noreen Hunt (London, 1971), 98–122.

6. Linage Conde, *Los Orígenes* and "El monacato visigotico."

associate themselves even more actively with pilgrimage to Santiago.[7] The order exerted influence through connections of patronage with the great northern Spanish nobility, and as a consequence, Cluny became involved in the promotion of the shrine of Santiago de Compostela.[8] The monks did not perform pilgrimages themselves, but they built guesthouses along the pilgrimage roads that provided the infrastructure of high medieval pilgrimage.[9]

Eventually a Cluniac monk, Dalmatius, became bishop of Santiago in 1094.[10] He was raised to the episcopacy through long negotiations between Pope Urban II and King Alfonso VI, who had imprisoned the previous bishop. Dalmatius, as a monk of Cluny, was an acceptable candidate to both the reform-minded pope and Alfonso, who actively promoted Compostela pilgrimage. By this time, however, Compostela pilgrimage had an international appeal; Cluniac monks, with their base in France, promoted pilgrimage along the *Camino* that wove through its network of roads and hostels throughout France and into Spain. In Paris, the principal north-south road through the city was the Rue St. Jacques, and it marked the beginning of the pilgrimage route to Compostela. Cluniac houses and Cluniac shrines dotted the *Camino,* from its beginnings in Paris, through Aquitaine and the Pyrenees, finally across northern Spain to the far western reaches of Europe, stopping at the small town of Compostela.

Monasticism and pilgrimage had clearly diverged in their history: monasticism in the West, through the Cluniac reform movement, was now defined by stability, while pilgrimage became a form of religious travel practiced by the laity, focusing on a specific goal or quest. Medieval Christian pilgrimage had replaced religious wandering, but it was increasingly a lay phenomenon. It also became increasingly standardized and regulated. Monasteries would regulate travel and the reception of guests, as monks in the West led increasingly cloistered lives. The monastery at Cluny and the shrine at Compostela in Spain were both instrumental in this transformation.

7. For an opposing view, see Etienne Delaruelle, "The Crusading Idea in Cluniac Literature of the Eleventh Century," in *Cluniac Monasticism in the Central Middle Ages,* ed. Noreen Hunt (London, 1971), 191–216. Delaruelle warns against "panclunism," or seeing Cluniac influence everywhere. For an excellent introduction to Cluniac historiography, see Rosenwein, *Rhinoceros Bound,* 3–29.

8. O. K. Werckmeister, "Cluny III and the Pilgrimage to Santiago de Compostela," *Gesta* 27, no. 1/2 (1988): 103–12; John Williams, "Cluny and Spain," ibid., 93–101; Juan G. Atienza, *Monjes y monasterios españoles en la edad media: De la heterodoxia al integrismo, Historia de la España sorprendente* (Madrid, 1992).

9. See H. E. J. Cowdrey, *The Cluniacs and the Gregorian Reform* (Oxford, 1970).

10. Ibid., 244–46; Sumption, *Pilgrimage,* 119.

The growing popularity of the new pilgrimage to Santiago de Compostela in northwestern Spain, with its beginnings in the tenth century, helped to inspire new travelers, primarily lay people, to journey to Jerusalem.[11] In late antiquity and the early Middle Ages, religious writers had emphasized visiting or experiencing the spiritual Jerusalem in preference to a journey to the physical city. This changed at the beginning of the eleventh century, when the laity began *locus*-centered, long-distance pilgrimage to Jerusalem. The participants were mostly lay nobles from the provinces of France: Normandy, Aquitaine, Burgundy, Lorraine, and Gascony.[12] Unlike the earlier travelers to Jerusalem and the Holy Land, they traveled in large groups, often hundreds of travelers, and were far different from the traveling monks who had visited the holy places and holy people.

A reform papacy and a more rigid caliphate in the eleventh century changed the nature of Christian-Muslim relations in the East and West. Society in general was less fluid in the period before the Crusades. These factors whittled away at the freedom of movement across the Mediterranean that was characteristic of the late antique and early medieval worlds. It should come as no surprise that it was a pope and former monk of Cluny, Urban II, who called the first crusade. Urban's sermon at Clermont in 1095 was a call for another mass pilgrimage to the Holy Land, an idea his noble French audience was already familiar with. What was new was that this was to be an armed pilgrimage, a journey of conquest and purification—in short, a Holy War. The influence of the Spanish *Reconquista* is clear; the French knights listening to Pope Urban in Clermont were very familiar with stories of battles with Muslims. The anonymous author of the *Song of Roland,* a vernacular *chanson de geste* composed shortly before Urban's call to crusade, had substituted Muslims for Basques as the hated enemy responsible for the death of Roland and the destruction of Charlemagne's rear guard during the Battle of Roncevaux. The theme of holy warfare in the *Song of Roland* came from the stories circulated along the *Camino* about the victories and defeats of the Spanish nobility in their war with the Spanish Muslims. Urban's audience at Clermont understood quite well what the pontiff was asking from them. The first crusade was also the first pilgrimage to the Holy Land sponsored by the pope. In return for traveling on this

11. Santiago de Compostela pilgrimage had its greatest early patron in King Sancho the Great of Navarre. Cowdrey, *The Cluniacs,* 215.

12. Sumption, *Pilgrimage,* 117.

religious journey to Jerusalem and freeing the city, the pope offered the pilgrims a commutation of penance, a papal indulgence. These armed pilgrims were going to Jerusalem in order to fulfill a vow.

Almost a hundred years before the Crusaders came to the Holy Land, the caliph al-Hakim ordered the destruction of the remaining churches and synagogues in the city of Jerusalem.[13] His reasons are unclear, and most medieval chroniclers, Christian and Muslim, thought he was simply mad, especially after he proclaimed his own divinity. His decrees resulted in the almost complete destruction of the Martyrium, and the other parts of the Holy Sepulcher complex lay in ruins. The Byzantine emperor Constantine IX Monomachus funded the rebuilding of the church beginning in 1030, but on a much smaller scale.[14]

It was beginning in the eleventh century, when most long distance travel to the East had ended and the Holy Sepulcher was destroyed, that Jerusalem as a singular goal took prominence in the imagination of the West and became the embodiment of the heavenly Jerusalem as described by Augustine. Western medieval builders were constructing copies of Holy Land monuments, and new pilgrimage quests began, including the popular shrine of Santiago in Spain. The representation of Jerusalem, both as a real and as an imagined holy city, sheds light on the way travelers perceived the city and the way in which those controlling the representation wanted the city perceived.[15]

In 1099, Crusaders from the Latin West conquered Jerusalem, and a Christian kingdom lasted there for almost one hundred years. During this time the Crusaders launched an active "reclamation" of Christian Jerusalem that created a "Latin" Jerusalem.[16] This time they did not shy away from using the Temple Mount. They converted the Dome of the Rock into a church, which the pilgrim Theodorich denoted as "the Temple of the Lord" in 1172.[17] Maps from this period also refer to the building as either the "Temple of the Lord" or the "Temple of Solomon." Theodorich described the building's octagonal shape and rich mosaic decoration, yet he did not mention the

13. See the accounts in Peters, *Jerusalem*, 258–67.
14. Ibid., 267.
15. Bianca Kühnel, *From the Earthly to the Heavenly Jerusalem: Representations of the Holy City in Christian Art of the First Millennium* (Rome, 1987); P. de Palol Salellas and M. Hirmer, *Early Medieval Art in Spain* (London, 1967).
16. See Bernard Hamilton, "The Impact of Crusader Jerusalem on Western Christendom," *Catholic Historical Review* 80, no. 4 (1994): 695–713; idem, "Ideals of Holiness: Crusaders, Contemplatives, and Mendicants," *International History Review* 17, no. 4 (1996): 693–712.
17. Theoderich, *Guide to the Holy Land*, 23.

giant rock housed within or discuss the building's Muslim past. He did, however, record eight inscriptions that appeared on the eight interior walls of the building, one of which read, "The house of the Lord is well built upon a firm rock."[18]

The twelfth-century Jewish traveler Benjamin of Tudela came to Jerusalem while Crusaders occupied the city.[19] The only building he saw on Mount Sion was a church, though he also said that the tombs of David and the other kings were there. Workmen, hired by the patriarch, had discovered the tombs during the repair of a church's fallen wall only fifteen years prior to Benjamin's visit.

Benjamin of Tudela provides interesting evidence as to the fate of Hebron during the Islamic period and under Crusader control. The Tomb of the Patriarchs was still contested space when Benjamin visited in the twelfth century. The city of Hebron was in ruins, but there was a "great church called St. Abram, and this was a Jewish place of worship at the time of the Mohammedan rule, but the Gentiles have erected there six tombs, respectively called those of Abraham and Sarah, Isaac and Rebekah, Jacob and Leah."[20] Jews had clearly continued to visit the Tomb of the Patriarchs during the early Islamic period. The Crusader takeover of the area resulted in the restoration of these tombs. Christians who visited the site paid the custodians to see these six tombs, but guards secretly showed Jews different tombs, hidden down a long flight of steps. These led to a cave which contained the actual tombs of the Patriarchs, on the opposite side of the cave from their wives.[21] Jewish ossuaries filled the cave, and the custodians kept a lamp burning there day and night. Jews and Christians no longer shared space at the tombs as they did during the visit of the Piacenza Pilgrim; by the twelfth century at least, they had divided the sacred space. Theodorich, writing in the twelfth century, likewise described the Tomb of

18. Ibid., 25.

19. Benjamin of Tudela, *The Itinerary of Benjamin of Tudela,* ed. Michael A. Signer (Malibu, Calif., 1987).

20. Ibid., 86. For Islamic pilgrimage to Hebron, see Elad, "Pilgrims and Pilgrimage," 21–62.

21. "If a Jew comes, however, and gives a special reward, the custodian of the cave opens unto him a gate of iron, which was constructed by our forefathers, and then he is able to descend below by means of steps, holding a lighted candle in his hand. He then reaches a cave, in which nothing to be found, and a cave beyond, which is likewise empty, but when he reaches the third cave behold there are six sepulchers, those of Abraham, Isaac and Jacob, respectively facing those of Sarah, Rebekah, and Leah." *Itinerary of Benjamin of Tudela,* 86. This cave is echoed in his account of Rome where Benjamin of Tudela mentions a secret cave under the Lateran where the Temple treasures were hidden.

the Patriarchs as a "double cave," one that included the tombs of Adam and Eve, in addition to the six tombs mentioned by the other authors. He also mentions that the Oak of Mamre, which, he writes, had died in the reign of Theodosius, had put forth another branch, though somewhat withered, from its stump.[22]

The Crusaders viewed the city in a way much different from that of earlier Christians. For them, the Christianization of Jerusalem was a purification of holy space.[23] They were not beginning with a blank slate; the Holy Sepulcher and other churches were still standing, and Christians were free to live and worship in the city. The Crusaders exercised their claim on the religious topography of the city through purification. They wanted to cleanse the city of its Islamic identity. They did this by killing thousands of the Muslim residents of the city and driving out the Jews and Greek Christians and cleansing and transforming the buildings of the city. This co-option of religious space and structure in the city was a new phenomenon. Even during the Muslim takeover of Jerusalem there was not such large-scale "cleansing." The new Muslim buildings coexisted with Christian and Jewish structures. The post-Crusade guidebooks describe Jerusalem for the first time as completely Christian.

The Crusaders can, in many ways, be compared to the Romans, who expelled the Jewish population, destroyed the Temple, and then took over Jewish holy space. The changing of the name of the city to that of the emperor Hadrian's family and the building of a temple to Capitoline Jupiter, possibly containing an imperial cult shrine as well, was not an attempt to add new religious space or a new sacred identity to the city, but rather an attempt to erase its Jewish identity. Twelfth-century Jerusalem, full of Islamic holy places, underwent a similar change under Crusader rule.

Each of the travelers discussed in this book had a unique path over the religious and physical geography around them, and much in their stories was driven by their own personal sense of religious meaning. Yet certain coherent patterns and themes emerge from their travels when seen together. Meeting monks and other travelers, constant travel and homelessness, imitating the earthly homelessness of the Christian, patronage, and conceiving of

22. Theoderich, *Guide to the Holy Land,* 34.
23. See Hamilton, "Impact of Crusader Jerusalem," 699–704; idem, "Ideals of Holiness," 693–712. Hamilton overstates the ruined condition of Christian shrines and churches within the city.

Jerusalem as a Christian city and a destination of travel were all common experiences to late antique monastic travelers.

The large number of women among these travelers indicates first the accessibility and popularity of this form of monastic escape, but wandering monasticism also held a particular appeal for women. Throughout this study, female travelers have emerged as a central part in the creation of a Christian Jerusalem and of pilgrimage. It is impossible to know just how popular travel was among women, but there is nothing in the sources to indicate that these female wanderers seemed out of the ordinary to their contemporaries. Monasticism in general was one of the only forms of deep religious expression allowed to women as they were excluded from the ecclesiastical hierarchy and from participation in the daily liturgy. Monasticism also supplied an alternative to marriage, providing a structure for the pursuit of other activities, such as establishing and maintaining hospitals and monasteries. Women travelers were able to meet holy people, including other women, and participate in meaningful interactions such as gift exchanges.

For all the early Christian travelers, travel was a way of achieving separation from society and family. Together, their stories reveal the coherence of itinerant spirituality. Though their stories shed light on the places and people around them, these wanderers lived in a world of their own devising. Though their travels often consisted of visiting holy people, giving gifts, venerating relics, and setting up monastic foundations, they had no prescribed structure so familiar in modern pilgrimage. In their freedom from the strictures of stable society, from Benedictine monasticism, and from formulaic pilgrimage, they created their own form of spiritual expression through travel, an asceticism of wandering unique to the late antique world. The stricter adherence to the Benedictine ideal of *stabilitas* and an increasingly more rigid sociopolitical and religious Mediterranean world helped to end monastic travel and led to the promotion of lay pilgrimage.

BIBLIOGRAPHY

ABBREVIATIONS

CC	*Corpus Christianorum. Series latina.* Turnhout, 1953– .
CIL	*Corpus Inscriptionum Latinarum.* Berlin, 1862– .
ConZA	*Consultationes Zacchei christiani et Apollonii philosophi*
CSEL	*Corpus scriptorum ecclesiasticorum latinorum.* Vienna, 1866– .
CTh	*Codex Theodosianus*
HE	Eusebius *Historia Ecclesiastica*
HL	Palladius *Historia Lausiaca*
Itin.	Egeria *Itinerarium*
Itin. Plac.	*Itinerarium Placentini*
Itin. Burd.	*Itinerarium Burdigalense*
LP	*Liber Pontificalis*
MGH	*Monumenta Germaniae historica.* Berlin, 1877– .
AA	*Auctores antiquissimi*
Epp.	*Epistolae*
SRM	*Scriptores rerum merovingicarum*
PG	*Patrologia graeca.* Edited by J. P. Migne. Paris, 1857– .
PL	*Patrologia latina.* Edited by J. P. Migne. Paris, 1844– .
PLRE	A. H. M. Jones, J. R. Martindale, and J. Morris, *Prosopography of the Later Roman Empire.* Vol. 1, A.D. 260–395. Cambridge, 1971.
RA	*Regula Augustini*
RB	*Regula Benedictina*
RBT	Basil *Regulae Brevius Tractatae*
RFT	Basil *Regulae Fusius Tractatae*
RIVP	*Regula IV Patrum*
RM	*Regula Magistri*
SC	*Sources chrétiennes.* Paris, 1940– .
VPE	*Vitas Sanctorum Patrum Emeretensium*
VSF	*Vita Sancti Fructuosi*

PRIMARY SOURCES

Adomnán of Iona. *De locis sanctis.* Edited by P. Geyer and O. Cuntz. In *Itineraria et alia geographica,* CC 175:175–234. Translated by Denis Meehan as *Adamnan's De Locis Sanctis* (Dublin, 1958).

———. *Vita S. Columbae.* Edited by A. O. Anderson and M. O. Anderson. London, 1961. Translated by Richard Sharpe as *Adomnán of Iona: Life of St. Columba* (New York, 1995), and by Alan Orr Anderson and Marjorie Ogilvie Anderson as *Adomnán's Life of Columba* (Oxford, 1991).

Ambrose of Milan. *Oratio de obitu Theodosii. CSEL* 73.371–401.

Ammianus Marcellinus. *Res Gestae.* Edited and translated by John C. Rolfe. In *Rerum Gestarum qui supersunt.* 3 vols. Loeb Classical Library. Cambridge, Mass., 1971.

Antiochus Strategos. "Antiochus Strategos' Account of the Sack of Jerusalem in A.D. 614." Translated by F. C. Conybeare. *English Historical Review* 25 (1910): 502–17.

Apophthegmata Patrum. Edited by J. B. Cotelier. *PL* 65:71–440. Translated by Benedicta Ward as *The Sayings of the Desert Fathers: The Alphabetical Collection* (Kalamazoo, Mich., 1975) and as *The Wisdom of the Desert Fathers: Systematic Sayings from the Anonymous Series of the Apophthegmata Patrum* (Fairacres, Oxford, 1986).

Athanasius of Alexandria. *Vita Antonii.* Edited by G. J. Bartelink and translated into Italian by Pietro Citati and Salvatore Cilla as *Vita di San Antonio.* Volume 1 of *Vite dei Santi,* ed. C. Mohrmann. Milan, 1974. Translated by Robert C. Gregg as *Athanasius: The Life of Saint Antony and the Letter to Marcellinus* (New York, 1980).

Augustine of Hippo. *Confessiones. CC* 27. Translated by Henry Chadwick as *Augustine's Confessions* (Oxford, 1992).

———. *De civitate Dei. CC* 47–48. Translated by Henry Bettenson as *Concerning the City of God Against the Pagans* (Harmondsworth, U.K., 1984).

———. *De opere monachorum. CSEL* 41. An English translation can be found in *Saint Augustine: Treatises on Various Subjects,* ed. Roy J. Deferrari (New York, 1952).

———. *Enarrationes in Psalmos, CI–CL. CC 40.*

———. *Epistolae 1*–29*.* In *Lettres 1*–29*, Nouvelle édition de texte critique et introduction.* Edited by J. Divjak. Bibliothèque Augustinienne, vol. 46B. Paris, 1987. Translated by Robert B. Eno as *Saint Augustine, Letters, Volume VI (1*–29*)* (Washington, D.C., 1989).

———. *Epistulae. CSEL* 57. An English translation by Philip Schaff can be found in *The Confessions and Letters of St. Augustin, with a Sketch of His Life and Work,* vol. 1 of *A Select Library of Nicene and Post-Nicene Fathers of the Christian Church* (Grand Rapids, Mich., 1994).

———. *Regula.* Edited and translated by George Lawless as *Augustine of Hippo and His Monastic Rule* (Oxford, 1987).

———. *Retractationum Libri II. CC 57.*

———. *Sermons.* Translated by Edmund Hill as *Newly Discovered Sermons,* part 3, volume 11, of *The Works of Saint Augustine: A Translation for the 21st Century,* ed. John E. Rotelle (Hyde Park, N.Y., 1997).

Avitus. *Epistola ad Palchonium, de reliquiis Sancti Stephani, et de Luciani epistola a se e graeco in latinum versa. PL* 41:805–8.

Bachiarius. *De reparatione lapsi ad Januarium. PL* 20:1019–63.

———. *Libellus de Fide. PL* 20:1019–63.

Basil of Caesarea. *Epistolae.* Translated by Roy J. Deferrari as *Saint Basil: The Letters: Address to Young Men on Reading Greek Literature,* 4 vols., Loeb Classical Library (Cambridge, Mass., 1934).

———. *Regulae Fusius Tractatae* and *Regulae Brevius Tractatae.* Translated by W. K. L. Clarke as *The Ascetic Works of Saint Basil* (London, 1925), 9–55.

Bede. *Historia Ecclesiastica.* In *Baedae Opera Historica,* ed. J. E. King. 2 vols. Cambridge, Mass., 1979.

Benedict of Aniane. *Concordia Regularum.* Edited by Pierre Bonnerue. *CC,* Continuatio Mediavalis. Turnhout, 1999.

Benjamin of Tudela. *The Itinerary of Benjamin of Tudela.* Edited and translated by Michael A. Signer. Malibu, Calif., 1987. Selections of the *Itinerary* can be found in *Jewish Travellers in the Middle Ages,* ed. Elkan Nathan Adler (New York, 1987).

Braulio of Saragossa. *Epistulae. PL* 80:649–700. An English translation can be found in *Iberian Fathers, volume 2: Braulio of Saragossa, Fructuosus of Braga,* ed. Claude W. Barlow (Washington, D.C., 1969).

———. *Life of St. Emilian. PL* 80:699–714. An English translation by Claude W. Barlow can be found in *Iberian Fathers volume 2: Braulio of Saragossa, Fructuosus of Braga* (Washington, D.C., 1969).

Breviarius de Hierosolyma. Edited by P. Geyer and O. Cuntz. In *Itineraria et alia geographica, CC* 175:109–12.

Caesarius of Arles. *Oeuvres Monastiques: Oeuvres pour les Moniales.* Edited and translated by Adalbert de Vogüé and Joël Courreau. Paris, 1988. Translated by Maria Caritas McCarthy as *The Rule for Nuns of St. Caesarius of Arles* (Washington, D.C., 1960).

Cassian, John. *Conférences.* Edited by E. Pichery and translated as *Conférénces, SC* 42, 54, and 64 (Paris, 1955–59). Translated into English by Colm Luibheid as *John Cassian: Conferences* (New York, 1985).

———. *Institutiones.* Edited and translated by Jean-Claude Guy as *Jean Cassien: Institutions Cénobitiques. SC* 109 (Paris, 1965). Translated into English by Edgar C. S. Gibson as "The Works of John Cassian," in *A Select Library of Nicene and Post-Nicene Father of the Christian Church, second series,* 183–641 (Grand Rapids, Mich., 1955).

The Celtic Monk: Rules and Writings of Early Irish Monks. Edited by Uinseann Ó Maidín. Kalamazoo, Mich., 1996.

Codex Theodosianus. Edited by Th. Mommsen as *Theodosiani Libri XVI cum Constitutionibus Sirmondianis* (Berlin, 1905). Translated into English by Clyde Pharr as *The Theodosian Code and Novels and the Sirmondian Constitutions* (Princeton, N.J., 1952).

Concilios Visigóticos e Hispano-Romanos, España Cristiana. Edited by José Vives. Barcelona, 1963. Second edition. Barcelona, 1969.

Consultationes Zacchei christiani et Apollonii philosophi. Edited and translated into French by Jean Louis Feiertag and Werner Steinmann as *Questions d'un païen à un chrétien (Consultationes Zacchei christiani et Apollonii philosophi),* 2 vols., *SC* 401 (Paris, 1994). Translated into English by Caedmon Holmes as *Discussions of Zacchaeus and Apollonius,* revised by Adalbert de Vogüé, *Monastic Studies* 12 (1976).

Corpus of Balearic Inscriptions up to the Arab Conquest. Edited by Cristóbal Veny. Translated by Louis Cavell. Wetteren, Belgium, 1972.

Cosmas Idicopleustes. *The Christian Topography of Cosmas.* Edited by J. W. McCrindle. New York, 1897. Extracts translated by John Wilkinson in *Jerusalem Pilgrims Before the Crusades,* 2d ed. (Warminster, 2002), 122–23.

Crónica Seudo Isidoriana. Edited by Antonio Benito Vidal. Vol. 5 of *Textos Medievales.* Valencia, 1961.

Cyril of Jerusalem. *Catecheses.* Translated and edited by Edward Hamilton Gifford as *Catechetical Lectures.* In *A Select Library of Nicene and Post-Nicene Fathers of the Christian Church.* Second series. Vol. 7. Grand Rapids, Mich., 1979.

Cyril of Scythopolis. *Lives of the Monks of Palestine by Cyril of Scythopolis.* Edited and translated by R. M. Price. Kalamazoo, Mich., 1991.

Decrees of the Ecumenical Councils. Edited by Norman P. Tanner. 2 vols. Washington, D.C., 1990.

Didache, Epistle of Barnabas, Epistles and Martyrdom of St. Polycarp, Fragments of Papias, Epistle to Diognetus. Edited and translated by James A. Kleist. Westminster, Md., 1948. Another translation, by Kirsopp Lake, appears in volume 1 of *The Apostolic Fathers* (New York, 1930).

Early Monastic Rules. Edited and translated by Carmela Vircillo Franklin, Ivan Havener, and J. Alcuin Francis. Collegeville, Minn., 1982.

Egeria. *Itinerarium.* Edited by P. Geyer and O. Cuntz. In *Itineraria et alia geographica,* CC 175:37–90. Two other editions are the *Itinerarium Egeriae (Peregrinatio Aetheriae),* ed. Otto Prinz, in *Sammlung Vulgärlateinischer Texte* (Heidelberg, 1960), and the *S. Silviae Aquitanae, Peregrinatio ad Loca Sancta,* ed. J. F. Gamurrini (Rome, 1888). Translated into English by G. E. Gingras as *Egeria: Diary of a Pilgrimage* (New York, 1970) and John Wilkinson as *Egeria's Travels,* 3d ed. (Warminster, 1999). Translated into French by Pierre Maraval as *Égérie: Journal de Voyage (Itinéraire),* SC 296 (Paris, 1982), and into Spanish by Agustín Arce as *Itinerario de la Virgen Egeria* (Madrid, 1980).

Enchiridion Locorum Sanctorum: Documenta S. Evangelii Loca Respicientia. Edited by P. Donatus Baldi. Jerusalem, 1935.

Eucherius. *Epistola ad Faustum de locis sanctis.* CC 175:236–43. An English translation by John Wilkinson appears in *Jerusalem Pilgrims Before the Crusades* (Warminster, 1977).

Eunapius of Sardis. *Lives of the Philosophers and Sophists.* Edited and translated by Wilmer Cave Wright as *Philostratus and Eunapius: The Lives of the Sophists.* Cambridge, Mass., 1961.

Eusebius. *Historia Ecclesiastica.* Translated and edited by Arthur Cushman McGiffert as *The Church History of Eusebius,* in *A Select Library of Nicene and Post-Nicene Fathers of the Christian Church,* second series, vol. 1 (Grand Rapids, Mich., 1979).

Eusebius. *Vita Constantini.* Translated by Averil Cameron and Stuart G. Hall as *Eusebius, Life of Constantine* (Oxford, 1999).

Eugippii Regula. Edited by Fernando Villegas and Adalbert de Vogüé. CSEL 87.

Fructuosus of Braga. *Epistola ad Regem Recesvindum.* MGH Epp. 3. Berlin, 1892. An English translation can be found in *Iberian Fathers, volume 2: Braulio of Saragossa, Fructuosus of Braga,* ed. Claude W. Barlow (Washington, D.C., 1969).

———. *Regula Monachorum Complutensis.* Edited and translated by Julio Campo Ruiz and Ismael Roca Melia in "La regla de monjes de San Fructuoso de Braga," in *San Leandro, San Isidoro, San Fructuoso,* volume 2 of *Santos Padres Españoles* (Madrid, 1971). An English translation by Claude W. Barlow can be found in *Iberian Fathers, volume 2: Braulio of Saragossa, Fructuosus of Braga* (Washington, D.C., 1969).

———. *Regula Monastica Communis.* Edited and translated by Julio Campo Ruiz and Ismael Roca Melia in "La regla de monjes de San Fructuoso de Braga," in *San Leandro, San Isidoro, San Fructuoso,* volume 2 of *Santos Padres Españoles* (Madrid, 1971). An English translation by Claude W. Barlow can be found in *Iberian Fathers, volume 2: Braulio of Saragossa, Fructuosus of Braga* (Washington, D.C., 1969).

Gerontius. *Life of Melania.* Edited by D. Gorce. *SC* 90. Paris, 1962. An English translation can be found in *Handmaids of the Lord: Contemporary Descriptions of Feminine Asceticism in the First Six Christian Centuries,* ed. Joan M. Petersen (Kalamazoo, Mich., 1996).

Gregory of Tours. *De virtutibus s. Martini.* *MGH SRM* 1. Hanover, 1885. An English translation by Raymond Van Dam can be found in *Saints and Their Miracles in Late Antique Gaul* (Princeton, N.J., 1993).

———. *Historia Francorum.* *MGH SRM* 1. Hanover, 1885. Translated by Lewis Thorpe as *Gregory of Tours: The History of the Franks* (New York, 1974).

Gregory the Great. *Registrum epistolarum VIII.* CC 140A.

Huneberc of Heidenheim. *Vita Willibaldi Episcopi Eichstetensis.* Edited by O. Holder-Egger. *MGH* 15, 86–106. Hanover, 1887. Translated into English by C. H. Talbot as "The *Hodoeporicon* of St. Willibald by Huneberc of Heidenheim," in *The Anglo-Saxon Missionaries in Germany* (New York, 1954). Revised and reprinted in Thomas Head and Thomas F. X. Noble, eds., *Soldiers of Christ: Saints and Saints' Lives from Late Antiquity and the Early Middle Ages* (University Park, Pa., 1995).

Hydatius. *Chronica.* Translated by R. W. Burgess as *The Chronicle of Hydatius and the Consularia Constantinopolitana: Two Contemporary Accounts of the Final Years of the Roman Empire,* Oxford Classical Monographs (Oxford, 1993).

Ildefonsus of Toledo. *De itinere deserti.* A Spanish translation by Vicente Blanco Garcia and Julio Campos Ruiz can be found in *Santos Padres Españoles,* vol. 1, *San Ildefonso de Toledo.* Madrid, 1971.

———. *De viris illustribus.* Translated by Carmen Codoñer Merino as *El "De viris illustribus" de Ildefonso de Toledo: Estudio y Edicion critica* (Salamanca, 1972).

Inscripciones Cristianas de la España Romana y Visigoda. Edited by José Vives. Second edition. In volume 2 of *Monumenta Hispaniae Sacra, Serie patrística.* Barcelona, 1969.

Inscripciones Latinas de la España Romana: Antología de 6,800 textos. Edited by José Vives. 2 vols. Universidad de Barcelona, consejo superior de investigaciones científicas. Barcelona, 1971–72.

Isidore of Seville. *Commonitiuncula ad Sororem.* Edited by A. E. Anspach. In volume 4 of *Scriptores Ecclesiastici Hispano-Latini veteris et medii aevi.* Madrid, 1935.

———. *De viris illustribus.* Edited by Carmen Codoñer-Merino as *El "de viris illustribus" de Isidoro de Sevilla: Estudio y edicion critica.* Salamanca, 1964.

——. *Epistulae. PL* 84. Translated by Gordon B. Ford as *The Letters of Isidore of Seville* (Amsterdam, 1970).

——. *Etimologías.* Edited by Jose Oroz Reta and Manuel-A. Marcos Casquero. Vol. 1. Madrid, 2000.

——. *Historica Gothorum, Wandalorum, Seuborum.* Edited by Th. Mommsen. *MGH AA,* 11. Berlin, 1894. Translated into English by Guido Donini and Gordon B. Ford as *Isidore of Seville's History of the Kings of the Goths, Vandals, and Suevi* (Leiden, 1966).

Itineraria et Alia Geographica. Edited by P. Geyer. 2 vols. *CC* 175–176. Turnhout, 1965.

Itinerarium Burdigalense. Edited by P. Geyer and O. Cuntz. In *Itineraria et alia geographica, CC* 175:1–26.

Itinerarium Placentini. Edited by P. Geyer and O. Cuntz. In *Itineraria et alia geographica, CC* 175:127–74. Translated by John Wilkinson in *Jerusalem Pilgrims Before the Crusades* (Warminster, 1977).

Jerome. *De viris illustribus. PL* 23:603. Translated by Ernest Cushing Richardson as "Jerome and Gennadius: Lives of Illustrious Men," in *A Select Library of Nicene and Post-Nicene Fathers of the Christian Church* (Grand Rapids, Mich., 1979).

——. *Epistulae.* Edited by I. Hilberg. 3 vols. *CSEL* 54–56. Translated by Jérôme Labourt as *Saint Jérôme: Lettres,* vols. 1–8 (Paris, 1949–63), and by F. A. Wright as *Select Letters of St. Jerome* (1933; reprint, Cambridge, Mass., 1991).

——. *Life of Paul, the First Hermit.* Translated by Paul B. Harvey Jr., in *Ascetic Behavior in Greco-Roman Antiquity: A Sourcebook,* ed. Vincent L. Wimbush. Minneapolis, 1990.

John Chrysostom. *Contra oppugnatores vitae monasticae. PG* 47.

John of Biclar. *Chronica.* Edited by Th. Mommsen. *MGH AA* 11. Berlin, 1894. Translated by Kenneth Baxter Wolf in *Conquerors and Chroniclers of Early Medieval Spain* (Liverpool, 1990).

John of Ephesus. *Lives of the Eastern Saints: Mary, Euphemia and Susan.* In *Holy Women of the Syrian Orient,* ed. Sebastian P. Brock and Susan Ashbrook Harvey. Berkeley and Los Angeles, 1987.

John Rufus. *Life of Peter the Iberian.* Edited by R. Raabe as *Petrus der iberer* (Leipzig, 1885). Extracts translated by John Wilkinson in *Jerusalem Pilgrims Before the Crusades,* 2d ed. (Warminster, 2002), 99–102.

Jordanes. *Romana et Getica.* Edited by Th. Mommsen. *MGH AA* 5. Berlin, 1882. Translated by Charles C. Mierow as *Jordanes: The Origin and Deeds of the Goths, in English version* (Princeton, N.J., 1908).

Julian. *The Works of the Emperor Julian.* Edited by Wilmer Cave Wright. 3 vols. Loeb Classical Library. New York, 1913.

Leander of Seville. *De institutione virginum et contemptu mundi.* Edited and translated by Julio Campo Ruiz and Ismael Roca Melia in "La regla de monjes de San Fructuoso de Braga," in *San Leandro, San Isidoro, San Fructuoso,* volume 2 of *Santos Padres Españoles* (Madrid, 1971). An English translation can be found in *Iberian Fathers, volume 1: Martin of Braga, Paschasius of Dumium, Leander of Seville,* ed. Claude W. Barlow (Washington, D.C., 1969). Also published under the editorship of Jaime Velazquez under the title *De la instruccion de las virgenes y desprecio del mundo,* Corpus patristicum Hispanum (Madrid, 1979).

Libanius. *Orationes.* Edited by R. Foerster. Berlin, 1909–27. Translated by A. F. Norman as *Libanius: Selected Works.* Vol. 2. Cambridge, Mass., 1977.

Liber Pontificalis. The standard edition is L. Duchesne and Cyrille Vogel, eds., *Le Liber Pontificalis, Texte, introduction et commentaire,* 3 vols. (Paris, 1955–57). Translated into English by Raymond Davis as *The Book of the Pontiffs (Liber Pontificalis)* (Liverpool, 1989), and also by Raymond Davis as *The Lives of the Eighth-century Popes (Liber Pontificalis): The Ancient Biographies of Nine Popes from A.D. 715 to A.D. 817* (Liverpool, 1992).

"The Life and Works of Our Holy Father, St. Daniel the Stylite." In *Three Byzantine Saints: Contemporary Biographies Translated from the Greek,* ed. E. Dawes and N. H. Baynes. Crestwood, N.Y., 1977.

The Life of Pelagia of Antioch. In *Holy Women of the Syrian Orient,* ed. Sebastian P. Brock and Susan Ashbrook Harvey. Berkeley and Los Angeles, 1987.

The Life of Saint Nicholas of Sion. Edited and translated by Ihor Sevcenko and Nancy Patterson Sevcenko. Brookline, Mass., 1984.

Marinus of Neapolis. *Life of Proclus.* Translated by Kenneth Sylvan Guthrie and edited by David R. Fideler. Grand Rapids, Mich., 1986.

Martin of Braga. *Martini Episcopi Bracarensis: Opera omnia.* Edited by Claude W. Barlow. New Haven, Conn., 1950. Also see *Martin de Braga: Obras Completas,* ed. Ursicino Domínguez del Val, volume 4 of *Corpus Patristicum Hispanum* (Madrid, 1990). Translated by Claude W. Barlow in *Iberian Fathers, volume 1: Martin of Braga, Paschasius of Dumium, Leander of Seville* (Washington, D.C., 1969).

Navigatio S. Brendani Abbatis. Edited by C. Selmer. Notre Dame, Ind., 1959. Translated by J. F. Webb and edited by D. H. Farmer in *The Age of Bede* (Harmondsworth, U.K., 1985).

Orosius. *Consultatio sive Commonitorium Orosii ad Augustinum.* In *Paulo Orosio su vida y sus obras,* ed. Casimiro Torres Rodriguez. Galicia Historica. Santiago de Compostela, 1985. Also see Klaus-D. Daur, ed., *Sancti Aurelii Augustini, Commonitorium Orosii et Sancti Aurelii Augustini contra Priscillianistas et Origenistas, CC* 49 (Turnholt, 1985).

———. *Historiarum adversum paganos libri VII.* In *Paulo Orosio su vida y sus obras,* ed. Casimiro Torres Rodriguez. Galicia Historica. Santiago, 1985. Translated by Roy J. Deferrari as *Paulus Orosius: The Seven Books of History Against the Pagans* (Washington, D.C., 1964).

———. *Liber apologeticus.* In *Paulo Orosio su vida y sus obras,* ed. Casimiro Torres Rodriguez. Galicia Historica. Santiago, 1985.

Pachomius. *Pachomian Koinonia: The Lives, Rules and Other Writings of Pachomius and His Disciples.* 3 vols. Translated by Armand Veilleux. Kalamazoo, Mich., 1981.

Palladius. *Historia Lausiaca.* Edited by Cuthbert Butler, Cambridge, 1898–1904. Translated by W. K. Lowther Clarke as *The Lausiac History of Palladius* (New York, 1918) and by R. T. Meyers as *Lausiac History* (London, 1965).

Paulinus of Nola. *Epistolae. CSEL* 29. Translated by P. G. Walsh as *Letters of St. Paulinus of Nola,* 2 vols. (New York, 1966).

Possidius. *Vita Augustini.* Translated by A. A. R. Bastiansen as *Vita di Agostino,* in *Vita dei santi,* ed. Christine Mohrmann (Verona, 1989). Translated by Thomas F. X. Noble and Thomas Head in *Soldiers of Christ: Saints and Saints' Lives from Late Antiquity and the Early Middle Ages* (University Park, Pa., 1995).

Procopius of Caesarea. *Justinian's Buildings*. Edited and translated by H. B. Dewing and G. Downey. Loeb Classical Library. Cambridge, Mass., 1961.

Prudentius. *Peristephanon Liber*. In *Prudentius*, ed. H. J. Thomson. 2 vols. Cambridge, Mass., 1949.

———. *Tituli historiarum (Dittochaeon)*. In *Prudentius*, ed. H. J. Thomson. 2 vols. Cambridge, Mass., 1949.

Les Règles des Saints Pères: Trois règles du VI siècle incorporant des Textes Lériniens. Edited by Adalbert de Vogüé. 2 vols. SC 297. Paris, 1982.

Regula Benedicti. Edited and translated by Justin McCann under the title *The Rule of Saint Benedict*. London, 1952.

Regula Magistri. Edited by Adalbert de Vogüé under the title *La Règle du maître*. 3 vols. SC 105–7. Paris, 1964. Also see *La Règle du Maître: Édition diplomatique des manuscrits latins 12205 et 12634 de Paris*, ed. Hubert Vanderhoven and François Masai, with collaboration by P. B. Corbett (Paris, 1953). Translated by Luke Eberle under the title *The Rule of the Master* (Kalamazoo, Mich., 1977).

Revelatio Sancti Stephani. Edited by S. Vanderlinden. *Revue des études byzantines* 4 (1946): 178–217.

Rufinus. *Basili regula a Rufino latine versa*. Edited by Klaus Zelzer. *CSEL* 86. Translated by William Henry Fremantle as "Life and Works of Rufinus with Jerome's Apology against Rufinus," in *A Select Library of Nicene and Post-Nicene Fathers of the Christian Church* (Grand Rapids, Mich., 1979).

Severus of Minorca. *Epistola Severi Episcopi*. Edited by Eusebio Lafuente Hernández in *Edición paleográfica y Transcripción latina seguidas de las versiones castellana y catalana de su texto*, vol. 1, *Documenta Historica Minoricensia*. Menorca, 1981. Translated by Scott Bradbury as *Severus of Minorca: Letter on the Conversion of the Jews* (Oxford, 1996).

Sidonius Apollinaris. *Epistolae*. Edited by W. B. Anderson. 2 vols. Cambridge, Mass., 1936.

Socrates Scholasticus. *Historia ecclesiastica*. Edited by W. Bright. Oxford, 1978. Translated by A. C. Zenos as "Church History from A.D. 305–439," in *A Select Library of Nicene and Post-Nicene Fathers of the Christian Church* (Grand Rapids, Mich., 1979).

Sophronius. *Anacreonticon*. Edited by M. Gigante. In *Soprhonii Anacreontica*. Rome, 1957.

Sozomen. *Historia ecclesiastica*. Edited and translated by C. D. Hartrauft. In *A Select Library of Nicene and Post-Nicene Fathers of the Christian Church*. Grand Rapids, Mich., 1979.

Symmachus. *Relationes*. Translated and edited by R. H. Barrow as *Prefect and Emperor: The Relationes of Symmachus, A.D. 384*. Oxford, 1973.

Theoderich. *Guide to the Holy Land*. Translated by Aubrey Stewart. New York, 1986.

Theodoret of Cyrrhus. *Historia ecclesiastica*. An English translation may be found in Blomfield Jackson, "The Ecclesiastical History, Dialogues, and Letters of Theodoret." In *A Select Library of Nicene and Post-Nicene Fathers of the Christian Church*. Grand Rapids, Mich., 1979.

———. *Historia monastica*. Edited and translated by R. M. Price as *A History of the Monks of Syria by Theodoret of Cyrrhus*. Kalamazoo, Mich., 1985.

Theodosius. *De situ terrae sanctae.* In *Itineraria et alia geographica,* ed. P. Geyer and
     O. Cuntz, *CC* 175:113–25. An English translation by John Wilkinson appears
     in *Jerusalem Pilgrims Before the Crusades* (Warminster, 1977).
Valerius of Bierzo. *Epistola Beatissime Egerie laude conscripta fratrum Bergidensium
     monachorum a Valerio conlata.* Edited and translated by Manuel C. Díaz y
     Díaz as *Valerius du Bierzo: Lettre sur la Bsa Égerie. SC* 296. Paris, 1982.
——. *Ordo Querimoniae.* In *Valerio of Bierzo: An Ascetic of the Late Visigothic Period,*
     ed. and trans. Consuelo Maria Aherne. Washington, D.C., 1949.
Venantius Fortunatus. *Carminum libri.* Edited by F. Leo. *MGH AA* 4. Berlin 1881.
     Translated by Claude W. Barlow in *Martini Episcopi Bracarensis. Opera omnia*
     (New Haven, 1950), appendix 4.
Vie des Pères du Jura. Edited by François Martine. *SC* 142. Paris, 1968.
The Vita Sancti Fructuosi: Text with a Translation, Introduction, and Commentary.
     Edited and translated by Sister Frances Clare Nock. Washington, D.C., 1946.
     Spanish edition and translation by Manuel C. Díaz y Díaz as *La Vida de San
     Fructuoso de Braga* (Braga, 1974).
Vitas Sanctorum Patrum Emeretensium. Edited by A. Maya Sanchez. Turnholt, 1992.
     Also see *The "Vitas Sanctorum Patrum Emeretensium,"* ed. Joseph N. Garvin.
     Washington, D.C., 1946.
Zosimus. *Historia Nova.* Translated into French and edited by François Paschoud as
     Zosime. Histoire nouvelle. 3 vols. Paris, 2003. Translated into English by
     Ronald T. Ridley as *New History* (Canberra, 1982).

SECONDARY SOURCES

Accademia Nazionale dei Lincei, ed. *Passaggio dal mondo antico al medio evo da
     Teodosio a San Gregorio Magno.* Vol. 45, Atti dei Convegni Lincei (Roma,
     25–28 maggio 1977). Rome, 1980.
Amengual i Batle, Josep. "Manifestaciones del Monacato Balear y Tarraconense
     según la correspondencia entre San Agustín y Consencio (415–420)." In
     *Il Monachesimo Occidentale dalle origini alla Regula Magistri. XXVI Incontro di
     studiosi dell'antichità Cristiana,* Roma, 8–10 maggio 1997, 341–59. Rome, 1998.
Angenendt, Arnold. *Monachi Peregrini: Studien zu Pirmin und den Monastischen
     Vorstellungen des frühen Mittelalters.* Munich, 1972.
Anson, John. "The Female Transvestite in Early Monasticism: The Origin and
     Development of a Motif." *Viator* 5 (1974): 1–32.
Arce, Javier. "The City of Mérida (Emerita) in the *Vitas Patrum Emeritensium* (VIth
     Century A.D.)." In *East and West: Modes of Communication: Proceedings of the
     First Plenary Conference at Mérida,* ed. Evangelos Chrysos and Ian Wood,
     1–14. Leiden, 1999.
——. *El último siglo de la España romana: 284–409.* Madrid, 1982.
Armstrong, G. T. "Fifth and Sixth-century Church Buildings in the Holy Land."
     Greek Orthodox Theological Review 14 (1969): 17–30.
Arnold, Duane W. H. *The Early Episcopal Career of Athanasius of Alexandria.* Notre
     Dame, Ind., 1991.
Atienza, Juan G. *Monjes y monasterios españoles en la edad media: De la heterodoxia al
     integrismo, Historia de la España sorprendente.* Madrid, 1992.

Avi-Yonah, Michael. *Gazetteer of Roman Palestine.* Edited by N. Avigad, Y. Yadin, J. Aviram, A. Ben-Tor, and Y. Tsafrir. Vol. 5, *Qedem: Monographs of the Institute of Archaeology.* Jerusalem, 1976.

———. *The Holy Land from the Persian to the Arab Conquests: A Historical Geography.* Grand Rapids, Mich., 1966.

———. *The Madaba Mosaic Map.* Jerusalem, 1954.

———. *Map of Roman Palestine.* Jerusalem, 1940.

Bagnall, Roger S. *Egypt in Late Antiquity.* Princeton, N.J., 1993.

Baldovin, John F. *The Urban Character of Christian Worship. The Origins, Development, and Meaning of Stational Liturgy.* Rome, 1987.

Bammel, C. P. "Problems of the Historia Monachorum." *Journal of Theological Studies* 47, no. 1 (1996): 92–104.

Bango Torviso, Isidro G. "El camino jacobeo y los espacios sagrados durante la Alta Edad Media en España." In *Viajeros, Peregrinos, Mercaderes en el Occidente Medieval.* XVIII Semana de Estudios Medievales Estella, 22 a 26 de Julio de 1991, 121–55. Pamplona, 1992.

Bardy, Gustave. "Pèlerinages a Rome vers la fin du iv siècle." *Analecta Bollandiana* 67 (1949): 224–35.

Barnes, Timothy D. *Athanasius and Constantius: Theology and Politics in the Constantinian Empire.* Cambridge, Mass., 1993.

———. *Constantine and Eusebius.* Cambridge, Mass., 1981.

———. *The New Empire of Diocletian and Constantine.* Cambridge, Mass., 1982.

Baroni, Anselmo. "Cronologia della storia romana dal 235 al 476." In *Storia di Roma,* volume 3, *L'età tardoantica,* ed. Andrea Carandini, Lellia Cracco Ruggini, and Andrea Giardina, part 1, "Crisi e trasformazioni," 1017–45. Turin, 1993.

Barral I Altet, Xavier. "L'image littèraire de la ville dans la Péninsule Ibèrique pendant l'antiquité tardive." In *Actes du XIe Congrès International d'Archéologie Chrétienne,* 2:1393–1400. Rome, 1989.

Bartelink, G. J. M. "Les Démons comme Brigands." *Vigiliae Christianae* 21 (1967): 12–24.

Beckwith, John. *Early Christian and Byzantine Art.* New Haven, Conn., 1979. Reprint, 1993. Page references are to the 1979 edition.

Besozzi, Raimondo. *La storia della Basilica di Santa Croce in Gerusalemme.* Rome, 1750.

Binns, John. *Ascetics and Ambassadors of Christ: The Monasteries of Palestine, 314–631.* Oxford, 1994.

Birch, Debra J. *Pilgrimage to Rome in the Middle Ages: Continuity and Change.* Woodbridge, Suffolk, 1998.

Bishko, Charles Julian. "The Date and Nature of the Spanish *Consensoria Monachorum.*" *American Journal of Philology* 69. Also in *Variorum Reprints* (1948): 377–95.

———. "Gallegan Pactual Monasticism in the Repopulation of Castile." In *Variorum Reprints,* 513–36A. London, 1951.

———. "The Pactual Tradition in Hispanic Monasticism." In *Spanish and Portuguese Monastic History, 600–1300,* ed. Charles Julian Bishko, 1–43. London, 1984.

———. "Spanish Abbots and the Visigothic Councils of Toledo." In *Spanish and Portuguese Monastic History, 600–1300,* ed. Charles Julian Bishko, 139–52. London, 1984.

Bitel, Lisa M. *Isle of the Saints: Monastic Settlement and Christian Community in Early Ireland*. Ithaca, N.Y., 1990.

Blázquez-Martínez, J. M. "Prisciliano introductor del ascetismo en Gallaecia." In *Primera Reunion Gallega de Estudios Clasicos*, 210–36. Santiago de Compostela, 1981.

Bonnerue, Pierre. "Concordance sur les activités manuelles dans les règles monastiques anciennes." *Studia Monastica* 35, no. 1 (1993): 69–96.

Bover, José M. "Bachiarius Peregrinus?" *Estudios eclesiasticos* 7 (1928): 361–66.

Braegelmann, Sister Athanasius. *The Life and Writings of Saint Ildefonsus of Toledo*. Washington, D.C., 1942.

Brenk, Beat. "La cristianizzazione della Domus dei Valerii sul Celio." In *The Transformations of Urbs Roma in Late Antiquity*, ed. W. V. Harris, 33, 69–84. Portsmouth, R.I., 1999.

Brock, Sebastian P. "The Rebuilding of the Temple under Julian, a New Source." *Palestine Exploration Quarterly* 108 (1976): 103–7.

———. *Syriac Perspectives on Late Antiquity*. London, 1984.

Brock, Sebastian P., and Susan Ashbrook Harvey, eds. *Holy Women of the Syrian Orient*. Berkeley and Los Angeles, 1987.

Brown, Peter. *Augustine of Hippo: A Biography*. Berkeley and Los Angeles, 1969. Revised edition with epilogue. Berkeley and Los Angeles, 2000.

———. *Authority and the Sacred: Aspects of the Christianisation of the Roman World*. Cambridge, 1995.

———. *The Body and Society: Men, Women and Sexual Renunciation in Early Christianity*. New York, 1988.

———. *The Cult of the Saints: Its Rise and Function in Latin Christianity*. Chicago, 1981.

———. "Il filosofo e il monaco: due scelte tardoantiche." In *Storia di Roma*, volume 3, *L'età tardoantica*, ed. Andrea Carandini, Lellia Cracco Ruggini, and Andrea Giardina, part 1, "Crisi e trasformazioni," 877–94. Turin, 1993.

———. "Images as a Substitute for Writing." In *East and West: Modes of Communication. Proceedings of the First Plenary Conference at Merida*, ed. Evangelos Chrysos and Ian Wood, 15–34. Leiden, 1999.

———. *The Making of Late Antiquity*. Cambridge, Mass., 1978.

———. *Power and Persuasion in Late Antiquity: Towards a Christian Empire*. Madison, Wis., 1992.

———. "The Rise and Function of the Holy Man in Late Antiquity." *Journal of Roman Studies* 61 (1971): 80–101.

———. *The Rise of Western Christendom: Triumph and Diversity, A.D. 200–1000*. Cambridge, Mass., 1996. 2d ed. London, 2003.

Brunert, Maria-Elisabeth. *Das Ideal der Wüstenaskese und seine Rezeption in Gallien bis zum Ende des 6. Jahrhunderts*. Edited by Ildefons Herwegen. Münster, 1994.

Bruyne, Dom de. "Nouveaux fragments de l'*Itinerarium Eucheriae*." *Revue Benedictine* 26 (1909): 481–84.

Budriesi, Roberta. "I 'Santuari del mare' a Ravenna, Caesarea e Classe. Miracoli, luoghi di culto e pellegrini prima del mille." *Il Carrobbio* 21 (1995): 13–32.

Bulliet, Richard W. *The Camel and the Wheel*. Cambridge, Mass., 1975.

Bullough, Donald A. "Social and Economic Structure and Topography in the Early Medieval City." In *Topografia Urbana e Vita Cittadina nell'alto medioevo in occidente,* 351–99. Spoleto Centro Italiano di Studi Sull'Alto Medioevo. Spoleto, 1974.

Burgess, R. W. "From *Gallia Romana* to *Gallia Gothica:* The View from Spain." In *Fifth-century Gaul: A Crisis of Identity?* ed. John Drinkwater and Hugh Elton, 19–27. Cambridge, 1992.

Burrus, Virginia. *The Making of a Heretic: Gender, Authority, and the Priscillianist Controversy.* Berkeley and Los Angeles, 1995.

Burton-Christie, Douglas. *The Word in the Desert: Scripture and the Quest for Holiness in Early Christian Monasticism.* Oxford, 1993.

Byrne, Richard. "The Cenobitic Life: A Digression in Jerome's Letter Twenty-Two to Eustochium." *The Downside Review* 105 (1987): 277–93.

Caballero-Zoreda, Luis. "Un tipo cruciforme de iglesia visigoda: Melque, La Mata y Bande." In *Papers in Iberian Archaeology,* ed. R. F. J. Jones, T. F. C. Blagg, and S. J. Keay, 578–98. Oxford, 1984.

Cameron, Averil. *The Later Roman Empire,* A.D. *284–430.* Cambridge, Mass., 1993.

———. *The Mediterranean World in Late Antiquity,* A.D. *395–600.* London and New York, 1993.

———. *Procopius and the Sixth Century.* Berkeley and Los Angeles, 1985.

Campana, Augusto. "La storia della scoperta del Codice Aretino nel Carteggio Gamurrini-De Rossi." In *Atti del Convegno Internazionale sulla Peregrinatio Egeriae, nel centenario della pubblicazione del Codex Aretinus 405 (già Aretinus VI, 3),* ed. Arezzo Accademia Petrarca di Lettere Arti e Scienze, 77–84. Arezzo, 1990.

Campbell, Sheila D. "Armchair Pilgrims: Ampullae from Aphrodisias in Caria." *Mediaeval Studies* 50 (1988): 539–45.

Campenhausen, H. F. von. "The Ascetic Idea of Exile in Ancient and Early Medieval Monasticism." In *Tradition and Life in the Church.* London, 1968.

Campos, Julio. *Juan de Biclaro, Obispo de Gerona: Su Vida y Su Obra.* Madrid, 1960.

Caner, Daniel. *Wandering, Begging Monks: Spiritual Authority and the Promotion of Monasticism in Late Antiquity.* Berkeley and Los Angeles, 2002.

Capper, Brian J. "'With the Oldest Monks . . .' Light from Essene History on the Career of the Beloved Disciple?" *Journal of Theological Studies* 49, no. 1 (1998): 1–55.

Carandini, Andrea, Lellia Cracco Ruggini, and Andrea Giardina, eds. *L'età tardoantica.* Vol. 3 of *Storia di Roma,* ed. Aldo Schiavone. Turin, 1993.

Cardini, Franco. "Cruzada y peregrinación." In *Viajeros, Peregrinos, Mercaderes en el Occidente Medieval,* 115–20. XVIII Semana de Estudios Medievales Estella, 22 a 26 de julio de 1991. Pamplona, 1992.

———. "La Gerusalemme di Egeria e il pellegrinaggio dei Cristiani d'occidente in terrasanta fra IV e V secolo." In *Atti del Convegno Internazionale sulla Peregrinatio Egeriae, nel centenario della pubblicazione del Codex Aretinus 405 (già Aretinus VI, 3),* ed. Arezzo Accademia Petrarca di Lettere Arti e Scienze, 333–41. Arezzo, 1990.

———. "Reliquie e Pellegrinaggi." In *Santi e Demoni nell'Alto Medioevo Occidentale (secoli V–XI),* 981–1041. Spoleto, 1989.

Cardman, Francine. "The Rhetoric of Holy Places: Palestine in the Fourth Century." *Studia Patristica* 17 (1982): 18–25.

Casson, Lionel. *The Ancient Mariners: Seafarers and Sea Fighters of the Mediterranean in Ancient Times.* Princeton, N.J., 1991.

——. *Libraries in the Ancient World.* New Haven, Conn., 2001.

——. *Ships and Seamanship in the Ancient World.* Princeton, N.J., 1971.

——. *Travel in the Ancient World.* Toronto, 1974.

Castellanos, Santiago. "The Significance of Social Unanimity in a Visigothic Hagiography: Keys to an Ideological Screen." *Journal of Early Christian Studies* 11, no. 3 (2003): 387–419.

Cernadas, José M. Andrade. "El Monasterio de Samos y la hospitalidad Benedictina con el peregrino (siglos XI–XIII)." In *El Camino de Santiago, la hospitalidad monástica y las peregrinaciones,* ed. Horacio Santiago-Otero, 273–83. Salamanca, 1992.

Chadwick, Henry. "New Sermons of St Augustine." *Journal of Theological Studies* 47, no. 1 (1996): 69–91.

——. *Priscillian of Avila: The Occult and the Charismatic in the Early Church.* Oxford, 1976.

Chadwick, Owen. *John Cassian.* London, 1968.

Charles-Edwards, Thomas. "The Social Background of Irish *Peregrinatio.*" *Celtica* 11 (1976): 43–59.

Charlesworth, M. P. *Trade-Routes and Commerce of the Roman Empire.* Cambridge, 1924.

Chastagnol, André. *La Préfecture Urbaine à Rome sous le bas-empire.* Paris, 1960.

Chelini, Jean, and Henry Branthomme. *Les Chemins de Dieu: Histoire des Pèlerinages Chrétiens des origines à nos jours.* Paris, 1982.

Chitty, Derwas J. *The Desert a City: An Introduction to the Study of Egyptian and Palestinian Monasticism under the Christian Empire.* Crestwood, N.Y., 1966.

Chuvin, Pierre. *A Chronicle of the Last Pagans.* Translated by B. A. Archer. Cambridge, Mass., 1990.

Chrysos, Evangelos, and Ian Wood, eds. *East and West: Modes of Communication.* Proceedings of the First Plenary Conference at Merida. Leiden, 1999.

Clark, Elizabeth A. *Ascetic Piety and Women's Faith: Essays on Late Ancient Christianity.* Lewiston, N.Y., 1986.

——. "Ascetic Renunciation and Feminine Advancement: A Paradox of Late Ancient Christianity." *Anglican Theological Review* 63 (1981): 240–57.

Clark, Gillian. "Going Home: Soul Travel in Late Antiquity." In *Travel, Communication and Geography in Late Antiquity,* ed. L. Ellis and F. L. Kidner. Ashgate, 2004.

——. *Women in Late Antiquity: Pagan and Christian Lifestyles.* Oxford, 1993.

Cloke, Gillian. *This Female Man of God: Women and Spiritual Power in the Patristic Age, A.D. 350–450.* London, 1995.

Collins, Roger. "The 'Autobiographical' Works of Valerius of Bierzo: Their Structure and Purpose." In *Los Visigodos: Historia y Civilización,* 425–42. Murcia, 1986.

——. *The Basques.* Cambridge, Mass., 1990.

——. "Doubts and Certainties on the Churches of Early Medieval Spain." In *God and Man in Medieval Spain: Essays in Honour of J. R. L. Highfield,* ed. Derek W. Lomax and David Mackenzie, 1–18. Warminster, 1989.

——. *Early Medieval Spain: Unity in Diversity, 400–1000.* 2d ed. New York, 1995.

——. "Mérida and Toledo: 550–585." In *Visigothic Spain: New Approaches,* ed. Edward James, 189–219. Oxford, 1980.

Conant, J. "The Original Buildings at the Holy Sepulchre in Jerusalem." *Speculum* 31 (1956): 1–48.

Consolino, Franca Ela. "Ascetismo e monachesimo femminile in Italia dalle origini all'età longobarda (IV–VIII secolo)." In *Donne e fede. Santità e vita religiosa in Italia,* ed. Lucetta Scaraffia and Gabriella Zarri, 4–41. Bari, 1994.

Constable, Giles. *Medieval Monasticism: A Select Bibliography.* Toronto, 1976.

——. "Monachisme et pèlerinage au Moyen Age." *Revue Historique* 258, no. 1 (1977): 3–27.

——. "Opposition to Pilgrimage in the Middle Ages." In *Religious Life and Thought (11th–12th centuries),* ed. Giles Constable, 125–46. London, 1979.

Cooper, Kate. *The Virgin and the Bride: Idealized Womanhood in Late Antiquity.* Cambridge, Mass., 1996.

Corbett, P. B. "The *Regula Magistri* and Some of Its Problems." *Studia Patristica* 1, no. 1 (1957): 82–93.

Corsini, Eugenio. *Introduzione alle "Storie" di Orosio.* Turin, 1968.

Courtois, Christian. "L'évolution du monaschisme en Gaule de St. Martin à St. Colomban." In *Il Monachesimo nell'alto medioevo e la formazione della civiltà occidentale,* 47–72. Spoleto, 1957.

Cowdrey, H. E. J. *The Cluniacs and the Gregorian Reform.* Oxford, 1970.

Cox, Edward Godfrey. *A Reference Guide to the Literature of Travel.* 3 vols. Seattle, 1935–49.

Cox, Patricia. *Biography in Late Antiquity: A Quest for the Holy Man.* Berkeley and Los Angeles, 1983.

Crook, John. *Law and Life of Rome.* Ithaca, N.Y., 1967.

Crowfoot, J. W. *Early Churches in Palestine.* London, 1941.

Curchin, Léonard A. "Élite urbaine, élite rurale en Lusitanie." In *Les Villes de Lusitanie Romaine: Hiérarchies et territoires,* ed. Jean-Gérard Gorges, 265–76. Paris, 1990.

——. *Roman Spain: Conquest and Assimilation.* London, 1991.

Curran, John R. *Pagan City and Christian Capital: Rome in the Fourth Century.* Oxford, 2000.

D'Emilio, James. "The Building and the Pilgrims' Guide." In *The Codex Calixtinus and the Shrine of St. James,* ed. John Williams and Alison Stones, 185–206. Tübingen, 1992.

Dagron, Gilbert. "Constantinople. Les sanctuaires et l'organisation de la vie religieuse." In *Actes du XIe Congrès International d'Archéologie Chrétienne,* 2:1069–85. Rome, 1989.

Daly, Lowrie J. *Benedictine Monasticism: Its Foundation and Development Through the Twelfth Century.* New York, 1965.

Davidson, Linda Kay, and Maryjane Dunn-Wood. *Pilgrimage in the Middle Ages: A Research Guide.* New York, 1993.

Davies, Horton, and Marie-Hélène Davies. *Holy Days and Holidays: The Medieval Pilgrimage to Compostela.* Toronto, 1982.

Davies, J. G. "*Peregrinatio Egeriae* and the Ascension." *Vigiliae Christianae* 8 (1954): 94–100.

de Blaauw, Sible. "Jerusalem in Rome and the Cult of the Cross." In *Pratum Romanum. Richard Krautheimer zum 100. Geburtstag,* ed. Meredith J. Gill, Renate L. Colella, Lawrence A. Jenkens, and Petra Lamers, 55–73. Wiesbaden, 1997.

de Jong, Mayke. "Carolingian Monasticism: The Power of Prayer." In *The New Cambridge Medieval History, Volume II c. 700–c. 900,* ed. Rosamond McKitterick, 622–53. Cambridge, 1996.

Dekkers, E. "De datum der *Peregrinatio Egeriae* en het feest van Ons Heer Hemelvaart." *Sacris erudiri* 1 (1948): 181–205.

Delaruelle, Etienne. "The Crusading Idea in Cluniac Literature of the Eleventh Century." In *Cluniac Monasticism in the Central Middle Ages,* ed. Noreen Hunt, 191–216. London, 1971.

——. "La Spiritualité des Pèlerinages a Saint-Martin de Tours du Ve au Xe siècle." In *Pellegrinaggi e Culto dei Santi in Europa fino alla Iª Crociata, Convegni del Centro di Studi sulla Spiritualità Medievale,* ed. Giuseppe Ermini, 201–43. Perugia, 1963.

Devos, Paul. "La date du voyage d'Égérie." *Analecta Bollandiana* 85 (1967): 165–94.

——. "Égérie a Bethléem: le 40e jour aprés Pâques à Jérusalem, en 383." *Analecta Bollandiana* 86 (1968): 87–108.

——. "Il y a vingt ans. Les années du Pèlerinage d'Égérie: 381–84. Souvenirs du mois de Février 1967." In *Atti del Convegno Internazionale sulla Peregrinatio Egeriae, nel centenario della pubblicazione del Codex Aretinus 405 (già Aretinus VI, 3),* ed. Arezzo Accademia Petrarca di Lettere Arti e Scienze, 305–14. Arezzo, 1990.

——. "Une nouvelle Égérie." *Analecta Bollandiana* 101 (1983): 43–66.

Di Nino, Antonella Maria. "Sul Sinai con Egeria." In *Atti del Convegno Internazionale sulla Peregrinatio Egeriae, nel centenario della pubblicazione del Codex Aretinus 405 (già Aretinus VI, 3),* ed. Arezzo Accademia Petrarca di Lettere Arti e Scienze, 343–53. Arezzo, 1990.

Díaz Martínez, P. C. "Comunidades monásticas y comunidades campesinas en la España visigoda." In *Los Visigodos: Historia y Civilizacion,* 189–95. Actas de la Semana Internacional de Estudios Visigóticos. Murcia, 1986.

——. "Monasticism and Liturgy in Visigothic Spain." In *The Visigoths: Studies in Culture and Society,* ed. Alberto Ferreiro, 169–99. Leiden, 1999.

Díaz y Díaz, Manuel C. "Aspectos de la tradición de la *Regula Isidori." Studia Monastica* 5, no. 1 (1963): 27–57.

——. "El Codex Calixtinus: Volviendo sobre el Tema." In *The Codex Calixtinus and the Shrine of St. James,* ed. John Williams and Alison Stones, 1–9. Tübingen, 1992.

——. "Fructuosiana." In *De Tertullien aux Mozarabes. Antiquité Tardive et Christianisme Ancien Mélanges offerts à Jacques Fontaine membre de l'Institut à l'occasion de son 70e anniversaire, par ses élèves, amis et collègues,* ed. Louis Holtz and Jean-Claude Fredouille, vol. 1, *IIIe–VIe siècles,* 31–40. Paris, 1992.

——. "Puntos de vista sobre la vida cultural peninsular en los siglos V y VI." In *Innovacion y Continuidad en la España Visigotica,* ed. Ramón Gonzálvez-Ruiz, 1–21. Toledo, 1981.

——. "Las Reglas monásticas españolas allende los Pirineos." In *L'Europe Héritière de l'Espagne Wisigothique,* ed. Jacques Fontaine and Christine Pellistrani, 159–76. Madrid, 1992.

――. *Visiones del más alla en Galicia durante la alta edad media*. Santiago de Compostela, 1985.

Dietz, Maribel. "Itinerant Spirituality and the Late Antique Origins of Christian Pilgrimage." In *Travel, Communication, and Geography in Late Antiquity*, ed. L. Ellis and F. L. Kidner. Ashgate, 2004.

Dihle, Albrecht, ed. *L'église et l'empire au IVe siècle*. Geneva, 1987.

Dillon, Matthew. *Pilgrims and Pilgrimage in Ancient Greece*. London, 1997.

Dionisi, Davide, and Gennaro Della Pietra. *Torpignattara. I luoghi della memoria*. Rome, 1994.

Dixon, Philip. "'The Cities Are Not Populated as Once They Were.'" In *The City in Late Antiquity*, ed. John Rich, 145–60. London, 1992.

Dodds, Jerrilyn D. *Architecture and Ideology in Early Medieval Spain*. University Park, Pa., 1990.

Dolbeau, François. "Une refonte Wisigothique du De viris illustribus d'Isidore." In *De Tertullien aux Mozarabes. Antiquité Tardive et Christianisme Ancien Mélanges offerts à Jacques Fontaine membre de l'Institut à l'occasion de son 70e anniversaire, par ses élèves, amis et collègues*, ed. Louis Holtz and Jean-Claude Fredouille, vol. 1, *IIIe–VIe siècles*, 41–56. Paris, 1992.

Domínguez del Val, Ursicino. "Algunos temas monásticos de San Leandro de Sevilla." *Studia Patristica* 16, no. 2 (1985): 1–14.

――. *Estudios sobre Literatura Latina Hispano-Cristiana*, vol. 1, *1955–1971*. Madrid, 1986.

――. *Leandro de Sevilla y la lucha contra el Arrianismo*. Madrid, 1981.

――. "Perspectivas de unidad en el 'de institutione virginum' de Leandro de Sevilla." In *Innovacion y Continuidad en la España Visigotica*, ed. Ramón Gonzálvez-Ruiz, 23–47. Toledo, 1981.

D'Onofrio, Mario. *Romei and Giubilei: il pellegrinaggio medievale a San Pietro (350–1350)*. Rome, 1999.

Douglas, Laurie. "A New Look at the *Itinerarium Burdigalense*." *Journal of Early Christian Studies* 4, no. 3 (1996): 313–33.

Drake, H. A. *Constantine and the Bishops. The Politics of Intolerance*. Baltimore, 2000.

――. "Eusebius on the True Cross." *Journal of Ecclesiastical History* 36 (1985): 1–22.

Drijvers, Jan Willem. *Helena Augusta: The Mother of Constantine the Great and the Legend of Her Finding of the True Cross*. Leiden, 1992.

Drijvers, Jan Willem, and David Hunt, eds. *The Late Roman World and Its Historian: Interpreting Ammianus Marcellinus*. London, 1999.

Drinkwater, J. F. "The Bacaudae of Fifth-century Gaul." In *Fifth-century Gaul: A Crisis of Identity?* ed. John Drinkwater and Hugh Elton, 208–17. Cambridge, 1992.

Driscoll, Jeremy. *The Mind's Long Journey to the Holy Trinity: The Ad Monachos of Evagrius Ponticus*. Collegeville, Minn., 1993.

Dronke, Peter. *Women Writers of the Middle Ages: A Critical Study of Texts from Perpetua (203) to Marguerite Porete (1310)*. Cambridge, 1984.

Ducan-Flowers, Maggie. "A Pilgrim's Ampulla from the Shrine of St. John the Evangelist at Ephesus." In *The Blessings of Pilgrimage*, ed. Robert Ousterhout, 125–39. Urbana, Ill., 1990.

Duhr, Joseph. *Aperçus sur l'Espagne chrétienne du IVe siecle ou le 'De Lapso' de Bachiarius*. Louvain, 1934.

Duncan-Jones, Richard. *The Economy of the Roman Empire: Quantitative Studies.* Cambridge, 1982.

———. *Structure and Scale in the Roman Economy.* Cambridge, 1990.

Dunn, Marilyn. *The Emergence of Monasticism: From the Desert Fathers to the Early Middle Ages.* Oxford, 2000.

———. "Mastering Benedict: Monastic Rules and Their Authors in the Early Medieval West." *English Historical Review* 416 (1990): 567–94.

Dunn, Maryjane, and Linda Kay Davidson. *The Pilgrimage to Santiago de Compostela: A Comprehensive, Annotated Bibliography.* New York, 1994.

———, eds. *The Pilgrimage to Compostela in the Middle Ages: A Book of Essays.* New York, 1996.

Dupront, Alphonse. *Du Sacré: Croisades et pèlerinages, images et langages.* Paris, 1987.

Eade, John, and Michael J. Sallnow, eds. *Contesting the Sacred: The Anthropology of Christian Pilgrimage.* London, 1991.

Edelstein, Ludwig, and Emma J. Edelstein. *Asclepius.* Baltimore, 1998.

Eickelman, Dale F., and James Piscatori, eds. *Muslim Travelers: Pilgrimage, Migration, and the Religious Imagination.* Berkeley and Los Angeles, 1990.

Eisenberg, E. "Jerusalem: The Church of the Dormition." *Excavations and Surveys in Israel* 3 (1984): 47.

Elad, Amikam. "Pilgrims and Pilgrimage to Hebron (al-Khalil) During the Early Muslim Period (638?–1099)." In *Pilgrims and Travelers to the Holy Land,* ed. Bryan F. LeBeau and Menachem Mor, 21–62. Omaha, Nebr., 1996.

Elliott, Alison Goddard. *Roads to Paradise: Reading the Lives of the Early Saints.* Hanover, N.H., 1987.

Elm, Susanna. "Perceptions of Jerusalem Pilgrimage as Reflected in Two Early Sources on Female Pilgrimage (3rd and 4th centuries a.d.)." *Studia Patristica* 20 (1989): 219–23.

———. "The Sententiae ad Virginem by Evagrius Ponticus and the Problem of Early Monastic Rules." *Augustinianum* 30 (1990): 393–404.

———. *Virgins of God: The Making of Asceticism in Late Antiquity.* Oxford, 1994.

Ericsson, Christoffer H. *Navis Oneraria: The Cargo Carrier of Late Antiquity.* Åbo, 1984.

Ermini, Giuseppe, ed. *Pellegrinaggi e Culto dei Santi in Europa fino alla I^a Crociata.* Perugia, 1963.

Étienne, Robert. *Le Culte Impérial dans la péninsule ibérique d'Auguste à Dioclétien.* Paris, 1958.

———. "Le culte impérial, vecteur de la hiérarchisation urbaine." In *Les Villes de Lusitanie Romaine: Hiérarchies et territoires,* ed. Jean-Gérard Gorges, 216–31. Paris, 1990.

Fabbrini, Fabrizio. "La Cornice Storica della 'Peregrinatio Egeriae." In *Atti del Convegno Internazionale sulla Peregrinatio Egeriae, nel centenario della pubblicazione del Codex Aretinus 405 (già Aretinus VI, 3),* ed. Arezzo Accademia Petrarca di Lettere Arti e Scienze, 21–75. Arezzo, 1990.

Felle, Antonio Enrico. "Testimonianze Epigrafiche del Pellegrinaggio Garganico in età altomedievale: la memoria e la scrittura." *Mitteilungen zur christlichen Archäologie* 7 (2001): 60–77.

Ferguson, Everett. *Backgrounds of Early Christianity.* Grand Rapids, Mich., 1993.

Fernández Alonso, Justo. *La Cura Pastoral en la España Romanovisigoda.* Rome, 1955.

Fernández del Pozo, José M. "Razones económicas de un conflicto en el Camino de Santiago." In *El Camino de Santiago, la hospitalidad monástica y las peregrinaciones*, ed. Horacio Santiago-Otero, 211–16. Salamanca, 1992.

Férotin, M. "Le Véritable auteur de la *Peregrinatio Silviae*, la vierge espagnole Ethéria." *Revue des Questions Historiques* 74 (1903): 367–97.

Ferrari, Guy. *Early Roman Monasteries: Notes for the History of the Monasteries and Convents at Rome from the V Through the X Century.* Vatican City, 1957.

Ferreiro, Alberto. "The Cult of Saints and Divine Patronage in Gallaecia Before Santiago." In *The Pilgrimage to Compostela in the Middle Ages: A Book of Essays*, ed. Maryjane Dunn and Linda Kay Davidson, 3–22. New York, 1996.

———. "The Missionary Labors of St. Martin of Braga in Sixth-century Galicia." *Studia Monastica* 23 (1981): 11–26.

———. "The Omission of St. Martin of Braga in John of Biclaro's *Chronica* and the Third Council of Toledo." In *Los Visigodos: Historia y Civilizacion*, 145–50. Murcia, 1986.

———. *The Visigoths in Gaul and Spain, A.D. 418–711, A Bibliography.* Leiden, 1988.

———. "The Westward Journey of St. Martin of Braga." *Studia Monastica* 22 (1980): 243–51.

———, ed. *The Visigoths: Studies in Culture and Society.* Leiden, 1999.

Figueras, Pau. "Découvertes récentes d'épigraphie Chrétienne en Israel." In *Actes du XIe Congrès International d'Archéologie Chrétienne*, 2:1771–85. Rome, 1989.

Fischer, Moshe. "An Early Byzantine Settlement at Kh. Zikrin (Israel). A Contribution to the Archaeology of Pilgrimage in the Holy Land." In *Actes du XIe Congrès International d'Archéologie Chrétienne*, vol. 2, 1787–807. Rome, 1989.

Fletcher, R. A. *The Conversion of Europe: From Paganism to Christianity, 371–1386 A.D.* New York, 1997.

———. *Saint James's Catapult: The Life and Times of Diego Gelmírez of Santiago de Compostela.* Oxford, 1984.

Flobert, Pierre, ed. *La vie ancienne de Saint Samson de Dol.* Paris, 1997.

Folliet, Georges. "Le monachisme en Afrique de Saint Augustin à Saint Fulgence." In *Il Monachesimo Occidentale dalle origini alla Regula Magistri*, 291–315. XXVI Incontro di studiosi dell'antichità cristiana, Roma, 8–10 maggio 1997. Rome, 1998.

Fontaine, Jacques. "El ascetismo. ¿Manzana de discordia entre latifundistas y obispos en la Tarraconense del siglo IV?" In *Culture et Spiritualité en Espagne du IVe au VIIe siècle*, 201–6. London, 1986.

———. "El *De viris illustribus* de San Ildenfonso de Toledo: tradición y originalidad." In *Culture et Spiritualité en Espagne du IVe au VIIe siècle*, 59–96. London, 1986.

———. "King Sisebut's *Vita Desiderii* and the Political Function of Visigothic Hagiography." In *Culture et Spiritualité en Espagne du IVe au VIIe siècle*, 93–129. London, 1986.

Fontaine, Jacques, and Christine Pellistrani, eds. *L'Europe Héritière de l'Espagne Wisigothique.* Madrid, 1992.

Foss, Clive. *Byzantine and Turkish Sardis.* Cambridge, Mass., 1976.

Fowden, Garth. "The Pagan Holy Man in Late Antique Society." *Journal of Hellenic Studies* 102 (1982): 33–59.

Frank, Georgia. *The Memory of the Eyes: Pilgrims to Living Saints in Christian Late Antiquity.* Berkeley and Los Angeles, 2000.

Frankfurter, David, ed. *Pilgrimage and Holy Space in Late Antique Egypt*. Leiden, 1998.

Frazee, Charles A. "Late Roman and Byzantine Legislation on the Monastic Life from the Fourth to the Eighth Centuries." *Church History* 51 (1982): 263–79.

Frend, W. H. C. *Archaeology and History in the Study of Early Christianity*. London, 1988.

———. "The Church in the Reign of Constantius II (337–361): Mission, Monasticism, Worship." In *L'église et l'empire au IVe siècle*, ed. Albrecht Dihle, 73–111. Geneva, 1987.

———. "Circumcillions and Monks." *Journal of Theological Studies*, n.s., 20 (1969): 542–49.

———. *Religion Popular and Unpopular in the Early Christian Centuries*. London, 1976.

Frenkel, Yehoshua. "Muslim Pilgrimage to Jerusalem in the Mamluk Period." In *Pilgrims and Travelers to the Holy Land*, ed. Bryan F. LeBeau and Menachem Mor, 63–87. Omaha, Nebr., 1996.

Frolow, Anatole. *La relique de la Vraie Croix. Recherches sur le Développement d'un culte*. Paris, 1961.

Frutaz, Amato Pietro. *Il complesso monumentale di Sant'Agnese*. 5th ed. Rome, 1992.

Gafni, Isaiah. "Reinterment in the Land of Israel: Notes on the Origin and Development of the Custom." *Jerusalem Cathedra* 1 (1981): 96–104.

Galiano, Manuel Fernández, ed. *Los Visigodos: Historia y Civilizacion*. Murcia, 1986.

Gamurrini, G. F. "Della inedita peregrinazione ai luoghi santi." *Studii e documenti di storia e diritto* 6 (1885): 145–68.

———. "I misteri e gl'imni di s. Ilario vescovo di Poitiers ed una peregrinazione ai luoghi santi nel quarto secolo." *Studii e documenti di storia e diritto* 5 (1884): 81.

Garaffa, Filippo, ed. *Monasticon Italiae: Repertorio topo-bibliografico dei monasteri italiani*. Cesena, 1981.

García de Cortázar, José Angel. "Viajeros, peregrinos, mercaderes en la Europa Medieval." In *Viajeros, Peregrinos, Mercaderes en el Occidente Medieval*, 15–51. Pamplona, 1992.

García Moreno, Luis A. "El estado protofeudal visigodo: precedente y modelo para la Europa carolingia." In *L'Europe Héritière de l'Espagne Wisigothique*, ed. Jacques Fontaine and Christine Pellistrandi, 17–43. Madrid, 1992.

———. *Prosopografía del Reino Visigodo de Toledo*. Salamanca, 1974.

———. "Spanish Gothic Consciousness among the Mozarabs in Al-Andalus (VIII–Xth Centuries)." In *The Visigoths: Studies in Culture and Society*, ed. Alberto Ferreiro, 303–23. Leiden, 1999.

Garcia Rodriguez, Carmen. *El Culto de los Santos en la España Romana y Visigoda*. Madrid, 1966.

Garcia Villada, Zacarias. *Historia Eclesiástica de España*. Vols. 1 and 2. Madrid, 1929–33.

———. "La lettre de Valérius aux moines du Bierzo sur la bienheureuse Aetheria." *Analecta Bollandiana* 29 (1910): 377–99.

Gargano, Innocenzo. "Cultura e Spiritualità nel monachesimo antico." In *Cultura e Spiritualità nella tradizione monastica*, ed. Gregorio Penco, 9–65. Rome, 1990.

Garnsey, Peter, Keith Hopkins, and C. R. Whittaker, eds. *Trade in the Ancient Economy*. London, 1983.

Garnsey, Peter, and Richard P. Saller. *The Roman Empire: Economy, Society and Culture*. London, 1987.

Geary, Patrick. *Before France and Germany: The Creation and Transformation of the Merovingian World.* Oxford, 1988.

——. *Furta Sacra: The Theft of Relics in the Central Middle Ages.* Princeton, N.J., 1990.

Giardina, Andrea, ed. *Società romana e impero tardoantico: Roma Politica Economia Paesaggio Urbano.* Rome, 1986.

Gil, Johannes, ed. *Miscellanea Wisigothica.* Seville, 1972.

Glick, Thomas F. *Islamic and Christian Spain in the Early Middle Ages.* Princeton, N.J., 1979.

Goehring, James E. "Withdrawing from the Desert: Pachomius and the Development of Village Monasticism in Upper Egypt." *Harvard Theological Review* 89, no. 3 (1996): 267–85.

Goitein, S. D. *A Mediterranean Society: The Jewish Communities of the Arab World as Portrayed in the Documents of the Cairo Geniza.* 3 vols. Berkeley and Los Angeles, 1967.

Goffart, Walter. *Barbarians and Romans, A.D. 418–584: The Techniques of Accommodation.* Princeton, N.J., 1980.

——. *The Narrators of Barbarian History (A.D. 550–800): Jordanes, Gregory of Tours, Bede, and Paul the Deacon.* Princeton, N.J., 1988.

Gomez Moreno, Manuel. *Monumentos romanos y visigoticos de Granada.* Granada, 1988.

González García, Vicente José. "La Hospitalidad Asturiana durante la primera época del Camino de Santiago." In *El Camino de Santiago, la hospitalidad monástica y las peregrinaciones,* ed. Horacio Santiago-Otero, 157–83. Salamanca, 1992.

Gonzálvez Ruiz, Ramón, ed. *Innovacion y Continuidad en la España Visigotica.* Toledo, 1981.

Gorges, Jean-Gérard, ed. *Les Villes de Lusitanie Romaine: Hiérarchies et territoires.* Paris, 1990.

Gough, Mary, ed. *Alahan, an Early Christian Monastery in Southern Turkey, Based on the Work of Michael Gough.* Toronto, 1985.

Gould, Graham E. *The Desert Fathers on Monastic Community.* Oxford, 1993.

——. "Moving on and Staying Put in the Apophthegmata Patrum." *Studia Patristica* 20 (1989): 231–37.

Grabar, André. *Ampoules de Terre Sainte.* Paris, 1958.

——. *Christian Iconography: A Study of Its Origins.* Princeton, N.J., 1968.

——. *Martyrium: Recherches sur le culte des reliques et l'art chrétien antique.* 2 vols. London, 1946. Reprint, 1972.

Grabar, Oleg. "The Meaning of the Dome of the Rock." In *The Medieval Mediterranean: Cross-Cultural Contacts,* ed. Marilyn J. Chiat and Kathryn L. Reyerson, 1–10. St. Cloud, Minn., 1988.

Greene, Kevin. *The Archaeology of the Roman Economy.* Berkeley and Los Angeles, 1986.

Grew, Francis, and Brian Hobley. "Introduction: The Study of Classical Urban Topography." In *Roman Urban Topography in Britain and the Western Empire,* ed. Francis Grew and Brian Hobley, viii–xvi. London, 1985.

Groh, D. E. "The Onomastikon of Eusebius and the Rise of Christian Palestine." *Studia Patristica* 18 (1983): 28.

Grosse, Roberto, ed. *Las fuentes de la época visigoda y bizantinas*. Barcelona, 1947.

Guidobaldi, Federico. "Ricerche di Archeologia Cristiana a Roma (dentro le mura)." In *Actes du XIe Congrès International d'Archéologie Chrétienne*, vol. 2, 2127–48. Rome, 1989.

Guillaumont, Antoine. "Le dépaysement comme forme d'ascèse, dans le monachisme ancien." *Ecole pratique des Hautes Etudes, Ve section, Sciences religieuses: Annuaire* 76 (1968–69): 31–58. Also in *Aux Origines du Monachisme Chrétien: Pour une phénoménologie du monachisme*, 89–116. Bellefontaine, 1979.

Guyon, Jean. "Dal praedium imperiale al santuario dei martiri. Il territorio *ad duas lauros*." In *Società romana e impero tardoantico*, ed. Andrea Giardina, 299–332. Rome, 1986.

———. "Roma. Emerge la città cristiana." In *Storia di Roma*, volume 3, *L'età tardoantica*, ed. Andrea Carandini, Lellia Cracco Ruggini, and Andrea Giardina, part 2, "I luoghi e le culture," 53–68. Turin, 1993.

Hahn, Cynthia. "*Loca Sancta* Souvenirs: Sealing the Pilgrim's Experience." In *The Blessings of Pilgrimage*, ed. Robert Ousterhout, 85–96. Urbana, Ill., 1990.

Halbwachs, Maurice. *La topographie légendaire des évangiles en terre sainte: Etude de mémoire collective*. Paris, 1971.

Haldon, J. F. *Byzantium in the Seventh Century: The Transformation of a Culture*. Cambridge, 1990.

Hamilton, Bernard. "Ideals of Holiness: Crusaders, Contemplatives, and Mendicants," *International History Review* 17, no. 4 (1996): 693–712.

———. "The Impact of Crusader Jerusalem on Western Christendom." *Catholic Historical Review* 80, no. 4 (1994): 695–713.

Harbison, Peter. *Pilgrimage in Ireland: The Monuments and the People*. Syracuse, N.Y., 1991.

Harl, K. W. "Sacrifice and Pagan Belief in Fifth- and Sixth-Century Byzantium." *Past and Present* 128 (1990): 7–27.

Harper, James. "John Cassian and Sulpicius Severus." *Church History* 34, no. 4 (1965): 371–80.

Harries, Jill. "Christianity and the City in Late Roman Gaul." In *The City in Late Antiquity*, ed. John Rich, 77–98. London, 1992.

Harrison, Martin. *A Temple for Byzantium: The Discovery and Excavation of Anicia Juliana's Palace Church in Istanbul*. Austin, Tex., 1989.

Hauschild, Theodor. "Archaeology and the Tomb of St. James." In *The Codex Calixtinus and the Shrine of St. James*, ed. John Williams and Alison Stones, 89–103. Tübingen, 1992.

Haverkamp, Alfred, and Alfred Heit, eds. *Mönchtum, Kultur und Gesellschaft: Beiträge zum Mittelalter: zum sechzigsten Geburtstag des Autors- Friedrich Prinz*. Munich, 1989.

Hawley, R., and B. Levick, eds. *Women in Antiquity: New Assessments*. London, 1995.

Hazlett, Ian, ed. *Early Christianity: Origins and Evolution to A.D. 600. In Honour of W. H. C. Frend*. Nashville, Tenn., 1991.

Heather, Peter. "The Emergence of the Visigothic Kingdom." In *Fifth-century Gaul: A Crisis of Identity?* ed. John Drinkwater and Hugh Elton, 84–96. Cambridge, 1992.

———. *The Goths.* Oxford, 1996.

Hefele, Carl Joseph. *Histoire des conciles d'après les documents originaux. Nouvelle traduction française.* Translated by H. Leclercq. Hildesheim, 1908. Reprint, 1973.

Heitz, Carol. *L'architecture religieuse carolingienne. Les formes et leurs fonctions.* Paris, 1980.

———. *Recherches sur les rapports entre Architecture et Liturgie à l'époque carolingienne.* Bibliothèque générale de l'École Pratique des Hautes Études, VIe section. Paris, 1963.

Herbers, Klaus, and Robert Plötz. "Einführung: Spiritualität des Pilgerns im frühen Mittelalter." In *Spiritualität des Pilgerns: Kontinuität und Wandel,* ed. Klaus Herbers and Robert Plötz, 7–25. Tübingen, 1993.

Herbert, Máire. *Iona, Kells and Derry. The History and Hagiography of the Monastic Familia of Columba.* Dublin, 1996.

Herrin, Judith. *The Formation of Christendom.* Princeton, N.J., 1987.

Hertling, L., and E. Kirschbaum. *The Roman Catacombs and Their Martyrs.* Translated by M. Joseph Costelloe. London, 1956.

Hickey, Anna Ewing. *Women of the Roman Aristocracy as Christian Monastics.* Ann Arbor, Mich., 1987.

Hillgarth, J. N. "The Historiae of Orosius in the Early Middle Ages." In *De Tertullien aux Mozarabes: Antiquité Tardive et Christianisme Ancien Mélanges offerts à Jacques Fontaine membre de l'Institut à l'occasion de son 70e anniversaire, par ses élèves, amis et collègues,* ed. Louis Holtz and Jean-Claude Fredouille, vol. 1, *IIIe–VIe siècles,* 157–70. Paris, 1992.

———. "Historiography in Visigothic Spain." In *La storiografia altomedievale,* 261–311. Spoleto, 1970.

———. "Modes of Evangelization of Western Europe in the Seventh Century." In *Irland und die Christenheit: Bibelstudien und Mission / Ireland and Christendom: The Bible and the Missions,* ed. Próinséas Ní Chatháin and Michael Richter, 311–31. Stuttgart, 1987.

———. "Popular Religion in Visigothic Spain." In *Visigothic Spain: New Approaches,* ed. Edward James, 3–60. Oxford, 1980.

———. "Towards a Critical Edition of the Works of St. Julian of Toledo." *Studia Patristica* 1, no. 1 (1957): 37–43.

———. "Visigothic Spain and Early Christian Ireland." In *Visigothic Spain, Byzantium and the Irish,* ed. J. N. Hillgarth, 167–94. London, 1985.

———, ed. *Visigothic Spain, Byzantium and the Irish.* London, 1985.

Hirschfeld, Yizhar. "Imperial Building Activity During the Reign of Justinian and Pilgrimage to the Holy Land in Light of the Excavations on Mt. Berenice, Tiberias." *Revue Biblique* 106, no. 2 (1999): 236–49.

———. *The Judean Desert Monasteries in the Byzantine Period.* New Haven, Conn., 1992.

———. "List of the Byzantine Monasteries in the Judean Desert." In *Christian Archeology in the Holy Land, New Discoveries: Essays in Honour of Virgilio C. Corbo, OFM,* ed. L. Di Segni, G. C. Bottini, and E. Alliata, 1–89. Jerusalem, 1990.

Hitchner, R. B. "Meridional Gaul, Trade and the Mediterranean Economy in Late Antiquity." In *Fifth-century Gaul: A Crisis of Identity?* ed. John Drinkwater and Hugh Elton, 122–31. Cambridge, 1992.

Hochstetler, Donald. *A Conflict of Traditions: Women in Religion in the Early Middle Ages 500–840*. Lanham, Md., 1992.

Hodges, Richard. *Dark Age Economics: The Origins of Towns and Trade*, A.D. 600–1000. *New Approaches in Archaeology*. London, 1989.

Hodges, Richard, and David Whitehouse. *Mohammed, Charlemagne and the Origins of Europe: Archaeology and the Pirenne Thesis*. Ithaca, N.Y., 1983.

Hohlwein, N. "Déplacements et Tourisme dans l'Egypte romaine." *Chronique d'Egypte* 15 (1940): 253–78.

Holum, Kenneth G. "Hadrian and St. Helena: Imperial Travel and the Origins of Christian Holy Land Pilgrimage." In *The Blessings of Pilgrimage*, ed. Robert Ousterhout, 66–81. Urbana, Ill., 1990.

———. *Theodosian Empresses: Women and Imperial Dominion in Late Antiquity*. Berkeley and Los Angeles, 1982.

Holum, Kenneth G., and Gary Vikan. "The Trier Ivory, *Adventus* Ceremonial, and the Relics of St. Stephen." *Dumbarton Oaks Papers* 33 (1979): 114–33.

Holum, Kenneth G., and Robert L. Hohlfelder, eds. *King Herod's Dream: Caesarea on the Sea*. New York, 1988.

Horden, Peregrine, and Nicholas Purcell. *The Corrupting Sea: A Study of Mediterranean History*. Oxford, 2000.

Hotchkiss, Valerie R. *Clothes Make the Man: Female Cross-dressing in Medieval Europe*. New York, 1999.

Huelsen, Cr. *La Pianta di Roma dell'Anonimo Einsidlense*. Rome, 1907.

Hughes, Kathleen. "The Changing Theory and Practice of Irish Pilgrimage." In *Church and Society in Ireland*, A.D. 400–1200, ed. David Dumville, 143–51. London, 1987.

———. "On an Irish Litany of Pilgrim Saints." In *Church and Society in Ireland*, A.D. 400–1200, ed. David Dumville, 302–31. London, 1987.

Hunt, E. D. "Gaul and the Holy Land in the Early Fifth Century." In *Fifth-century Gaul: A Crisis of Identity?* ed. John Drinkwater and Hugh Elton, 264–74. Cambridge, 1992.

———. *Holy Land Pilgrimage in the Later Roman Empire*, A.D. 312–460. Oxford, 1982.

———. "St. Silvia of Aquitaine: The Role of a Theodosian Pilgrim in the Society of East and West." *Journal of Theological Studies*, n.s., 23 (1972): 351–73.

———. "St. Stephen in Minorca: An Episode in Jewish-Christian Relations in the Early 5th Century A.D." *Journal of Theological Studies* 33, no. 1 (1982): 106–23.

Hunt, Noreen. "Cluniac Monasticism." In *Cluniac Monasticism in the Central Middle Ages*, ed. Noreen Hunt, 1–10. London, 1971.

———. *Cluny under Saint Hugh, 1049–1109*. Notre Dame, Ind., 1968.

Hyland, Ann. *Equus: The Horse in the Roman World*. London, 1990.

Idinopulos, Thomas A. "Sacred Space and Profane Power: Victor Turner and the Perspective of Holy Land Pilgrimage." In *Pilgrims and Travelers to the Holy Land*, ed. Bryan F. LeBeau and Menachem Mor. Omaha, Nebr., 1996.

Iogna-Prat, Dominique. "Influences spirituelles et culturelles du monde wisigothique: Saint-Germain d'Auxerre dans la seconde moitié du IXe siècle." In *L'Europe Héritière de l'Espagne Wisigothique*, ed. Jacques Fontaine and Christine Pellistrandi, 243–57. Madrid, 1992.

James, Edward. *The Franks*. Oxford, 1988.

——, ed. *Visigothic Spain: New Approaches*. Oxford, 1980.

Janeras, S. "Contributo alla bibliografia Egeriana." *Atti del convegno Internazionale sulla Peregrinatio Egeriae*, 355–66. Arezzo, 1987.

Jeffery, George. *A Brief Description of the Holy Sepulchre: Jerusalem and Other Christian Churches in the Holy City, with Some Account of the Mediaeval Copies of the Holy Sepulchre Surviving in Europe*. Cambridge, 1919.

Jenal, Georg. *Italia ascetica atque monastica. Das Asketen- und Mönchtum in Italien von den Anfängen bis zur Zeit der Langobarden (ca. 150/250–604)*. 2 vols. Stuttgart, 1995.

Jerusalem dans les Traditions Juives et Chrétiennes. Leuven, 1987.

Jestice, Phyllis G. *Wayward Monks and the Religious Revolution of the Eleventh Century*. Leiden, 1997.

Jimenez Duque, Baldomero. *La Esprivitualidad Romano-Visigoda y Muzarabe*. Madrid, 1977.

Jimenez Garnica, Ana Maria. *Origenes y desarrollo del reino visigodo de Tolosa (a. 418–507)*. Valladolid, 1983.

Join-Lambert, Michel. *Jerusalem*. Translated by Charlotte Haldane. London, 1958.

Jones, A. H. M. *Constantine and the Conversion of Europe*. 1948. Reprint, Toronto, 1989.

——. *The Later Roman Empire, 284–602: A Social, Economic, and Administrative Survey*. 2 vols. 1964. Reprint, Baltimore, 1990.

Jones, A. H. M., J. R. Martindale, and J. Morris, eds. *The Prosopography of the Later Roman Empire*. Vol. I, A.D. 260–395. Cambridge, 1971.

Jorge, Ana Maria. "Church and Culture in Lusitania in the V–VIII Centuries: A Late Roman Province at the Crossroads." In *The Visigoths: Studies in Culture and Society*, ed. Alberto Ferreiro, 99–121. Leiden, 1999.

Kampers, Gerd. *Personengeschichtliche Studien zum Westgotenreich in Spanien*. Münster, 1979.

Kasper, Clemens M. *Theologie und Askese. Die Spiritualität des Inselmönchtums von Lérins im 5. Jahrhundert*. Münster, 1991.

Keay, Simon J. "Decline or Continuity? The Coastal Economy of the Conventus Tarraconensis from the Fourth Century until the Late Sixth Century A.D." In *Papers in Iberian Archaeology*, ed. R. F. J. Jones, T. F. C. Blagg, and S. J. Keay, 552–70. Oxford, 1984.

——. *Roman Spain*. Berkeley and Los Angeles, 1988.

Kennedy, Hugh. "From Polis to Madina: Urban Change in Late Antique and Early Islamic Syria." *Past and Present* 106 (1985): 3–27.

——. *The Prophet and the Age of the Caliphates: The Islamic Near East from the Sixth to the Eleventh Century*. London, 1986.

Kessler, Herbert L. "Pictures as Scripture in Fifth-century Churches." In *Studies in Pictorial Narrative*, 357–79. London, 1994.

Kinzig, Wolfram. "'Non-separation': Closeness and Co-operation Between Jews and Christians in the Fourth Century." *Vigiliae Christianae* 45 (1991): 27–53.

Kirschner, Robert. "The Vocation of Holiness in Late Antiquity." *Vigiliae Christianae* 38 (1984): 105–24.

Kirshner, Julius, and Suzanne F. Wemple, eds. *Women of the Medieval World: Essays in Honor of John H. Mundy*. Oxford, 1985.

Kitzinger, Ernst. *Byzantine Art in the Making. Main Lines of Stylistic Development in Mediterranean Art, 3rd–7th century.* Cambridge, Mass., 1980.

Klingshirn, William. "Caesarius's Monastery for Women in Arles and the Composition and Function of the 'Vita Caesarii.'" *Revue Bénédictine* 4 (1990): 441–81.

——. "Charity and Power: Caesarius of Arles and the Ransoming of Captives in Sub-Roman Gaul." *Journal of Roman Studies* 75 (1985): 183–203.

Knowles, David. *Great Historical Enterprises: Problems in Monastic History.* London, 1963.

Kötting, Bernhard. *Peregrinatio Religiosa: Wallfahrten in der Antike und das Pilgerwesen in der alten Kirche.* Münster, 1950.

Krautheimer, Richard. *Corpus Basilicarum Christianarum Romae: The Early Christian Basilicas of Rome.* 5 vols. Vatican City, 1937–77.

——. *Rome: Profile of a City, 312–1308.* Princeton, N.J., 1980.

——. "Santo Stefano Rotondo: conjectures." *Romisches Jahrbuch der Bibliotheca Hertziana* 29 (1994): 1–18.

——. *Three Christian Capitals: Topography and Politics.* Berkeley and Los Angeles, 1983.

Krautheimer, Richard, and Slobodan Curcic. *Early Christian and Byzantine Architecture.* 4th ed. London, 1986.

Küchler, Max, and Christoph Uehlinger, eds. *Jerusalem: Texte—Bilder—Steine.* Freiburg, 1987.

Kühnel, Bianca. *From the Earthly to the Heavenly Jerusalem: Representations of the Holy City in Christian Art of the First Millennium.* Rome, 1987.

Kulikowski, Michael. "The Identity of Bachiarius." *Medieval Prosopography.* Forthcoming.

Krueger, Derek. "Writing as Devotion: Hagiographical Composition and the Cult of the Saints in Theodoret of Cyrrhus and Cyril of Scythopolis." *Church History* 66, no. 4 (1997): 707–19.

La Rocca, Cristina. "Public Buildings and Urban Change in Northern Italy in the Early Mediaeval Period." In *The City in Late Antiquity,* ed. John Rich, 161–80. London, 1992.

Lacarra, José Maria. "Panorama de la Historia Urbana en la Peninsula Iberica desde el siglo V al X." In *La Città nell'alto medioevo,* 319–55. Spoleto, 1959.

Ladner, Gerhart B. "*Homo Viator:* Mediaeval Ideas on Alienation and Order." *Speculum* 42, no. 2 (1967): 233–59.

Lambert, A. "L'Itinerarium Egeriae vers 414–416." *Revue Mabillon* 28 (1938): 49–69.

Lambert, Elie. "Ordres et confréries dans l'histoire du pèlerinage de Compostelle." *Annales du Midi* 55 (1943): 369–403.

Lanciani, Rodolfo. *Ancient Rome in the Light of Recent Discoveries.* London, 1889.

——. *The Destruction of Ancient Rome: A Sketch of the History of the Monuments.* New York, 1901. Reprint, 1967.

——. *Pagan and Christian Rome.* Boston, 1892.

——. *The Ruins and Excavations of Ancient Rome.* New York, 1897. Reprint, 1967.

Lane Fox, Robin. *Pagans and Christians in the Mediterranean World from the Second Century A.D. to the Conversion of Constantine.* London, 1986.

Lang, D. M. "Peter the Iberian and His Biographers." *Journal of Ecclesiastical History* 2 (1951): 158–68.

Lawrence, C. H. *Medieval Monasticism: Forms of Religious Life in Western Europe in the Middle Ages.* London, 1989.

LeBeau, Bryan F., and Menachem Mor, eds. *Pilgrims and Travelers to the Holy Land.* Omaha, Nebr., 1996.

Leclercq, Jean. *The Love of Learning and the Desire for God: A Study of Monastic Culture.* Translated by Catherine Misrahi. 1961. Reprint, New York, 1981.

———. "Monachisme et Pérégrination du IXe au XIIe siècle." *Studia Monastica* 3, no. 1 (1961): 33–52.

———. "Y a-t-il une culture monastique?" In *Il Monachesimo nell'alto medioevo e la formazione della civiltà occidentale,* 339–56. Spoleto, 1957.

Leighton, Albert C. *Transport and Communication in Early Medieval Europe,* A.D. *500–1100.* Devon, 1972.

Lenski, Noel. "Empresses in the Holy Land: The Making of a Christian Utopia in the Fourth and Fifth Centuries." In *Travel, Communication and Geography in Late Antiquity,* ed. L. Ellis and F. L. Kidner. Ashgate, 2004.

Lepelley, Claude. "The Survival and Fall of the Classical City in Late Roman Africa." In *The City in Late Antiquity,* ed. John Rich, 50–76. London, 1992.

Levi, Annalina, and Mario Levi. *Itineraria Picta: Contributo allo Studio della Tabula Peutingeriana.* Rome, 1967.

Levine, Lee I., ed. *The Synagogue in Late Antiquity.* Philadelphia, 1987.

Lewis, Archibald R., and Timothy J. Runyan. *European Naval and Maritime History, 300–1500.* Bloomington, Ind., 1990.

Leyser, Conrad. *Authority and Asceticism from Augustine to Gregory the Great.* Oxford, 2000.

———. "St. Benedict and Gregory the Great: Another Dialogue." In *Sicilia e Italia suburbicaria tra IV e VIII secolo: Atti del Convegno di Studi (Catania, 24–27 ottobre 1989),* ed. Salvatore Pricoco, Francesca Rizzo Nervo, and Teresa Sardella, 21–43. Soveria Mannelli, 1991.

———. "The Temptations of Cult: Roman Martyr Piety in the Age of Gregory the Great." *Early Medieval Europe* 9, no. 3 (2000): 289–307.

Liebeschuetz, J. H. W. G. *Barbarians and Bishops: Army, Church, and State in the Age of Arcadius and Chrysostom.* Oxford, 1990.

———. "The End of the Ancient City." In *The City in Late Antiquity,* ed. John Rich, 1–49. London, 1992.

Lienhard, Joseph T. *Paulinus of Nola and Early Western Monasticism.* Cologne, 1977.

Lim, Richard. "People as Power: Games, Munificence, and Contested Topography." In *The Transformations of Urbs Roma in Late Antiquity,* ed. W. V. Harris, 265–81. Portsmouth, R.I., 1999.

Limor, Ora. "The Origins of a Tradition: The Tomb of David on Mount Zion (Religious Confrontation and Compromise between Christian, Muslim and Jew)." *Traditio* 44 (1988): 453–62.

———. "Reading Sacred Space: Egeria, Paula, and the Christian Holy Land." In *De Sion exibit lex et verbum domini de Hierusalem: Essays on Medieval Law, Liturgy, and Literature in Honour of Amnon Linder,* ed. Yitzhak Hen, 1–15. Turnhout, 2001.

Linage Conde, Antonio. "La difusión de la *Regula Benedicti* en la Península Ibérica." *Regulae Benedicti Studia* 1 (1971): 297–325.

————. "El monacato bético del Sevillano San Isidoro." *Studia Monastica* 32, no. 1 (1990): 131–38.

————. "El monacato femenino entre la clausura y la peregrinación: en torno a Egeria." *Studia Monastica* 34, no. 1 (1992): 29–40.

————. "El monacato visigotico, hacia la Benedictinizacion." In *Los Visigodos: Historia y Civilizacion,* 235–59. Murcia, 1986.

————. *Los Origenes del monacato Benedictino en la peninsula Iberica.* 3 vols. Leon, 1973.

————. "Pobreza, Castidad y Obediencia en el monacato visigotico." In *Los Consejos evangelicos en la tradicion monastica,* 29–55. Silos, 1975.

————. "San Benito y las Fuentes Literarias de la Obra Monastica de Fructuoso De Braga." *Studia Patristica* 20 (1989): 264–73.

————. "La tardía supervivencia de los monasterios doubles en la península Ibérica." *Studia Monastica* 32, no. 2 (1990): 365–79.

Linehan, Peter. *History and the Historians of Medieval Spain.* Oxford, 1993.

Lintott, Andrew W. *Violence in Republican Rome.* 2d ed. Oxford, 1999.

Lizzi, Rita. "Ambrose's Contemporaries and the Christianization of Northern Italy." *Journal of Roman Studies* 80 (1990): 156–73.

Llewellyn, P. A. B. "The Roman Church in the Seventh Century: The Legacy of Gregory I." *Journal of Ecclesiastical History* 25, no. 4 (1974): 363–80.

————. *Rome in the Dark Ages.* London, 1993.

López Alsina, Fernando. "Los espacios de la devoción: peregrinos y romerías en el antiguo reino de Galicia." In *Viajeros, Peregrinos, Mercaderes en el Occidente Medieval,* 173–92. Pamplona, 1992.

Loseby, S. T. "Bishops and Cathedrals: Order and Diversity in the Fifth-century Urban Landscape of Southern Gaul." In *Fifth-century Gaul: A Crisis of Identity?* ed. John Drinkwater and Hugh Elton, 144–55. Cambridge, 1992.

Louis, R. "La visite des saintes femmes au tombeau." *Mémoires de la Société Nationale des Antiquaires de France,* 9th series, 3 (1954): 109–22.

Lourdaux, W., and D. Verhelst, eds. *Benedictine Culture, 750–1050.* Leuven, 1983.

Lyman, Thomas W. "The Politics of Selective Eclecticism: Monastic Architecture, Pilgrimage Churches, and 'Resistance to Cluny.'" *Gesta* 27, no. 1/2 (1988): 83–92.

MacCormack, Sabine G. *Art and Ceremony in Late Antiquity.* Berkeley and Los Angeles, 1981.

————. "*Loca Sancta:* The Organization of Sacred Topography in Late Antiquity." In *The Blessings of Pilgrimage,* ed. Robert Ousterhout, 7–40. Urbana, Ill., 1990.

Mackie, Gillian. "A New Look at the Patronage of Santa Costanza, Rome." *Byzantion* 67 (1997): 383–406.

MacMullen, Ramsay. *Christianizing the Roman Empire, A.D. 100–400.* New Haven, Conn., 1984.

Magen, Y. "The Church of Mary Theotokos on Mount Gerizim." In *Christian Archaeology in the Holy Land, New Discoveries. Essays in Honour of Virgilio C. Corbo, OFM,* ed. G. C. Bottini, L. Di Segni, and E. Alliata. Jerusalem, 1990.

Malamut, Elisabeth. *Sur la route des saints byzantins.* Paris, 1993.

Maraval, Pierre. "Egérie et Grégoire de Nysse, pèlerins aux lieux saints de Palestine." In *Atti del Convegno Internazionale sulla Peregrinatio Egeriae, nel centenario della pubblicazione del Codex Aretinus 405 (già Aretinus VI, 3),* ed. Arezzo Accademia Petrarca di Lettere Arti e Scienze, 315–31. Arezzo, 1990.

————. *Lieux Saints et pèlerinages d'Orient: Histoire et Géographie des Origines à la Conquête Arabe*. Paris, 1985.

Marchetta, Antonio. *Orosio e Ataulfo nell'ideologia dei rapporti Romano-Barbarici*. Rome, 1987.

Marcos, Mar. "Monjes ociosos, vagabundos y violentos." In *Cristianismo Marginado: Rebeldes, Excluidos, Persuguidos.*, ed. Ramón Teja, vol. 1, *De los origenes al año 1000*, 55–75. Madrid, 1998.

Mare, W. Harold. *The Archaeology of the Jerusalem Area*. Grand Rapids, Mich., 1987.

Margalit, S. "Aelia Capitolina." *Judaica* 1 (1989): 45–56.

Marique, Joseph M. F., ed. *Leaders of Iberean Christianity (50 to 650 A.D.)*. Boston, 1962.

Markus, Robert A. *The End of Ancient Christianity*. Cambridge, 1990.

————. *Gregory the Great and His World*. Cambridge, 1997.

————. *Saeculum: History and Society in the Theology of St. Augustine*. Cambridge, 1970.

Martindale, J. R., ed. *The Prosopography of the Later Roman Empire, Vol. 3, A.D. 527–641*. Cambridge, 1992.

Martinez Sopena, P. "Sobre los cultos del Camino de Santiago en los reinos de Castilla y León. Génesis y evolución." In *Viajeros, Peregrinos, Mercaderes en el Occidente Medieval*, 157–72 . Pamplona, 1992.

Mathews, Thomas F. *The Clash of the Gods: A Reinterpretation of Early Christian Art*. Princeton, N.J., 1993.

————. *The Early Churches of Constantinople: Architecture and Liturgy*. University Park, Pa., 1971.

Mathisen, Ralph W. *Ecclesiastical Factionalism and Religious Controversy in Fifth-century Gaul*. Washington, D.C., 1989.

Matthews, John. *The Roman Empire of Ammianus*. Baltimore, Md., 1989.

McCormick, Michael. *Eternal Victory: Triumphal Rulership in Late Antiquity, Byzantium, and the Early Medieval West*. Cambridge, 1990.

————. *Origins of the European Economy: Communications and Commerce, A. D. 300–900*. Cambridge, 2001.

McKenna, Stephen. *Paganism and Pagan Survivals in Spain up to the Fall of the Visigothic Kingdom*. Washington, D.C., 1938.

McKitterick, Rosamond. *The Frankish Church and the Carolingian Reforms, 789–895*. London, 1977.

————, ed. *The New Cambridge Medieval History, vol. 2, c. 700–c. 900*. Cambridge, 1996.

McLynn, Neil B. *Ambrose of Milan: Church and Court in a Christian Capital*. Berkeley and Los Angeles, 1994.

McNamara, Jo Ann. "Cornelia's Daughters: Paula and Eustochium." *Women's Studies* 11 (1984): 9–27.

————. "A Legacy of Miracles: Hagiography and Nunneries in Merovingian Gaul." In *Women of the Medieval World: Essays in Honor of John H. Mundy*, ed. Julius Kirshner and Suzanne F. Wemple, 36–52. Oxford, 1985.

————. "Muffled Voices: The Lives of Consecrated Women in the Fourth Century." In *Medieval Religious Women: Distant Echoes*, ed. John A. Nichols and Lillian Thomas Shank, 11–29. Kalamazoo, Mich., 1984.

Meeks, Wayne A. *The First Urban Christians: The Social World of the Apostle Paul.* New Haven, Conn., 1983.

Meeks, Wayne A., and Robert L. Wilken. *Jews and Christians in Antioch in the First Four Centuries of the Common Era.* Ann Arbor, Mich., 1978.

Meinardus, Otto F. A. *Monks and Monasteries of the Egyptian Deserts.* 1961. Reprint, Cairo, 1989.

Meister, K. "De itinerario Aetheriae abbatissae perperam nomini s. Silviae addicto." *Rheinisches Museum für Philologie,* n.s., 64 (1909): 337–92.

Meyer, Robert T. "Holy Orders in the Eastern Church in the Early Fifth Century as Seen in Palladius." *Studia Patristica* 16, no. 2 (1985): 38–49.

———. "Palladius as Biographer and Autobiographer." *Studia Patristica* 17 (1982): 66–71.

Millar, Fergus. *The Roman Near East, 31 B.C.–A.D. 337.* Cambridge, Mass., 1993.

Momigliano, Arnaldo. *Essays in Ancient and Modern Historiography.* 1977. Reprint, Middletown, Conn., 1987.

———, ed. *The Conflict between Paganism and Christianity in the Fourth Century.* Oxford, 1963.

Moorhead, John. *Theoderic in Italy.* Oxford, 1992. Reprint, 1997.

More, John Blake. "Problems in the Study of Early Monasticism." *Diakonia* 17, no. 1 (1982): 233–42.

Morghen, Raffaello. "Monastic Reform and Cluniac Spirituality." In *Cluniac Monasticism in the Central Middle Ages,* ed. Noreen Hunt, 11–28. London, 1971.

Morin, Germain. "Pages inédites de deux pseudo-Jéromes des environs de l'an 400. I: Deux lettres mystiques d'un ascète espagnol." *Revue Bénédictine* 40 (1928): 289–310.

Mundó, Anscari M. "Estudios sobre el *De fide* de Baquiari." *Studia Monastica* 7, no. 2 (1965): 247–303.

———. "Il monachesimo nella penisola iberica fino al sec. VII." In *Il Monachesimo nell'alto medioevo e la formazione della civiltà occidentale,* 73–108. Spoleto, 1957.

———. "Monastic Movements in the East Pyrenees." In *Cluniac Monasticism in the Central Middle Ages,* ed. Noreen Hunt, 98–122. London, 1971.

Murphy, Francis X. "Julian of Toledo and the Fall of the Visigothic Kingdom in Spain." *Speculum* 27, no. 1 (1952): 1–21.

———. "Melania the Elder: A Biographical Note." *Traditio* 5 (1947): 59–77.

Muschiol, Gisela. "Zur Spiritualität des Pilgerns im frühen Mittelalter." In *Spiritualität des Pilgerns: Kontinuität und Wandel,* ed. Klaus Herbers and Robert Plötz, 25–38. Tübingen, 1993.

Natalucci, Nicoletta. "Egeria ed il monachesimo femminile." *Benedictina* 35 (1988): 37–52.

———. "L'Epistola del monaco Valerio e l'Itinerarium Egeriae." *Giornale italiano di Filologia* 35, no. 14 (1983): 3–24.

Neuman, Abraham A. *The Jews in Spain: Their Social, Political and Cultural Life during the Middle Ages.* 2 vols. Philadelphia, 1942.

Newton, Arthur Percival, ed. *Travel and Travelers of the Middle Ages.* 1926. Reprint, Freeport, N.Y., 1967.

Nichols, John A., and Lillian Thomas Shank, eds. *Medieval Religious Women: Distant Echoes.* Kalamazoo, Mich., 1984.

Niermeyer, J. F. *Mediae Latinitatis Lexicon minus.* Leiden, 1976.

Noble, Thomas F. X. *The Republic of St. Peter: The Birth of the Papal State, 680–825.* Philadelphia, 1984.

Ohler, Norbert. *The Medieval Traveller.* Translated by Caroline Hillier. Southhampton, 1989.

Oort, Johannes Van. *Jerusalem and Babylon: A Study into Augustine's City of God and the Sources of His Doctrine of the Two Cities.* Leiden, 1991.

Oost, Stewart Irvin. *Galla Placidia Augusta: A Biographical Essay.* Chicago, 1968.

Orlandis, Jose. "Abades y Concilios en la Hispania visigotica." In *Los Visigodos: Historia y Civilizacion,* 221–33. Murcia, 1986.

———. *Estudios sobre Instituciones Monasticas Medievales.* Pamplona, 1971.

———. *Historia de España: La España Visigótica.* Madrid, 1977.

———. *La Iglesia en la España Visigotica y Medieval.* Pamplona, 1976.

———. "Le royaume wisigothique et son unité religieuse." In *L'Europe Héritière de l'Espagne Wisigothique,* ed. Jacques Fontaine and Christine Pellistrandi, 9–16. Madrid, 1992.

Ortolani, Sergio. *S. Croce in Gerusalemme.* 3d ed. Rome, 1997.

Osborne, John, and Amanda Claridge. *Early Christian and Medieval Antiquities. Mosaics and Wallpaintings in Roman Churches.* Vol. 1, *Series A—Antiquities and Architecture.* London, 1996.

O'Sullivan, Jeremiah F. "Early Monasticism in Gaul." *American Benedictine Review* 16 (1965): 32–46.

Oudart, Hervé. "L'ermite et le prince. Les débuts de la vie monastique à Conques (fin VIIIe–début IXe siècle)." *Revue Historique* 297, no. 1 (1997): 3–39.

Oursel, Raymond. *Les Pèlerins du Moyen Age: les hommes, les chemins, les sanctuaires.* Paris, 1963.

Ousterhout, Robert, ed. *The Blessings of Pilgrimage.* Urbana, Ill., 1990.

Ovadiah, Asher. *Corpus of the Byzantine Churches in the Holy Land.* Bonn, 1970.

Palol Salellas, Pedro de. *Arqueologia Cristiana de la España Roman.* Madrid, 1967.

———. "La Arqueología Cristiana en la Hispana Romana y Visigoda. Descubrimientos recientes y nuevos puntos de vista." In *Actes du XIe Congrès International d'Archéologie Chrétienne,* 2:1975–2021. Rome, 1989.

Palol Salellas, Pedro de, and M. Hirmer. *Early Medieval Art in Spain.* London, 1967.

Palol Salellas, Pedro de, and Gisela Ripoll. *Los Godos en el Occidente Europeo: Ostrogodos y Visigodos en los siglos V–VIII.* Madrid, 1988.

Pani Ermini, Letizia. "Roma da Alarico a Teoderico." In *The Transformations of Urbs Roma in Late Antiquity,* ed. W. V. Harris, 33, 35–52. Portsmouth, R.I., 1999.

Papi, Anna Benvenuti. "*Homo Viator:* La tradizione del pellegrinaggio nell'alto medioevo." In *990–1990: Millenario del viaggio di Sigeric, Arcivescovo di Canterbury,* 5–19. Rome, 1990.

Pardo-Fernández, A. "La condición de viuda en el mundo visigodo a través de las actas conciliares." In *Los Visigodos: Historia y Civilizacion,* 209–19. Murcia, 1986.

Penco, Gregorio. "Il capitolo *de generibus monachorum* nella tradizione medievale." In *Medievo Monastico,* ed. P. Giustino Farnedi, 493–513. Rome, 1988.

———. *Il monachesimo fra spiritualità e cultura.* Milan, 1991.

———. "S. Benedetto nella storia della Cristianitá occidentale." In *Medievo Monastico,* ed. P. Giustino Farnedi, 61–80. Rome, 1988.

Percival, John. "Villas and Monasteries in Late Roman Gaul." *Journal of Ecclesiastical History* 48, no. 1 (1997): 1–21.

Pérez de Urbel, Justo. *Los Monjes Españoles en la edad media*. 2 vols. Madrid, 1933.

Peroni, Adriano. "Raffigurazione e Progettazione di strutture urbane e architettoniche nell'alto medio evo." In *Topografia Urbana e Vita Cittadina nell'alto medioevo in occidente*, 679–710. Spoleto, 1974.

Peters, F. E. *Jerusalem: The Holy City in the Eyes of Chroniclers, Visitors, Pilgrims, and Prophets from the Days of Abraham to the Beginnings of Modern Times*. Princeton, N.J., 1985.

———. *Jerusalem and Mecca: The Typology of the Holy City in the Near East*. New York, 1986.

Philippart, Guy, ed. *Hagiographies. International History of the Latin and Vernacular Hagiographical Literature in the West from Its Origins to 1550*. Turnholt, 1996.

Piccirillo, Michele. "Il Pellegrinaggio di Egeria al Monte Nebo in Arabia." In *Atti del Convegno Internazionale sulla Peregrinatio Egeriae, nel centenario della pubblicazione del Codex Aretinus 405 (già Aretinus VI, 3)*, ed. Arezzo Accademia Petrarca di Lettere Arti e Scienze, 193–214. Arezzo, 1990.

———. "Recenti scoperte di Archeologia Cristiana in Giordania." In *Actes du XIe Congrès International d'Archéologie Chrétienne*, 2:1697–1735. Rome, 1989.

Pietri, Charles. *Roma Christiana. Recherches sur l'Eglise de Rome, son organisation, sa politique, son idéologie de Miltiade à Sixte III (311–440)*. 2 vols. Rome, 1976.

Plötz, Robert. "Peregrinatio ad Limina Sancti Jacobi." In *The Codex Calixtinus and the Shrine of St. James*, ed. John Williams and Alison Stones, 37–50. Tübingen, 1992.

Pohl, Walter, Ian Wood, and Helmut Reimitz, eds. *The Transformation of Frontiers from Late Antiquity to the Carolingians*. Leiden, 2001.

Pohlsander, Hans A. *Helena: Empress and Saint*. Chicago, 1995.

Prawer, Joshua. *The History of the Jews in the Latin Kingdom of Jerusalem*. Oxford, 1988.

Price, Simon R. F. *Rituals and Power: The Roman Imperial Cult in Asia Minor*. Cambridge, 1984.

Pricoco, Salvatore. "Il Monachesimo Occidentale dalle origini al maestro lineamenti storici e percorsi storiografici." In *Il Monachesimo Occidentale dalle origini alla Regula Magistri*, 7–22. Rome, 1998.

Prinz, Friedrich. *Askese und Kultur. Vor- und frühbenediktinisches Mönchtum an der Wiege Europas*. Munich, 1980.

———. "Columbanus, the Frankish Nobility and the Territories East of the Rhine." In *Columbanus and Merovingian Monasticism*, ed. H. B. Clarke and Mary Brennan, 73–87. London, 1981.

———. *Frühes Mönchtum im Frankenreich. Kultur und Gesellschaft in Gallien, den Rheinlanden und Bayern am Beispiel der monastischen Entwicklung (4. bis 8. Jahrhundert)*. Munich, 1965.

———. "Il Monachesimo occidentale." In *Passaggio dal mondo antico al medio evo da Teodosio a San Gregorio Magno*, 415–34. Rome, 1980.

———. "Papa Gregorio Magno, il monachesimo siciliano e dell'Italia meridionale e gli inizi della vita monastica presso gli anglosassoni." In *Sicilia e Italia suburbicaria tra IV e VIII secolo: Atti del Convegno di Studi (Catania, 24–27 ottobre 1989)*, ed. Salvatore Pricoco, Francesca Rizzo Nervo, and Teresa Sardella, 7–20. Soveria Mannelli, 1991.

Pryor, John H. *Geography, Technology and War: Studies in the Maritime History of the Mediterranean, 649–1571.* Cambridge, 1988.

Rabanal Alonso, Manuel Abilio. *El Camino de Santiago en Leon: Precedentes Romanos y Epoca Medieval.* Leon, 1992.

Raven, Susan. *Rome in Africa.* 3d ed. London, 1993.

Rebecchi, Fernando. "Ravenna, ultima capitale d'Occidente." In *Storia di Roma,* volume 3, *L'età tardoantica,* ed. Andrea Carandini, Lellia Cracco Ruggini, and Andrea Giardina, part 2, "I luoghi e le culture," 121–30. Turin, 1993.

Reekmans, Louis. "L'implantation monumentale Chrétienne dans le paysage urbain de Rome de 300 à 850." In *Actes du XIe Congrès International d'Archéologie Chrétienne,* 2:861–915. Rome, 1989.

Reilly, Bernard F. *The Medieval Spains.* Cambridge, 1993.

———, ed. *Santiago, Saint-Denis, and Saint Peter: The Reception of the Roman Liturgy in León-Castile in 1080.* New York, 1985.

Reinhart, Wilhelm. *Historia General del Reino Hispanico de los Suevos.* Madrid, 1952.

Renna, Thomas. "Jerusalem in Late Medieval *Itineraria.*" In *Pilgrims and Travelers to the Holy Land,* ed. Bryan F. LeBeau and Menachem Mor, 119–31. Omaha, Nebr., 1996.

Rich, John, ed. *The City in Late Antiquity.* London, 1992.

Richards, Jeffrey. *Consul of God: The Life and Times of Gregory the Great.* London, 1980.

Richardson, L. *A New Topographical Dictionary of Ancient Rome.* Baltimore, Md., 1992.

Riché, Pierre. "Columbanus, His Followers and the Merovingian Church." In *Columbanus and Merovingian Monasticism,* ed. H. B. Clarke and Mary Brennan, 59–72. London, 1981.

Rike, R. L. *Apex Omnium: Religion in the Res Gestae of Ammianus.* Berkeley and Los Angeles, 1987.

Ripoll-López, Gisela. "Las relaciones entre la Península Ibérica y la Septimania entre los siglos V y VIII, según los hallazgos arqueológicos." In *L'Europe Héritière de l'Espagne Wisigothique,* ed. Jacques Fontaine and Christine Pellistrandi, 285–301. Madrid, 1992.

Rivera Recio, Juan Francisco. *San Ildefonso de Toledo: Biografía, época y posteridad.* Madrid, 1985.

Rivers, Joseph T. "Pattern and Process in Early Christian Pilgrimage." Ph.D. diss., Duke University, 1983.

Rivet, A. L. F. *Gallia Narbonensis with a Chapter on Alpes Maritimae: Southern France in Roman Times.* London, 1988.

Roberts, Michael J. *Poetry and the Cult of the Martyrs: The "Liber Peristephanon" of Prudentius.* Ann Arbor, Mich., 1993.

Rohrbacher, David. *The Historians of Late Antiquity.* London, 2002.

Roldán Hervás, José Manuel. *Itineraria Hispana: Fuentes Antiguas para el estudio de las vías romanas en la península Ibérica.* Madrid, 1975.

Romero, Juan Ramón. *Los monasterios en la España Medieval.* Madrid, 1987.

Rosen-Ayalon, Myriam. *The Early Islamic Monuments of Al-Haram Al-Sharif.* Jerusalem, 1989.

Rosenwein, Barbara H. *Rhinoceros Bound: Cluny in the Tenth Century.* Philadelphia, 1982.

Ross, James Bruce. "A Study of Twelfth-century Interest in the Antiquities of Rome." In *Medieval and Historiographical Essays in Honor of James Westfall Thompson,* ed. James Lea Cate and Eugene N. Anderson, 302–21. Chicago, 1938.

Rouche, Michel. "Du royaume de Tolède à la future Europe (VIIe–VIIIe siècles)." In *L'Europe Héritière de l'Espagne Wisigothique,* ed. Jacques Fontaine and Christine Pellistrandi, 45–50. Madrid, 1992.

Rousseau, Philip. *Ascetics, Authority, and the Church in the Age of Jerome and Cassian.* Oxford, 1978.

——. *Basil of Caesarea.* Berkeley and Los Angeles, 1994.

——. "Christian Asceticism and the Early Monks." In *Early Christianity: Origins and Evolution to A.D. 600. In Honour of W. H. C. Frend,* ed. Ian Hazlett, 112–22. Nashville, 1991.

——. *Pachomius: The Making of a Community in Fourth-century Egypt.* Berkeley and Los Angeles, 1985.

Rubin, Zeev. "Sinai in the Itinerarium Egeriae." In *Atti del Convegno Internazionale sulla Peregrinatio Egeriae, nel centenario della pubblicazione del Codex Aretinus 405 (già Aretinus VI, 3),* ed. Arezzo Accademia Petrarca di Lettere Arti e Scienze, 177–91. Arezzo, 1990.

Rubió-I-Balaguer, Jordi. *Vida Española en la época gótica.* Barcelona, 1985.

Safrai, S. "The Holy Congregation of Jerusalem." *Scripta Hierosolymitana* 23 (1972): 62–78.

Saint-Laurent, George. "St. Basil of Caesarea and the Rule of St. Benedict." *Diakonia* 16 (1981): 71–79.

Saitta, Biagio. *Società e potere nella Spagna Visigotica.* Catania, 1987.

Salway, R.W.B. "Itineraries in Use." In *Travel, Communication and Geography in Late Antiquity,* ed. L. Ellis and F. L. Kidner. Ashgate, 2004.

Salzman, Michele R. "Aristocratic Women: Conductors of Christianity in the Fourth Century." *Helios* 16 (1989): 207–20.

——. "Competing Claims to 'Nobilitas' in the Western Empire of the Fourth and Fifth Centuries." *Journal of Early Christian Studies* 9, no. 3 (2001): 359–85.

——. *On Roman Time: The Codex-Calendar of 354 and the Rhythms of Urban Life in Late Antiquity.* Berkeley and Los Angeles, 1990.

Santiago-Otero, Horacio, ed. *El Camino de Santiago, la hospitalidad monástica y las peregrinaciones.* Salamanca, 1992.

Saranyana, Josep-Ignasi, and Eloy Tejero, eds. *Hispania Christiana: Estudios en honor del Prof. Dr. Jose Orlandis Rovira en su septuagesimo aniversario.* Barañaín-Pamplona, 1988.

Saxer, Victor. "L'utilisation par la liturgie de l'espace urbain et suburbain: L'exemple de Rome dans l'antiquité et le haut moyen âge." In *Actes du XIe Congrès International d'Archéologie Chrétienne,* 2:917–1033. Rome, 1989.

Scarpi, Paolo. *La Fuga e il Ritorno: Storia e Mitologia del Viaggio.* Venice, 1992.

Schapiro, Meyer. *Late Antique, Early Christian and Mediaeval Art: Selected Papers.* New York, 1979.

Schulenburg, Jane Tibbetts. "Strict Active Enclosure and Its Effects on the Female Monastic Experience (ca. 500–1100)." In *Medieval Religious Women: Distant Echoes,* ed. John A. Nichols and Lillian Thomas Shank, 51–86. Kalamazoo, Mich., 1984.

Scrinari, Valnea Santa Maria. "Contributo all'Urbanistica tardo antica sul Campo Laterano." In *Actes du XIe Congrès International d'Archéologie Chrétienne,* 2:2101–220. Rome, 1989.

Semmler, Josef. "Benedictus II: una regula—una consuetudo." In *Benedictine Culture, 750–1050,* ed. W. Lourdaux and D. Verhelst, 1–49. Leuven, 1983.

Sepulcre, Jaime. *"Dos 'etimologías' de monachus: Jerónimo y Agustín."* In *Il Monachesimo Occidentale dalle origini alla Regula Magistri.* XXVI Incontro di studiosi dell'antichità cristiana, Roma, 8–10 maggio 1997, 197–211. Rome, 1998.

Serna González, Clemente de la. *"Regula Benedicti* 73 y el prologo de *Regula Isidori.* A proposito de las fuentes literarias de las reglas monasticas." In *Los Visigodos: Historia y Civilizacion,* 387–95. Murcia, 1986.

———, ed. *Mujeres del Absoluto: el monacato femenino, historia, instituciones, actualidad.* Burgos, 1986.

Shalem, Avinoam. "Bi'r al-Waraqa: Legend and Truth. A Note on Medieval Sacred Geography." *Palestine Exploration Quarterly* 127, no. 1 (1995): 50–61.

Sharf, Andrew. *Byzantine Jewry from Justinian to the Fourth Crusade.* London, 1971.

Sirago, Vito Antonio. *Cicadae Noctium: Quando le donne furono monache e pellegrine.* Soveria Mannelli, 1986.

Sivan, Hagith. "Holy Land Pilgrimage and Western Audiences: Some Reflections on Egeria and Her Circle." *Classical Quarterly* 38, no. 2 (1988): 528–35.

———. "Pilgrimage, Monasticism, and the Emergence of Christian Palestine in the Fourth Century." In *The Blessings of Pilgrimage,* ed. Robert Ousterhout, 54–65. Urbana, Ill., 1990.

———. "Who was Egeria? Piety and Pilgrimage in the Age of Gratian." *Harvard Theological Review* 81, no. 1 (1988): 59–72.

Smiraglia, Pasquale. "Il testo di Egeria: Problemi di Struttura." In *Atti del Convegno Internazionale sulla Peregrinatio Egeriae, nel centenario della pubblicazione del Codex Aretinus 405 (già Aretinus VI, 3),* ed. Arezzo Accademia Petrarca di Lettere Arti e Scienze, 93–108. Arezzo, 1990.

Smith, C. Delano. "Geography or Christianity? Maps of the Holy Land Before A.D. 1000." *Journal of Theological Studies,* n.s., 42 (1991): 143–52.

Starowieyski, M. "Bibliografia Egeriana." *Augustinianum* 19 (1979): 297–317.

Stone, Michael E. "Holy Land Pilgrimage of Armenians before the Arab Conquest." *Revue Biblique* 93 (1986): 93–110.

Stopani, Renato. *Le vie di Pellegrinaggio del Medioevo: Gli itinerari per Roma, Gerusalemme, Compostella.* Florence, 1991.

Stowers, Stanley K. *Letter Writing in Greco-Roman Antiquity.* Philadelphia, 1986.

Straw, Carole. *Gregory the Great: Perfection in Imperfection.* Berkeley and Los Angeles, 1988.

Sumption, Jonathan. *Pilgrimage: An Image of Mediaeval Religion.* Totowa, N.J., 1975.

Taft, Robert F. "Women at Church in Byzantium: Where, When—and Why?" *Dumbarton Oaks Papers* 52 (1998): 27–87.

Talbot, Alice-Mary. "Women's Space in Byzantine Monasteries." *Dumbarton Oaks Papers* 52 (1998): 113–27.

Talbot, C. H., ed. *The Anglo-Saxon Missionaries in Germany.* New York, 1954.

Taylor, Joan E. *Christians and the Holy Places: The Myth of Jewish-Christian Origins.* Oxford, 1993.

Testini, Pasquale. "Egeria e il S. Sepolcro di Gerusalemme." In *Atti del Convegno Internazionale sulla Peregrinatio Egeriae, nel centenario della pubblicazione del Codex Aretinus 405 (già Aretinus VI, 3),* ed. Arezzo Accademia Petrarca di Lettere Arti e Scienze, 215–30. Arezzo, 1990.

Theissen, Gerd. *Social Reality and the Early Christians: Theology, Ethics, and the World of the New Testament.* Translated by Margaret Kohl. Minneapolis, 1992.

———. *The Social Setting of Pauline Christianity.* Philadelphia, 1982.

Thelamon, Françoise. *Païens et Chrétiens au IVe siècle: L'apport de "l'Histoire ecclésiastique" de Rufin d'Aquilée.* Paris, 1981.

Thompson, E. A. "The End of Roman Spain." Parts 1–4. *Nottingham Mediaeval Studies* 20 (1976): 3–28; 21 (1977): 3–30; 22 (1978): 3–22; 23 (1979): 3–21.

———. *The Goths in Spain.* Oxford, 1969.

———. *Romans and Barbarians.* Madison, Wis., 1982.

Tolotti, Francesco. "Il S. Sepolcro di Gerusalemme e le coeve basiliche di Roma." *Mitteilungen des Deutschen Archaeologischen Instituts, Roemische Abteilung* 93 (1986): 471–512.

Tomlinson, Richard. *From Mycenae to Constantinople: The Evolution of the Ancient City.* London, 1992.

Trout, Dennis. *"Et sic vadis . . . deindes pervenies:* Rome of the Pilgrims." In *Travel, Communication and Geography in Late Antiquity,* ed. L. Ellis and F. L. Kidner. Ashgate, 2004.

Tsafrir, Yoram. "Christian Archaeology in Israel in Recent Years." In *Actes du XIe Congrès International d'Archéologie Chrétienne,* 2:1735–70. Rome, 1989.

———. "Maps Used by Theodosius: On Pilgrim Maps of the Holy Land and Jerusalem in the Sixth Century C.E." *Dumbarton Oaks Papers* 40 (1986).

Turbessi, Giuseppe. *Ascetismo e monachesimo prebenedettino.* Rome, 1961.

Turner, Victor. *Dramas, Fields, and Metaphors: Symbolic Action in Human Society.* Ithaca, N.Y., 1974.

Turner, Victor, and Edith Turner. *Image and Pilgrimage in Christian Culture.* New York, 1978.

Utterback, Kristine T. "The Vision Becomes Reality: Medieval Women Pilgrims to the Holy Land." In *Pilgrims and Travelers to the Holy Land,* ed. Bryan F. LeBeau and Menachem Mor, 159–68. Omaha, Nebr., 1996.

Valade, Bernard, ed. *Saint Jacques de Compostelle: La Quête du Sacré.* Turnhout, 1985.

Van Dam, Raymond. *Leadership and Community in Late Antique Gaul.* Berkeley and Los Angeles, 1985.

———. "The Pirenne Thesis and Fifth-century Gaul." In *Fifth-century Gaul: A Crisis of Identity?* ed. John Drinkwater and Hugh Elton, 321–33. Cambridge, 1992.

———. *Saints and Their Miracles in Late Antique Gaul.* Princeton, N.J., 1993.

Van Engen, John. "The 'Crisis of Cenobitism' Reconsidered: Benedictine Monasticism in the Years 1050–1150." *Speculum* 61, no. 2 (1986): 269–304.

Van Esbroeck, Michel. "Jean II de Jérusalem et les cultes de S. Étienne, de la Sainte-Sion et de la Croix." *Analecta Bollandiana* 102 (1984): 99–134.

Varagnoli, Claudio. *S. Croce in Gerusalemme.* Rome, 1995.

Vermeer, G.F.M. *Observations sur le vocabulaire du pèlerinage chez Egerie et chez Antonin de Plaisance.* Utrecht, 1965.

Vikan, Gary. *Byzantine Pilgrimage Art.* Washington, D.C., 1982.

——. "Guided by Land and Sea: Pilgrim Art and Pilgrim Travel in Early Byzantium." *Jahrbuch für Antike und Christentum* 18 (1991): 74–92.

——. "Pilgrims in Magi's Clothing: The Impact of Mimesis on Early Byzantine Pilgrimage Art." In *The Blessings of Pilgrimage,* ed. Robert Ousterhout, 97–107. Urbana, Ill., 1990.

Viñayo González, Antonio. "La Hospitalidad Monástica en las Reglas de San Isidoro de Sevilla y de San Fructuoso del Bierzo." In *El Camino de Santiago, la hospitalidad monástica y las peregrinaciones,* ed. Horacio Santiago-Otero, 39–51. Salamanca, 1992.

——. "San Fructuoso y San Valerio: Dos archiveros Bercianos del siglo VI." In *Memoria Ecclesiae II. Las raices visigoticas de la iglesia en España: en torno al concilio III de Toledo,* 57–62. Oviedo, 1991.

Violante-Branco, Maria João. "St. Martin of Braga, the Sueves and Gallaecia." In *The Visigoths: Studies in Culture and Society,* ed. Alberto Ferreiro, 63–97. Leiden, 1999.

Vogt, Joseph. "Pagans and Christians in the Family of Constantine the Great." In *The Conflict between Paganism and Christianity in the Fourth Century,* ed. Arnaldo Momigliano, 38–55. Oxford, 1963.

Vogüé, Adalbert de. "The Cenobitic Rules of the West." *Cistercian Studies* 12 (1977): 175–83.

——. "Cesáreo de Arlés y los orígenes de la clausura de las monjas." In *Mujeres del Absoluto: el monacato femenino, historia, instituciones, actualidad,* ed. Fray Clemente de la Serna Gonzalez, 183–95. Burgos, 1986.

——. *Community and Abbot.* Kalamazoo, Mich., 1979.

——. *Histoire Littéraire du Mouvement Monastique dans L'Antiquité.* Part 5, *De l'épitaphe de sainte Paule à la consécration de Démétriade (404–414).* Paris, 1998.

——. *Histoire Littéraire du Mouvement Monastique dans L'Antiquité.* Part 1, *De la mort d'Antoine à la fin du séjour de Jérôme à Rome (356–385).* Paris, 1991.

——. *Les Règles Monastiques Anciennes (400–700).* Turnhout, 1985.

——. "Sub regula vel abbate: A Study of the Theological Significance of the Ancient Monastic Rules." In *Rule and Life: An Interdisciplinary Symposium,* ed. M. Basil Pennington, 21–64. Spencer, Mass., 1971.

——. "To Study the Early Monks." *Monastic Studies* 12 (1976): 55–83.

Waddell, Helen, ed. *The Desert Fathers.* Ann Arbor, 1957.

Walker, Peter W. L. "Eusebius, Cyril and the Holy Places." *Studia Patristica* 20 (1989): 306–14.

——. *Holy City, Holy Places? Christian Attitudes to Jerusalem and the Holy Land in the Fourth Century.* Oxford, 1990.

Wallace-Hadrill, J. M. *The Frankish Church.* Oxford, 1983.

Wathen, Ambrose. "*Conversatio* and Stability in the Rule of Benedict." *Monastic Studies* 11 (1975): 1–44.

Ward, Benedicta. "Apophthegmata Matrum." *Studia Patristica* 16, no. 2 (1982): 63–66.

Ward-Perkins, Bryan. *From Classical Antiquity to the Middle Ages: Urban Public Building in Northern and Central Italy,* A.D. 300–850. Oxford, 1984.

Webb, Diana. *Pilgrims and Pilgrimage in the Medieval West.* London, 1999.

——. "St. James in Tuscany: The Opera di San Jacopo of Pistoia and Pilgrimage to Compostela." *Journal of Ecclesiastical History* 50, no. 2 (1999): 207–34.

Weitzmann, Kurt. "*Loca Sancta* and the Representational Arts of Palestine." *Dumb-arton Oaks Papers* 28 (1974): 31–55.

——. *Studies in the Arts at Sinai: Essays by Kurt Weitzmann.* Princeton, N.J., 1982.

Werckmeister, O. K. "Cluny III and the Pilgrimage to Santiago de Compostela." *Gesta* 27, no. 1/2 (1988): 103–12.

White, Carolinne. *The Correspondence (394–419) Between Jerome and Augustine of Hippo.* Lewiston, N.Y., 1990.

Whitelock, Dorothy. "The Interpretation of the Seafarer." In *The Early Cultures of North-West Europe,* ed. Sir Cyril Fox and Bruce Dickins, 261–72. Cambridge, 1950.

Whittow, Mark. "Ruling the Late Roman and Early Byzantine City: A Continuous History." *Past and Present* 129 (1990): 3–29.

Wickham, Chris. *Early Medieval Italy: Central Power and Local Society, 400–1000.* 1981. Reprint, Ann Arbor, Mich., 1989.

Wilken, Robert L. *John Chrysostom and the Jews: Rhetoric and Reality in the Late Fourth Century.* Berkeley and Los Angeles, 1983.

——. *The Land Called Holy: Palestine in Christian History and Thought.* New Haven, Conn., 1992.

——. "Melito, the Jewish Community at Sardis and the Sacrifice of Isaac." *Theological Studies* 37 (1976): 53–69.

Wilkinson, John. "Christian Pilgrims in Jerusalem During the Byzantine Period." *Palestine Exploration Quarterly* 108 (1976): 75–101.

——. *Jerusalem Pilgrims Before the Crusades.* Warminster, 1977.

——. "Jerusalem under Rome and Byzantium, 63 B.C.–637 A.D." In *Jerusalem in History,* ed. K. J. Asali, 75–104. Brooklyn, N.Y., 1990.

——. "Jewish Holy Places and the Origins of Christian Pilgrimage." In *The Blessings of Pilgrimage,* ed. R. Ousterhout, 41–53. Urbana, Ill., 1990.

Williams, John. "Cluny and Spain." *Gesta* 27, no. 1/2 (1988): 93–101.

Williams, John, and Alison Stones, eds. *The Codex Calixtinus and the Shrine of St. James.* Tübingen, 1992.

Wilson-Kastner, Patricia, ed. *A Lost Tradition: Women Writers of the Early Church.* Washington, D.C., 1981.

Wolfram, Herwig. *History of the Goths.* Translated by Thomas J. Dunlap. Berkeley and Los Angeles, 1988.

Wood, Ian. "Images as a Substitute for Writing: A Reply." In *East and West: Modes of Communication: Proceedings of the First Plenary Conference at Merida,* ed. Evangelos Chrysos and Ian Wood, 35–46. Leiden, 1999.

——. *The Missionary Life: Saints and the Evangelisation of Europe, 400–1050.* Harlow, Eng., 2001.

——. "The Use and Abuse of Latin Hagiography in the Early Medieval West." In *East and West: Modes of Communication. Proceedings of the First Plenary Conference at Merida,* ed. Evangelos Chrysos and Ian Wood, 93–109. Leiden, 1999.

Wood, Susan E. *Imperial Women: A Study in Public Images, 40 B.C.–A.D. 68.* Leiden, 1999.

Yarnold, E. "Who Planned the Churches at the Christian Holy Places in the Holy Land?" *Studia Patristica* 18 (1983): 108.

Ziegler, Aloysius K. *Church and State in Visigothic Spain.* Washington, D.C., 1930.

INDEX